"This is not just another t   s
and contusions. Rather, it ... .—mere
as genuine, not minimal—one that draws on the wisdom of the entire Christian
tradition. Well-written and clearly argued, this book offers a compelling way forward
for the evangelical church today."

Timothy George, founding dean, Beeson Divinity School of Samford University,
general editor, Reformation Commentary on Scripture

"Vanhoozer and Treier are calling for the development of a catholic evangelical theology by drawing from the resources of the Christian tradition. If their call is heeded,
we will likely see the emergence of a more robust ecclesiology and a consensual
orthodoxy unified around matters central to evangelical faith and practice. There is
a bright future for evangelical theology and genuine ecumenism if their proposals
are followed through."

Simon Chan, Trinity Theological College, Singapore

"In the last decade, Vanhoozer and Treier have been as busy as anyone else—arguably
more so—on theological prolegomena and the full range of questions contested in
that complex arena. *Theology and the Mirror of Scripture* gathers together the various
strands of their arguments but also charts a coherent forward trajectory. This account is a veritable starting point for all those who would be mere evangelical theologians amidst the present ferment."

Amos Yong, Fuller Theological Seminary, author of *The Future of Evangelical Theology*

"Kevin Vanhoozer and Daniel Treier, two of the leading theological voices in the
evangelical world, have combined their adroit skills and wise insights to produce a
lucid and thoughtful proposal designed to point evangelical theology toward a
hopeful and constructive future. These two brilliant authors have initiated an inviting project shaped by a commitment to the truthfulness of Scripture, informed
by the best of the Christian tradition and anchored in the trinitarian gospel. *Theology and the Mirror of Scripture* will delight many and challenge others, engaging
not only theologians and scholars, but students, pastors and church leaders alike."

David S. Dockery, president, Trinity International University

"A deft treatment of the relationship between Scripture and evangelical theology, this
book doubles as a lucid, winsome introduction to classic evangelical theology as a
whole. Readers will encounter here not only a wide-ranging discussion of hermeneutical matters but also a clear-eyed, calm, faithful testimony to the 'mere' evangelical truth of God's act in Jesus Christ for the life of the world."

Wesley Hill, Trinity School for Ministry, Ambridge, Pennsylvania

THEOLOGY *and the* MIRROR *of* SCRIPTURE

A Mere Evangelical Account

◆◆◆◆◆◆◆◆◆◆◆◆◆◆◆◆◆◆◆◆◆◆◆

Kevin J. Vanhoozer
and Daniel J. Treier

IVP Academic

An imprint of InterVarsity Press
Downers Grove, Illinois

InterVarsity Press
P.O. Box 1400, Downers Grove, IL 60515-1426
ivpress.com
email@ivpress.com

InterVarsity Press® is the book-publishing division of InterVarsity Christian Fellowship/USA®, a movement of students and faculty active on campus at hundreds of universities, colleges and schools of nursing in the United States of America, and a member movement of the International Fellowship of Evangelical Students. For information about local and regional activities, visit intervarsity.org.

Scripture quotations, unless otherwise noted, are from The Holy Bible, English Standard Version, copyright © 2001 by Crossway Bibles, a division of Good News Publishers. Used by permission. All rights reserved.

Cover design: Cindy Kiple
Interior design: Beth McGill
Images: Saint Matthew: Saint Matthew, from the Benedictine abbey of Hautvillers, France / De Agostini Picture Library / G. Dagli Orti / Bridgeman Images
   textured background: Bill Noll/Getty Images
   manhole cover: © lucato/iStockphoto

ISBN 978-0-8308-4076-2 (print)
ISBN 978-0-8308-9678-3 (digital)

Printed in the United States of America ∞

Library of Congress Cataloging-in-Publication Data

Treier, Daniel J., 1972-

 Theology and the mirror of scripture : a mere evangelical account / Daniel J. Treier and Kevin J. Vanhoozer.
  pages cm. -- (Studies in Christian doctrine and scripture)
 Includes bibliographical references and index.
 ISBN 978-0-8308-4076-2 (pbk. : alk. paper)
1. Reformed Church--Doctrines. 2. Evangelicalism. 3. Bible--Evidences, authority, etc. 4. Bible--Criticism, interpretation, etc. 5. Word of God (Christian theology) I. Title.
 BX9422.3.T74 2015
 230'.42--dc23

                    2015033925

P	23	22	21	20	19	18	17	16	15	14	13	12	11	10	9	8	7	6	5	4	3	2	1
Y	34	33	32	31	30	29	28	27	26	25	24	23	22	21	20	19	18	17	16	15			

To Doug Sweeney

Contents

UNSCIENTIFIC PREFACE TO
MERE EVANGELICAL THEOLOGY

CONFESSION IS GOOD FOR the evangelical soul, and it is only
fitting that I (Kevin) begin by coming clean on my own ambivalent
relationship to North American evangelicalism. If anyone else thinks he has
reason for confidence in this label ("evangelical"), I have more: graduated in
1978, of the college of Westmont, of the Christian College Consortium, a
born-again boomer of boomers; as to the faith, a scholar; as to zeal, a semi-
narian of the church; as to righteousness under the evangelical moral code,
a goody two-shoes. But whatever gain I thought I had, I now count as loss
because of the surpassing worth of knowing Christ and union with Christ.

SOCIOLOGICAL VERSUS THEOLOGICAL IDENTITY STATEMENTS

In non-Pauline terms: I was raised an evangelical, remained an evangelical
even during my graduate studies in Cambridge, and began my teaching
ministry at Trinity Evangelical Divinity School. However, five years living in
England and France had opened my eyes to the extent to which North
American culture had conditioned evangelicalism. The health-and-wealth
gospel fit hand in glove with the mentality of consumerist capitalism. Contemporary Christian music was in tune with the experiential expressivism
of the 1960s and '70s. The reduction of the Christian life to the code of a
moral majority fit well with a caricature of Puritanism. As to theology, in-
ternecine warfare about nonessentials was the badge of evangelical identity,
and the bane of evangelical existence.

"I am of Henry"; "I belong to Bloesch"; "I follow Pinnock." Who deserves to wear the label "evangelical" has become the topic of no little disagreement. The very term is today essentially disputed, a descriptor that has lost its saltiness. Yeats's famous line from his poem "The Second Coming" (1919), written in the wake of the First World War, describes the plight of present-day evangelicalism too: "Things fall apart; the center cannot hold." In spite of contemporary trends toward greater fragmentation and factionalism, we can nevertheless preserve the center, and perhaps redeem the label, by retrieving the original meaning ("of the gospel") and by refusing to identify ourselves with one or another faction, saying instead, "I belong to Christ."

We write this book with the hope and prayer of commending anew the evangel, and evangelical theology, to evangelicals. At their best, evangelicals have sought to hold Christ first. The present book proposes how we might do that again.

It is also a book that I (Kevin) never intended to write. To pick up the thread of my story: I left Trinity Evangelical Divinity School in 1990 (like everything else in America, evangelical culture was suffering from a bad case of the 1980s), with no plans to return, either to Trinity or the United States. I was happy to be a California Yankee in King Robert's (the Bruce) Scottish court. For eight years I taught Reformed theology at the University of Edinburgh, and rarely did I see the point of using the term *evangelical* in either my lectures or my writings. In retrospect, I may have been a bit like Jonah, trying to escape my calling and failing miserably. For, eventually, a whale (in truth, a Boeing 747) spit me up on dry Midwestern land, where I returned to teaching at a seminary that had "Evangelical" for its middle name.

North American evangelicals are, broadly speaking, still too much in thrall to (and too enthralled with) the broader culture, and evangelical theology still suffers from the self-inflicted wound of factionalism. Have I not come, like Ulysses, full (vicious) circle? Why therefore am I now willing not only to use the term *evangelical* as a qualifier to theology, but also to write a book commending it? It is because I now understand *evangelical* to refer to a guiding hope and eschatological reality, not an already-accomplished historical achievement. In brief: I now own the term in its *theological* rather than *sociological* sense. Evangelicalism is frequently defined as "a renewal movement within Protestant confessional orthodoxy," but today it is evangelicalism itself that needs renewal through retrieving the evangel. We wrote our book in the hope that the evangelical movement will live up to its name, and into its definition.

AN EDIFYING (AND UNIFYING) PROPOSAL

"Mere evangelical theology" is not the theology of a particular evangelical group. Deeper than our ancestry, or denominational DNA, or even our autobiographies, is another story, of creation and redemption in Christ, and this latter story is what ultimately defines us. Similarly, what defines evangelical theology is not the surface sociological phenomena (i.e., what evangelicals typically believe and how they behave) but rather the message of the gospel. In short: human words and deeds are not the reference point; what ultimately defines *evangelical* is God's Word and God's act.

Who are we to pontificate about evangelical theology? Are we "authorized" evangelicals? These are fair questions. Are we speaking *for* all evangelicals? No. Are we speaking *to* all evangelicals? Yes, but not to evangelicals only. We are self-critical evangelicals who wish to take our bearings not simply from the branch of the Christian family to which we belong but, more importantly, from the vine that nourishes each branch (Jn 15:5). We do not pretend to give a universally compelling description of what evangelicals *in fact* profess and practice. Our intention is rather to offer a normative proposal of what evangelicals *ought* to profess and practice, if they would be truly evangelical—if they would correspond to the gospel that is according to the Scriptures.

At the same time, we believe that evangelicals, perhaps more than any other people group, are the most fitting audience for our book. First, because, at their best, evangelicals understand themselves to be a trans-denominational *renewal movement* within the broader but denominated church.[1] Second, because, at their best, evangelicals understand themselves to be a *retrieving movement* that returns again and again to the Word of God written to regain their bearings.[2] Third, because, at their best, evangelicals understand themselves to be a *reviving movement* that encourages

---

[1] We shall suggest that renewal is not only spiritual but also imaginative.
[2] We shall suggest that what needs to be retrieved is not simply the biblical text itself but its orthodox interpretation.

heartfelt response, in the power of the Spirit, to God's authoritative word.[3]

We use the qualifier *mere* of evangelical theology for the same reason that C. S. Lewis used it of Christianity: when present controversies risk skewing things out of all proportion, the only safety "is to have a standard of plain, central Christianity ('mere Christianity' as Baxter called it) which puts the controversies of the moment in their proper perspective."[4] *Mere* does not mean "minimal" Christianity, as if Lewis were aiming for the lowest common denominator. On the contrary: *mere* stands for the *greatest* common denominator, that which ought to unify the denominations.

MERE EVANGELICAL FIRST THEOLOGY

Mere evangelical theology pertains to what is of first importance. For a philosopher like Descartes, what was of first importance was self-knowledge. The original Latin title of his seminal work, one of the landmarks of modern philosophy, is *Meditationes de prima philosophia* (*Meditations on First Philosophy*).[5] Descartes depicts the mind as the mirror of nature, with thoughts being images of what is external to the mind. By way of contrast, what is of first importance to the mere evangelical theologian, first theology, is well stated by the apostle Paul: "For I delivered to you as of first importance what I also received: that Christ died for our sins *in accordance with the Scriptures*" (1 Cor 15:3). Where *reason* is of first importance for Descartes, *Christ's death and resurrection according to the Scriptures* is of first importance for evangelicals. The Bible is therefore an important element in what we may call "first theology."[6]

Evangelicals are justly known for their concern with being biblical. "Biblicism," or the conviction of the supreme authority of Scripture, figures on everyone's list of defining evangelical characteristics. Previously I (Kevin) described first theology in terms of the reciprocal rela-

[3]We shall suggest that this revival should lead to evangelism in a broad rather than narrow sense, not simply proclaiming the gospel but pursuing radical correspondence to the gospel in individual and corporate life.

[4]C. S. Lewis, "Introduction," in Athanasius, *On the Incarnation* (Crestwood, NY: St. Vladimir's Seminary Press, 1993), p. 4.

[5]Descartes agreed with Augustine that what is of first importance is knowledge of God and the soul, but he departed from Augustine in the way he sought it.

[6]Cf. Kevin J. Vanhoozer, *First Theology: Essays on God, Scripture, and Hermeneutics* (Downers Grove, IL: InterVarsity Press, 2002), esp. chap. 1.

tionship between God and Scripture: we can only know the God of the gospel, the God of Jesus Christ, by attending to Scripture; but we attend to Scripture as a trustworthy word only because we believe it is "of God" (inspired). We therefore cannot begin doing evangelical theology from either the doctrine of God or the doctrine of Scripture alone, but rather with both simultaneously.

I now think that my first theology was too small, its "domain of the Word" too limited. I advocated for "mere evangelicalism" by following the example of Bernard Ramm, who spoke of the "evangelical heritage" and railed against what he called the "abbreviated Protestant principle." With this abbreviation evangelicals tried to base theology on the principle of biblical authority exclusively, as if the letter alone, apart from the Spirit who illumined it and the Christ to whom it pointed, were enough. Ramm viewed the evangelical heritage as built on the *unabbreviated* Protestant principle, which identified God's authority with "the Holy Spirit speaking in the Scripture," and the "christocentric principle," which insisted that what the Spirit speaks in the Scripture is ultimately Jesus Christ.[7] According to Ramm, "the temptation of biblicism is that it can speak of the inspiration of the Scriptures *apart from* the Lord they enshrine."[8]

Ramm helpfully articulated a threefold "pattern of authority" as his first theology: "Christ is the supreme object of the witness of the Spirit, and Christ is the supreme content of the Scriptures. The Spirit inspired the Scriptures and they witness supremely to Christ, the personal Word of God. Such is the pattern of authority."[9] We continue to find Ramm's work extraordinarily helpful, even ahead of its time.[10] However, we now believe that an evangelical account of first theology must extend the pattern of authority even further, to include the interpretation of Scripture in the church. As we shall see, the church too is part of the content of the gospel, and the pattern of theological authority. The pattern itself is thoroughly Trinitarian, structured by the missions of the Son and the Spirit, a theme to which we return

---

[7]"The Holy Spirit speaking in the Scripture" is from the Westminster Confession of Faith I.x.
[8]Bernard Ramm, *Special Revelation and the Word of God* (Grand Rapids: Eerdmans, 1961), p. 117.
[9]Bernard Ramm, *The Pattern of Religious Authority* (Grand Rapids: Eerdmans, 1957), p. 37.
[10]See Kevin J. Vanhoozer, "The Pattern of Evangelical Theology: Hommage à Ramm," in Bernard Ramm, *The Evangelical Heritage: A Study in Historical Theology* (Grand Rapids: Baker, 2000), pp. ix-xxvii.

in chapter one. To anticipate that discussion: mere evangelical first theology treats theological prolegomena, the biblical gospel and the church together by situating all three within the triune economy: the "collected works" of the triune God.

ACKNOWLEDGMENTS

W E ARE THANKFUL TO the good folks at InterVarsity Press—in particular Andy Le Peau, Gary Deddo and David Congdon—for being patient with us through the thick and thin of proposing, redefining and launching the Studies in Christian Doctrine and Scripture series. We are also thankful to our board of advisers—Oliver Crisp, Stephen Holmes, Suzanne McDonald, Paul Nimmo and Fred Sanders. Undoubtedly each of them would express certain points differently than we do here, but we are grateful that they share our core vision and are willing to come alongside us.

Craig Hefner and Anna Williams have provided tangible help in getting this manuscript ready for publication. So have our institutions and their leaders. Michael Allen, Jon Laansma and Darren Sarisky offered encouraging but constructively critical feedback on portions of this manuscript. Mark Bowald was courageous enough as a true friend to indicate that an early draft of several chapters was fundamentally flawed, leading to a crucial reorganization and rewrite.

Our wives have provided unyielding support through a project full of twists and turns over several years. Our daughters have provided not only their love but also reminders about why the future of mere evangelical theology matters. Doug Sweeney, to whom we dedicate this book, has reminded us both in person and in print that evangelical history matters too—all the while being a great encourager of two perennially idealistic theologians.

Abbreviations

CSCD	Cambridge Studies in Christian Doctrine
CT	*Christianity Today*
DTIB	*Dictionary for Theological Interpretation of the Bible*, ed. Kevin J. Vanhoozer. Grand Rapids: Baker Academic, 2005.
FET	Foundations of Evangelical Theology
JETS	*Journal of the Evangelical Theological Society*
NICNT	New International Commentary on the New Testament
NIGTC	New International Greek Testament Commentary
NSBT	New Studies in Biblical Theology
PNTC	Pillar New Testament Commentary
TIS	theological interpretation of Scripture

IN MY FATHER'S HOUSE,
MANY EVANGELICAL ROOMS

F OR "PEOPLE OF THE BOOK," evangelical identity and scriptural integrity are subjects of perennial, interwoven debate. Yet the volume and force of debate are increasing, not abating. Academic theologians may not settle the issues, but "ivory towers" can exert lasting, iconic influence. Thus in this book we propose an account of "mere evangelical" theology around which to rally. Theology's relation to Scripture has always been central to evangelical identity, yet increasingly this "biblicism" generates shouting matches that drown out rallying cries. The present situation calls for a fresh, galvanizing account of the ways in which evangelical theology can, and should, "mirror" the teaching of Scripture: "Anyone who listens to the word but does not do what it says is like someone who looks at his face in a mirror and, after looking at himself, goes away and immediately forgets what he looks like. But whoever looks intently into the perfect law that gives freedom, and continues in it . . . they will be blessed in what they do" (Jas 1:23-25 NIV).

No account of biblical doctrine can ignore the church, its proper context. James confronts the personal worldliness of cavalier listeners who fail to look carefully at their lives in Scripture's light. But his surrounding challenges repeatedly focus on love's communal wisdom. The canonicity of Scripture and the catholicity of the church imply each other. Evangelical theologies sometimes fail to appreciate this catholic context, focusing ecclesiologies on biblical images, polity controversies and congregational concerns. Usually lacking is a theological, not just pragmatic, rationale for pursuing orthodox and pietist Protestant ecumenism alongside, even as an aspect of, obedience to the God who speaks in Scripture. Absent an ecclesiological rationale, we are vulnerable to powerful leaders and passing fads. It can be evangelical genius to bypass institutional gridlock in favor of personal fellowship, when sharing in the gospel is readily apparent. But it can also be evangelical undoing to rest almost wholly on intuitive relationships. "Piety" is a uniter and a divider. Evangelical theology needs to account for not only sharing the basic gospel, but also collaborating to understand and minister that gospel more fully.

As perceptions of theological fragmentation increase within Anglo-American evangelicalism, many dissect evangelical theology into so-called traditionalist and reformist camps.[1] The more these labels gain currency, the more they shape perceptions; the more these perceptions become common currency, the more they shape reality—as the stock market frequently illustrates. Of course real disagreements exist within evangelical theology, with some taking binary shape. Nevertheless, adopting a two-party system is problematic, even at a descriptive level. Many fine evangelical scholars past and present defy polar categorization, particularly when certain figures wind up being pushed or pulled in both directions depending on who draws the map.

Almost by definition, therefore, mere evangelical theology pursues an elusive center that may hold by God's grace. Such a "third way" must invite dynamic collaboration between those positioned (by themselves or others) in the two camps, rather than setting up a static "camp" all its own. Indeed, recent years have already seen attempts from each side to "renew" or "reclaim" the center.[2] For evangelical theology to walk in any third way requires both a broad center (appealing to reformists) and acknowledged boundaries of some kind (appealing to traditionalists). The most basic boundaries marking the way of a healthy evangelical center would form around a theologically faithful, ecclesiastically habitable approach to

---

[1]See initially Roger E. Olson, "The Future of Evangelical Theology: Roger Olson Argues That a Division Between Traditionalists and Reformists Threatens to End Our Theological Consensus (Responses by Clark H. Pinnock, Thomas C. Oden, and Timothy George)," *CT* 42, no. 2 (Feb. 9, 1998): 40-48. More recently discussion ensued in *First Things* and elsewhere between Olson and Gerald R. McDermott (treated later in this book).

[2]Stanley J. Grenz, *Renewing the Center: Evangelical Theology in a Post-Theological Era* (Grand Rapids: Baker, 2000); Millard J. Erickson, Paul Kjoss Helseth and Justin Taylor, eds., *Reclaiming the Center: Confronting Evangelical Accommodation in Postmodern Times* (Wheaton, IL: Crossway, 2004).

Scripture and doctrine. It is impossible to address either ecclesiology or theological prolegomena in isolation, just as it is impossible to opt exclusively for either a centered (reformist) or bounded (traditionalist) set. Instead we propose that mere evangelical theology should aspire to be an anchored set: encompassing a Protestant ecumenical range of motion while anchored to the biblical, Trinitarian and crucicentric gospel. To mark out such a churchly and scriptural third way, this book depends on two fundamental metaphors in particular.

First, the ecclesiology of our subtitle: C. S. Lewis's talk of mere Christianity as a hall adjoining the rooms of specific church traditions ("communions") evokes the metaphor of the church as God's household.[3] If there is anyone for whom a wide spectrum of evangelicals share considerable appreciation, Lewis would be a strong candidate. In the present instance, his hallway motif for mere Christianity works out an ecclesiological implication of a key biblical concept—the church as family. Ecclesiology has rarely been an evangelical strength, to say the least, in part due to the impossibility of specifying all the relevant dimensions in generic detail.[4] However, for all its weaknesses, there may be neglected promise in such implicit aspects of an evangelical ecclesiology to which our account appeals.

Second, the aspiration of our title: mirroring involves both imaging God by reflecting scriptural truth in our living, and the corresponding intellectual task of evangelical theology—reflecting the Bible's forms and content in our teaching. Richard Rorty infamously construed Western philosophy as (mistakenly) attempting to mirror nature in the mind. He concluded that this mirroring was impossible and inappropriate, appealing instead for a focus on "wisdom."[5] Like Rorty, we appeal for wisdom; contra Rorty, we construe theological wisdom in terms of mirroring Scripture's forms and content as a means of grace. In Christ the Bible both represents the divine economy in which we humans find ourselves, and reflects our inadequate

---

[3]C. S. Lewis, *Mere Christianity* (San Francisco: HarperSanFrancisco, 2001), pp. xv-xvi (originally published by Macmillan in 1952).

[4]See, e.g., John G. Stackhouse Jr., ed., *Evangelical Ecclesiology: Reality or Illusion?* (Grand Rapids: Baker Academic, 2003); Mark Husbands and Daniel J. Treier, eds., *The Community of the Word: Toward an Evangelical Ecclesiology* (Downers Grove, IL: InterVarsity Press, 2005); Brad Harper and Paul Louis Metzger, *Exploring Ecclesiology: An Evangelical and Ecumenical Introduction* (Grand Rapids: Brazos, 2009).

[5]Richard Rorty, *Philosophy and the Mirror of Nature* (Princeton, NJ: Princeton University Press, 1979).

correspondence to its patterns. Evangelicals have sometimes aspired to represent Scripture as closely as possible in ways that are untenable and unhealthy. Yet reorienting mere evangelical theology involves a fresh account to galvanize, not abandon, biblical representation, with Christian communities serving as images of Christ, their drama of doctrine showing the Way to Truth in Life. Like many evangelical forebears, we still believe that imaging Christ, God's truth incarnate, requires wise understanding of God's truth in Scripture.

The two metaphors of household and mirror link via need for the Spirit's illumination: both the hallway and various rooms shed light on biblical truth. Here metaphor stretches almost to the breaking point, of course, because the mirror of Scripture moves with us as we journey. It is not a static object at which to gaze from only one perspective; the mirror does not reside solely in any one place. Given the lighting in the hallway, only large-scale patterns emerge visibly from the shadows; other details of identity in Christ come to light only in the brightness of a traditional room—with each shedding light on particular aspects and dimming others. Because mirroring works two ways—representing God to us in the biblical Christ, then reflecting our theological correspondence to the divine economy and resulting human pattern of life—the perspectives of church traditions affect our ability to see the big picture, and vice versa. We need illumination suited for more than passing glances.

Ecclesiologically, contra those who simply stay in a particular room, there is a need to live with and learn from the whole gospel family.[6] Alternatively,

---

[6]Protestant confessionalism garners scrutiny later, but here Catholicism and Orthodoxy merit brief treatment. If evangelicalism is "Protestant," at least historically, then are Orthodox and Catholic communions or their members by definition outside the household? No, most minimally a Protestant ecclesiology merely denies exclusive claims of those traditions regarding one true institutional church. That means refusing to make pronouncements concerning the salvation of any person or group based directly on ecclesiastical affiliation. Persons, congregations or structures outside evangelical Protestant networks have room(s) within the gospel house, neither defining the whole structure nor being displaced entirely to the outside. Denying Catholic and Orthodox claims about the church is not the same as denying that Orthodoxy and Catholicism can function as church communions construed in some Protestant sense, and of course no evangelical theologian should deny that our own sections of the gospel household are in disrepair.

Catholic and Orthodox believers can be "evangelical" in some senses of the word, but it is needlessly confusing to blend them into definitions of *evangelicalism* or *evangelical theology* as subcultures. George Weigel, with whom many evangelicals have been in fruitful dialogue, nevertheless illustrates the clear sense in which such Catholics still distinguish themselves from

contra those who try to see the mirror sufficiently in the hall, Lewis reminds us that no one lives there. Necessary resources, solitude and activities are only available in the rooms. Acknowledging what each brings to light, evangelical theologians need to find which room brings biblical truth most fully into view while listening to the hallway conversation about what others see.[7] In a certain sense Protestants call no one on earth "father," highlighting our oneness in Christ the head, through whom God is our Father. Appealing to spiritual oneness, we easily neglect the church as our mother: by divine design the Spirit's nurturing instruction comes in Scripture via her teaching ministry. The classic evangelical emphasis on biblical authority in 2 Timothy 3:16-17 fits into a surrounding context of wisdom unto salvation (2 Tim 3:15), inextricably linked with familial and churchly formation (2 Tim 3:14-15; 4:1-5). The family and house images cohere in the larger metaphor of the church as God's household. Its unfolding drama comes about as close as possible to a core biblical concept for ecclesiology.

Before getting our hands too dirty with detailed ecclesiological and hermeneutical work, however, this introductory chapter provides historical perspective for our theological proposal. We begin with a basic inspection of the many rooms in the evangelical household: first their contemporary fragmentation, then their theological history. Patchwork renovation without a careful design might produce a temporary fix, but neither lasting stability nor flexibility for continued growth.

Still, it needs to be said right up front that our theological design does not depend on the sociological realities of contemporary evangelicalism or a particular historiography of its identity. We propose a design for *evangelical theology*, not evangelicalism as such. When accounting at times for popular evangelicalism vis-à-vis such theology, we are appreciating the priesthood of all believers and therefore shading in surrounding contours, not drawing a more comprehensive blueprint. Ultimately, we aim to provide a theological

Protestant evangelicalism in his *Evangelical Catholicism: Deep Reform in the 21st-Century Church* (New York: Basic Books, 2013). In this case, whether "evangelical" language serves as an adjective or a noun affects the self-understanding of both.

[7]Richard Lints compares such a politics of evangelical ecclesiology with the opportunities and temptations of modern democracy, advocating principled pluralism, in "A Post-Partisan Partisan Ecclesiology," in *Renewing the Evangelical Mission*, ed. Richard Lints (Grand Rapids: Eerdmans, 2013), pp. 161-86.

prolegomenon and ecclesiological perspective for orthodox, pietist, Protestant ecumenism—historically dependent solely on the aspiration of some earlier evangelical theologians to mirror Scripture, while theologically discerning how we might do so again.

A Crumbling Hallway? An Initial Inspection

In order to sketch an evangelical theological tradition stable enough to handle winds of change, yet flexible enough to embrace a growing family, we begin by examining current structural reports. While many have the impression that contemporary evangelical identity rests on shifting sands, others worry about the historical credibility or theological propriety of appealing to solid foundations. Perceptions that mere evangelicalism's hallway is crumbling or chaotic reflect at least four recent developments. These developments identify challenges that any proposal for evangelical theology must address.

First among the most relevant forms of change is more robust academic engagement. Carl F. H. Henry and others pioneered an evangelical return to mainstream academic life.[8] Subsequent waves of religious historians, philosophers and biblical scholars—especially from the 1970s onward—are increasingly joined by natural and social scientists, theologians and others. This increase of intellectual faithfulness and missional presence inevitably confronts church leaders, laypersons and parachurch institutions—not to mention the scholars themselves—with puzzling difficulties. How does one discern whether changing views as a result are theologically faithful or unfaithful, identity-altering or indifferent?

Second, evangelicals have increased awareness of the so-called Great Christian Tradition and the variety of our subtraditions. Formerly associated primarily with Roman Catholicism and Eastern Orthodoxy, the creeds, texts and practices of early Christianity are newly interesting to many evangelicals—in the process altering how some see their Protestant identity

---

[8]Classically see Carl F. H. Henry, *The Uneasy Conscience of Modern Fundamentalism* (Grand Rapids: Eerdmans, 1947). More recently see Mark A. Noll, *The Scandal of the Evangelical Mind* (Grand Rapids: Eerdmans, 1994); a sequel with retrospective comments in idem, *Jesus Christ and the Life of the Mind* (Grand Rapids: Eerdmans, 2011); specifically concerning biblical scholarship, idem, *Between Faith and Criticism: Evangelicals, Scholarship, and the Bible in America* (San Francisco: Harper & Row, 1986).

and embody their faith. No longer do they simply claim that their beliefs match portions of the Great Tradition, primarily on basic questions about the triune God and the identity of Jesus Christ; now evangelicals begin to wonder if the very fact of such tradition somehow binds them. Evangelicals are also more aware of internal variety. Debate persists over how to honor both Reformed and Holiness contributions to evangelical history.[9] No longer does a quasi-Reformed basic consensus dominate evangelical texts and institutions as it once seemed to do in the middle of the twentieth century. Plus there have been significant developments of Southern Baptist self-definition, not to mention evangelical identity vis-à-vis Pentecostal movements here and abroad.[10]

Which leads, third, to interest in global Christianity. It is not as if God was doing little in Africa, Asia and Latin America for much of the twentieth century or beforehand. To the contrary, "the West" was slow to realize or celebrate how God is active—both through missionary efforts and quite apart from them.[11] A couple of decades ago, the chief evangelical challenge in this area involved sporadic debate over contextualization. Today's challenge concerns whether or how such a concept goes far enough.[12] Meanwhile, more substantial debate looms over what counts as "evangelical," and whether the term matters for mission.

Fourth among these changes is interfaces with emergent Christianity and culture. Theological method is at issue because evangelical identity is at issue—not just around the world, or vis-à-vis church traditions, or resulting

[9]Donald W. Dayton and Robert K. Johnston, *The Variety of American Evangelicalism* (Knoxville: University of Tennessee Press, 1991), is well-known for criticizing the historical perspective in George M. Marsden, *Reforming Fundamentalism: Fuller Seminary and the New Evangelicalism* (Grand Rapids: Eerdmans, 1987) and the theological perspective in Bernard L. Ramm, *The Evangelical Heritage* (Waco, TX: Word, 1973).

[10]See therefore the contrasting emphases when treating hermeneutics and doctrine in Malcolm B. Yarnell III, *The Formation of Christian Doctrine* (Nashville: B&H Academic, 2007), and Kevin L. Spawn and Archie T. Wright, eds., *Spirit and Scripture: Exploring a Pneumatic Hermeneutic* (London: T&T Clark, 2012), vis-à-vis their critical discussions of prominent evangelical figures and traditional tendencies.

[11]Though speaking of a north/south contrast might be more accurate than using the construct of "Western civilization," nevertheless it is handy to accede to common usage here.

[12]For a useful overview of evangelical perspectives, see David K. Clark, *To Know and Love God*, FET (Wheaton, IL: Crossway, 2003), pp. 99-131; on evangelical practices, see A. Scott Moreau, *Contextualization in World Missions: Mapping and Assessing Evangelical Models* (Grand Rapids: Kregel, 2012).

from scholarly presence, but also within Western churches. Evangelicalism has always had younger, theologically edgier, ministerial entrepreneurs and older, wiser or merely reactionary guardians. Now new media foster faster, more polarizing conversation, perhaps exaggerating perceptions of fragmentation; at the same time it remains possible to overstate previous consensus out of nostalgia.[13] Hence, emergent forms of Christianity—which are what they are, for good and ill, in response to cultural trends—put considerable pressure on any traditional concept of evangelical identity.

These four developments exacerbate the dilemma of distinguishing uniquely "evangelical theology" from the "theology done by evangelicals" (as members of various Christian traditions). Without trying to solve historical or sociological mysteries of evangelical identity, though, we merely establish here that fragmentation both affects and generates contemporary evangelical conversations about theological method. If many perceive fragmentation, it will come. If we can construe both fragmentation and evangelical identity theologically, however, then hidden opportunities may emerge from perceived crisis. Some further historical inspection will help to put this perceived fragmentation in theological perspective.[14]

BENEATH THE CRACKS: A HISTORICAL-THEOLOGICAL INSPECTION

Questions of evangelical identity are often pressed in the following way: Should our definition be historical and/or sociological (primarily descriptive), or else theological (primarily prescriptive)? If "evangelical" becomes a matter of description or self-attestation, then does the label slide toward "anything goes"—"whosoever will" may come forward? By contrast, if the label becomes property of those holding certain beliefs, then does that prescriptive approach deny the complexity of history, marginalize certain contributions to the evangelical movement and ignore the inescapable reality of theological traditions changing over time—even simply to stay the

[13]Championing strong consensus are J. I. Packer and Thomas C. Oden, in *One Faith: The Evangelical Consensus* (Downers Grove, IL: InterVarsity Press, 2004).
[14]The most prominent contemporary historiography is Molly Worthen, *Apostles of Reason: The Crisis of Authority in American Evangelicalism* (New York: Oxford University Press, 2013). Details aside, our approach seems to be broadly compatible with hers, in this respect: much of today's perceived fragmentation has longstanding roots in struggles over integrating traditional, personal piety and public rationality.

same? Not to mention: Does a prescriptive approach assume an overly cognitive account of the church? To what extent would evangelicals, in that case,
actually deny their heritage, which sometimes developed in spite of or even
over against formal theology? Moreover, what about the evangelical future,
since much global Christianity will not define itself with respect to an
Anglo-American heritage?

Little recent discussion wrestles with a specifically ecclesiological rationale for evangelical theology in the first place, which might put some of
the historical and sociological complexity in a theological light. The evident
rise of conflicts over theological identity—or at least the perception of losing
a classically "evangelical" doctrinal consensus—has an academic history that
can be narrated in terms of the following four animating questions. Important as these disputes are, they encourage developing an ecclesiological
rationale for identifying and sustaining evangelical theology: How does
being people of the gospel depend on being people not just of the Book but
of the church—precisely because of the drama the Book presents? Much of
the following history centers on North America, for there the identity debate
has been most vociferous. Our theological proposal, reorienting mere evangelicalism around a more robustly ecclesiological account of what it means
to mirror Scripture, tries to transcend a merely American locale, and for that
matter primarily historical or sociological desiderata. Nevertheless, the
history of the recent American debates proves to be instructive regarding
evangelical ecclesiological deficits that a theological proposal must address.

Can or should we define evangelical *theologically?* Was there once an
evangelical theological "consensus," worth retaining or recapturing? That
conversation starts with the writing of evangelical history. David Bebbington's ubiquitously cited quadrilateral of evangelical identifiers—activism,
biblicism, conversionism, crucicentrism—is somewhat theological but minimally so.[15] Subsequently George Marsden wrote a history of Fuller Seminary
called *Reforming Fundamentalism.* Some perceived that this sequel to *Fundamentalism and American Culture* cast evangelicalism in rather Reformed

---

[15]David W. Bebbington, *Evangelicalism in Modern Britain: A History from the 1730s to the 1980s*
(London: Unwin Hyman, 1989), pp. 2-17. Responses to Bebbington's criteria get further treatment in chapter five, which more directly proposes an ecclesiology for evangelical theology.
Bebbington placed these criteria within a particular historical framework that their citations
often neglect.

or (New School) Presbyterian terms, which Wesleyan and Holiness–
oriented scholars such as Donald Dayton opposed.[16] (That's not to mention
Baptists, although their stories and others are likewise complicated.)

Every so often theologians jump into the unfolding stages of this historical debate. Some Reformed thinkers have made peace with Dayton's
challenge to Marsden. They are willing to grant the lack of significant evangelical consensus around Protestant Reformation doctrines. Instead of
being a big theological tent with a four-sided boundary, says Michael
Horton, evangelicalism is more like a village green or town square.[17] People
gather to talk and perhaps to share certain activities, remaining quite clear
that their homes are elsewhere. In this context Horton appeals to the very
Mere Christianity reference around which we construct this book, likening
evangelicalism to a hallway. People meet in common space occasionally,
but they should not get confused and move their chairs or beds outside
their own rooms.

Horton makes this claim out of acute sensitivity to Reformed distinctiveness while, presumably, letting non-Reformed folks be themselves too.
Additionally, Horton is sensitive to that infamous evangelical weakness, the
doctrine of the church. Drawing on a Lewis Smedes essay, we can satirically
envision evangelical care for confessional discipline.[18] Annually, leaders of
large churches and parachurch ministries would fly from their Nebraska
headquarters, or wherever else, into O'Hare Airport, be taxied to Wheaton,
and meet around a hotel conference table. (This vision may be outdated,
with the meeting now transpiring in Colorado Springs or via the Internet.)
Anyway, these leaders would meet for an hour or two, vote on whose
teachings were false or dangerous, and head home. Then what: would *Christianity Today* publish the list? Would anything actually happen to the so-
called heretics?

The point here is to emphasize the parachurch-, and charismatic leader-,

---

[16]See George M. Marsden, *Fundamentalism and American Culture: The Shaping of Twentieth-
Century Evangelicalism 1870–1925* (Oxford: Oxford University Press, 1980).

[17]Michael S. Horton, "The Battles Over the Label 'Evangelical,'" *Modern Reformation* (March/April
2001): 15-21; more extensively, idem, "The Church After Evangelicalism," in Lints, *Renewing the
Evangelical Mission*, pp. 134-60. Also broadly in this vein is D. G. Hart, *Deconstructing Evangelicalism: Conservative Protestantism in the Age of Billy Graham* (Grand Rapids: Baker Academic, 2004).

[18]Lewis B. Smedes, "Evangelicalism: A Fantasy," *Reformed Journal* 30, no. 2 (Fall 1980): 2-3.

dominated nature of evangelicalism, as well as particularities of the Reformed and non-Reformed groups hovering about its edges. These dynamics raise the question of whether earlier evangelical consensus was apparent or real, theological or otherwise. Is Horton right to argue that the original consensus that (re)birthed evangelicalism (in its current form) in the 1940s was largely political, not theological—a vision of what America would be like (with serious implications for evangelical families and gospel witness) if cultural forms became thoroughly secular (as fundamentalists seemed to find inevitable)?[19] By contrast, in the judgment of others such as Timothy George and J. I. Packer, a rough-and-ready theological consensus once prevailed and still might: evangelicals agreed on proclaiming gospel basics, being rightful heirs of the church's classical Protestant heritage and treating other differences as secondary. So, with the name "evangelical," surely we must agree about the gospel . . . right?

Is there an evangelical "gospel"? A second debate, over the gospel, has similarly unfolded in stages. The Lausanne Covenant, to which worldwide evangelicals agreed in 1974 under the leadership of John Stott and others, did not dominate the American scene. Many who now style themselves "evangelical," or at least "conservative evangelical" when involved in contemporary theological discussions, were closer to the fundamentalist orbit during the 1970s. They felt wary of Lausanne's commitment to social action, which they maintained as subsidiary rather than integrally related to mission. Today the Lausanne movement itself faces queries about whether its pursuit of social justice goes far enough in dethroning Western hegemony.[20]

At any rate, in the mid-1990s the gospel debate sometimes became acrimonious over the Evangelicals and Catholics Together (ECT) dialogue. The first ECT proposal, for "co-belligerence" on social issues and mission where possible, along with discussion about remaining theological disagreements,

---

[19]In an interview accompanying Horton's *Modern Reformation* essay ("Are Charismatic-Inclined Pietists the True Evangelicals? And Have the Reformed Tried to Hijack the Movement? Interview with Donald Dayton," pp. 40-49), Dayton reads this development less in terms of missionary commitment and more in terms of social class advancement.

[20]See, e.g., a rough translation of comments from a well-respected leader among global evangelicals in Al Hsu, "Rene Padilla on the Cape Town Lausanne Congress," *The Suburban Christian* (blog), November 10, 2010, http://thesuburbanchristian.blogspot.com/2010/11/rene-padilla -on-cape-town-lausanne.html.

led later to *ECT II*, a statement on the gospel.[21] *ECT II* acknowledged remaining soteriological disagreements, especially ongoing differences over church practices such as sacraments and indulgences. But its signatories affirmed basic agreement on "justification by faith." Objections emanated from several evangelical quarters—both specifically Reformed and more generally separatist. Not wanting to cause division, but rather to galvanize evangelistic efforts in preparation for Amsterdam 2000 (a worldwide event connected to Billy Graham), ECT signatories such as George, Packer and John Woodbridge crafted a "statement on the gospel" affirming what evangelicals continued to agree on in-house. After much negotiating, rewriting, cajoling and pleading, "The Gospel of Jesus Christ: An Evangelical Celebration" was produced along with accompanying literature.[22] The Amsterdam 2000 leadership signed on. Nine evangelicals from different traditions wrote one-page summaries of the gospel for a special issue of *Christianity Today*.[23]

But not all Reformed conservatives signed on. Neither did crucial Southern Baptist leaders. Prominent academics, mostly non-Reformed, criticized the document from the other side—for including certain Reformed distinctives (such as Christ's "active obedience") and/or for excluding "nonexclusivists" (regarding the destiny of non-Christians). Indeed, although Arminians were represented, the drafting committee was overwhelmingly Reformed or Reformed Baptist. Ironically enough, Robert Gundry (a Baptist biblical scholar) criticized the document both for including Reformed particularities (too conservatively) and for not being clear enough on an "exclusivist" position (too progressively).[24]

Religious pluralism is newly contested from various angles. Evangelical attitudes toward even the possibility that Roman Catholics might be saved have relaxed dramatically between the last generation and the current one.

[21]"Evangelicals and Catholics Together: The Gift of Salvation," *CT* 41, no. 15 (Dec. 8, 1997): 35-38, presenting this statement. Defending *ECT I* was J. I. Packer in "Why I Signed It: The Recent Statement 'Evangelicals and Catholics Together' Recognizes an Important Truth: Those Who Love the Lord Must Stand Together," *CT* 38, no. 14 (Dec. 12, 1994): 34-37.
[22]It appeared in *CT* 43, no. 7 (June 14, 1999): 51-56, and later as an appendix in John N. Akers, John N. Armstrong and John D. Woodbridge, eds., *This We Believe: The Good News of Jesus Christ for the World* (Grand Rapids: Zondervan, 2000), pp. 238-49.
[23]"What's the Good News? Nine Evangelical Leaders Define the Gospel," *CT* 44, no. 2 (Feb. 7, 2000): 46-51.
[24]Robert H. Gundry, "Why I Didn't Endorse 'The Gospel of Jesus Christ: An Evangelical Celebration' . . . Even Though I Wasn't Asked to," *Books & Culture* 7, no. 1 (January/February 2001): 6-9.

Such contrasts become more striking after scanning catalogs from evangelical publishers advertising diverse viewpoints on the nature of hell or the fate of the unevangelized, not to mention various indicators from sociological research.[25] Meanwhile a growing chorus of Wesleyan-Arminians, Anabaptists and others highlights that their traditions have not always accepted a penal substitution theory of Christ's atonement. Thus controversies have ensued in mainstream evangelical circles over publication of such perspectives. Still further, debates over justification did not abate in the wake of ECT but morphed into controversies over the so-called New Perspective on Paul, especially the work of N. T. Wright, with that literature becoming too voluminous to cite. The point now adequately established by these examples is that, if various wings of evangelicalism ever agreed on "conversionist piety" (a frequent phrase stemming from Bebbington) centered on the biblical message of the cross, more than ever they now disagree about its language, its logic and its necessity for someone's eternal destiny.

Is there an evangelical doctrine of God? How should evangelicals deal with new theological proposals? The gospel debate intersects with a third controversy, regarding the doctrine of God, where this animating question of biblical creativity lurks behind the scenes. Some proponents of a less-than-exclusivist approach to religious pluralism also happen to be key proponents of the open or freewill theism debated over the last three decades. Open theists' appeals to plain-sense readings of the Bible and thereby to *sola Scriptura* were quickly deemed acceptable by certain leading evangelical institutions, despite the self-proclaimed departure from classic Christian theology. Some traditionalist responses were predictably reactionary, even excessively so, yet others struggled to find a mainstream evangelical publisher.

Debate over the substantive issues has died down, as positions have entrenched themselves. But key formal issues arise in this realm too. The Evangelical Theological Society (ETS), among other organizations, had to discern how it is like and unlike a church, or how if at all a Christian scholarly society should practice doctrinal discipline. The operative

---

[25]Earlier indications of this change came from James Davison Hunter, *Evangelicalism: The Coming Generation* (Chicago: University of Chicago Press, 1987), although its methodology has been challenged. Contemporary studies from Christian Smith, such as (with Patricia Snell) *Souls in Transition: The Religious and Spiritual Lives of Emerging Adults* (New York: Oxford University Press, 2009), are broadly consistent with this point.

implications of *sola Scriptura* on one hand, and respect for Christian tradition on the other, became newly pressing. The "Hellenization thesis," concerning classic Christian orthodoxy's supposed fall from a simpler, Jewish,
biblical gospel into Greek philosophical abstraction, suddenly had poignant
implications for evangelical theology.[26] Broad appeals to patristic orthodoxy
could no longer suffice, with evangelicals now having to address the authority of classical theistic consensus vis-à-vis the limits of contemporary
theological creativity.

Is there an evangelical theological "method"? How then should evangelical theology approach the Bible, supposedly its shared source of authority, concerning such doctrinal proposals? These questions of Scripture
and tradition giving definition to the gospel bring us full circle, back to the
formal Protestant principle amid increasing material diversity.

The stories may be relatively familiar, and details are no doubt accessible
elsewhere, regarding the battle for the Bible, from which collateral damage
still lingers. After the rise of Old Princeton theology and the fundamentalist-
modernist conflicts, the narrative picks up speed once again with Fuller
Theological Seminary's 1960s removal of required faculty adherence to full
biblical inerrancy; the rise of Trinity Evangelical Divinity School as an intellectual alternative; Harold Lindsell's "battle for the Bible" in the 1970s,
and the ensuing international councils on biblical inerrancy and hermeneutics; the claims of Jack Rogers and Donald McKim to support partial
inerrancy (limited to matters of faith and practice) from Reformed roots,
followed by rejection of their historical claims from Trinity's Woodbridge;
and then the 1980s ETS controversy over Gundry's commentary on Matthew.[27] Gundry claimed that events in Matthean infancy narratives might

---

[26]Associated fairly or unfairly with Adolf von Harnack, most notably his *History of Dogma*, trans.
Alexander Balmain Bruce (Boston: Roberts, 1896–1899), this narrative of decline had been
primarily the provenance of more liberal or progressive theologies. Once linked with the evangelical tendency toward post–New Testament and pre-Reformation decline narratives, though,
aspects of the thesis began to appear in evangelical scholarship—not least in open theist appeals
for plain reading over against traditional hermeneutical constraints.

[27]See Marsden, *Reforming Fundamentalism*; Harold Lindsell, *The Battle for the Bible* (Grand Rapids:
Zondervan, 1976); Jack Bartlett Rogers and Donald K. McKim, *The Authority and Interpretation
of the Bible: An Historical Approach* (San Francisco: Harper & Row, 1979); John D. Woodbridge,
Biblical Authority: A Critique of the Rogers/McKim Proposal (Grand Rapids: Zondervan, 1982);
Robert H. Gundry, *Matthew: A Commentary on His Literary and Theological Art* (Grand Rapids:
Zondervan, 1982).

not be straightforwardly historical; instead, as Jewish midrash on key Old Testament passages, their kind of truth fits their genre. Some within the ETS disputed Gundry's claims about midrash as a genre,[28] whereas others disputed the credence of his affirmation of inerrancy.[29] He was asked to leave the society.

Fast-forward another fifteen years, and debates over biblical authority regained energy: Norman Geisler, so influential in the earlier controversy, gave the ETS presidential address in 1998. His theme was the need to recognize (and resist) philosophies that prevent being biblical. Geisler named specific views—and evangelicals who succumbed to them.[30] The next year's address came from Wayne Grudem, then a Trinity faculty member who subsequently moved to Phoenix Seminary. Grudem is fascinating because he taught New Testament—the field of his PhD—for years before switching to systematic theology. Now his *Systematic Theology*, in various forms, is overwhelmingly the most popular evangelical doctrine textbook, at least in the United States. Grudem challenged ETS members to do more biblical work in their theologizing, more in-house evangelical reading and publication, and more work on practical concerns of evangelical churches—to view encounters with academic theology not as learning opportunities but as largely apologetic and/or evangelistic in nature. Both Geisler and Grudem influenced and epitomized a resurgence of conservative biblicism, within the Southern Baptist Convention and elsewhere.

In the process Grudem became a target of many on the evangelical left. In *Renewing the Center* (2000), Stanley Grenz (himself a frequent target of the evangelical right) used Grudem to epitomize hidebound traditionalism and biblicism. Grenz traced two (debatable) streams in evangelical thought, one from Henry through Millard Erickson to Grudem, and the other from Bernard Ramm through Clark Pinnock to John Sanders. A similar two-party arrangement—"postconservatives" versus everybody else—characterizes

---

[28]Douglas J. Moo, "Matthew and Midrash: An Evaluation of Robert H Gundry's Approach," *JETS* 26, no. 1 (March 1983): 31-39.

[29]Norman L. Geisler, "Methodological Unorthodoxy," *JETS* 26, no. 1 (March 1983): 87-94.

[30]Geisler again entered the fray over open theism, with Clark Pinnock and John Sanders winning close and closer votes (respectively) to remain in the Evangelical Theological Society. Even more recently Geisler opposed the treatment of Matthew 27:51-53 by Michael Licona (*The Resurrection of Jesus: A New Historiographical Approach* [Downers Grove, IL: InterVarsity Press, 2010]) as inconsistent with biblical inerrancy.

the analysis of Erickson, Roger Olson and nonevangelical Gary Dorrien.[31]

Alternatively, numerous scholars epitomize the possibility of an evangelical center, or perhaps a remnant, in between the two parties. One illustration of greater complexity involves Ramm's legacy. It is possible (like Grenz) to admire Ramm (himself pilloried by Dayton) and join contemporaries who are appreciative as well as critical of Karl Barth, without simply rejecting the work of Henry or embracing open theism, and while defending a nuanced form of biblical inerrancy.[32] Such positions characterize various evangelical scholars who simultaneously pursue increasing dialogue with academic theology as well as British and other global theologians outside the American orbit. These scholars may engage and critique both Grudem and Grenz, aligning fully with neither. As the Ramm case proves, there may be different ways of appealing to a theological legacy.

Even attempts to define a third way cannot merely draw lines in this muddled middle, as if simply bisecting traditionalists and reformists. No single set of issues—biblical inerrancy or not, postmodernism or not, open theism or not, and so forth—definitively draws such a map. Issues of underlying ethos—forms of engagement with classic Christian tradition(s), earlier evangelical theology and contemporary nonevangelical scholarship—are likewise too diffuse for clear map drawing. The label "postconservative" itself has varied uses. Some scholars are traditionalists on certain issues and reformists on others.

Sorting through these conversations, one discerns progression in how American evangelicals relate to Reformed theology. In the middle 1900s, many "traditions" wrote and used in-house materials (for instance, dispensationalists had their authors at Dallas Seminary). But formal evangelical theology per se was dominated by broadly Reformed sensibilities— the Princetonians dominated epistemology, apologetics and biblical authority; general outlines of magisterial Reformation teaching domi-

[31]See Millard Erickson, *Postmodernizing the Faith: Evangelical Responses to the Challenge of Postmodernism* (Grand Rapids: Baker, 1998) and especially *The Evangelical Left: Encountering Postconservative Evangelical Theology* (Grand Rapids: Baker, 1997). See the review of Gary Dorrien by Rodney Clapp, "The Remaking of Evangelical Theology," *Books & Culture* 5 (May/June 1999): 25.

[32]Note the Grenz/Dayton contrast regarding Ramm, plus the fact that neither Grenz nor Dayton embraced open theism. See also the appreciative treatment of Ramm by Kevin J. Vanhoozer (himself attached to the Henry tradition in many respects) in the foreword to *The Evangelical Heritage: A Study in Historical Theology* (Grand Rapids: Baker, 2000).

nated talk about "justification" in the gospel, consistent (in a personalized way) with the message preached by revivalists. Within these boundaries, differences over sanctification, the church and last things were tolerable. Relatively few theological works tackled the academic spirit of the age head-on, so that texts such as Henry's six-volume *God, Revelation, and Authority* garnered widespread evangelical scholarly attention. Popular evangelical theology may have been more diverse than the formal, Reformed-leaning discourse would indicate; at the same time, popular trends may eventually have been influenced by such elite discourse in ways that are easy to overlook.

Now, in any case, many without Reformed sensibilities engage intellectual culture; every tradition seeks to develop schools populated with publishing scholars. In addition, the "objective truth" of biblical "revelation" no longer gains much traction from select appeals to modern philosophy. The result is that non-Reformed sensibilities have a stronger voice in evangelical theological conversations, beyond enclosure within their own traditions. Evangelicals are so rooted in revivalism and activism (or even individualism and pragmatism?) that Calvinist tendencies of intellectual rigor and sometimes austere piety will be perennially problematic for many. Correspondingly, full-blooded Presbyterian and Reformed thought is sensitive about dilution of its identity by broader evangelical tendencies.

A central challenge for evangelical theology therefore involves pursuing newfound intellectual engagement from within different traditions. Will there be enough perceived consensus on gospel truth and theological method, now that (faux?) Reformed hegemony is over, for working or even talking together? Conversely, will various theological traditions contribute distinctively—will anyone care to say anything particular—if evangelicalism at the congregational level intermingles everyone so much that they become doctrinally indistinguishable?

In the American context, group struggles over religious identity follow as a matter of course. From the emerging global scene come additional challenges along with exciting opportunities. Hence this history serves as a vital pointer to the looming issue of how evangelical theology embraces the catholicity of the church. After theological conservatives serially lost key battles within American Protestant denominations, they withdrew to

retrench, in the process banding together as they created new institutions.[33]
This retrenchment had positive consequences for practical catholicity:
mutual edification, intellectually and otherwise, resulted when embattled
evangelicals supported each other in crisis.[34] As the preceding history demonstrates, though, the new coalition did not give sustained biblical and
theological attention to an ecclesiology with staying power—the staying
power of an account of Scripture and doctrine that appreciates "mere"
evangelical fellowship.

Recent collections reflecting an evangelical theological identity, which not
coincidentally try to move beyond just the American scene, extend the history
detailed above. They reflect progress in academic theological engagement,
some even coming from important university presses.[35] They reflect lingering
weakness in dogmatic theology, often depending heavily on appeals to nonevangelical resources.[36] They reflect progress, albeit with lingering weakness,

---

[33]See particularly Joel A. Carpenter, *Revive Us Again: The Reawakening of American Fundamentalism* (Oxford: Oxford University Press, 1997).

[34]On the theme of perceived marginalization helping evangelical identity, see Christian Smith,
American Evangelicalism: Embattled and Thriving (Chicago: University of Chicago Press, 1998).

[35]Gerald R. McDermott, ed., *The Oxford Handbook of Evangelical Theology* (Oxford: Oxford University Press, 2010), is perhaps the most academically stalwart, though its contributors are
overwhelmingly Western and male. McDermott's version of a two-party approach, favoring the
traditionalist side and dubbing the reformist side "meliorist," elicited fresh controversy with
Olson; see McDermott's "Evangelicals Divided: Gerald McDermott Describes the Battle Between Meliorists and Traditionalists to Define Evangelicalism," *First Things* 212 (April 2011):
45-50, and Olson's response in Roger E. Olson, "My Letter to First Things (Responding to the
McDermott Article)," *Roger E. Olson: My Evangelical Arminian Theologial Musings* (blog), March
23, 2011, www.patheos.com/blogs/rogereolson/2011/03/my-letter-to-first-things-responding
-to-the-mcdermott-article/. McDermott describes the meliorists (an appellation generally celebrating human progress) as those who "think we must improve and sometimes change substantially the tradition of historic orthodoxy" (p. 46). He uses the term *postconservative* as an
equivalent. Roger E. Olson, *The Westminster Handbook to Evangelical Theology* (Louisville: Westminster John Knox, 2004), not a compendium since it comes from a single author, fulfills a
similar function and proffers Olson's fullest statement of his own approach.

[36]Mark A. Noll's historical treatment in McDermott, *Oxford Handbook of Evangelical Theology*
("What Is 'Evangelical'?" pp. 19-32) advocates working with Bebbington's quadrilateral, manag-
ing its difficulties of definition (such as terminological slippage, application to black Protestantism and most poignantly "the increasing number of non-Western independent churches") with
"common sense." Timothy Larsen's "Defining and Locating Evangelicalism," in *The Cambridge
Companion to Evangelical Theology*, ed. Timothy Larsen and Daniel J. Treier (Cambridge: Cambridge University Press, 2007), pp. 1-14, turns Bebbington's quadrilateral into a pentagon by
adding the Holy Spirit's work. The added pneumatological emphasis coheres with increased
diversity: the Cambridge volume compares very favorably with others in its series regarding
female, minority and non-Western contributors, and in the global range of its essays. David
Fergusson counts the volume as evidence of the "vitality" of evangelical theology in "Theology

in global and minority theological engagement—in addition to lack of consensus about how to address gender in a healthy way.[37] Where the Bible speaks with apparent clarity, lending itself to proof texts, evangelical theologians have taught faithfully, and in some academic circles their work has been tolerated or even appreciated. But where the Bible does not speak so directly, evangelical theologians have not been very bold or capable, and their doctrinal efforts are received with more intellectual suspicion.

This dogmatic and constructive weakness is partially a deficit of catholicity: evangelical theology has not yet reckoned adequately with either time or place. Inadequate attention to tradition, minority voices and global cultures also puts apostolicity at stake, since we fail to hear the biblical Word in its fullness or to participate wholly in the mission on which the Spirit sends us. Dogmatic and constructive weakness further highlights longstanding contrasts between American evangelicals and British or Continental European theologians. With exceptions such as Jonathan Edwards, America has not produced leading theologians; it may not be in our religious temper to do so. As American evangelicals begin now to reengage academic theology, where and to whom do they look for models? To the European Bs, of course—to Barth, Bonhoeffer, Berkouwer, Brunner and the British. While explicitly self-identified evangelicals may be relatively few on that ecclesiastical scene, conservative or substantially orthodox Protestants have not been so marginal, keeping alive intellectual aspects of the Reformation heritage languishing among Americans. This contrast between America and Europe complicates use of the term *evangelical* past and future: some possibly willing to use the word have not been strongly affiliated with its historical network, yet serve as orthodox theologians within classic Protestant churches.

Today—Currents and Directions," *Expository Times* 123, no. 3 (2011): 105-12, at p. 108n5.

Yet Kevin Vanhoozer's "The Triune God of the Gospel" (pp. 17-34) and John Webster's "Jesus Christ" (pp. 51-64) both identify dogmatic weakness in evangelical theology, with its apologetics- and textbook-oriented tendencies simultaneously constricting constructive depth and untethering creative exploration from proper dogmatic constraints.

[37]William A. Dyrness and Veli-Matti Kärkkäinen, eds., *Global Dictionary of Theology* (Downers Grove, IL: InterVarsity Press, 2008), truly can boast an international contributor list, yet key articles (e.g., on systematic theology) contain sections separately written by Anglo-American and non-Western contributors. This separation manifests lingering complexities concerning "Western" influence over formal evangelical discourse, with points of overlap inside such articles also manifesting that enduring influence worldwide.

Attending then to the geographical fullness of Christ's church in the Global South, evangelical theology does not yet adequately manifest the democracy of either the dead or the living. Arriving late at deep engagement with the classic creedal and theological tradition, simultaneously encountering the breadth of global Christianity, evangelical theology feels a double strain at points of its earlier identity. The differences between so-called Western and non-Western evangelical theology frequently concern emphasis rather than method or even content.[38] Truth judgments on questions such as justification by faith may be similar, with conceptual priorities strikingly different—for instance, raising queries about Western terminology of "righteousness" instead of "justice"; overemphasis on individual salvation in the hereafter; or neglect of the justice about which the Old Testament prophets speak as directly as Paul speaks concerning justification. Some non-Western thinkers associated with the evangelical movement, according to historical definitions anyway, may be wary of the label—given the flawed emphases they associate with its Anglo-American dominance—yet in a sense evangelical they may still be.

Accordingly, progress in fostering and listening to diverse evangelical voices across place and time—what we might call operational catholicity—is possible but requires intentional effort. The European theological scene may bring orthodox Protestants closer to network evangelicals but, in the process, highlights need for growth in theology's dogmatic dimension. Undoubtedly, American concerns in addressing biblical authority vis-à-vis theological method have a particular history. The strengths of those commitments should be shared so that others might discern how to appropriate them in their contexts. Yet the West tends to export fixations and weaknesses alongside strengths. Anglo-American evangelicals on both sides of the Atlantic Ocean need to learn from global brothers and sisters to grow in theology's constructive dimension. Global questions about which Westerners have been less energetic highlight important theological priorities. When the Bible less explicitly addresses nontraditional subjects like technology—

---

[38]In this regard see, e.g., Tokunboh Adeyemo et al., eds., *Africa Bible Commentary: A One-Volume Commentary Written by 70 African Scholars* (Grand Rapids: Zondervan, 2006), or certain chapters from non-Western scholars in the aforementioned *Cambridge Companion to Evangelical Theology.*

an example already signaled by the Lausanne Covenant a generation ago—tendencies toward proof-texting do not help. In fact, this global lesson should hit closer to home on other matters of perspective as well: at least in America, the white male failure to listen to other voices manifests itself dramatically in evangelical theological history pertaining to race, gender and the like. In temporal, geographical and social ways, therefore, appreciating the catholicity of the church is vital for doing fully evangelical theology, for hearing and mirroring the apostolic Word.

WISE FOUNDATIONS? OUR PROPOSED DESIGN

How then to go forward? An account of the triune God's self-revelation by Word and Spirit is a vital component of evangelical theology. But, for all that we might share in Jesus Christ, doctrines of Scripture and the Holy Spirit increasingly reveal rather than resolve our differences.[39] If the key to an already common, inevitably stable, evangelical identity will not simply be discovered in a hidden theological core, then our quest must also pursue discernment for handling our differences. Evangelical theology requires an account of how understanding and ministering the gospel incorporates the unity and diversity of the church.

Of course it would be naive to suggest that various evangelical traditions could agree fully about the nature of the church despite numerous other disagreements. However, since at the very least we do not embrace Orthodox and Catholic definitions of the church's institutional unity, earthly holiness and hierarchical apostolicity, perhaps some minimal understanding of evangelical catholicity is implicit and could become more explicit. If evangelical theology could address catholicity in light of broadly Protestant commitment to the biblical gospel, buttressing its intermittent practice with a

---

[39]Whether various "evangelical" phenomena, including some global "Pentecostal" movements, count as "Protestant" is itself complex. A minimalist approach would treat "Protestant" negatively: neither formally Catholic nor Orthodox. Thus Christoph Schwöbel ("The Trinity," in *God's Advocates: Christian Thinkers in Conversation*, ed. Rupert Shortt [Grand Rapids: Eerdmans, 2005], p. 101) sees the ecumenical significance of Trinitarian doctrine in terms of three groups: liberals, theologians of the creed's first article; evangelicals, focused on the second; and charismatics, focused on the third. However oversimplified this may be, these relative priorities remain tricky for defining "Protestant" identity along with recognizably "evangelical" common life and ministry. Mark A. Noll addresses the newly complex ecumenical landscape in "Ecumenical Realities and Evangelical Theology," in Lints, *Renewing the Evangelical Mission*, pp. 51-68; there see also Tite Tiénou, "Renewing Evangelical Identity from the Margins," pp. 31-50.

clearer ecclesiological rationale, then internal disagreements might appear in proper perspective.

The evangelical failure to address ecclesiology and theological authority in tandem—not just to address the intricacies of particular traditions but also to acquire shared principles for ecumenical collaboration—leaves decisions about "community" to individual whim and maybe institutional principles. The result is frequent chaos. In former days, evangelicals did not linger over the ecclesiological rationale for activism. They may not have had the luxury. Times having changed, there is no longer luxury to neglect the fullness of the church as the context and aim of evangelical fellowship. As the company of the gospel, the church is both the creature of the Word and the fellowship of the Spirit—the primary end of the most dramatic divine action. Evangelical fellowship in turn performs an implied account of Scripture's theological authority and doctrine's formational power.

Having written extensively on theological prolegomena in the broader academic arena, here we present a united, clear distillation of *evangelical* theology as the pursuit of wisdom, via "theological interpretation of Scripture," in the drama of the church's worship and witness. The wisdom theme has the virtues of being scripturally central and holistically oriented, embracing all the ways in which Christian persons and congregations are called to mirror the biblical Christ. Evangelicals also need to pursue wisdom because decisions about theological fellowship cannot be made in light of either rational abstractions or relational appreciation alone. These decisions require wisdom to recognize how Scripture bears on ever-changing ecclesial situations. To count as fully Christian wisdom, though, such an account of evangelical theology needs the surrounding christocentric realism and ecclesiological approach contained in our design.

Part one sketches this christocentric realism and ecclesiological approach in two chapters that deal with the "economy of light" (the light that shines forth from the mirror of Scripture to illumine), presenting evangelical theology as an "anchored" set. Appropriately enough, the two chapters mirror each other: Each has the same eight-part structure that opens with a presenting problem and then examines *what is in Christ* from different angles. Chapter one presents a theological ontology, an investigation into the gospel of God and the God of the gospel. The focus here is on the reality *behind* the mirror of Scripture, namely, the economic Trinity (the missions of the Son and Spirit) that mirrors in turn the immanent Trinity (God's perfect eternal life). The chapter focuses on the Son as the very image of God and explains the place of Scripture and the church in the economy of light. Chapter two presents a theological epistemology that focuses on the way in which biblical testimony yields knowledge, and the way biblical truth is preserved as doctrines come into focus through time and across cultural space. The focus here is on the truth *in* and the authority *of* the mirror. What eventually comes into focus is the importance of the church's teaching and councils—in a word, *catholicity*—for assessing right development of doctrine.

Part two then shades in more specific contours of theological prolegomena in light of part one's christocentric realism. Part one sketches an agenda for evangelical theology, theologically considered; part two analyzes in greater detail how that agenda applies to the evangelical theology currently being practiced. Part two attempts to relate theological prolegomena and evangelical ecclesiology, depicting biblically rooted catholicity that not only respects particular churchly traditions but also pursues ecumenical opportunities from an orthodox and pietist Protestant perspective. Chapter three therefore defines and defends an account of theology as the wisdom of the whole people of God. Chapter four depicts the theological interpretation of Scripture that is central to seeking Christian wisdom. Chapter five moves directly to ecclesiology, sketching how theology serves God's people amid various kinds of missional fellowship. Finally, chapter six shifts the focus more fully to the academy, detailing how evangelical theology can benefit from and contribute to scholarly excellence. Wisdom remains crucial on both academic and churchly fronts, discerning proper responses to theological differences with fellow Christians as well as the various possibilities afforded by public intellectual engagement.

We do not speak for all whom the label "evangelical" may designate, and we do not speak to its subculture alone. We try instead to provide a theological interpretation of the label that, without applying to all insiders equally, may account for their debates, address the way forward and even appeal to outsiders. Such mere evangelical theology seeks to mirror in life and in teaching the whole counsel of God—gaining the mind of Christ as the Spirit ministers the Bible's literary and theological fullness. This truly evangelical "biblicism" requires refining the nuances of our "canonical" commitment to biblical theology, reading with the rule of faith and remembering our "creedal" heritage(s) more faithfully, as well as responding to the "cultural" contexts of our biblical interpretation more discerningly and creatively. To cultivate such canonical sense, catholic sensibility and contextual sensitivity[40] requires the humility integral to Christian wisdom. Engaging other saints and scholars to see the truth more clearly, we learn to focus on the logs revealed in our own eyes rather than the specks in others'. Evangelical theology reflects the necessity and blessing of biblical fellowship: while practicing the wisdom of particular traditions, together we pursue the fullest possible communion in gospel faith and collaboration in mission.

---

[40]The first of these triads appears in Daniel J. Treier, *Introducing Theological Interpretation of Scripture: Recovering a Christian Practice* (Grand Rapids: Baker Academic, 2008), addressed here in chapter four. The second appears in Kevin J. Vanhoozer, *The Drama of Doctrine: A Canonical-Linguistic Account of Christian Theology* (Louisville: Westminster John Knox, 2005). The two are obviously complementary, with this book unfolding their meaning more directly in terms of evangelical theology.

Part One

THE AGENDA

The Material and Formal
Principles of Evangelical Theology

Chapter One

THE GOSPEL OF GOD AND THE GOD OF THE GOSPEL

The Reality *Behind* the Mirror

EVANGELICAL theology designates an aspiration and ambition, not a fait (or even a faith) accompli. The chief task of evangelical theology is to say, on the basis of Scriptures, what God is doing *in* Christ, and then to indicate how to live it *out*. Stated differently: the purpose of evangelical theology is to help make communities of disciples, people who come to understand and correspond to the reality of the gospel—people who become "little Christs" and thus fulfill their vocation to live as images of God. The hope of the gospel impels us to look forward (always renewing); the knowledge that present-day Christians are not the first to receive the gospel urges us to look back and learn from the past (always retrieving). Evangelical theology is both hope and heritage. It is this dynamic position, poised between past and future, that makes the evangelical present a moment charged with eschatological significance (always responding): "Today, if you hear his voice, do not harden your hearts" (Heb 3:7-8, 15; 4:7; cf. Ps 95:7-8). The ambition of evangelical theology is to retrieve what God's people have heard in the past, to renew tired traditions and to respond with alacrity and obedience to God's forward call in the present. But we are getting ahead of ourselves . . .

A FIRST PRESENTING PROBLEM: EVANGELICAL THEOLOGY HAS NO AGREED-UPON DOCTRINAL CORE

In the field of medicine, a "presenting problem" refers to the initial symptom, either physical or psychological discomfort that leads a patient to seek out a doctor. It is the most prominent sign that all is not well. The presenting problem of evangelical theology is all too conspicuous: it has no doctrinal backbone. This too is a public health issue insofar as it complicates the project of preserving the unity of the body, that is, of the transdenominational, Bible-centered renewal movement that is modern, global evangelicalism.

The problem stated. This presenting problem is also a direct challenge to our project of articulating a "mere" evangelical theology. To be sure, there are family resemblances between evangelicals, and these can be described in sociological terms. According to Timothy George, "Evangelicals are a worldwide family of Bible-believing Christians committed to sharing with everyone everywhere the transforming good news of new life in Jesus Christ, an utterly free gift that comes through faith alone in the crucified and risen Savior."[1] David Bebbington's description of modern British evangelicals has become a useful point of reference for defining evangelicalism in general: conversionism (emphasis on being "born again"), biblicism (emphasis on biblical authority), crucicentrism (emphasis on the saving significance of Jesus' death) and activism (emphasis on sharing the gospel by witnessing in word and works of love).[2] Important as these emphases are, we already saw in the introduction that they are too broad to give rise to a single unified theology.[3] This should not be surprising when one realizes that evangelicals can be found in nearly all Protestant and Pentecostal denominations, and beyond. Evangelicals have an ecumenical bent toward unity. The question is whether they can reach unity as concerns the essentials of theological truth. A mere evangelical theology requires no less.

The story of twentieth- and twenty-first-century American evangelicalism is largely that of a struggle for the evangelical soul. Speaking broadly:

---

[1]Timothy George, "Directions: If I'm an Evangelical, What Am I?" *CT* 43, no. 9 (Aug. 9, 1999): 62.

[2]David W. Bebbington, *Evangelicalism in Modern Britain: A History from the 1730s to the 1980s* (London: Unwin Hyman, 1989), pp. 2-3. See also Timothy Larsen, "Defining and Locating Evangelicalism," in Larsen and Daniel J. Treier, eds., *The Cambridge Companion to Evangelical Theology* (Cambridge: Cambridge University Press, 2007), pp. 1-14, especially his proposed five-point definition.

[3]This is also true of Alister McGrath's helpful list of six governing evangelical convictions: biblical authority, the majesty of Jesus Christ, the lordship of the Holy Spirit, the need for personal conversion, the priority of evangelism, the importance of Christian community (*Evangelicalism and the Future of Christianity* [Downers Grove, IL: InterVarsity Press, 1995], pp. 55-56).

some (call them "pietists" for short) contend that the soul of evangelicalism, the unifying principle, is spiritual and experiential, rooted in love, while others (call them "propositionalists") contend that the unifying principle is doctrinal, rooted in truth. Still others (call them "peacemakers") contend that the unifying principle is political, rooted in justice.[4] For Stanley Grenz, a pietist, evangelicalism is at root a shared experience of conversion to Christ, an *ethos* rather than a system of belief.[5] Many hasten to agree on the ground that, as concerns the evangelical movement, spiritual experience unites, whereas doctrine divides.

In line with our introductory sketch, then, there are several reasons why any project that sets out to formulate the doctrinal core of the evangelical movement may be doomed in advance to failure: (1) there is no institutional mechanism or magisterium to declare what is essential; (2) evangelicals inhabit differing confessional traditions that reflect real theological disagreements; (3) identifying a stable doctrinal core might actually work *against* evangelicalism's ability to serve as a transdenominational renewal movement in the church; (4) no amount of sociological description of what evangelicals *do* believe is able to generate a theological prescription of what evangelicals *ought* to believe.

As Stephen Holmes observes with classic British understatement, "The standard definitions of evangelicalism are not doctrinal."[6] While one can identify Roman Catholics, Lutherans, Presbyterians and so on by consulting official documents (e.g., catechisms, confessions), one can find evangelicals all over the theological map: hence, "Distinguishing 'insiders' from 'outsiders' can prove to be tricky business."[7] In the words of William Abraham:

[4]See, for example, David P. Gushee, ed., *A New Evangelical Manifesto: A Kingdom Vision for the Common Good* (St Louis: Chalice, 2012). For more thoroughgoing historical accounts of American evangelicalism, see Douglas A. Sweeney, *The American Evangelical Story: A History of the Movement* (Grand Rapids: Baker, 2005); Donald W. Dayton and Robert K. Johnston, eds., *The Variety of American Evangelicalism* (Knoxville: University of Tennessee Press, 1991); Mark A. Noll, *American Evangelical Christianity: An Introduction* (Oxford: Blackwell, 2001).
[5]See Stanley Grenz, *Revisioning Evangelical Theology: A Fresh Agenda for the 21st Century* (Downers Grove, IL: InterVarsity Press, 1983), p. 31. Cf. John Stackhouse, whose "generic" evangelicalism inclines him too to define *evangelical* as "a type . . . of Christian ethos" ("Generic Evangelicalism," in *Four Views on the Spectrum of Evangelicalism*, ed. Andrew David Naselli and Collin Hansen [Grand Rapids: Zondervan, 2011], p. 119).
[6]Stephen R. Holmes, "Evangelical Doctrine: Basis for Unity or Cause for Division?" *Scottish Bulletin of Evangelical Theology* 30, no. 1 (2012): 62.
[7]Sweeney, *American Evangelical Story*, p. 20.

"There is no single essence or one particular condition that . . . will be agreed upon by all evangelicals."[8] In response to this inherent diversity, Donald Dayton has proposed a moratorium on the label "evangelical," on the grounds that it is "theologically incoherent, sociologically confusing, and ecumenically harmful."[9] D. G. Hart concurs: "Evangelicalism needs to be relinquished as a religious identity because it does not exist."[10]

The problem expanded: Floating centers and fuzzy boundaries. The evangelical empire has been quick to strike back. Albert Mohler agrees that a merely descriptive (i.e., historical or sociological) definition of evangelical identity is not enough to ensure the theological integrity of the movement. For that, we need a normative definition.[11] Whereas fundamentalists promote a static "bounded set" with clearly defined doctrinal borders, and revisionists a dynamic "centered set" with members who are closer or farther from the center (but neither "in" or "out"), Mohler's confessional evangelicalism represents what he calls a "center-bounded set." At the center is "devotion to Christ and joyful confidence in the gospel."[12] Yet the center, rightly understood, "defines the boundaries" and, without boundaries—without a discernible circumference—it is impossible to say what affirming the evangelical center rules *out*: what evangelicals are *not* (e.g., *not* theologically liberal; *not* heretics), and what positions are *not* evangelical. The center focuses on what the gospel *is*; the boundaries on what the gospel *is not*: "Attention to the boundaries is as requisite as devotion to the center."[13]

Mohler worries that if evangelicalism is defined merely by the center, it will be at best a "fuzzy set." Yet his critics worry that Mohler's boundaries are themselves fuzzy. Who gets to decide to draw the line that determines who is "in" or "out," and how can such a line be other than subjective, even arbitrary? John Stackhouse comments, "The notion of boundaries has to do with

[8]William J. Abraham, *The Coming Great Revival: Recovering the Full Evangelical Tradition* (San Francisco: Harper & Row, 1984), pp. 73-74.
[9]Donald W. Dayton, "Some Doubts About the Usefulness of the Category Evangelical," in Dayton and Johnston, *Variety of American Evangelicalism*, p. 251.
[10]D. G. Hart, *Deconstructing Evangelicalism: Conservative Protestantism in the Age of Billy Graham* (Grand Rapids: Baker, 2004), p. 16.
[11]R. Albert Mohler Jr., "Confessional Evangelicalism," in Naselli and Hansen, *Four Views on the Spectrum of Evangelicalism*, p. 74.
[12]Ibid., p. 95.
[13]Ibid.

whether there must be sharp definition at the edges, not whether there is clear definition at the core."[14] Mohler understands the importance of having more than arbitrary criteria for deciding which doctrines are essential and proposes a "theological triage" model that distinguishes first-, second- and third-level doctrines. Only first-level doctrines make up the boundaries that distinguish evangelicals from nonevangelicals, for without these doctrines "we are left with a denial of the gospel itself."[15]

David Bebbington's review of *Four Views on the Spectrum of Evangelicalism* rightly identifies the underlying conflict:

> The conservatives specify what evangelicalism ought to be; the progressives explain what the phenomena is. For the first pair, a theological conviction of their own trumps whatever anyone else may say; for the second twosome, the existence of other persuasions among self-described evangelicals dictates that nobody can make a firm prescription. There lies the nub of the question at issue.[16]

Again we are faced with the difficulty, serious and perhaps insurmountable, of deriving an evangelical *ought* from an evangelical *is*.[17]

"In essentials, unity; in non-essentials, liberty; in all things, charity."[18] Evangelicals are not the first Christians who have struggled to define the essentials. The challenge, again, is to do so in principled fashion. Stephen Holmes advances the discussion by answering the implied question: essential *for what*? Holmes argues that what makes evangelical doctrine distinctive is not the content (all Christians agree about orthodoxy) but rather its "conscious and serious decision about the relative importance of doctrines."[19] Specifically, the first-order or essential evangelical doctrines are

---

[14]John Stackhouse, "A Generic Evangelical Response," in Naselli and Hansen, *Four Views on the Spectrum of Evangelicalism*, p. 106.

[15]Mohler, "Confessional Evangelicalism," p. 79.

[16]D. W. Bebbington, "About the Definition of Evangelicalism . . ." *Institute for the Study of American Evangelicals* 83 (2012): 5.

[17]Call it the *supernaturalistic* fallacy—a nod to the "*naturalistic* fallacy," G. E. Moore's name for the mistaken attempt to derive a moral category (e.g., "good") from a natural property (e.g., "pleasurable").

[18]This famous saying, often mistakenly attributed to Augustine, now appears to have come from a seventeenth-century diatribe against the papacy written by a controversial archbishop, Marco Antonio Dominis (*De Republica Ecclesiastica* IV, 8). Despite its dubious origins, the phrase itself was disseminated by Richard Baxter and has become the motto of the Evangelical Presbyterian Church (see "History," Evangelical Presbyterian Church, www.epc.org/history? [accessed March 30, 2015]).

[19]Holmes, "Evangelical Doctrine," p. 64.

"just those necessary to maintain a particular soteriological scheme."[20] The soteriological scheme Holmes has in mind is associated with being "born again," namely, "punctilliar [sic] conversion and immediate assurance."[21] Doctrines that do not have a direct bearing on this soteriological scheme will ipso facto be secondary or tertiary. Holmes thinks that this consequence was only fitting, "because the mission of taking the gospel to the world mattered far more than the task of upholding inherited doctoral distinctives."[22] He therefore concludes, "That which does not serve the cause of mission is, necessarily, not important in a truly evangelical theology."[23]

Holmes is on to something. A mere evangelical theology must be able to say what the essentials are by answering the question, "Essential *for what*?" However, rather than limit our answer to what evangelicals may think is necessary for salvation, we find it more to the evangelical point to define essential doctrines in terms of what is necessary for the integrity of the gospel itself as set forth in the Scriptures and, by implication, what is necessary for speaking well of the God of the gospel. In this regard, Karl Barth's definition is worth pondering: "'Evangelical' means informed by the gospel of Jesus Christ, as heard afresh in the 16th-century Reformation by a direct return to Holy Scripture."[24] Here is, we believe, the key to both retrieving and renewing: to return to Scripture as it has been heard by the Protestant and, by extension, the catholic heritage the Reformers affirmed—all for the sake of preserving and promoting the logic of the gospel and the integrity of our God-talk.[25]

We are under no delusions: our account of mere evangelical theology is not a panacea but a proposal. We do not pretend to have a doctrinal slide-

[20]Ibid.
[21]Ibid.
[22]Ibid., p. 65.
[23]Ibid.
[24]Karl Barth, *The Humanity of God* (Atlanta: John Knox, 1960), p. 11.
[25]Cf. J. I. Packer and Thomas Oden: "Theologically, the roots of evangelicalism go back much further than its name, a nineteenth-century coinage, would suggest. Its account of God and godliness builds on the Trinitarian, incarnational and transformational consensus that the patristic period achieved, and then on the consensus of the magisterial Reformation about biblical authority and justification by faith only, by grace only, in virtue of Christ only" (*One Faith* [Downers Grove, IL: InterVarsity Press, 2004], p. 160). See also Michael Allen and Scott R. Swain, *Reformed Catholicity: The Promise of Retrieval for Theology and Biblical Interpretation* (Grand Rapids: Baker, 2015).

rule that would render first theology an exact science. Such a claim would, indeed, go against the need for prayerful wisdom and communal discernment that we advocate in these pages. Mere evangelical theology is an aim, not a possession; it is a promissory note, not money in the bank. Nevertheless, there is a "good deposit" to be guarded (2 Tim 1:14). The good deposit is "the faith that was once for all delivered to the saints" (Jude 3). The church has been "entrusted with the gospel" (1 Thess 2:4); hence the good deposit is nothing less than the good news. Mere evangelical theology takes this trust with the utmost seriousness—and passion. We are zealous of this trust: we trust this trust more than anything else. This trust is the apostolic testimony to the wondrous acts of God in the history of Jesus Christ.

An anchored set. Is the good deposit a bounded, centered or center-bounded set? The problem with a bounded set is that everything in it appears to be of equal importance: one's identity is a function of everything the set contains. The problem with the centered set, as Mohler points out, is that, in lacking a circumference, it also lacks definition. The problem with Mohler's center-bounded set, though, is that it ultimately lacks a clear principle for distinguishing essential from nonessential doctrine, inadvertently giving license for each evangelical theologian to do what seems right in his or her own eyes . . .

If we must define *evangelical* in terms of set theory, it will be in terms not of a mathematical but a nautical model: mere evangelical theology, we contend, is an *anchored set.* An anchor is like a center in that it is a fixed point whose purpose is to restrict a vessel from drifting. The church is not the anchor but the vessel—an ark that the anchor holds fast. It is only thanks to the anchor that this ark is not tossed to and fro by the waves of secularization and carried about by every wind of cultural doctrine (Eph 4:14). As we know, it is possible to make shipwreck of one's faith (1 Tim 1:19). While an anchor is grounded (not bounded), there are indeed limits on the surface as to how far a vessel can drift. An anchored set is thus defined not only by its anchor but also by the limited range of motion that it allows on the surface—and by the length of its rope, on which we shall say more below.

Scripture speaks of a certain hope as "a sure and steadfast anchor of the soul" (Heb 6:19). What is this anchor of hope? In context, it is God's promise to Abraham, a promise made even more certain by God's oath: "So when

God desired to show more convincingly to the heirs of the promise the unchangeable character of his purpose, he guaranteed it with an oath, so that by two unchangeable things, in which it is impossible for God to lie, we who have fled for refuge might have strong encouragement to hold fast to the hope set before us" (Heb 6:17-18). This is a deep passage, but for our purposes the salient point is this: the unchanging purpose of God is guaranteed by the unchanging Word of God, which in turn is guaranteed by the unchanging nature of God. The "anchor" in question is therefore God's very being, which, as we shall see below, means his being true: steadfast and faithful (Ex 34:6). We know that God is faithful and true because Jesus is the fulfillment of the promise of salvation. God has kept his word.

The rest of the present chapter explores the nature of this "sure and steadfast anchor" for mere evangelical theology. To the charge that evangelical theology has no doctrinal backbone, we shall respond that the gospel itself presupposes, implies and entails it; however, in addition to being crucicentric, we shall argue that evangelical theology is essentially *Trinity-centric*.[26] It is unfortunately telling that the doctrine of the Trinity is often missing from lists like Bebbington's that merely describe what evangelicals believe and prioritize.

Mere evangelical theology, as an anchored set, can initially be characterized in terms of two principles, one material (substantive), one formal (stylistic), each with three entailments. As to substance, mere evangelical theology is (1) *orthodox*, conforming to the early creeds; (2) *catholic*, spanning all the times and places where there has been a local church; and (3) *Protestant*, affirming of the Reformation *sola*s. As to style, it is (1) *radical*, first, because anchored in the root (*radix*) of the gospel—the triune God— and, second, because this rootedness leads it to confront the world with the claims of the gospel; (2) *irenic*, acknowledging that we need many perspectives and people groups fully to appreciate the gospel's wealth of meaning; and (3) *joyful*, first because it takes its bearings from the best of all words that can be heard and, second, because it takes its energy from the Spirit, the minister of God's word and the giver of God's life.

---

[26]Both of the first two chapters begin with a statement of their respective presenting problems, which we then answer with a pair of mere evangelical "notes": Trinitarian and crucicentric (chap. 1), biblicist and catholic (chap. 2).

To anticipate: mere evangelical theology is the constant source of renewal at the heart of the renewal movement with which evangelicalism has been identified, a permanent revolution that, under the authority of the word and in the power of the Spirit, helps the church to renew, retrieve and respond to the gospel in every age, culture and circumstance.

GOSPEL: GOD DOES WHAT HE SAYS AND IS AS HE DOES

In September 2012 the *Christian Century* magazine published several authors' best attempts at summarizing the gospel in seven words. A few stated general principles or moral maxims without even mentioning Jesus Christ: "We are who God says we are"; "Love your neighbor as yourself" (also known as a summary of the law!). Others mentioned Christ, but do not qualify as news: "Christ's humanity occasions our divinity"; "God, through Christ, welcomes you anyhow." Still others tied the message of Christ to a particular event: "God was born. We can be reborn"; "The wall of hostility has come down." None, to our mind, surpasses the apostle Paul's "In Christ God was reconciling the world" (2 Cor 5:19).

The God of the gospel. The gospel (*evangel*) is good news about what God has done in Jesus Christ for the sake of the world. As such, it presupposes two key theological truths: (1) *God has acted* (there is something good to report); (2) *God has spoken* (the news comes from God and is thus utterly reliable). That *God* has spoken and acted can never be the conclusion of natural theology, and neither is it the kind of happening that can be verified by investigative journalism. On the contrary, the gospel presupposes divine speech and action: revealed theology; God's self-communication. These divine initiatives constitute the doctrinal backbone of mere evangelical theology.

God's speech and act are on conspicuous display throughout the Scriptures. Indeed, Scripture is to a great extent the mirror of God's words and deeds. The Psalms are filled with passages praising God for his word or speech (Pss 18:30; 119) and his "wondrous deeds" (Pss 9:1; 40:5). In particular, God makes himself known to Israel as the One who fulfills his promise to Abraham by delivering his descendants from slavery in Egypt. God is identified by what one scholar has called "the gospel according to Moses": "I am the LORD your God, who brought you out of the land of Egypt, out of the

house of slavery" (Deut 5:6).[27] God makes himself known not through ideas
("I am the being than which nothing greater may be conceived") but by
piercing words and mighty works: not only by his act of deliverance but also
by revealing his will (the law) and entering into covenant with Israel. What
God did for Israel was unfathomably good and unquestionably newsworthy:
"For ask now of the days that are past . . . and ask from one end of heaven to
the other, whether such a great thing as this has ever happened or was ever
heard of" (Deut 4:32).

The later chapters of the book of Isaiah depict a "new exodus" event, involving a figure called the Servant of the Lord and having to do with the
restoration of Israel from exile in Babylon (see, for example, Is 42; 49; 52).
The New Testament authors appealed to this new exodus imagery to an-
nounce the good news of salvation in Jesus Christ—to explain the deliverance God makes not just for Israel but for the whole world on the cross of
Christ. The gospel is the news that God, out of his own free love, has made
a people for himself. The church, like Israel, is a chosen race (1 Pet 2:9),
chosen to be a kingdom of priests (Ex 19:6; cf. 1 Pet 2:9), God's treasured
possession (Ex 19:5; Deut 7:6; 14:2; 26:18; cf. Rev 21:2), and his adopted
children (Deut 14:1; Rom 8:23; Gal 4:5; Eph 1:5). The gospel of Jesus Christ
does not introduce something entirely novel but is rather the continuation
and climax of the good news about the one true God. God delivers.

In the New Testament, the good news is particularly associated with the
announcement of the arrival of God's kingdom. Matthew's Gospel depicts
Jesus as proclaiming "the gospel of the kingdom" (Mt 4:23; 9:35; 24:14). The
term *gospel* (εὐαγγέλιον) also shows up in the Greco-Roman context, where
it marked the birth of the emperor Augustus, as a "god" who would bring
peace to the world. The term also referred to announcements of victory in
battle, and of what life would now be like.[28] This is how Irenaeus and other
church fathers understood what has come to be known as the *protevangelium*—the first intimation of the gospel—in Genesis 3:15:

> I will put enmity between you and the woman,
>   and between your offspring and her offspring;

---

[27]Daniel I. Block, *The Gospel According to Moses* (Eugene, OR: Cascade, 2012), p. xii.
[28]See N. T. Wright on "Roman good news" in his *Simply Good News: Why the Gospel Is News and What Makes It Good* (New York: HarperOne, 2015), pp. 9-13.

> he shall bruise your head,
>> and you shall bruise his heel.

To trample a snake underfoot is to strike a moral blow, which is why the church fathers were able to associate this text with the *Christus Victor* motif (cf. Col 2:13-15).[29]

What Jesus proclaims in Matthew as "the gospel of the kingdom" Paul can refer to as "the gospel of Christ" (Rom 15:19; 1 Cor 9:12; 2 Cor 2:12; 9:13; 10:14; Gal 1:7; Phil 1:27; 1 Thess 3:2). There is no contradiction when we see that the kingdom has indeed come in the person and work of Jesus ("L'état, c'est moi!"). N. T. Wright has argued at length that the Gospels are not instructions about how to go to heaven but rather announcements that heaven—the reign of God—has come to earth. The story of Jesus is "the story of Israel's God coming back to his people as he had always promised."[30] The gospel is thus the good news that God has made good on his promise to restore Israel and renew creation. It is the good news that God has come to set the world right, yet with a different kind of exodus than Israel had been expecting. *This* exodus took place as Jesus expired on the cross (Lk 9:31), and what God parted was not the Red Sea but the curtain of the temple (Mt 27:51; Mk 15:38; Lk 23:45), thus enabling new access to God.[31] The good news is that, through the cross and resurrection, God has overcome the powers and principalities of this world to establish his rule of justice, administered by his Prince of Peace (Is 9:6), *on earth as it is in heaven.*[32] Again, the gospel is not about "going to heaven" as much as it is bringing heaven to earth to renew and transform creation itself.

This is a lot to fit into seven words. The message that Jesus' death delivers sinners from death, though it is propositional, can only be rightly understood in the context of the story of Israel and, indeed, of creation itself. We

---

[29]Cf. Graham Cole: "The *protevangelium* of Genesis 3:15 signals the divine intent to defeat evil, and the cross constitutes the blow" (*God the Peacemaker: How Atonement Brings Shalom* [Downers Grove, IL: InterVarsity Press, 2009], p. 127).

[30]N. T. Wright, *How God Became King: The Forgotten Story of the Gospels* (New York: HarperCollins, 2012), p. 83.

[31]For a suggestion that the tearing of the temple curtain marks the climax of the gospel story, see Kevin J. Vanhoozer, *Faith Speaking Understanding: Performing the Drama of Doctrine* (Louisville: Westminster John Knox, 2014), pp. 210-11.

[32]Wright, *Simply Good News*, p. 43. See also Jeremy R. Treat, *The Crucified King: Atonement and Kingdom in Biblical and Systematic Theology* (Grand Rapids: Zondervan, 2014).

rightly grasp the meaning of the crucifixion scene on Golgotha only against
the narrative backdrop of creation and the covenants with Abraham and
David.[33] For the good news is in large measure a function not only of what
God has done, but also of who God is.

The gospel of God. In addition to the gospel being "of the kingdom" and
"of Christ," there are also references to the gospel "of your salvation" (Eph
1:13) and "of peace" (Eph 6:15). More striking still is a phrase that occurs
seven times and appears to make God himself the content of the gospel: "the
gospel of God" (Mk 1:14; Rom 1:1; 15:16; 1 Thess 2:2, 8, 9; 1 Pet 4:17). The
gospel *of* God means the good news *about* God.[34] To say "gospel of God" is
to sum up how the gospel involves Christ, the kingdom, salvation and peace.
Mere evangelical theology takes its fundamental orientation from this insight that the good news about God's kingdom—the coming of salvation and
shalom—has largely to do with how God the Father has set things right in
God the Son, through the cross and resurrection, by the power of God the
Holy Spirit. *The gospel is unintelligible apart from the Trinity, and the Trinity
is unknowable apart from the gospel,* though how this is so awaits further
explanation below.

The gospel is the announcement that God has fulfilled his promise. Paul
makes this perfectly clear in Romans 1:1-4. The "gospel of God" was promised
beforehand "through his prophets" (Rom 1:2). The "gospel of God" concerns
God's Son, a descendant of David according to the flesh (Rom 1:3). This same
Son, though he died in the flesh, was declared to be the Son of God "in
power according to the Spirit of holiness by his resurrection from the dead"
(Rom 1:4). The good news is that God did what he said he would do, through
his Son and his Spirit. God is true to himself, as good as his word: God does
what he says, and he is as he does—and what he does, and is, involves his
Son and Spirit.

---

[33]For more on the relation of kingdom and covenant, see Peter J. Gentry and Stephen J. Wellum,
Kingdom Through Covenant: A Biblical-Theological Understanding of the Covenants (Wheaton, IL:
Crossway, 2012).

[34]At least this appears to be the sense in Mk 1:14; 1 Thess 2 and 1 Pet 4:17, if not in Rom 1:1 and
Rom 15:16, where it probably means *originated* with God (i.e., it was θεόπνευστος [2 Tim 3:16],
"God-breathed" through the prophets and apostles). Interestingly, though Ernest Best takes the
"of God" in 1 Thess 2:2 to be a subjective genitive (God's gospel), he goes on to say that God is
"in a real sense . . . the good news himself, both its author and its object" (*A Commentary on The
First and Second Epistles to the Thessalonians* [London: Adam & Charles Black, 1977], p. 91).

The good news is a narrative report: God the Father of all things has established his reign in Christ's death and resurrection and, through faith, incorporates through his Spirit those who put their trust in the Son, making them coheirs who share in his reign. Behind this narrative report—or rather, over and above it—is an ontological presupposition about the God of this gospel.

Earlier we cited the exodus from Egypt as the gospel according to Moses. There is a long tradition of taking God's covenant name, revealed to Moses from the burning bush, as a metaphysical claim: "I am the one who is." This, at least, is the way the Septuagint translates Exodus 3:14, and it has generated speculation that God is being itself, and thus immutable. We prefer another interpretive tradition that reads the divine name ("I am that I am") in the context of God's ongoing relationship with the children of Abraham. In this context, at stake is not simply God's existence but God's identity. God's name is as much promise as proposition: "I will be who I prove myself to be." The ontological implication of God's name is less metaphysical than covenantal: God is unchanging because he is steadfast and faithful. The gospel is the good news not that God is "the one who is" but that God is *who* he says he is, and has done something wonderful that proves it.[35]

MIRRORING GOD: THE SON AS *IMAGO DEI*

We are now in a position to state, and then explicate over several sections, the principal thesis of the present chapter concerning the God of the gospel.

The substance of mere evangelical theology is the God presupposed and implied by the gospel. The task of mere evangelical theology is to understand who God is, what he has done and why it counts as good news. Mere evangelical theology depends on God's self-communication in Christ and the Scriptures as the primary source and norm of this understanding. The God who reveals himself in the person and work of Jesus Christ is from all eternity Father, Son and Holy Spirit. The gospel is thus grounded in, and an expression of, God's triune being. The way God reveals himself in time is a dramatic representation (a moving image) of the way God is in eternity. The good news of what God has done in history thus has a counterpart in the way God has always been

---

[35]For a similar though more pastoral proposal, see John Piper, *God Is the Gospel: Meditations on God's Love* (Wheaton, IL: Crossway, 2005).

disposed toward humanity. Jesus Christ is the mirror of God and the gospel: mere evangelical theology is evoked, sustained, governed, challenged and judged by the good news that we can have union with Christ and thus eternal communion with God.

Light and mirrors. A mirror is a surface that receives and reflects light. Any kind of reflecting surface, whether polished metal or glass, can serve as a mirror to the extent that it catches light and thus reflects the things before it. Mirrors image the world outside their surface. Richard Rorty roundly criticizes the Enlightenment idea that the human mind is the mirror of nature. We can raise a similar concern about the human mind as mirror of grace: Whence come our images of what God is like? Mere evangelical theology wants to avoid at all costs Ludwig Feuerbach's critique that God is nothing more than a projection of our best human thoughts on what would otherwise be a blank heavenly screen.[36] To the extent that it seeks to think of God with its own resources only (e.g., ideas of perfect being), the mind is a mirror not of nature but of natural theology.

Who is mirroring whom? Contra Feuerbach, mere evangelical theology insists that whatever source of light we have about God comes from God, not ourselves. The light of reason projects only a faint glow compared to the glorious light of God's self-communication. God is light (1 Jn 1:5) and, though creation reflects some of this light (Rom 1:19-20), stubborn and sinful human hearts distort the mind's reflective surface (Rom 1:21-22). Un-aided reason cannot find out the gospel because the mind is a darkened mirror: "The god of this world has blinded the minds of the unbelievers, to keep them from seeing the light of the gospel of the glory of Christ, who is the image of God" (2 Cor 4:4).

The light of the gospel of the glory of Christ is the anchor of mere evangelical theology. We want to see the light; we want to know the God who is light; we earnestly desire "the light of life" (Jn 8:12). Above all, we want to understand and participate in what we might call the "economy of light," that is, the way God administers or distributes his self-knowledge, and the way God delivers us from the domain of darkness and transfers us to his kingdom of light (cf. Col 1:13). In this chapter we examine the (ontological) source of

---

[36]For more on Feuerbach's critique, see Kevin J. Vanhoozer, *Remythologizing Theology: Divine Action, Passion, and Authorship* (Cambridge: Cambridge University Press, 2010), pp. 18-21, 388-90.

the light in the triune God. In the following chapter our focus will be on the (epistemological) light of knowledge and the role that Scripture and its interpretation play in the economy of light. Mention should also be made of the role that the Holy Spirit plays in conforming us (ethically) to Christ, thereby making saints into "little lights" that reflect God's own light.[37] But we begin with the "true light [that] . . . was coming into the world" (Jn 1:9).

Christ (revelation), not the mind (reason), is the mirror of grace. Jesus Christ is the revelation of God. He is, in the words of the Nicene Creed, "Light of Light, very God of very God." He is, in his words, "the light of the world" (Jn 8:12; 9:5). The author of Hebrews makes a connection between light and mirror, claiming that Christ is "the radiance of the glory of God and the exact imprint [Gk. χαρακτήρ] of his nature" (Heb 1:3). We learn, therefore, that the Father is "essentially *outgoing*," an extrovert, so to speak.[38] Jesus' body, the surface of his flesh, mirrors God; he is, as it were, the "spitting image" of his Father, not least because he is the Word that proceeds from the Father's mouth: "In these last days he has spoken to us by his Son" (Heb 1:2). The Son is an echo, a verbal reflection of the speaker. But we were speaking of mirrors . . .

The Son as mirror of the Father. The Son is the Father's self-communicative act, an uttered Word that, in taking flesh, becomes the bodily reflection ("exact representation") of God's unapproachable light—in a word, an *image*. Calvin's comment on the claim that the Son is "the exact imprint of his nature" (Heb 1:3) is apt: "The substance of the Father is in some way engraven on Christ."[39] Christ shares in the light that is God but reflects it in the mirror of his humanity and flesh. What Jesus does in his human form mirrors divinity: "He displayed the nature (or form) of God *in* the nature (or form) of a servant."[40] The humanity of Jesus Christ is the polished (sinless!) surface in which we see reflected the very image of God (Heb 4:15). This is a rich biblical theme, and here we can only touch on two key passages: the pro-

---

[37]We return to this theme in chapter three regarding wisdom, and in the conclusion.

[38]Michael Reeves, *Delighting in the Trinity: An Introduction to the Christian Faith* (Downers Grove, IL: InterVarsity Press, 2012), p. 43.

[39]John Calvin, *The Epistle of Paul the Apostle to the Hebrews and the First and Second Epistles of Peter* (Grand Rapids: Eerdmans, 1994), p. 8. See also John Webster, "One Who Is Son: Theological Reflections on the Exordium to the Epistle to the Hebrews," in *The Epistle to the Hebrews and Christian Theology*, ed. Richard Bauckham et al. (Grand Rapids: Eerdmans, 2009), pp. 69-94.

[40]F. F. Bruce, *Philippians* (Grand Rapids: Baker, 1989), p. 70 (commenting on Phil 2:7).

logue to the Fourth Gospel and the hymn to Christ in Colossians 1:15-20.

The Word that in the beginning was with God and was God (Jn 1:1), the "true light" (Jn 1:9), "became flesh and dwelt among us" (Jn 1:14). Brooke Foss Westcott is right to note that there was "word" (λογός) even before God's self-communication to humanity.[41] Though no one has seen God, this Word—God "the one and only [Gk. μονογενής = unique]" (Jn 1:18 NIV)—he has made him known: "We have seen his glory, glory as of the only Son from the Father, full of grace and truth" (Jn 1:14). This "grace and truth" that characterizes the incarnate Son recalls the חֶסֶד and אֱמֶת of Exodus 34:6 that Moses saw when God passed before him and proclaimed his name. The truth pertains to revelation, the grace to redemption, perhaps even the gift of sonship.[42] As Jesus serves to mirror God, so the prologue of the Fourth Gospel "serves as a mirror of what is ours in Christ."[43]

It is because God is seen in the mirror of Jesus' humanity that Christ is called the "image" (Gk. εἰκών) of God (2 Cor 4:4). The terminology is initially shocking: after all, the Second Commandment says, "Thou shalt not make . . . any graven image" (Ex 20:4 KJV) of God. Such attempts to image the invisible God are idolatrous, Feuerbachian projections. In the ancient Near East it was the custom for kings to erect images representing themselves when they could not be physically present (cf. Dan 3:1-7). This may explain the purpose behind God's creation of men and women "in" God's image (Gen 1:26-27), to rule over creation in his stead (Gen 1:28). This appears to have been the intended destiny for humankind: to reflect God in and to creation. In the words of the psalmist: "You have made him a little lower than the heavenly beings and crowned him with glory and honor" (Ps 8:5). Tragically, the species has not lived up to its divinely intended purpose. We have not ruled rightly but rebelled against our design plan. Consequently, we do not image God.[44]

---

[41]Westcott also says, anticipating our next section, "Thus the economic Trinity, the Trinity of revelation, is shown to answer to an essential Trinity" (Brooke Foss Westcott, *The Gospel According to St. John* [Grand Rapids: Baker, 1980], p. 5).

[42]So Henri Blocher, "John 1," in *Theological Commentary: Evangelical Perspectives*, ed. R. Michael Allen (New York: T&T Clark, 2011), p. 127.

[43]Ibid., p. 128.

[44]John Kilner argues that human beings are "in" the image of God even when they have lost their ability to reflect God: "The likeness involved in being created in God's likeness-image is about the likeness that God is intending at creation, not a descriptive statement about the way people

The true God, the High King, is immortal and invisible (1 Tim 1:17). As Paul reminds the idol-mongering Athenians, "we ought not to think that the divine being is like gold or silver or stone, an image formed by the art and imagination of man" (Acts 17:29). Nevertheless, God has an image: "He [Jesus Christ] is the image of the invisible God" (Col 1:15). The Son is not God's image because he is a man, but because he is the eternal template of which human beings are but fainter tokens. That God has an image who was with him in the beginning, in his own interior life, means "that God incorporates otherness within God's own life, and . . . that God communicates the fullness of God's own being to this other."[45] The Son is the eternally reflecting image of the Father: very God from very God. Humans created "in" God's image are thus created to be *like Christ*, to magnify God's glory by reflecting it even further. This is our human destiny, indeed, our predestination: "For those whom he foreknew he also predestined *to be conformed to the image of his Son*" (Rom 8:29).[46]

The Son as mirror of God and the gospel. The Christ hymn in Colossians 1 suggests that Christ is the mirror image not simply of God, but of the gospel itself, and indeed of all reality.[47] The good news is that God the Father has enabled believers "to share in the inheritance of the saints in light" (Col 1:12). He has done this by transferring them into the kingdom of his beloved Son (Col 1:13). In the hymn that follows, the stanzas move from Christ being the "firstborn of all creation" (Col 1:15) to his being the "firstborn from the dead" (Col 1:18), that is, the firstfruits of the new creation. He is both agent and goal of creation and redemption alike, for "all things were created through him and for him" (Col 1:16), and it is "through him [that God pleased] to reconcile to himself all things" (Col 1:20). Accordingly, this passage too, like the prologue to the Fourth Gospel, acts as a mirror that shows us the riches we have in Christ.

---

actually are" (*Dignity and Destiny: Humanity in the Image of God* [Grand Rapids: Eerdmans, 2015], p. 131).

[45]Ian A. McFarland, *The Divine Image: Envisioning the Invisible God* (Minneapolis: Augsburg Fortress, 2005), p. 157.

[46]As we shall see, it is the Spirit's role to unite and conform us to Christ. The Spirit, we might say, is the efficacy of the divine imagery. We shall return to the Trinitarian scope of mirroring God in the next section.

[47]Cf. Marianne Meye Thompson: "One of the distinctive contributions—if not the distinctive contribution—of Colossians is its comprehensive vision of reality with the focal point of christology" (*Colossians & Philemon*, Two Horizons New Testament Commentary [Grand Rapids: Eerdmans, 2005], p. 155).

Colossians 1:15-20 is itself a mirror of earlier Scripture inasmuch as it draws on earlier Scriptures to describe Christ—particularly Genesis 1, and perhaps Proverbs 8.[48] The figure of Jesus Christ best comes into focus only against a canonical canvas, as does the gospel itself. For example, "firstborn" alludes both to Israel's divine election (Ex 4:22) and to the divine appointment of Israel's king (Ps 89:27): "[Paul] is teaching the Colossians from the inherited scriptures who Christ is, what he has done for them . . . transporting them into the dominion of David, which is properly the Son's."[49]

The truly startling feature of this hymn to Christ, written within living memory of Jesus' death, is Paul's assertion that Jesus Christ is not only the image of God but actively imaged God in doing things that only God could do, namely, creating heaven and earth.[50] As Richard Bauckham observes, "What the passage does is to include Jesus Christ in God's unique relationship to the whole of created reality and thereby to include Jesus in the unique identity of God as Jewish monotheism understood it."[51] God is not simply "the one who delivered Israel from slavery" but also "the one who created the heavens and the earth," and the Son whom Paul extols in Colossians 1 is somehow included in this identity.

Christ is the mirror image not only of God the Creator, but also of God the Redeemer. Paul's Christ hymn celebrates the good news that the one who made all things "good" (Gen 1:31) has acted again to reconcile all things to himself through the blood of Jesus' cross (Col 1:20). Christ is thus the beginning of the beginning (creation) and the beginning ("firstborn from the dead") of the end, the remaking of creation (redemption). Christ is the image of God and the mirror of the gospel because he is the point— the person—that integrates creation and redemption.

---

[48]C. F. Burney suggests that the whole passage may be Paul's way of adapting for Christian purposes a rabbinic commentary of sorts on Proverbs 8:22, and the role of Wisdom in the world's creation, in light of Genesis 1:1 ("Christ as the ARXH of Creation," *Journal of Theological Studies* 27 [1926]: 160-67). For a fuller discussion of this issue, see Douglas J. Moo, *The Letters to the Colossians and to Philemon*, PNTC (Grand Rapids: Eerdmans, 2008), pp. 107-20.

[49]Christopher R. Seitz, *Colossians*, Brazos Theological Commentary on the Bible (Grand Rapids: Brazos, 2014), p. 91.

[50]Moo points out that the idea that all things have been created "for him" (Col 1:16) "goes beyond any Jewish tradition about wisdom" (*Letters to the Colossians and to Philemon*, p. 124).

[51]Richard Bauckham, "Where Is Wisdom to Be Found? Colossians 1:15-20 (2)," in *Reading Texts, Seeking Wisdom: Scripture and Theology*, ed. David F. Ford and Graham Stanton (Grand Rapids: Eerdmans, 2003), p. 133.

We come to know God by what he has said and done. God has spoken and acted for a purpose "which he set forth in Christ as a plan [Gk. οἰκονομίαν] for the fullness of time, to unite all things in him" (Eph 1:9-10). The operative concept here is plan, also known as the divine "economy"—the divine strategy by which God communicates his goodness to the created order. Irenaeus saw Christ as the "recapitulation" of all God's creative and redemptive purposes. Every aspect of Jesus' life, but especially his incarnation, had cosmic significance, for it was all part of the divine project to "unite all things in him" (Eph 1:10). The gospel concerns the outworking of God's saving purpose, "the ways and means of God's enactment of the new creation."[52] Creation itself is but the beginning of a divine drama in which the beginning—"all things were created through him and for him" (Col 1:16)—already anticipates the end.

Christ is the image of God, but in Christ there is a whole economy—an outworking of the divine purpose to share God's light, life and love with the entire cosmos, and the human creature in particular. Jesus Christ is the revelation of God: what Jesus says and does makes God known and accomplishes God's will. The incarnation thus becomes "the 'play within the play' of the whole economy of creation and salvation."[53] The good news is that God has communicated his light and life. More to the point: God communicates his light and life through himself. Hence, the gospel of God is the God of the gospel. A mere evangelical theology, to the extent that its anchor is Christ, is thus ultimately anchored in the whole economy by which God communicates his light and life to a world that would otherwise be dark and dead. To see how this is so, we now turn to a brief exposition of the divine economy.

TRINITARIAN TESTIMONY: THE ECONOMIC AS "MOVING IMAGE" OF THE IMMANENT

When you start from the Jesus of the Bible,
it is a triune God that you get.
MICHAEL REEVES, *DELIGHTING IN THE TRINITY*

---

[52]Paul Blowers, *Drama of the Divine Economy: Creator and Creation in Early Christian Theology and Piety* (Oxford: Oxford University Press, 2012), p. 15.
[53]Ibid., p. 14.

The Trinity is the gospel.

FRED SANDERS, *THE DEEP THINGS OF GOD*

The prologue to the Fourth Gospel "affirms the roots and foundations in Eternal Being of the Gospel Events."[54] This eternal being—God's perfect life *in se*—is what anchors the "set" of doctrines that comprise mere evangelical theology. Our contention is that *the anchor is not simply the gospel of God (the events) but the God of the gospel (the eternal being).* The image of Christ in the mirror of the gospel is inextricably related to the reality of the triune God: Father, Son and Spirit.

The gospel according to Father, Son and Spirit. The gospel is the announcement that God has made it possible for human creatures to enjoy fellowship with God forever because of the life, death and resurrection of Jesus Christ. The main claim we wish to stake in the present section is that what God has done in Christ (the gospel) is unintelligible unless Jesus Christ is indeed part of the identity of God (i.e., the second person of the Godhead), together with the Holy Spirit. Why should the gospel be unintelligible unless the Son and the Spirit are part of the divine identity? Because the gospel is the good news that God the Father has reached out with both hands—Son and Spirit—to a world lost in darkness in order to lift it up into the light of his life and hold it in a loving embrace. This reaching out, lifting and embracing is a nontechnical way of referring to the divine economy: the shared work of Father, Son and Spirit to enlarge their familial circle. The gospel, then, is thoroughly Trinitarian: "The good news of the gospel is that God has opened up the dynamics of his triune life and given us a share in that fellowship."[55]

We understand both the person and work of Jesus Christ, the Son incarnate, only in relation to the Father and the Spirit. Jesus was conceived by the Spirit, was anointed by the Spirit at his baptism, did miracles by the power of the Spirit, and after his ascension sent his Spirit to empower the church. But this does not go far enough: the gospel is not about a Spirit-filled man. We only understand the gospel when we come to see Jesus Christ as the eternal Son of God on a missionary journey, a journey into

---

[54]Blocher, "John 1," p. 121.
[55]Fred Sanders, *The Deep Things of God: How the Trinity Changes Everything* (Wheaton, IL: Crossway, 2010), p. 62.

humanity (flesh) and into human history (a Roman crucifixion). The Father declares at Jesus' baptism and again at his transfiguration: "This is my beloved Son" (Mt 3:17; 17:5). Jesus is the eternal Son of God who was with God in the beginning, who humbled himself to the point of giving himself away altogether, to the point of death (Phil 2:5-11), becoming flesh (Jn 1:14) for the sake of the divine rescue mission for which he was a willing volunteer. The Son forsook his perfect life—his basking in the glory (Jn 17:5), union (Jn 17:11) and love of his Father in heaven—precisely in order to enlarge the scope of heaven's fellowship.

Rightly to understand the gospel requires us to see the events of Jesus' history as elements in a divine plan conceived "before the foundation of the world" (Eph 1:4; Rev 13:8; cf. 1 Pet 1:20). Plato called time "a moving image of eternity."[56] Going beyond Plato: our thesis is that the way God is in time is a "moving image" of the way God is in eternity. Stated differently, the economic Trinity—what the Father, Son and Spirit do in history—is a dramatic representation of what God's eternal life is (the immanent Trinity) *and* of his eternally gracious disposition toward the world. For example, the love the Father shows the Son during his sojourn on earth is the historical realization of their eternal relationship: "You loved me before the foundation of the world" (Jn 17:24). The events of the gospel show us who and what God eternally is. Behind the good news ("God for us"), therefore, is the reality of the perfection of God's own life ("God in himself").[57]

The economy as mirror of eternity. We best see the way in which the economy mirrors God's eternity by contemplating how what Jesus does in his earthly ministry mirrors what the Father is always doing, just as the divine missions of the Son and Spirit mirror the eternal relations that make up God's perfect life. In John 5 Jesus heals a sick man on the Sabbath, much to the consternation of the Jews. Jesus answers them, "My Father is working until now, and I am working" (Jn 5:17).[58] The Jews (rightly) heard him as

---

[56]Plato, *Timaeus*, trans. R. G. Bury, Loeb Classical Library (Cambridge, MA: Harvard University Press, 1929), p. 77.

[57]Cf. Sanders, who speaks of something "better than the good news: the goodness that is the perfection of God himself" (*Deep Things of God*, p. 62).

[58]On the Trinitarian interpretation of John 5, see Kevin J. Vanhoozer, "At Play in the Theodrama of the Lord: The Triune God of the Gospel," in *Theatrical Theology: Explorations in Performing the Faith*, ed. Wesley Vander Lugt and Trevor Hart (Eugene, OR: Cascade, 2014), pp. 1-29.

making himself equal with God, thus prompting this response from Jesus: "Truly, truly, I say to you, the Son can do nothing of his own accord, but only what he sees the Father doing. For whatever the Father does, that the Son does likewise. For the Father loves the Son and shows him all that he himself is doing. . . . For as the Father raises the dead and gives them life, so also the Son gives life to whom he will" (Jn 5:19-21). The Father "has life in himself" (Jn 5:26), but he gives life, in the Son and through the Spirit, to others. Hence our thesis: God's saving work in time (the economic Trinity) mirrors God's being in eternity (the immanent Trinity). *What lies behind the gospel of God is the triune God of the gospel.*[59]

What glimpse we have of the eternal God derives only from the light of his revelation. For example, we only know that Jesus is the Son of God, and that the Son of God is included in God's identity, thanks to the events of the gospel. Yet, from these events, and the experience of the earliest Christians, we can reason back to what must be the case if revelation does indeed reveal God. From the fact that the Son was "sent" by the Father, the early church concluded that the Son must be "eternally begotten." In other words, the temporal *mission* of the Son is grounded—anchored!—in an eternal *procession*.

Theologians are rightly reluctant to speculate about God-in-himself. In no way do we wish to be heard as condoning such speculation. However, while abstract speculation is one thing, it is quite another to ask what must be true of God for the gospel to be the good news that it is. It is vitally important that the being of God lies "behind" (or above) the events of the gospel. In the first place, this is the only way to preserve the Creator/creature distinction. Some theologians, in their zeal to celebrate the God of the gospel, collapse God's being into the gospel events. In this case, the economic does not mirror or dramatically represent the immanent Trinity but simply *is* the Trinity. However, to collapse the immanent into the economic Trinity in this way is to inscribe conflict (i.e., the cross) into God's very life, thus subverting the good news.[60]

---

[59]See further Vanhoozer, *Remythologizing Theology*, chap. 5, "God in Three Persons: The One Who Lights and Lives in Love."

[60]Robert Jenson insists on identifying God not *by* the events of the gospel, as does the present proposal, but *with* the events of the gospel. See Vanhoozer, "At Play in the Theodrama of the Lord," pp. 7-11. Cf. Scott R. Swain: "If evangelical theology is to account for the pure gratuity of

A second point: the economy begins with a primordial choice (Eph 1:4). If God reaches out to the world, it is not because he is obliged to do so: on the contrary, God freely determines to extend his two hands—hence the "plan" from before the foundation of the world to sum up all things in Christ (Eph 1:10). Hence, in reaching out to the world with both hands, God is simply being himself: God is love, a ceaseless communicative activity in which Father, Son and Spirit share their light and life in a never-ending dance of mutual glorification (Jn 17:1-5). In peering intently into the mirror of the gospel, we come to understand that the God who speaks and acts in Jesus Christ is eternally self-communicative. In Jonathan Edwards's words: "God is a communicative being."[61]

The third, and most important, reason for anchoring the gospel in the immanent Trinity is that only the perfect life of the triune God preserves the integrity of the gospel and the gratuity of grace. Again, the good news is that God has graciously opened up his eternal life to us and become our adoptive Father. Consider: Jesus' Father is "our Father" only if (1) Jesus is the eternal Son of God, and (2) the Holy Spirit gives us a share in his sonship by uniting us to the Son. Union with Christ is itself the good news that God gives us the gift of his Son's relationship to the Father, and thus the means by which we share in the very life of the Trinity itself.[62] Furthermore, the gospel—that all those who believe in the Son may have eternal life (Jn 3:16)—presupposes that there is eternal life to be had. There is: the life of God in himself—Father, Son and Spirit. The eternal life of God is his ceaseless, loving communication of his life and light in which all three persons communicate all that they have and are to one another in glorious, joyful, inexhaustible communion. It is into this eternal fellowship that the Spirit incorporates those who put their trust in and are baptized into Christ.

Everything the Son does is testimony to the plan of God and the character of the Father. What we see, returning to John 5, is the Son engaged in the most

---

the relation between God and the divine acts of election, incarnation, and indwelling, God's triune identity must be wholly actual . . . prior to the act wherein he gives himself to us and welcomes us into his trinitarian bliss" (*The God of the Gospel: Robert Jenson's Trinitarian Theology* [Downers Grove, IL: InterVarsity Press, 2013], p. 232).

[61]Jonathan Edwards, "Miscellany 332," in *The Works of Jonathan Edwards*, vol. 13 (New Haven, CT: Yale University Press, 1994), p. 410.

[62]Donald Fairbairn, *Life in the Trinity: An Introduction to Theology with the Help of the Church Fathers* (Downers Grove, IL: InterVarsity Press, 2009).

characteristic activity of the triune God: giving life and light (i.e., sight) to
others (Jn 5:21). What there is in the immanent Trinity is a *doing* than which
nothing better can be conceived: free and loving communication of God's
light and life between Father, Son and Spirit. God's perfect life is being-in-
communion, and it is this that anchors the set "mere evangelical theology."

Making the lame walk and the blind see is only the beginning: "And
greater works than these will he show him" (Jn 5:20). The works that the
Father shows and the Son sees—the incarnate Son's life-giving works of
salvation—are the result of what the Father and Son eternally determined
to do to communicate their perfect life to human creatures. The eternal Son
is personally present as the image (mirror) of God the Father. God enacts
his threefold perfection, his communicative activity, on earth (i.e., in the
economy) as it is in heaven (i.e., the immanent Trinity). Stated axiomati-
cally: the economic Trinity mirrors and communicates the immanent
Trinity.[63] The gospel events are nothing less than a space-time dramatic
mirroring—a moving fleshly image—of the triune God's eternal being in
communicative activity and communion, sharing his own light and life for
the sake of a world gone dark and dead. The Trinity is the gospel because
the good news announces the truth that Father, Son and Spirit have opened
up, through Jesus' incarnation, cross and resurrection, a way to share in
God's own perfect life.

WHAT IS IN CHRIST: A THEATER OF RECONCILIATION

"In Christ God was reconciling the world" (2 Cor 5:19). There it is: a seven-
word statement of the gospel. We can pair it with another seven-word
Pauline phrase: "In Christ, there is a new creation" (2 Cor 5:17 NRSV). God
in Christ; reconciliation in Christ; new creation in Christ; we in Christ.
The operative term in each instance is *in Christ*. *In Christ* there is "the
fullness of God" (Col 1:19); *in Christ* there is true humanity, the image of
God; *in Christ* there is a reconciled relationship with God and the perfection of his image.

---

[63]Cf. Fred Sanders: "Because the Son is the image of the Father within the immanent Trinity, the
Son's presence in salvation history makes the economic Trinity the image of the immanent Trinity" (*The Image of the Immanent Trinity: Rahner's Rule and the Theological Interpretation of Scripture* [New York: Peter Lang, 2005], p. 173).

The subject and substance of the gospel: What is "in Christ." The gospel is essentially the announcement—the setting forth in speech—of *what is in Christ*, of all that Christ is and has done for us. In secular philosophy, metaphysics is the study of *what is*. Metaphysics was first philosophy for the ancient Greeks. By way of contrast, a mere evangelical account takes as its first theology *what is in Christ*. The study of *what is in Christ* is more serious than metaphysics, for being—heaven and earth—will pass away, but neither Jesus Christ nor his words will ever pass away (Mt 24:35). Furthermore, *what is in Christ* is nonpartisan: it does not belong to one single confessional tradition or one denomination alone but rather serves as an anchor, not only to the soul, but to evangelical soteriology.[64]

The present chapter attempts to set forth the reality behind the mirror of Scripture—the reality reflected in the historical mirror of Christ's flesh—by specifying the content of the gospel and what it presupposes and entails about the God of the gospel. "What is in Christ" anchors mere evangelical theology. But this raises the question: What exactly is in Christ? How does God share his light and life with us in Christ? How does God reconcile the world "in his body of flesh by his death" (Col 1:22)? In sum: How does God love us in Christ? Let us count the ways—or at least begin to count the ways, for, as we shall see, there is far more "in Christ" than can be done justice in a few pages.

"In Christ God was reconciling the world" (2 Cor 5:19). We know that "in him" all created things are held together (Col 1:17), but the gospel is the good news that things not only cohere but also have been made right with God. The eternal Son is the "place" where creation happens; the incarnate Son is the "place" where sins are forgiven and creation made new. As Jesus says on the verge of his "departure" from earth (i.e., his crucifixion): "Now is the Son of Man glorified, and God is glorified in him" (Jn 13:31). As Calvin's comment on this text beautifully puts it:

> For in the cross of Christ, as in a splendid theater, the incomparable goodness
> of God is set before the whole world. The glory of God shines, indeed, in all

---

[64]For representative works on the subject, see J. Todd Billings, *Union with Christ: Reframing Theology and Ministry for the Church* (Grand Rapids: Baker, 2011); Marcus Peter Johnson, *One with Christ: An Evangelical Theology of Salvation* (Wheaton, IL: Crossway, 2013); Michael J. Thate, Constantine R. Campbell and Kevin J. Vanhoozer, eds., *"In Christ" in Paul* (Tübingen: Mohr Siebeck, 2014).

creatures on high and below, but never more brightly than in the cross, in which there is a wonderful change of things—the condemnation of all men was manifested, sin blotted out, salvation restored to men; in short, the whole world was renewed and all things restored to order.[65]

What God was doing in Christ makes the cross and the empty tomb key scenes in the theater of reconciliation.

What is "in Christ" is therefore a theater of operations, a place where powers and principalities are "disarmed" (Col 2:15) and where God's triune being comes into its own, even as the Son "came unto his own, and his own received him not" (Jn 1:11 KJV). Recall the prologue to the Fourth Gospel: the eternal Logos "became flesh and dwelt among us" (Jn 1:14). The Son of God "pitched his tent" (Gk. ἐσκήνωσεν) on earth and performed his play—the triune play of God's eternal determination to be not only with but "for us"— among us. What is in Christ is nothing less than the earthly, physical and fleshly theater of God's communicative action—a temporal acting out of God's eternal being, "full of grace and truth" (Jn 1:14). This, at least, is what the previous section argued: that what we see in the life of the incarnate Son are relations to the Father and the Spirit that bespeak and display the perfect life of the triune God.

Christ as mirror of our salvation. "In Christ" is the place where the gospel gets played out, the place where the economic Trinity dramatically represents the immanent Trinity, giving historical shape to God's being by performing the divine perfections. "In Christ" there is the image of God and the mirror of the gospel. Jaroslav Pelikan has commented on just how central a metaphor "mirror" is in Reformation thought.[66] For Martin Luther, Jesus is "a mirror of the Father's heart."[67] For John Calvin, "Christ, then, is the mirror where we must . . . contemplate our own election."[68] When we do, we realize that God has destined us "for adoption as his children" (Eph 1:5 NRSV). In his sermon on Ephesians 1:4-6, Calvin says, "I

---

[65]John Calvin, *The Gospel According to St. John 11-21 and The First Epistle of John*, trans. T. H. L. Parker, ed. David W. Torrance and Thomas F. Torrance (Grand Rapids: Eerdmans, 1961), p. 68.

[66]Jaroslav Pelikan, *Jesus Through the Centuries: His Place in the History of Culture* (New Haven, CT: Yale University Press, 1999), p. 158. Note the chapter title "The Mirror of the Eternal."

[67]Luther, Large Catechism Article II, 65 (1529).

[68]John Calvin, *Institutes of the Christian Religion*, trans. Ford Lewis Battles, ed. John T. McNeill, Library of Christian Classics (Philadelphia: Westminster Press, 1960), III.xxiv.5.

told you that Jesus Christ is the mirror in which God beholds us when he wishes to find us acceptable to himself. Likewise, on our side, he is the mirror on which we must cast our eyes and look, when we desire to come to the knowledge of our election."[69]

"In him [Christ] we have obtained an inheritance" (Eph 1:11). Indeed. In Christ are "all the treasures of wisdom and knowledge" (Col 2:3); in him is "the righteousness of God" (Rom 3:21, 22). In Christ there is both right status before God and right relatedness to God, right objective standing before God (forensic righteousness) and right subjective orientation toward God (renovative holiness). There is justification and sanctification, forgiveness and holiness: the "double grace" of union with Christ.[70] There is grace and truth, the steadfast love and covenant faithfulness of God. The gospel is that Christ has made himself like us so that we could become like him: "fellow heirs with Christ"; "heirs of God" (Rom 8:17). To be in Christ, to have a share in his death and resurrection, makes us beneficiaries of his personal history and inheritance.

Believers are elect not only unto adoption into the family of God but to kingship. At the gospel's consummation the Son of Man will sit on his glorious throne to judge the nations. After separating the sheep from the goats, "the King will say to those on his right [his sheep], 'Come, you who are blessed by my Father, inherit the kingdom prepared for you from the foundation of the world'" (Mt 25:34; cf. Lk 22:29). To be in Christ is to have a share in his ascension and his heavenly session too. Paul says that we are blessed in Christ "in the heavenly places" (Eph 1:3), and God has "seated us with him in the heavenly places in Christ Jesus" (Eph 2:6). There is no better inheritance. Hence, "future glory . . . will be nothing other than the con-

---

[69]John Calvin, *Sermons on the Epistle to the Ephesians* (Edinburgh: Banner of Truth, 1973), p. 47.
[70]So Calvin, *Institutes* 3.11.1. Cf. John Murray: "Union with Christ is really the central truth of the whole doctrine of salvation" (*Redemption, Accomplished and Applied* [Grand Rapids: Eerdmans, 1955], p. 161). Union with Christ is central in both Reformed and Wesleyan soteriology. The concluding stanza of Charles Wesley's hymn "And Can It Be" makes this clear: "No condemnation now I dread; / Jesus, and all in him, is mine; / Alive in Him, my living head, / And clothed in righteousness divine, / Bold I approach th' eternal throne, / And claim the crown, through Christ my own." See further William Burt Pope's systematic treatment of salvation, which he discusses under the heading "the unity of evangelical privileges." The unity is "in Christ": "Now all the prerogatives of the estate of grace are ours in virtue of our union with the Lord" (*A Compendium of Christian Theology*, rev. ed. (New York: Hunt & Eaton, 1889], 2:394). Our thanks to Tom McCall for this reference.

tinued unfolding of the riches of our union with Christ."[71]

"In Christ" by the Spirit of Christ. Of course, what is *in* Christ avails us
nothing if we are not united *to* Christ. But this, too, is part of the good news:
believers enjoy union with Christ thanks to the Holy Spirit, who communicates Christ to believers through faith in the proclamation of the gospel. The
Spirit is, in Calvin's words, "the bond by which Christ efficaciously unites
himself to us."[72] Here, too, we are reminded of the anchoring role the immanent Trinity plays.

Salvation is union *with* Christ, the second person of the Trinity, the obedient Son of God who poured out his life on the cross so that we would enjoy
resurrection life, *through* the Spirit, the third person of the Trinity, who gives
life by uniting us to and thereby communicating Christ.[73] If Jesus Christ
were not the eternal Son, his death would be simply one more tragedy. If
Jesus Christ were not the second person of the Trinity, union with him
would not unite us to God the Father. The good news is that, because of who
he is, the work of the Son enables what was his by nature (sonship) to be the
believer's by grace. To be united to Christ is to be adopted as the Father's
own child and thus incorporated into God's family through the Spirit, with
all the rights and privileges pertaining thereunto. The most astounding of
these privileges is communion—friendship—with God, and with all the
saints in Christ. Again, it is imperative to note the way in which the immanent Trinity anchors the gospel: "The good news of salvation is that God,
who in himself is eternally the Father, the Son, and the Holy Spirit, has
become for us the adoptive Father, the incarnate Son, and the outpoured
Holy Spirit."[74]

In sum: insofar as the Spirit unites us to Christ, he incorporates us into
the family of God, the Trinitarian fellowship in which there is an abundance
of light, life and love. The good news is that, in Christ through the Spirit, the
Father has adopted us as his own children, forever to celebrate Christmas

---

[71]Anthony Hoekema, *Saved by Grace* (Grand Rapids: Eerdmans, 1989), p. 64.
[72]Calvin, *Institutes* 3.1.1. William Burt Pope is equally clear that though Christ "accomplishes"
    salvation, the Spirit "administers" it: "He is the Saviour's Agent in dispensing individual salva-
    tion" (*Compendium of Christian Theology*, 2:324).
[73]Cf. Fred Sanders: "This fact of union with Christ is the core of Christian soteriology" (*Deep
    Things of God*, p. 172).
[74]Ibid., p. 165.

with the holy family, exchanging gifts—of grace, gratitude and glorification—around the tree of life (Rev 2:7; 22:14).

SCRIPTURE IN THE ECONOMY OF LIGHT

The present chapter sets out the reality *behind* the mirror of Scripture. Strictly speaking, Christians do not believe "in" Scripture but in Jesus Christ on the basis of the Scriptures. Yet there is an important sense in which Christians do place their trust in Scripture's testimony, the verbal anchor of our knowledge of Christ. Recall that the gospel is good news, and *news* means "verbal report." The integrity of the gospel therefore depends on the reliability of the sources. We shall treat the Bible as a norm for evangelical theology in the next section. It will suffice for present purposes to give a brief account of the ontology of Scripture, and its place in the divine economy of revelation and redemption—in what we have termed the "economy of light."

From one perspective, the Bible is like any other book, casting only a weak light on the past. It is possible to read it as one would any other humanly authored text, a text that may reveal more about its authors and their contexts than about God or anything else. The language and literature that make up the Bible are clearly on the creaturely side of the Creator/creation distinction. In Karl Barth's words: "The secularity proper to God's Word is not in itself and as such transparent or capable of being the . . . mirror of God's Word."[75] From a faith perspective, however, one perceives the Bible as it truly is: a text that is authored (ultimately) by God, with God (Jesus Christ) as its ultimate content, and with God (Holy Spirit) as its ultimate interpreter. God has deigned to address humanity in and through his servants, the prophets and apostles who authored Scripture. Peter likens the prophetic word "to a lamp shining in a dark place" (2 Pet 1:19). The Bible is "a light to my path" (Ps 119:105), but the true light it emits comes from the Spirit speaking in the Scriptures.

Whose word is it? John Webster argues that both the Bible and its interpretation "are elements in the domain of the Word."[76] Scripture is not an

---

[75]Karl Barth, *Church Dogmatics*, trans. G. W. Bromiley et al., ed. G. W. Bromiley and T. F. Torrance (Edinburgh: T & T Clark, 1936–1977), I/1, p. 166.

[76]John Webster, *The Domain of the Word: Scripture and Theological Reason* (New York: T&T Clark, 2012), p. viii.

autonomous oracle with powers of its own, a well of revelation from which
its users draw in order to glean supernatural knowledge for their own purposes. We must resist the temptation to make Scripture "a static, rational-
izing norm divorced from personal acceptance of the living Christ and from
the active presence of Christ's Spirit."[77] Instead, we must see Scripture for
what it is: part of a divinely administered economy of light by which the
triune God establishes and administers covenantal relations with its readers.
Put simply: the ontology of Scripture is a function of what God has done in
and is doing with it, not of what its human users do with it. Webster rightly
observes, "Holy Scripture is dogmatically explicated in terms of its role in
God's self-communication, that is, the acts of Father, Son, and Spirit which
establish and maintain that saving fellowship with humankind in which
God makes himself known to us and by us."[78]

The salient point is that God has appointed the Scriptures to play a vital
role in the economy of light. "God is light" (1 Jn 1:5), and only in his light do
we see light (Ps 36:9). The triune God is Lord of his lighting, we might say.
God "the Father of lights" (Jas 1:17) sends his Son, "the radiance of the glory
of God" (Heb 1:3), into the world to be "the light of the world" (Jn 8:12; 9:5).
The gospel, too, enlightens—communicates light (2 Cor 4:4). Scripture is
verbally inspired (i.e., "God-breathed"—2 Tim 3:16) triune discourse that
communicates in diverse ways "the light of the knowledge of the glory of
God in the face of Jesus Christ" (2 Cor 4:6). The Spirit inspires and illumines;
light does not enlighten unless people have eyes to perceive it. The Spirit is
the one who enlightens "the eyes of the heart" (cf. Eph 1:18). J. I. Packer
perfectly captures the place of Scripture in the triune economy: "God the
Father is the giver of Holy Scripture; God the Son is the theme of Holy
Scripture; and God the Spirit . . . is the author, authenticator, and interpreter
of Holy Scripture."[79]

Scripture is holy, then, because God, its ultimate author, commissions just
these texts to play a vital and authoritative role in the triune economy of
covenantal communication whereby the Lord dispenses his light (i.e., rev-

[77]Richard Muller, "The Foundation of Calvin's Theology: Scripture as Revealing God's Word,"
    Duke Divinity School Review 44, no. 1 (1979): 21.
[78]John Webster, *Holy Scripture: A Dogmatic Sketch* (Cambridge: Cambridge University Press,
    2006), p. 8.
[79]J. I. Packer, *God Has Spoken: Revelation and the Bible* (Grand Rapids: Baker, 1979), p. 97.

elation, knowledge, truth) and life (i.e., redemption, fellowship, salvation). The Father initiates, the Son effectuates and the Spirit consummates the discourse that Holy Scripture preserves in writing. Scripture is a means of God's self-presentation, a collection of diverse forms of discourse that, taken together, are ingredient in the extraordinary ministry of God's Word by which the risen Christ announces the gospel, administers his new creational kingdom and imparts his light and life to readers made right-minded and right-hearted—fit for communion with God—through the illumination of the Holy Spirit.[80]

The Church and the Economy: A Theater of Reconciliation (*Reprise*)

And he is the head of the body, the church.
Colossians 1:18

The gospel is good news for men and women individually, but to identify the good news with the promise of my "going to heaven" to be with Jesus reduces its grandeur. It is not simply that "God has a wonderful plan for *my* life" but that "God has a wonderful plan for all creation."[81] In the reduced version of the gospel, the church is either a place from which to recruit new converts or an antechamber in which to share one's excitement while waiting for one's ride to heaven. These are, admittedly, poorly drawn caricatures: the church is far more wonderful than these. Yet the serious point is that, in the framework of the reduced gospel, it is difficult to see why, or even that, the church is necessary.

The New Testament presents a different picture. So does Calvin. In his 1545 Catechism of the Church of Geneva, the question concerning the line in the Apostles' Creed, "I believe in . . . the holy catholic Church" simply reads, "Is this article necessary to be believed?" The answer is worth pondering: "Yes, truly, unless we would render the death of Christ without effect,

---

[80]For further elaboration of this thesis, see Kevin J. Vanhoozer, "Holy Scripture: Word of God; Word of Christ; Sword of the Spirit," in *Christian Dogmatics*, ed. R. Michael Allen and Scott R. Swain (Grand Rapids: Baker, forthcoming).

[81]N. T. Wright has written about this "slimmed-down" version of the gospel at length. See especially his *Simply Good News*.

and account for all that we have said, for nothing. For this is the sole purpose of all, *that there should be a Church*."[82] Though we cannot make a full-fledged biblical case for it here, we believe that the church is part and parcel of the economy and, yes, perhaps the very reason for the economy itself.

In the first place, the church is the "body" of Christ (Col 1:24), and hence what we could call the theater of evangelical operations. Christ is the "head" of the body (Col 1:18), and everything we said above about the blessings the saved enjoy "in Christ" pertains to the church. The church too is a theater of reconciliation, not only a place of the forgiven but a place where forgiveness happens.

Second, the coming-to-be of the church is an *event* in the drama of redemption. Indeed, the sending of the Spirit at Pentecost to create the church is one of the key divine missions in the economy. Something new happens "in Christ" through Pentecost: Gentiles, who were formerly not-God's-people, "strangers to the covenants of promise" (Eph 2:12), have in Christ "been brought near by the blood of Christ" (Eph 2:13). Paul goes on to say that Christ is himself our peace, for he has made both Jews and Gentiles one, "and has broken down in his flesh the dividing wall of hostility" (Eph 2:14). The church is the result of this wall coming down: the Father in Christ through the Spirit has created "one new man in place of the two" (Eph 2:15). We see here that the whole purpose of the cross was not only to reconcile sinners to God, but also to create a new humanity. The church is the eschatological harbinger of this new reality, a living demonstration of *what is in Christ*.

Third, the church is neither an accident nor a parenthesis in God's plan. Arguably the central plot of the entire Bible is that God is at work "to bring into being a people under his rule in his place."[83] God spent years forming Israel into a holy nation that would reflect his holiness in the world, just as the first humans were created to be his εἰκών. Israel was unable to become God's people after the flesh. Significantly, Paul calls the church the "Israel of God" (Gal 6:16), and Peter identifies the church as "a chosen race, a royal priesthood, a holy nation, a people for his own possession" (1 Pet 2:9). The purpose of this people, moreover, is to "proclaim the excellencies of him

---

[82]Geneva Catechism, Q. 94 (emphasis added).
[83]J. G. Millar, "People of God," in *New Dictionary of Biblical Theology*, ed. T. D. Alexander and Brian S. Rosner (Downers Grove, IL: InterVarsity Press, 2000), p. 684.

who called you out of darkness into his marvelous light" (1 Pet 2:9). The church is *part* of the economy of light.

The church is the place where Jesus now reigns, and so is a foretaste of heaven on earth. Note well: we are describing the church not on sociological but theological terms, as it is *in Christ*, through the power of the Spirit. The church is a theological entity: Paul several times refers to the "church of God" (1 Cor 11:22; 15:9; Gal 1:13; 2 Thess 1:4; 1 Tim 3:5). This is not to deny its earthly particularity, for Paul can also speak about its location: "To the church of God that is at Corinth" (2 Cor 1:1). What this means is that the local church is an instantiation—a reflection, perhaps a mirror—of the universal church.

We can go further. The local church, precisely because it is "of God," is the reality of the new creation in the midst of the old. The church—the fellowship of the saints gathered in a particular place—is now the house where God lives, and where God's will is done. The church is a God-ordained means of realizing his plan "to unite all things in him [Christ]" (Eph 1:10) and thus create "a dwelling place for God by the Spirit" (Eph 2:22). Far from being an accident or appendix to God's plan of salvation, then, the church is at its *apex*: the church is part of the mystery made known in Christ. It is through the church that "the manifold wisdom of God might now be made known to the rulers and authorities in the heavenly places. This was according to the eternal purpose that he has realized in Christ Jesus our Lord" (Eph 3:10-11). The church is both part of the economy and one of its chief dividends.

MERE EVANGELICAL THEOLOGY: THE TRIUNE GOD AND THE CROSS OF CHRIST IN THE MIRROR OF SCRIPTURE

Our intent in this chapter has been to address the oft-heard argument that evangelicalism lacks a distinct doctrinal backbone—that there is no such thing as a distinctly "evangelical" theology or, if theology *is* said to be evangelical, that this refers only to the energetic spirit in which it is done, not to any particular doctrinal focus. To recall the problem: "There is no single essence or one particular condition that . . . will be agreed upon by all evangelicals."[84]

---

[84]Abraham, *Coming Great Revival*, pp. 73-74.

Definitions such as Bebbington's, insofar as they are descriptions of a complex sociological group, focus not simply on shared beliefs but on values and habitual practices as well. By way of contrast, our proposal distinguishes what we could call the material, formal and final principles of mere evangelical theology. The present chapter has focused only on the material principle: the theological substance of the gospel. We believe that, behind the mirror of Scripture, there are indeed theological realities without which the evangel would no longer be good news. What therefore gives mere evangelical theology its distinct identity is passionately returning again and again to its anchor in the gospel of God and the God of the gospel—and therefore, in particular, to the wisdom of God made manifest in the foolishness of the cross (1 Cor 1:25). Indeed, *a concern to stay anchored in the gospel of God and the God of the gospel*, and the biblical discussion that concern generates in various times and places, may be the defining characteristic of the mere evangelical tradition.

In the first place, mere evangelical theology espouses "strong" rather than "weak" Trinitarianism.[85] An understanding of the Trinity is "weak" when it treats the Trinity as simply one doctrine among others. It is not. We have argued that the economic Trinity is the necessary framework for preserving the integrity of the gospel, and that the immanent Trinity is the necessary presupposition for preserving the integrity of the economy. *Mere evangelical theology holds to "strong" Trinitarianism that maintains the doctrine of the Trinity, ontological and economic, as the structure, substance and summary of the gospel.* The Trinity is Father, Son and Spirit sharing their light and life in love—in communicative activity oriented to communion. The debates in the early church at Nicaea and Chalcedon about the ontology of the Son were not idle metaphysical speculations but rather urgent soteriological safeguards. What was ultimately at stake in these debates was not "substance" (*ousios*) but *salvation*.

This leads, second, to a second hallmark of mere evangelical theology: a "strong" rather than "weak" crucicentrism. "Weak" crucicentrism views the

---

[85]There is also "radical" Trinitarianism that mistakenly collapses the immanent Trinity into the historical interactions of Father, Son and Spirit. See further Kevin J. Vanhoozer, "Three (or More) Ways of Triangulating Theology: On the Very Idea of a Trinitarian System," in *Revisioning, Renewing, Rediscovering the Triune Center: Essays in Honor of Stanley J. Grenz*, ed. Derek J. Tidball, Brian S. Harris and Jason S. Sexton (Eugene, OR: Cascade, 2014), pp. 31-58, esp. pp. 32-33.

cross as an example of a universal principle, either God's love for us or our love for God.[86] By way of contrast, "strong" crucicentrism views the cross as the event and place that becomes the hinge of history, the decisive turning point in the God-world relationship. Mere evangelical theology is first and foremost "passional"—passionate about the passion of Christ—assuming that we also take the resurrection to be part and parcel of the cross event. To be sure, incarnation and Pentecost are absolutely vital, yet their vitality stems from their relationship to the cross. The Son took on human form in order to humble himself to the point of death (Phil 2:8). Moreover, the risen and ascended Son pours out his Spirit in order to conform his disciples to his cruciform life.[87]

Though many aspects of the gospel deserve attention and adoration, at its heart is the message that because of God the incarnate Son's cross and resurrection, people from every tribe and nation can have filial fellowship with God the Father through God the Holy Spirit. Mere evangelical theology is thus *Trinity-centric* and *crucicentric*. At the center of both these centers stands the person of Jesus Christ.[88] Jesus Christ is the triune God's communicative activity oriented to communion *made flesh*. Thus, implicit in our two material principles is a third: union with Christ. Salvation, and thus the good news, ultimately comes to a "head" in him. Jesus Christ is the unifying principle: in him all things hold together—including the Trinity-centric and crucicentric principles. For what the Son makes possible on the cross is sharing in his own relationship to the Father: filial communion with God.

The substance of mere evangelical theology, then, includes the material first principles of the immanent Trinity (the *who*), the cross and resurrection of Christ (the *what*), and union with Christ (the *where*). Mere evangelical theology is a worldwide renewal movement within the one church of Jesus

---

[86]There is also "radical" crucicentrism that, under the rubric "the crucified God," mistakenly identifies the suffering of the incarnate Son of God with the suffering of God. See further Vanhoozer, *Remythologizing Theology*, pp. 109-12, for a critique of Jürgen Moltmann's radical crucicentrism and, more generally, see David Luy, *Dominus Mortis: Martin Luther on the Incorruptibility of God in Christ* (Minneapolis: Fortress, 2014).

[87]See further Michael J. Gorman, *Inhabiting the Cruciform God: Kenosis, Justification, and Theosis in Paul's Narrative Soteriology* (Grand Rapids: Eerdmans, 2009), esp. chap. 3, "You Shall Be Cruciform, for I Am Cruciform."

[88]"The right soteriology comes from a Christocentrism that is not in contradiction to a Trinity-centeredness" (Sanders, *Deep Things of God*, p. 175).

Christ, a renewal not of a particular confessional statement *but of the anchoring framework itself.* Mere evangelical theology is the passion to keep confessional and pietist theology strongly grounded in the Trinity and the cross—in a word, *in the person and work of Jesus Christ.*

We turn now to consider the formal principle of mere evangelicalism, and the challenge of wisely discerning whether a particular doctrine, practice or form of life is in accordance with the Scriptures, or whether it has broken loose from its anchor in first evangelical theology and thereby failed to preserve the integrity of the gospel. Cultivating this wisdom—and the wisdom to discern which doctrines are essential for the preservation of the gospel and which are only expedient or expendable—will involve following the economy of light into the domain of the Word, namely, Scripture's authority and interpretation in the church.

Chapter Two

FROM CANONICAL CRADLE
TO DOCTRINAL DEVELOPMENT

The Authority *of* the Mirror

I N THE PREVIOUS CHAPTER we set forth the evangelical reality *behind* the mirror of Scripture: the theological sum, substance and subject matter of the gospel. We there argued that the gospel events (the gospel of God) were grounded in the eternal being of God (the God of the gospel). The present chapter turns from the ontology to the epistemology of the gospel, from the material to the formal principle of mere evangelical theology, and hence to an examination of the mirror of Scripture itself.

As we have seen, mirrors reflect light. The main burden of the present chapter is to explicate Scripture's role in the economy of light and how the light of the knowledge of the gospel shines forth from Scripture to be reflected in Christian doctrine. Mere evangelical theologians stand both *within* and *under* the domain of Scripture, not *outside* or *over* it, intent on both understanding and submitting to the living and active word of God. Scripture alone is supreme (*suprema Scriptura*); mere evangelical theology exists to understand, minister and respond to God's word in ways that embody and expand the Word's domain, which is to say, the domain of the risen Christ.[1]

Mere evangelical theology affirms the supremacy and sufficiency of Scripture, then, but also acknowledges the necessity of ongoing doctrinal

---

[1]The Latin term *suprema Scriptura* is James Leo Garrett's suggestion for expressing the supreme authority of Scripture (*Systematic Theology: Biblical, Historical, and Evangelical* [Grand Rapids: Eerdmans, 1990], 1:206-9).

formulation in the context of the church, a set-apart people and the privileged place of the Word's domain. The challenge is to set forth in speech "all the treasures of wisdom and knowledge" (Col 2:3) as concerns *what is in Christ*. The church and church tradition figure prominently in this task, and in the economy of light, that is, the pattern of theological authority in which God communicates the truth of the gospel in and through the biblical texts. As Scripture is a mirror of the reality of the gospel, so doctrine too reflects what it sees in the mirror. Yet, because the church occupies a different place in time and culture, its testimony cannot be an exact duplicate of Scripture's. Accordingly, this chapter takes up the task of giving a theological account of theological reflection, and especially of how doctrine both develops and remains the same as a result of the church down through space and time peering prayerfully and intently into the mirror of Scripture.

A SECOND PRESENTING PROBLEM: INTERPRETIVE ANARCHY NULLIFIES BIBLICAL AUTHORITY

Our second presenting problem once again arises from a perception about evangelicalism, the social group. Evangelicals typically have high views of Scripture. This fits their self-conception as a "people of the gospel" and thus a "people of the Book." The problem is one to which evangelicals themselves are often oblivious, though it is obvious enough to their critics. There are two aspects: (1) holding a high view of Scripture does not guarantee its right use; (2) those who share a high view of Scripture often disagree as to what it means.

Doctrines versus uses of Scripture. To begin with: it is one thing to hold a high view of Scripture, quite another to know how, where and when to use Scripture to establish a theological proposal.[2] To think that having a high doctrine of Scripture leads to a right use of Scripture is to fall prey to a non sequitur. It is one thing to admire a Boeing 787, quite another to pilot it. It is simply false to think that affirming the verbal plenary inspiration and inerrancy of the Bible gives one proprietary rights over its interpretation. More is required of the biblical interpreter than *belief that*. As we shall see, being *biblical* means not simply holding views about the Bible, but also the

---

[2]See further Kevin J. Vanhoozer, "Scripture and Theology: On Proving Doctrine Biblically," in *Routledge Companion to the Practice of Christian Theology*, ed. Mike Higton and James Fodor (London: Routledge, 2015).

ability to handle it rightly, and that requires being a certain kind of person.

Stanley Hauerwas thinks that the Bible is too important to let just anyone use it: "*It should only be made available to those who have undergone the hard discipline of existing as God's people.*"[3] In particular, Hauerwas thinks that evangelicals too often "fail to acknowledge the *political* character of their account of the Bible. . . . They want to disguise how their 'interpretations' underwrite the privileges of the constituency they serve."[4] This is a valid insight, though there is no reason to limit it to evangelicals. The problem of determining whose use of Scripture is legitimate is hardly new. Mark Noll describes the American Civil War as a crisis of biblical authority, for Christians in both the North and the South appealed to the Bible to condemn or support slavery, respectively: "The country had a problem because its most trusted religious authority, the Bible, was sounding an uncertain note. . . . The supreme crisis over the Bible was that there existed no apparent biblical resolution to the crisis."[5] What was true of the Civil War is equally as true of our present-day culture wars.

Biblicism and the problem of pervasive interpretive pluralism. Christian Smith argues that contemporary evangelicals hold to a theory of biblical authority that is self-refuting: impractical, incoherent and thus impossible. *Biblicism* is a theory about the Bible "that emphasizes its exclusive authority, infallibility, perspicuity, self-sufficiency, internal consistency, self-evident meaning, and universal applicability."[6] This is indeed a high view, and Smith, a sociologist, has no problem marshaling plenty of evidence that evangelicals have appealed to the Bible as an authority on everything from economics and politics to dieting, dating and, of course, doctrine.

An initial problem with biblicism, thus defined, is its tendency to press the Bible into addressing issues that it has little or no interest in discussing. For present purposes, a much larger concern is what Smith calls *pervasive interpretive pluralism*: "Even among presumably well-intentioned readers—

---

[3]Stanley Hauerwas, *Unleashing the Scripture: Freeing the Bible from Captivity to America* (Nashville: Abingdon, 1993), p. 9, emphasis original.

[4]Ibid., p. 35.

[5]Mark Noll, *The Civil War as a Theological Crisis* (Chapel Hill: University of North Carolina Press, 2006), p. 50.

[6]Christian Smith, *The Bible Made Impossible: Why Biblicism Is Not a Truly Evangelical Reading of Scripture* (Grand Rapids: Brazos, 2011), p. viii.

including many evangelical biblicists—the Bible, after their very best efforts
to understand it, says and teaches very different things about most significant topics."[7] As William Blake poetically puts it: "Both read the Bible day
and night / But thou read'st black where I read white."[8] In short: biblicism
as a practice of biblical authority founders on the phenomenon that the
evangelical interpreters of goodwill cannot agree about what the Bible is
asking them to do and believe. Even inerrantists—those who affirm the
entire truth and trustworthiness of Scripture on all matters it addresses—
cannot always agree as to what that truth is. As evidence, Smith cites more
than thirty books with titles like *Three Views on the Millennium, Four Views
on Divine Providence* and *The Lord's Supper: Five Views*. Of course, this is
hardly newsworthy. Long after Albert Schweitzer's famous comment about
those on the modern "quest for the historical Jesus" peering into the well of
history and seeing only their own faces, Jaroslav Pelikan said something
similar about the early Protestant experiment with biblical authority: "The
Reformers all found different reflections in that Mirror [i.e., Scripture]."[9]
Indeed, such interpretive disputes have long been the target of anti-
Protestant polemics. Whereas the Roman Catholic church has a magisterial
authority that can ultimately address interpretive questions, evangelical
Protestantism appears downright anarchic.

Toward a critical (evangelical) biblicism. Smith's deconstruction of biblicism is not without its own problems. Most notably, he overlooks those
doctrinal areas on which there is widespread evangelical agreement.[10]
Neither is it clear whether what he terms "biblicism" is a centered or a
bounded set. In particular, must one hold to all ten assumptions that comprise the theory, or can one be a nine-point or five-point biblicist?[11] As it
stands, this key category lacks adequate precision. Finally, Smith fails to
distinguish what he calls biblicism from the Reformers' *sola Scriptura*, and
thus throws out the Protestant baby with the biblicist bathwater. Moreover,

---

[7]Ibid., pp. viii-ix.
[8]William Blake, "The Everlasting Gospel," in *The Oxford Book of English Mystical Verse*, ed. D. H.
S. Nicholson and A. H. E. Lee (Oxford: Clarendon, 1917), lines 13-14.
[9]Jaroslav Pelikan, *Jesus Through the Centuries: His Place in the History of Culture* (New Haven, CT:
Yale University Press, 1999), p. 158.
[10]See, e.g., the various evangelical confessions compiled in J. I. Packer and Thomas Oden, *One
Faith* (Downers Grove, IL: InterVarsity Press, 2004).
[11]See the list of ten assumptions in Smith, *Bible Made Impossible*, pp. 4-5.

we believe that Smith's so-called biblicism is better off described as *naive (subevangelical) biblicism*, that is, a theory that dissociates Scripture from the purposes for which God has given it in his economy of light (revelation).

Still, evangelicals ignore the warnings of Hauerwas and Smith to their own peril, for the problem toward which they gesture is real. The real problem is not simply interpretive pluralism, pervasive or not, but rather the locus of interpretive authority. The Westminster Confession of Faith states that Scripture interprets Scripture, but who interprets Scripture's self-interpretations? What gives to one evangelical exegete or theologian (or community) the interpretive authority that others lack? Or does the harsh reality of a conflict of interpretive authorities go all the way down, in which case we may ask, "Wretched interpreter that I am! Who will deliver me from this learned body of vicious hermeneutic circularity?"

Here our schema of the economy of light comes into its own. The problem with naive biblicism is that it attempts to short-circuit the economy of light, that is, the pattern of theological authority by which God communicates his knowledge through the prophets and apostles to the saints, and eventually to us today. We believe that the way forward is a *critical (evangelical) biblicism* that situates biblical authority in a broader pattern of authority, one that recognizes the purpose for which the Scriptures have been sent. The economy of light includes *sola Scriptura*, the work of biblical interpreters, teachers and theologians, and church tradition.[12] But anchoring it all is "the word of truth, the gospel of your salvation" (Eph 1:13).

BELIEVING IN THE GOSPEL: APOSTOLIC TESTIMONY AND EVANGELICAL RATIONALITY

The "gospel according to Moses" is that God speaks and acts to deliver his people from bondage ("I am the LORD your God, who brought you out of the land of Egypt, out of the house of slavery"—Deut 5:6). Yet this gospel was a prototype, an object lesson for an even more wonderful act of deliverance—a doing greater than which nothing greater can be conceived: God the Father reconciling creation and establishing his kingdom on earth as it

---

[12]Stated differently: *critical biblicism* affirms the supreme authority and unified truth of Scripture (hence "biblicism") while simultaneously acknowledging the ministerial authority, plurality and fallibility of human interpretations (hence "critical").

is in heaven through his Son's cross and resurrection, in the power of the Spirit. The Bible provides the background and authoritative account of this good news, summoning its readers and hearers to believe. The task of evangelical theology is to set forth the truth of the gospel in speech, seeking and promoting understanding of *what is in Christ*.

Evangelical theology informs and reinforces belief by making as explicit as possible the gospel's own intelligibility, thereby uncovering its many-splendored truth, goodness and beauty. In this respect, evangelical theology is something of an extended expository sermon on the whole of Scripture, a rendering in speech of the presuppositions, implications and entailments of *what is in Christ*. The mandate of evangelical theology is not to invent but to expound: God's word is its bond. Evangelical theology is speech about God according to the gospel, which is to say, according to the Scriptures.

We are not forgetting the problem of pervasive interpretive pluralism. Neither are we blind to the epistemological challenge of saying whether and how it is rational to believe in testimony without the kinds of evidence modern or postmodern people crave. The two problems are connected: each has to do with the role of authority, in interpretation and knowledge, respectively. We believe that the gospel has its own internal resources to respond to these challenges. The gospel by definition is not something men and women can find out for themselves; it is rather something one has to be told. The question, then, is whether it is rational to believe in something one has been told. Even this, however, is too general: though a number of contemporary philosophers regard testimony as a legitimate means of knowledge, few avail themselves of what Scripture says about the role of Christ and the Spirit in the economy of light.

The present section situates belief in the gospel in the broader economy of light, that is, the way in which the Father communicates knowledge of himself and our salvation in the Son through the Spirit. We unfold this economy in five stages: we begin by setting forth Jesus as light of the world and Lord of his lighting. Next we frame the whole discussion about believing in the gospel in properly dogmatic terms, which is to say, in the context of the triune economy; here the light of reason is seen to be utterly dependent on the "Father of lights" (Jas 1:17). Third, we set forth the nature of faith, and the rationality proper to faith. Fourth, we suggest that the gospel is inherently missional: intrinsic to the good news is the imperative both to understand it and to pass it on. Finally, we recall the ever-present danger of false teachers who distort the gospel. The fact of false teaching is a powerful incentive to the mere evangelical theologian to give an account of faithful theology and sound doctrine.

The gospel as taught and told. The first person to proclaim the gospel was Jesus. It is first and foremost his gospel: his to proclaim ("Jesus came into Galilee, proclaiming the gospel of God"—Mk 1:14) and him the proclamation ("the gospel of Jesus Christ, the Son of God"—Mk 1:1). John the Baptist preceded him, yet he proclaimed not the gospel but "a baptism of repentance" (Mk 1:4). John the Baptist "was not the light, but came to bear witness about the light" (Jn 1:8).

Jesus' authority as a teacher is a function of his being "the light of the world" (Jn 9:5). Jesus was acknowledged by others as a teacher ("Rabbi"—Jn 1:38) and referred to himself as "the Teacher" (Gk. διδάσκαλος—Mt 26:18; Mk 14:14). Moreover, Jesus' teaching was on an entirely unique level: "The crowds were astonished at his teaching, for he was teaching them as one who had authority, and not as their scribes" (Mt 7:28-29; cf. Mk 1:27). The content of his teaching, especially in the parables, was the kingdom of God. Yet the kingdom had come in his own person, so Jesus was also teaching about himself and his messianic work: "While you have the light, believe in the light, that you may become sons of light" (Jn 12:36). It is partly by his teaching that Jesus delivers from the domain of darkness and transfers his disciples into the kingdom of light (cf. Col 1:13). Jesus' teaching about being the light of the world (Jn 9:5) receives a startling confirmation when he heals a man blind from birth (Jn 9).

Jesus taught his disciples that "all authority in heaven and on earth" had become his (Mt 28:18). Yet Jesus distributed his authority, commissioning disciples in his name to teach and make more followers (Mt 28:18-20; Lk 24:46-49). An *apostle* is "one sent" (Gk. ἀπόστολος). Jesus "appoints" the Twelve (Mk 3:14) and foretells their "anointing" by the Spirit, thereby giving them the office and the power of commissioned witnesses (Acts 1:8).[13] The circle is complete: "As the Father has sent me, even so I am sending you" (Jn 20:21). Søren Kier-

---

[13]We shall say more about the particular anointing in the next section.

kegaard distinguished the apostle from the genius: the genius discovers what she knows through unaided reason; in contrast, the apostle discovers what he knows by being told.[14] The gospel is by definition something we cannot find out by ourselves; if it were, then it would not be "news." Even eyewitnesses of the risen Christ had to be told what his resurrection meant. Though the Twelve were not all uneducated, their authority stems from their status as apostles, not geniuses.[15] As we shall see, Jesus is lord even of the gospel's hearing insofar as he sends not only apostles but also the Spirit of truth.[16]

The gospel in the economy of light. God, the unauthored Author of all, is the primal and final authority: "For there is no authority except from God, and those that exist have been instituted by God" (Rom 13:1). We agree with Bernard Ramm: "*In Christianity the authority-principle is the Triune God in self-revelation.*"[17] Opinions diverge widely, however, as to the way in which the triune God delegates authority. To ask, "Who speaks for God?" is to inquire into the pattern of theological authority, the economy of light.

Theology is possible only because God shines his light on those who are not God. The gospel—the verbal proclamation of what is in Christ—is a part of the economy of light, the way God communicates himself through himself: "For God, who said, 'Let light shine out of darkness,' has shone in our hearts to give the light of the knowledge of the glory of God in the face of Jesus Christ" (2 Cor 4:6). This apostolic ministry of the gospel belongs to revealed, not natural, theology: the light of unaided reason is not able to search out the gospel. The primary means for coming to know the God of the gospel is by attending to testimony: the Father's to the Son, the Son's to the Father and the Spirit's to the Son. The latter is of special interest here: both the composition and interpretation of the Scriptures are elements of the Spirit's mission.

---

[14]Søren Kierkegaard, "The Difference Between a Genius and an Apostle," in *Without Authority,* translated by Howard V. Hong and Edna H. Hong (Princeton, NJ: Princeton University Press, 1997), pp. 91-108. See also Kevin J. Vanhoozer, "The Trials of Truth: Mission, Martyrdom, and the Epistemology of the Cross," in *First Theology: God, Scripture and Hermeneutics* (Downers Grove, IL: InterVarsity Press, 2001), pp. 337-73.

[15]See Richard Bauckham, *Jesus and the Eyewitnesses: The Gospels as Eyewitness Testimony* (Grand Rapids: Eerdmans, 2006), pp. 94-96.

[16]Cf. Francis Watson, who says that the event of God's revelation in Christ "includes its own reception" (*Text and Truth: Redefining Biblical Theology* [Grand Rapids: Eerdmans, 1997], p. 165).

[17]Bernard Ramm, *The Pattern of Religious Authority* (Grand Rapids: Eerdmans, 1957), p. 21, emphasis original.

The economy of light refers to the work of the Father, Son and Spirit alike in communicating the knowledge of the glory of the God of the gospel. Thomas Aquinas used light language to speak of the grace given to creaturely intelligence: "The illumination of our minds is primarily the mission of the Son."[18] The "true light, which gives light to everyone" (Jn 1:9), is the Word who has become flesh (Jn 1:14). Yet all three persons are involved in communicating the saving knowledge of Christ: light proceeds from the Father, proceeds through the Son and is perfected by the Spirit. God is the agent, act and effect of his self-communication: light, lighting and enlightenment.

Jesus not only appointed apostles to transmit the light of the gospel through words; he also *anointed* them with his Spirit, thereby empowering them to be his witnesses (Acts 1:8; cf. Acts 2:2-4). This fulfilled Jesus' earlier promise to send his disciples a "Helper" from the Father: "The Spirit of truth, who proceeds from the Father, he will bear witness about me" (Jn 15:26), not speaking "on his own authority, but whatever he hears he will speak" (Jn 16:13). The Spirit takes what is the Son's and declares it to the Son's appointed witnesses, with the Spirit enlightening their minds as well as the "eyes of your hearts" (Eph 1:18). The Spirit is the internal witness who ministers understanding of the "external" witness to Christ, namely, the Scriptures.[19]

Jesus Christ remains the head teacher. However, at this present point in the economy, between his first and second comings, he has sent a substitute teacher: the Holy Spirit. The Spirit's role is not to add to the curriculum: again, "whatever he *hears* he will speak" (Jn 16:13). Nevertheless, the Spirit's role in the economy of light is crucial. In the first place, the Spirit's internal witness means that biblical interpretation, like biblical inspiration, falls squarely in the domain of the economy of light. Reading Scripture requires more than the light of unaided reason.[20]

The Spirit with which Christ anoints his disciples is a permanent gift: "But the anointing that you received from him abides in you, and you have no

---

[18]David L. Whidden III, *Christ the Light: The Theology of Light and Illumination in Thomas Aquinas* (Minneapolis: Fortress, 2015), p. 8.

[19]See further Bernard Ramm, *The Witness of the Spirit: An Essay on the Contemporary Relevance of the Internal Witness of the Holy Spirit* (Grand Rapids: Eerdmans, 1959).

[20]See further Kevin J. Vanhoozer, "The Spirit of Light After the Age of Enlightenment: Reforming/Renewing Pneumatic Hermeneutics via the Economy of Illumination," in *Spirit of God: Renewal in the Community of Faith*, ed. Jeffrey W. Barbeau and Beth Felker Jones (Downers Grove, IL: InterVarsity Press, 2015), pp. 149-67.

need that anyone should teach you" (1 Jn 2:27). No one is privy to any rev-elation necessary for salvation that they do not already have thanks to the Spirit speaking in the Scriptures. This permanence leads to a second point about the Spirit's role in the economy: the Spirit opens the hearts and minds of those in Christ's church to *see* the light of Christ reflected in the mirror of Scripture, and what the church has seen of the light also "abides" in the form of tradition. Tradition—handing on what has been received—involves human formulations the Spirit uses to transmit truth from one generation to the next: "The products and processes of tradition may be regarded as natural signs of the Spirit's illuminating presence because they constitute true and proper effects of his pedagogical grace."[21]

The gospel as fiduciary: The epistemic authority of testimony. "Faith comes from hearing, and hearing through the word of Christ" (Rom 10:17). Christian faith is a matter of believing God when he speaks.[22] It is not simply that the one who believes holds the gospel to be true, but that one holds it true *because it comes from God*. As we have seen, Scripture is an appointed instrument, a mirror of knowledge, in the economy of triune light. Our present concern is to say more about the nature of saving faith and its proper rationality as the right response to the word of Christ.

Faith is more than intellectual assent to revealed propositions: "Even the demons believe" (Jas 2:19). Intellectual assent—theoretical knowledge—falls short of true faith if unaccompanied by action or "works" (Gk. ἔργον; Jas 2:20-22). To believe the gospel is to have not only a theoretical posture but a practical disposition to act in ways that befit the belief in question.[23] While faith is "the conviction of things not seen" (Heb 11:1), genuine faith takes visible form insofar as it is acted on and acted out.[24] Knowledge

---

[21]Michael Allen and Scott R. Swain, *Reformed Catholicity: The Promise of Retrieval for Theology and Biblical Interpretation* (Grand Rapids: Baker Academic, 2015), p. 45.

[22]See John Lamont, *Divine Faith* (Aldershot, UK: Ashgate, 2004), p. 28.

[23]For an extended account of believing as dispositional, see Anthony C. Thiselton, *The Hermeneutics of Doctrine* (Grand Rapids: Eerdmans, 2007), pp. 19-28.

[24]Chris Boesel says that, for Karl Barth, believing "is not fundamentally the cognitive assent to propositional statements, or even the confession of a creed. It is the concrete *living of a life*" ("Better News Hath No Evangelical Than This: Barth, Election, and the Recovery of the Gospel from Evangelicalism's Territorial Disputes," in *Karl Barth and the Future of Evangelical Theology*, ed. Christian T. Collins Winn and John L. Drury [Eugene, OR: Cascade, 2014], p. 185). See also Oliver O'Donovan, who treats faith as "the root of action" (*Ethics as Theology*, vol. 1, *Self, World, and Time* [Grand Rapids: Eerdmans, 2013], p. 107).

without obedience gets no further than theoretical understanding: by way of contrast, mere evangelical theology aims at wisdom, which includes both right knowledge and right response—theoretical and practical understanding alike.

That Scripture plays a divinely appointed role in the economy of light as divine-apostolic discourse has important repercussions for theologians in their pursuit of understanding. Renewed reason sees but does not generate the light. There is no need to "prove" Scripture's truth, as if one could find incontrovertible evidence that God is the ultimate author. On the contrary, the role of reason is to accept what Scripture says as "of God," and thus true, simply on its reliable testimony. *Knowledge of the gospel of God and the God of the gospel is necessarily testimonial.* This was the moral of Kierkegaard's comparison of the apostle and the genius. What modern evangelical theologians might not have sufficiently appreciated, however, is the extent to which accepting testimony on trust is eminently rational.

A number of philosophers have recently explored testimony as a way of knowing. C. A. J. Coady's thesis gets to the heart of the matter: "Our trust in the word of others is fundamental to the very idea of serious cognitive activity."[25] Such trust stands in marked contrast to the tendency of modern philosophers to wait for sufficient evidence before investing their belief. However, if we always suspended belief until we verified what others told us or experienced it for ourselves, we would have a greatly reduced stock of knowledge. The philosophers of testimony argue that believing what we are told is an irreducible source of knowledge in the way that perception and memory are. Trust is therefore an epistemic virtue, a habit conducive to getting knowledge of truth. Like memory and perception, believing testimony is a means by which we relate to the external world. I can have a true belief about a traffic accident by believing a report; I do not have to see it for myself. Most importantly: I do not need a reason to believe the testimony; rather, the testimony *is* the reason for my belief. Of course, not all testimony is reliable—but neither is perception or memory. Yet reliable testimony connects us to reality as well as reliable perception and memory do, unless we have good reason to think otherwise.[26]

---

[25]C. A. J. Coady, *Testimony: A Philosophical Study* (Oxford: Clarendon, 1992), p. vii.
[26]For a good discussion of John McDowell's account of testimony, on which some of the material

If even secular philosophers can defend trusting testimony as rational, how much more ought evangelical theologians apply their reason to trusting the testimony of the prophets and apostles who speak for God? Human knowers too have a place in the economy of light, as recipients of the apostolic testimony commissioned by Christ and superintended by the Spirit: "And he who was seated on the throne said, 'Behold, I am making all things new. . . . Write this down, for these words are trustworthy [πιστός] and true" (Rev 21:5; cf. 1 Tim 1:15; 3:1; 4:9; 2 Tim 2:11; Tit 1:9; 3:8). The point is that God has designed our minds to receive communicative overtures from other persons, ultimately including the variegated testimony of the triune God to himself.[27] Scripture is part of this economy: faith comes from hearing the word of God as light comes from light.

The gospel as missional. The nature of physical light remains somewhat elusive, with some mathematical explanations suggesting it behaves under certain conditions like particles (photons) and under others more like waves. In any case light is "radiant energy"—a form of electromagnetic radiation that transfers energy through space. Accordingly light offers a way of thinking about a key dimension of evangelical epistemology: the Christian mission to communicate and understand the gospel.

The gospel is intrinsically expansive: good news exists to be proclaimed and published. The gospel is expansive, first, inasmuch as the more one reflects on it the more significant it appears. What began as news about the fate of a corpse (the empty tomb) eventually exploded into news about the renewal of the entire cosmos. One aspect of the mission of communicating the gospel is to appreciate its height, length, breadth and depth. The gospel calls for understanding—theology.

The gospel is expansive, second, because the Spirit is the energy that communicates its radiance from Jerusalem to the ends of the earth (Acts 1:8). Admittedly, the good news does not travel at the speed of light, yet Luke-

---

in this paragraph is based, see Mats Wahlberg, *Revelation as Testimony: A Philosophical-Theological Study* (Grand Rapids: Eerdmans, 2014), pp. 132-43. For an argument that self-trust leads to trusting others, see Linda Trinkhaus Zagzebski, *Epistemic Authority: A Theory of Trust, Authority, and Autonomy in Belief* (Oxford: Oxford University Press, 2012), chaps. 2-3.

[27]For an intriguing argument that combines the insights of Alvin Plantinga and Karl Barth for the sake of a theological epistemology in which testimony figures prominently, see Kevin Diller, *Theology's Epistemological Dilemma: How Karl Barth and Alvin Plantinga Provide a Unified Response*, Strategic Initiatives in Evangelical Theology (Downers Grove, IL: InterVarsity Press, 2014).

Acts clearly traces its forward progress in the Spirit's power through Asia Minor and all the way to Rome: "But the word of God increased and multiplied" (Acts 12:24). In the economy of light, the Spirit uses people as conduits of the gospel's radiant energy (2 Cor 5:20; Eph 6:20).

The mission of light is to enlighten. Paul urged the communities he founded not merely to believe the gospel but also to become its citizens, living worthy of the gospel (Phil 1:27), reflecting its radiant (eschatological) energy. Like light, the gospel is essentially missional: "To be in Christ is to be in mission; to participate in the gospel is to participate in the advance of the gospel."[28]

The singular gospel and the darkness of desertion. The light of the gospel advances, then, but not without opposition: "The light shines in the darkness, and the darkness has not overcome it" (Jn 1:5). In the beginning, God spoke light into being and then "*separated* the light from the darkness" (Gen 1:4). In Jesus and his followers, however, the light shines *in* the darkness, and the darkness opposes it. The spread of the gospel is not without conflict.

The New Testament contains numerous warnings concerning false teachings, false teachers and false gospels: "Many deceivers have gone out into the world, those who do not confess the coming of Jesus Christ in the flesh" (2 Jn 7). To deny that Christ has come in the flesh is to deny that there *is* good news. The incarnation of Jesus was a particular problem for gnostics and other religious groups who refused to associate divinity with what they considered to be the source of evil: materiality.

To refuse to see *what is in Christ* is to fail to see the light of the world. The rest is darkness. Those who are not anchored in the truth will drift off into falsehood. There is false teaching wherever there is denial of *what is in Christ* (2 Pet 2:1). False teaching is anything that is "not according to Christ" and, for precisely that reason, is a matter of "empty deceit" (Col 2:8). Philosophy is vain when it is centered on the autonomous self. Disciples must beware things that have "an appearance of wisdom" (Col 2:23). False teaching is futile because, like idolatry, there is nothing behind it. In contrast, the gospel—the word of the truth—is bearing fruit (Col 1:5-6).

If evangelical theology involves explicating the gospel and preserving its

---

[28]Michael Gorman, "Participation and Mission in Paul," *Cross Talk ~ crux probat omnia* (blog), December 12, 2011, www.michaeljgorman.net/2011/12/12/participation-and-mission-in-paul/.

integrity against pretenders, then the apostle Paul was a paradigmatic evangelical theologian. Paul endured consistent opposition to his mission of taking the gospel to the Gentiles, including "super-apostles" (2 Cor 11:5) who derided his apostolic ministry. Paul's main concern, however, was over distortions of the gospel. Those who proclaim something other than *what is in Christ* ("another Jesus than the one we proclaimed") play the satanic part of the serpent, deceiving others with "a different spirit" from the Holy Spirit and "a different gospel" (2 Cor 11:3-4).

Though Paul mentions "a different gospel," he quickly corrects himself ("not that there is another one"—Gal 1:6-7). The sober truth is that there is no other good news about the relationship of God and humanity besides the grace and truth in Jesus Christ. To deny this truth (what *is* in Christ) is to desert the God of the gospel ("him who called you in the grace of Christ"— Gal 1:6). Evangelical theology is necessary because there are false teachers who proclaim a nongospel of an anti-Christ for a kingdom of darkness.[29]

Mere evangelical theology teaches "sound doctrine"—life-giving teaching that does not distort but rather corresponds to the gospel (1 Tim 1:10; 6:3; Tit 1:9; 2:1). Sound doctrine is the necessary anchor that prevents making "shipwreck" of one's faith (1 Tim 1:19). Sound doctrine is "in accordance with the gospel" (1 Tim 1:11), and the gospel—the good news that Christ died, was buried and was raised on the third day—is "in accordance with the Scriptures" (1 Cor 15:3-4). It follows that mere evangelical theology *must* be biblicist: it is not possible to give unambiguous or undistorted accounts of *what is in Christ* if one does not anchor such descriptions in Scripture's apostolic testimony. More pointedly: unless we acknowledge authoritative Scripture, the confession "Jesus is Lord and Savior" will be either meaningless or else prey to pervasive interpretive pluralism.

While skeptics depict the development of orthodox doctrine in terms of the will-to-power, a largely political process, it is more accurate to see it as an exercise of the church's corporate will-to-truth, which is to say, a will-to-be-biblical. Mere evangelicals can agree with Barth on the need for a solid

---

[29]Cf. H. Richard Niebuhr's criticism of the liberal social gospel of his day, which proclaimed "a God without wrath brought men without sin into a kingdom without judgment through the ministrations of a Christ without a cross" (*The Kingdom of God in America* [New York: Harper & Row, 1959], p. 193).

exegetical foundation for understanding the gospel: "[Theology] can know the Word of God only at second hand, only in the mirror and echo of the biblical witnesses."[30] We therefore turn to examine what it means to do theology "in accordance with" the mirror of Scripture.

TESTIMONY: CANONICAL PEDAGOGY AND THE FORMATION OF WISDOM

"But who do you say that I am?" (Mt 16:15). Jesus' question is not a true-or-false question but fill-in-the-blank, and the disciples had many options from which to choose: John the Baptist, Elijah, some other prophet—not to mention less flattering opinions like "carpenter's son" (Mt 13:55) or one who is "blaspheming" (Mk 2:7). Twenty-first-century biblical scholars list even more possibilities, including charismatic healer, revolutionary sage, Mediterranean peasant-prophet and Jewish zealot. Opinions multiply, knowledge less so. How are we able to say who Christ is, or what is in Christ?

As we saw in the previous section, the apostles were prepared not only to answer Jesus' question, but to shout their answer from the rooftops—and to preserve it for future generations in Scripture. We do well to observe closely what form their answer takes, and to remember that Christ himself authorizes apostles to speak on his behalf. We heed Scripture out of loyalty to Jesus.

Narrative testimony. The apostles identified Jesus Christ for us, to begin with, by writing Gospels, stories about what Jesus and said and did that give narrative density to his identification. Narratives are also the form of discourse appropriate to history. This is important: not all kinds of truth, or theology, require narration. There is no need for narrative in perfect being theology, for example. However, at the heart of Christian theology are certain events: events like the exodus make a difference in the world as they identify God ("who brought you out of the land of Egypt"—Deut 5:6).

Stories and histories are more than chronologies: in addition to relating what happened, they also *configure* characters and events, thereby *making sense* of what happened. Narratives are more than pretty packaging for the events they recount. Narratives have cognitive import—explanatory power—all their own: "emplotment."[31] The most important stories (metanarratives,

---

[30]Karl Barth, *Evangelical Theology* (Grand Rapids: Eerdmans, 1963), p. 31.
[31]The term comes from Paul Ricoeur. See Kevin J. Vanhoozer, *Biblical Narrative in the Philosophy*

like Darwinian evolution) purport to explain the whole of reality. The role of stories in articulating worldviews is now widely appreciated. Indeed, N. T. Wright claims that we come to have knowledge when we *"find things that fit"* with the particular story that serves as our overarching interpretive framework.[32] To believe in the gospel according to the Scriptures is ultimately to accept, and indwell, the biblical story that begins with creation, climaxes in Jesus' cross and resurrection, and concludes with new creation, the marriage of heaven and earth.

Canonical testimony. There is much more in Scripture than story. *What is in Christ* may be said in many ways. Let us call the different types of testimony in the Bible, the various writings of the prophets and apostles, *forms of discourse*, where discourse is "something said to someone about something in some way for some purpose."[33] The discourse is human, written in human languages and literary forms, though ultimately by these creaturely means and servant forms the Spirit speaks Christ to the church in every age.

A theology that seeks to be biblical must do justice to Scripture's forms and content alike. As Jesus took on the "form of a servant" (Phil 2:7), so God's word takes on a variety of servant forms (literary genres). We should no more deny their revelatory significance than we should deny the redemptive significance of Jesus' flesh. The Spirit takes up just these forms as instruments of his communicative presence, activity and authority. To think biblically, then, is to think along the literary grain of the various forms of biblical discourse. Simply extracting relevant information from these forms, while well intentioned, misses much of what the authors communicate.[34]

It is true that, in addition to story, there are also assertive statements, straightforward informative claims, both particular ("He is not here, but has

---

of Paul Ricoeur (Cambridge: Cambridge University Press, 1990), chap. 4, pp. 86-118. For more on the epistemological significance of narrative for theology, see Stanley Hauerwas and L. Gregory Jones, eds., *Why Narrative? Readings in Narrative Theology* (Grand Rapids: Eerdmans, 1989).

[32]N. T. Wright, *The New Testament and the People of God* (London: SPCK, 1993), p. 37, emphasis original.

[33]See further Kevin J. Vanhoozer, "The Apostolic Discourse and Its Developments," in *Scripture's Doctrine and Theology's Bible: How the New Testament Shapes Christian Dogmatics*, ed. Markus Bockmuehl and Alan J. Torrance (Grand Rapids: Baker Academic, 2008), pp. 191-207.

[34]For an argument that biblical authority involves not only revealed content (propositions) but also meaningful forms (poetics), see Kevin J. Vanhoozer, "Love's Wisdom: The Authority of Scripture's Form and Content for Faith's Understanding and Theological Judgment," *Journal of Reformed Theology* 5 (2011): 247-75.

risen"—Lk 24:6) and universal ("For all have sinned and fall short of the glory of God"—Rom 3:23). Yet there are also songs, hymns, prophecies, commandments, warnings, questions, proverbs, apocalyptic visions and so on. Jesus taught mainly in parables, many of which are not susceptible to easy propositional paraphrase. Clearly, being biblical must mean something more (but not less!) than preserving the information Scripture conveys. In the words of Herman Bavinck: "There is room in Scripture for every literary genre . . . and every genre retains its own character and must be judged in terms of its own inherent logic."[35] The authority of a story is different from that of a statement, or a song. Doing justice to the variety of biblical testimony means preserving not only the content but also the form, which is to say the particular force or energy with which the truth is conveyed.

If we trust the divine author, we should also trust the diverse forms of divine discourse that make up the biblical canon. All its books are useful for training in godliness, and for helping disciples walk the way of Jesus Christ. It may be helpful to think of the canon as an atlas composed of different kinds of maps. All the maps chart the way of truth and life, in various ways. A road map highlights different features of the world than a political map or a plat of survey, but they all provide orientation to this or that aspect of reality. Being biblical requires canonical competence: the ability to read, and find one's way, with the right maps for the right moments. Like literary forms, maps too have their conventions (e.g., scale, key to symbols), and to follow a map one has to understand these communicative conventions.[36] Those who would rightly handle the word of truth and walk its way do well to acquire cartographical (canonical) competence.

True testimony. The New Testament contains four Gospels, four narrative answers to Jesus' question, "Who do you say that I am?" One narrative begins "from below," with Jesus' earthly genealogy, another "from above," with the Son's eternal credentials. The point is not to decide which of the four is most true: the four Gospels are portraits, not photographs, each high-

---

[35]Herman Bavinck, *Reformed Dogmatics*, vol. 1, *Prolegomena*, ed. John Bolt (Grand Rapids: Baker, 2003), p. 434.

[36]For more on canonical competence, see Kevin J. Vanhoozer, *The Drama of Doctrine: A Canonical-Linguistic Approach to Christian Theology* (Louisville: Westminster John Knox, 2005), pp. 295-99.

lighting distinct aspects of its subject.[37] Truth involves the correspondence of language to reality, between what is written and what is written about, yet the metaphor of maps reminds us that there is more than one kind of correspondence, more than one kind of fit.[38] *No one map captures everything that is true about the world.* If the face of the earth can be mapped in different ways to highlight its different features, the cartography of the human face is even more complex, especially when, as in the case of Jesus' face, it reflects the glory of God (2 Cor 4:6).

No human can see the unadulterated glory of God's own face and live (Ex 33:20). When God shows Moses all his goodness, it is for his own protection that Moses sees only God's back (Ex 33:22-23). God accommodates his revelation to human capacity so that it can be perceived and understood: "For now we see in a mirror dimly" (1 Cor 13:12). John Calvin comments, "We . . . behold the image of God as it is presented before us in the word."[39] This revelation is only dim in comparison with the eschatological brightness yet to come. What we have in the mirror of Scripture is in fact a prism of inspired discourse: the white light of God's truth is refracted into different literary hues (genres). Something similar pertains to each Gospel: each story provides a lens that adds "color"—thick description—to the portrait of Jesus.

True testimony is reliable because it corresponds to reality; it communicates something about *what is.* New Testament testimony is reliable because it is ultimately divinely authored and communicates *what is in Christ* through a variety of perspectives.[40] God is light, yet his revealed truth does not come in the hot white light of its frontal glory, but is rather diffracted (accommodated) to make it visible. The mirror of Scripture is the prism: the light of truth shines through, dispersed into a rainbow of forms of human discourse. The only wise God has provided a canonical coat of many colors,

---

[37]See Francis Watson, *Gospel Writing: A Canonical Perspective* (Grand Rapids: Eerdmans, 2013).

[38]For a recent account, see Joshua Rasmussen, *Defending the Correspondence Theory of Truth* (Cambridge: Cambridge University Press, 2014).

[39]John Calvin, *Commentary on the First Epistle to the Corinthians* (Edinburgh: Calvin Translation Society, 1848), p. 430.

[40]Cf. Abraham Kuyper: "No one single subject could receive in himself the full impression of a mighty event. To see an image from all sides, one must place himself at several points and distances" (*Encyclopedia of Sacred Theology: Its Principles* [New York: Charles Scribner's Sons, 1898], p. 549).

each one true, though perhaps more appropriate in some pastoral situations than others. No single form can catch the sacred fish.

Edifying testimony. The canon resounds with many forms of human discourse because, as Abraham Kuyper says, there is "more than one string to the harp of [the human] soul."[41] Specifically, there is more to the soul, and to rationality, than information processing. Yes, the gospel is news—and thus assertive reports figure prominently—but the proper response to its truth is not mere affirmation but *acclamation*: Scripture solicits not merely begrudging assent but our joyful delight in the message of salvation in Christ. Scripture lays claims not only to our minds, but to our hearts and imaginations as well.

The testimony of the prophets and apostles—and ultimately of the Spirit speaking Christ in the Scriptures—does communicate truths we need to know: that Jesus came in the flesh; he was crucified for our sins; God raised him from the dead; he will come again to judge. Just as important, however, is how these truths fit together. Here the story form of Scripture comes into its own, with earlier persons and events (types) anticipating, and partially explaining, their eventual fulfillments in Christ, the antitype. Such connections display canonical competence, the pattern of biblical reasoning. Following these patterns in Scripture "make[s] you wise for salvation" (2 Tim 3:15) and is profitable "for training [παιδείαν] in righteousness" (2 Tim 3:16).

That Scripture's various kinds of discourse all are profitable for training (παιδείαν) suggests that biblical authority involves a divinely superintended canonical pedagogy. God gives us his word and Spirit not simply to inform but to form and transform, to renew our knowledge and refresh our love for God (Rom 12:2): to cultivate not only new thoughts but *habits* of thought, a way of thinking in accordance with the gospel. The canon trains us to think evangelically, *tuning* each string in our soul so that we vibrate in harmony with what God is doing in Christ.[42] Taken together, the stories, songs, teachings, apocalyptic visions and so forth orient desires, form beliefs, shape imagination and prompt action—in a word, they cultivate *wisdom*: knowledge that gets lived out. Scripture's role, therefore, in the economy of

---

[41]Kuyper, *Encyclopedia of Sacred Theology*, p. 520.
[42]Sympathetic vibration occurs when a passive string responds to external vibrations from another source.

light is to radiate the multicolored truth of what is in Christ into ready hearts and minds, and thus to form new habits of right thinking and desiring—in a word, the mind of Christ (cf. 1 Cor 2:16; Phil 2:5).

SCRIPTURE AS THE MIRROR OF TRUTH: CANONICAL REFLECTIONS

Acts 9 recounts Saul's enlightenment and apostolic commissioning on the road to Damascus, where a blinding light from heaven flashed, spoke and identified itself as Jesus (Acts 9:3-8). After three days without sight, Saul meets Ananias, regains his sight, is filled with the Holy Spirit and immediately begins proclaiming Jesus. Saul quickly does advanced theology, penetrating to the heart of the christological matter: "He is the Son of God" (Acts 9:20)! Indeed, he "confounded the Jews who lived in Damascus by proving that Jesus was the Christ" (Acts 9:22). The Greek verb for "prove" is συμβιβάζω, a term that suggests putting together or uniting (as in "gathering" one's thoughts). Luke does not say how Saul made his case, but in Paul's later epistles the pattern of reasoning is evident.

Biblical reasoning/thinking/theology: Connecting the canonical dots. Evangelical theology is essentially a matter of biblical thinking or canonical reasoning. "Thinking" indicates that mental activity whereby we do not merely perceive or react by instinct but rather reflect on and make judgments about things visible and invisible. In speaking of biblical thinking, we have in mind primarily thinking *with* the Bible rather than merely *about* it.[43] As we shall see, this is a matter of thinking along the canonical grain. It is less a matter of "drawing out" discrete theological propositions than of drawing together ("gathering") material from across the canon in ways that bring unifying patterns into focus.

We have mentioned Paul as a paradigmatic evangelical theologian who refutes false teaching. He is also a paradigmatic evangelical exegete and biblical theologian who displays canonical excellence in figuring out the Old Testament Scriptures even as he sought to "figure out" the identity of Jesus Christ. His "proof" to the Jews at Damascus that Jesus was the Christ involved reading the Jewish Scriptures in light of their fulfillment in the history

---

[43]See further R. R. Reno, "Biblical Theology and Theological Exegesis," in *Out of Egypt: Biblical Theology and Biblical Interpretation*, ed. Craig Bartholomew et al. (Grand Rapids: Zondervan, 2004), pp. 385-408.

of Jesus (and vice versa). Paul tells the Corinthians that Israel's history was written to instruct the church, "*on whom the end of the ages has come*" (1 Cor 10:11). The end of the ages refers to the eschatological salvation that is in Christ, namely, the climax of God's covenant with Israel.

Paul's "proof" is a product of exegetical reasoning, of connecting the canonical dots to form a meaningful pattern that centers on Jesus Christ. Prior to his conversion Paul could not see how Jesus or his "Way" fit into the story of Israel; they seemed rather to subvert it. After his conversion, however, Paul understood how Jesus' death and resurrection fit into the story of Israel while also reinterpreting it to see how the Gentiles fit as well.[44]

Paul did not invent Christianity, and neither was he the first to demonstrate canonical excellence. Throughout his public ministry, Jesus regularly spoke in biblical terms. Recall his use of ἔξοδος to refer to his "departure" (death), which he was about to "accomplish" at Jerusalem (Lk 9:31). By using fulfillment terminology for "accomplish," Luke calls attention to Jesus' use of the key Old Testament symbol for salvation to talk about his impending crucifixion. Similar examples abound. C. H. Dodd thinks that the practice of using Old Testament Scriptures to "figure out" the identity of Jesus ultimately goes back to Jesus himself.[45]

The Evangelists are also exemplars of canonical competence, skilled at seeing the broader symbolic, thematic and historical patterns that crisscross on Jesus Christ and unify the Scriptures: "The Gospels teach us to read the OT and—at the same time—the OT teaches us how to read the Gospels."[46] Again, exegetical reasoning is largely a matter of interpreting the story of Jesus by means of the symbolic world of the Old Testament Scriptures. The Evangelists read the Old Testament *figurally*: "The literal historical sense of the OT is not denied or negated; rather, it becomes the vehicle for latent figural meanings unsuspected by the original author and readers."[47] As Richard Hays suggests, "Their way of . . . 'doing theology' was to produce

---

[44]For examples of Paul's exegetical reasoning, see Richard B. Hays, *The Conversion of Imagination: Paul as Interpreter of Israel's Scripture* (Grand Rapids: Eerdmans, 2005).

[45]C. H. Dodd, *According to the Scriptures* (London: James Nisbet, 1952).

[46]R. W. L. Moberly, *The Bible, Theology, and Faith: A Study of Abraham and Jesus* (Cambridge: Cambridge University Press, 2000), p. 51.

[47]Richard B. Hays, *Reading Backwards: Figural Christology and the Fourfold Gospel Witness* (Waco, TX: Baylor University Press, 2014), p. 15.

richly intertextual narrative accounts of the significance of Jesus."[48]

Like Paul, readers today need a "conversion of the imagination" to see how the canonical patterns converge on the figure of Jesus. Mere evangelical theologians, especially, must become adept in figuring out the way the Bible's words, symbols, figures, stories and so forth go. Biblical thinking is largely a matter of figuring out the literal sense and then letting the literal sense "figure out" how Jesus Christ is the center of it all (cf. Lk 24:27). Here is Hays once more: "To read Scripture well, we must bid farewell to plodding literalism and rationalism in order to embrace *a complex poetic sensibility.*"[49] What Hays calls *poetic sensibility* we call *theology.* Theology lives and moves and has its being in discerning canonical patterns. At the very least, theology is not less than the kind of biblical reasoning that Jesus, Paul and the Evangelists themselves display.

We see in the mirror of Scripture one unified story—the economy of redemption—yet we see this one story from many authorial perspectives, through various literary lenses (genres), and with complementary thematic concerns (e.g., kingdom, temple, covenant).

Sola Scriptura *and the sufficiency of Scripture.* The biblical reasoning just examined, featuring intracanonical patterns, goes a long way in explaining why Protestants believe that "Scripture interprets Scripture."[50] Yet this adage itself allows for strong, weak and radical interpretations. The "strong" sense refers to the way in which Jesus, the Evangelists and apostles read the Christ story as the climax of Israel's story: canonical figuration focusing on Jesus. The "weak" sense claims simply that Scripture does not contradict itself, so that interpreters can read more difficult passages in light of clearer ones. The "radical" sense suggests that theology could get along fine with Scripture alone: *solo Scriptura,* not to be confused with the authentic *sola Scriptura.* This radical interpretation of the rule sometimes issues in another saying: "No creed but Christ, no book but the Bible." This sounds evangelical, and biblical, but we believe that it is ultimately subevangelical and unbiblical, falling afoul of the proper pattern of theological authority.

---

[48]Ibid., p. 103.

[49]Ibid., p. 105.

[50]This principle received what is perhaps its definitive formulation in the Westminster Confession of Faith: "The infallible rule of interpretation of Scripture is the Scripture itself" (1.9).

At issue in this broader pattern is how the triune God administers his authority. Scripture interprets Scripture, but the "radical" sense of this principle suffers most acutely from the problem of pervasive interpretive pluralism, for it is unable to resolve it. If we cannot together say what Scripture means, we short-circuit its authority: the bugle that gives an indistinct sound cannot summon the Lord's army to spiritual battle (1 Cor 14:8). Scripture is indeed the primary source and supreme norm of evangelical theology. Doing evangelical theology means coming to understand God, world and the self with the symbolic resources of Scripture, especially as these figures come to a head in the history of Jesus Christ. Doing evangelical theology under the supreme authority of Scripture means indwelling the richly patterned story-world and symbolic universe of the canon, imagining the world that Scripture imagines, mirroring in our lives the reality that Scripture mirrors.[51]

"Scripture interprets Scripture" is not a claim to absolute self-sufficiency. *Sola Scriptura* is the Reformation shorthand for the supreme authority of Scriptures. It is not, however, a claim that theologians ought to have recourse to Scripture alone. The crucial question about Scripture's sufficiency is: *sufficient for what*? To answer that Scripture is sufficient for *everything*— stock-market investments, leaky faucets, clogged arteries—saddles it with unrealistic expectations, eventually succumbing to naive biblicism and the quagmire of pervasive interpretive pluralism. We advocate a different response: *sufficient to accomplish in its entirety the divine purpose for which it was sent* (Is 55:11). In particular, Scripture is sufficient for at least three important purposes: (1) identifying Jesus as the Christ, (2) making readers wise unto salvation, and (3) narrating the true story of the world and its relation to God.[52]

The pattern of theological authority: Toward dogmatic reasoning. Strictly speaking, then, Scripture is not alone but rather *above* other sources and norms, for at least two reasons, one extrinsic and one intrinsic to Christian faith. In the first place, it is no longer obvious how contemporary

---

[51]See Luke Timothy Johnson, "Imagining the World Scripture Imagines," in *Theology and Scriptural Imagination*, ed. L. Gregory Jones and James J. Buckley (Oxford: Blackwell, 1998), pp. 3-18.

[52]See also John M. Frame's discussion of "general" and "particular" sufficiency (*The Doctrine of the Word of God* [Phillipsburg, NJ: P&R, 2010], pp. 225-28) and Timothy Ward, *Words of Life: Scripture as the Living and Active Word of God* (Downers Grove, IL: InterVarsity Press, 2009), pp. 106-15.

readers should indwell Scripture's symbolic universe, especially in view of the new cultural contexts and intellectual issues that confront present-day churches. The biblical symbols call for *thought* if they are to continue serving as our interpretive framework. As to the second reason for consulting norms and sources other than Scripture, it is given in Scripture itself—in Jesus' promise to send the Spirit to guide the church "into all the truth" (Jn 16:13). There is good reason to think that church tradition figures among the means the Spirit uses to minister this truth, but only when it extends Scripture's literal sense in what we might call "a long obedience in the same direction."[53]

Before addressing church tradition, however, it is important to say something about systematic theology. Given what we have said about biblical reasoning and *sola Scriptura*, the reader may be forgiven for wondering whether systematic theology is necessary (for what?). Is it not wrong to "go beyond" or "add" to what has been written in Scripture (1 Cor 4:6; Rev 22:18)? Not necessarily! But to see why not, we need to understand the nature of doctrine.[54]

SECONDARY MIRRORING: HOW THEOLOGICAL TRUTH COMES INTO DOCTRINAL FOCUS

For now we see in a mirror dimly.

1 CORINTHIANS 13:12

Christ is a mirror image (εἰκών) that reflects the glory of God; Scripture is a mirror that reflects the glory of Christ (2 Cor 3:18). Is theology likewise a mirror that reflects the glorious truth of Scripture? Those who peer into the mirror of Scripture must beware lest they see their own reflections only, exchanging "the glory of the immortal God for images resembling mortal man" (Rom 1:23). This double-edged, potentially idolatrous quality of mirrors is worth keeping in mind. There is always the Feuerbachian danger

---

[53]A phrase Eugene Peterson co-opts from Friedrich Nietzsche to describe Christian discipleship (*A Long Obedience in the Same Direction: Discipleship in an Instant Society*, 2nd ed. [Downers Grove, IL: InterVarsity Press, 2000], p. 13).

[54]See further Kevin J. Vanhoozer, "May We Go Beyond What Is Written After All? The Pattern of Theological Authority and the Problem of Doctrinal Development," in *"My Words Will Never Pass Away": The Enduring Authority of the Christian Scriptures*, ed. D. A. Carson (Grand Rapids: Eerdmans, forthcoming).

that biblical interpreters will see only themselves and their own ideas.[55]

The mirror of Scripture: A verbal εἰκών of what is in Christ. Scripture is as vital an ingredient to the practice of Christian theology as are the stars to nautical navigation, or a play script to dramatic performance. We have chosen the metaphor of the mirror not only because both Paul and James employ it, but also because the mirror is a medium for reflecting images and light. As Christ is an icon of God (a visible mirror image of the invisible), so Scripture is a verbal icon (a textual mirror) of Christ.

In an icon, the light appears to come from the figure, often a face, itself. Icons do not call attention to themselves but reflect what lies beneath or beyond their surface. The icon is a witness to transcendence or, in the case of a biblical text, the divine personal presence that shines through it and the divine voice that sounds through it. In the medieval period, the biblical texts were literally iconic: so-called illuminated manuscripts included decorations around the letters or even miniature illustrations. These were exquisitely produced, often with gold or silver. The net effect is akin to a stained glass window, only the light appears to be coming from the text itself. Hugh of St. Victor says that "wisdom illuminates" and asks readers of Scripture to expose themselves to the light (sense) emanating from the sacred page.[56]

At their wisest, then, theological interpreters stand with unveiled faces before the light of Scripture, soak it up and say what they see. Doctrine is not a dull and dry substitute for biblical discourse but a means of catching its light, and perhaps of seeing further into the mirror. Indeed, those who examine only the surface of the text with various exegetical methods may be in danger of thinking that their light (of critical reason) illuminates the text rather than vice versa. The challenge is to look into the mirror of Scripture to see the theological as well as historical realities imaged therein, and this means seeing *past* first-century Palestine and *further* than the ancient Near East.

Why doctrine? Thus, for at least three reasons beyond correcting false teaching, systematic theology is part and parcel of the ministry of the gospel,

---

[55]Jean-Luc Marion uses the image of the mirror in his discussion of conceptual idols and icons in his *God Without Being* (Chicago: University of Chicago Press, 1991), pp. 11-14, 19-22.
[56]See Ivan Illich, *In the Vineyard of the Text: A Commentary to Hugh's* Didascalicon (Chicago: University of Chicago Press, 1996), pp. 17-23.

and thus the economy of light: (1) Christian doctrine helps us answer questions about the story of salvation (e.g., why did Jesus *have* to die?); (2) doctrine helps us better to understand the realities presupposed and implied by the story (e.g., how does Jesus' cross atone for sins?); (3) doctrine helps the church today to understand how we in our place and time ought to participate in the ongoing story.

Critical biblicists agree with the Westminster Confession of Faith's understated observation that "all things in Scripture are not alike plain in themselves, nor alike clear unto all" (I, 7). Theology serves the church by ministering the understanding faith seeks. Sometimes one has to do more than repeat what Scripture says in order to explain it: "The genesis of doctrine lies in the exodus from uncritical repetition of the narrative heritage of the past."[57] There is a time for storytelling, and a time for interpreting the story; there is a time for recounting history, and a time for saying what events mean. Systematic theology is the time for interpreting the biblical story, and saying what it means.

To insist only on repeating the narrative or even didactic portions of the Bible is no guarantee of understanding, for contemporary Christians speak different languages and inhabit different contexts. Scripture provides the right interpretive framework for understanding God, the world and ourselves, but theology's task is to make this framework intelligible, both by clarifying its internal structure and by bringing it critically and constructively to bear on other prevailing interpretive frameworks.[58] The direction of flow is all-important: Scripture is an illuminated manuscript whose light flows through it onto us. Evangelical theology aims not to make sense of Scripture in the light of our world, but rather to make sense of our world in the light of Scripture.

What doctrine is: A photon in the economy of light. Christian doctrine attempts to set forth in communicative action *what is in Christ* on the basis of the Scriptures. *What is in Christ* is capacious: were everything to be said, "the world itself could not contain the books that would be written" (Jn 21:25). In

---

[57] Alister McGrath, *The Genesis of Doctrine: A Study in the Foundation of Doctrinal Criticism* (Oxford: Basil Blackwell, 1990), p. 7.

[58] Cf. Richard Lints: "The modern evangelical theological framework ought to seek to mirror the interpretive matrix that is found in the redemptive revelation of the Scriptures" (*The Fabric of Theology: A Prolegomena to Evangelical Theology* [Grand Rapids: Eerdmans, 1993], p. 310).

Christ is not only the "fullness of God" (Col 1:19) but also the true "human form" (Phil 2:8). In Christ is the reconciliation of God and the world (2 Cor 5:19): peace with God (Rom 5:1), every spiritual blessing (Eph 1:3), the beginning and the end (Rev 21:6)—the list goes on. Doctrine tells us *what has been, what now is* and *what will be* "in Christ." Doctrine tells us what we should believe (*credenda*), hope (*speranda*) and do (*agenda*). It is a special kind of instruction that teaches the head, orients the heart and guides the hand.

Doctrine is "sound" or health-giving to the extent that it indicates reality, for we are unhealthy when we are delusional. As Christ mirrors God and Scripture mirrors the divine economy, so doctrine mirrors Scripture—with its unified story, its various perspectival testimonies and its patterns that elicit biblical reasoning. To the extent that doctrine preserves the same story and the same thinking, it reflects the economy of light.

Most Christian doctrines focus either on the protagonists of the drama of redemption (God, humanity, Jesus Christ and, to a lesser extent, angels, demons and Satan), its key events (the cross, Pentecost), its background assumptions (divine providence) or its explicit claims ("God is one"; "Jesus is the Christ"; "Believe in his name and you will be saved"). We cannot fully understand the person and work of Jesus Christ until we are able to say both *who* he is and *what kind* of who (human? divine? both? neither? hybrid?). To begin to spell out the nature of Jesus Christ is to look deep into the mirror of Scripture, into its implied ontology.[59]

How doctrine develops. *That* Christian doctrine has "developed"—that theologians use new concepts for understanding the faith "once for all delivered" (Jude 3)—is indisputable. That some of these doctrinal formulations have settled into creeds and confessions, thus attaining a virtual career of their own, is also indisputable. What is in dispute is how best to evaluate these developments. Are doctrines *less* biblical than the words of Scripture itself? Can theology continue to mirror Scripture faithfully with new technical terms?

---

[59]C. F. D. Moule notes that on occasion the New Testament authors use explicitly ontological language (Heb 1:3), and Jesus does too (Jn 8:58), though for the most part the Bible's language straddles the "borderlands" of ontology ("The Borderlands of Ontology in the New Testament," in *The Philosophical Frontiers of Christian Theology: Essays Presented to D. M. MacKinnon*, ed. Brian Hebblethwaite and Stewart Sutherland [Cambridge: Cambridge University Press, 1982], pp. 1-11).

Consider the pastoral problem and theological crisis that emerged in the fifth century, when Nestorius, a church leader in Constantinople, was asked whether it was suitable to refer to Mary as *theotokos* ("God-bearer"). Nestorius reasoned that God cannot have a mother (perfect being theologians would no doubt agree), and countered by suggesting *Christotokos* ("Christ-bearer") instead. This answer, however, jeopardized the integrity of the gospel. If Jesus were not God in the flesh, how could his death be salvific? So Cyril of Alexandria reasoned against Nestorius. Cyril pointed out that if Mary were *not* the mother of a divine person (the second person of the Trinity), then Jesus could be considered divine only if he were adopted by the Son later in his life, which meant that "Jesus Christ" named two persons, not one.[60]

The Council of Ephesus resolved the controversy in 431, declaring Mary *theotokos* because her son Jesus was one divine person with two natures (divine and human). The development of this doctrine is instructive. Though it appears to be about Mary, its main concerns are really Christology and soteriology. Further, though apparently a piece of abstract speculation, in fact it is the product of good canonical judgment, an ontological clarification that was necessary to preserve the integrity of the main story about Jesus Christ.[61]

No matter how evangelical theologians try to minister fuller understanding of what is seen in the mirror of Scripture, their first commandment must always be: You shall not bear false witness to *what is in Christ*. Hence the principal challenge for the systematic theologian is to say the *same* thing as Scripture in *other* terms—or to "acknowledge" (Gk. ὁμολογέω—Mt 10:32; Rom 10:9; 1 Jn 4:15) in a new vocabulary what has already been said, either implicitly or explicitly, in Scripture. To say the same thing (ὁμο + λέγω) in other terms is the hallmark of dogmatic reasoning, which "produces a conceptual representation of what reason has learned from its exegetical following of the scriptural text."[62] Systematic theology attempts to say *what is in Christ* in terms that expound the biblical text on a deeper level, that

---

[60]For a fuller treatment of this debate, see John McGuckin, *Saint Cyril of Alexandria and the Christological Controversy* (Crestwood, NY: St. Vladimir's Seminary Press, 2004).

[61]It is much less obvious that other Marian dogmas (e.g., the immaculate conception) are either valid ontological implications from, or necessary to the integrity of, the story of Jesus.

[62]John Webster, *The Domain of the Word: Scripture and Theological Reason* (New York: T&T Clark, 2012), p. 130.

"gather together" various testimonies from throughout the canon to minister understanding in new idioms for new contexts.

To return to our example: *theotokos* seeks in a new situation to say the same thing as Scripture is saying about the child to whom Mary gave birth. The new pastoral problem concerned what is appropriate to assert about Mary as the mother of our Savior. To bear true witness is to remain faithful to what one sees in the mirror of Scripture in such new pastoral contexts. Simply repeating the words of Scripture is no guarantee of faithfulness and often fails to resolve the pastoral problem at hand. Yet neither is theology poetic or creative, if these mean going beyond or against Scripture. Theology is rather a special kind of mirroring, a secondary mirroring, that both reflects and magnifies what it sees in the text—a conceptual mimesis or imitation, nonidentical though faithful human repetition of the divine.[63]

Doctrine develops, then, when disciples have to think about what faithful imitation looks like in new situations. In setting forth in speech *what is in Christ*, doctrine helps direct disciples to follow the Way along previously untrodden paths. In this context, mirroring the mirror of Scripture is not a matter of exact replication, but rather of coming to understand the mystery in the mirror so deeply that one is able to enter into it—the new reality in Christ that the gospel announces—despite external circumstances that do not exactly mirror the Bible's original contexts. The key to faithfulness is to continue the same story despite the new setting and scenery. Evangelicals do affirm *sola Scriptura*: Scripture is the supreme criterion for discerning which doctrinal formulations are faithful and which are not. By contrast, "solo" *Scriptura* does not resolve the problem of pervasive interpretive pluralism, that is, discerning *whose interpretation of Scripture is right*.

Evangelical biblicists may initially be inclined to agree with the seventeenth-century Englishman William Chillingworth, who declared that the doctrine on which all Protestants agree, as a rule of faith and action, is Scripture alone: "The Bible, I say, the Bible only, is the religion of protestants!"[64] The problem of course, as Vincent of Lérins knew centuries

---

[63]A. N. Williams, *The Architecture of Theology: Structure, System & Ratio* (Oxford: Oxford University Press, 2011), p. 19.

[64]William Chillingworth, *The Religion of Protestants: A Safe Way to Salvation* (London: Henry G. Bohn, 1846), p. 463.

earlier, is that "we can find almost as many interpretations as there are men."[65] Alister McGrath refers to this as "the Achilles' heel" of contemporary evangelicalism: "Evangelicalism, having affirmed the supreme authority of Scripture, finds itself without any meta-authority by which the correct interpretation of Scripture could be determined."[66] Precisely for this reason does doctrine develop, and so we must consider the role of the church in the economy of light.

A CREATURE OF THE WORD: THE CHURCH
IN THE ECONOMY OF LIGHT

We have already seen that the existence of the church is part of the gospel: in Christ God has made Jew and Gentile into a new humanity. However, the church is not only of ontological but also of epistemological significance, occupying a place in the economy of light, illuminated by the Spirit. Evangelicals have typically failed to appreciate the church's significance. Hence our thesis: the church is the domain of the gospel, a divinely appointed means for coming to understand, corresponding to and passing on the good news of salvation in Christ—a means through which the risen Christ, through the Spirit, exhibits and extends his own domain. In this way the church will ultimately be an end and not just a means—a new humanity enjoying the consummation of the new creation. But for now, as a means, the ministry of the church does not compete with but rather serves and embodies *sola Scriptura* rightly understood.

Catechism: Teaching as ministerial authority. "Make disciples . . . baptizing them . . . teaching them" (Mt 28:19-20). Jesus' Great Commission is a *Magna Carta*, a Great Charter for the church to be the schoolhouse of Christ. The early church took its teaching responsibilities seriously: for centuries, believers received one to three years of oral instruction in preparation for baptism. Catechesis gave disciples what they needed to know before becoming active participants in the life of the church—actors in the drama of redemption.[67] Calvin believed catechisms to be so important that he agreed

---

[65]Vincent of Lérins, *Commonitorium* 2.2.

[66]Alister McGrath, "Faith and Tradition," in *The Oxford Handbook to Evangelical Theology*, ed. Gerald R. McDermott (Oxford: Oxford University Press, 2010), p. 82.

[67]For further exploration of the model of drama to discipleship, see Kevin J. Vanhoozer, *Faith Speaking Understanding: Performing the Drama of Doctrine* (Louisville: Westminster John Knox, 2014).

to return to his church in Geneva only on the condition that the magistrates made such instruction mandatory: "The church of God will never preserve itself without a catechism."[68]

The New Testament itself regards the church's foundation as the truth of Jesus Christ. Paul speaks of laying a "foundation" for the church (1 Cor 3:10), of James, Peter and John as "pillars" (Gal 2:9), and, more generally, of the church as "built on the foundation [θεμέλιος] of the apostles and prophets" (Eph 2:20). Yet the apostles themselves are not the foundation; this role belongs to Jesus Christ (1 Cor 3:11), so that the apostolic foundation is the truth of gospel set forth in their speech and writing. Again, the apostles did not arrive at this truth by the light of their own reason; rather, the Spirit of truth communicated this testimony to and through them (Jn 16:14-15).

The apostles also appointed others to lead and teach the church in their wake (Tit 1:5; cf. Acts 14:23). Human teachers are part of the economy of light, as the pastoral epistles amply testify. Indeed, the risen and ascended Christ himself "gave gifts" (Eph 4:8), namely, "the apostles, the prophets, the evangelists, the shepherds and teachers" (Eph 4:11). According to Calvin, each of these offices represents a form of the ministry of the Word.[69] Each of these offices plays a role in the economy of light precisely as a *ministerial* authority. Christ's authority is foundational, while the authority of the Spirit's inspired apostolic testimony to Christ is magisterial. Yet churchly teachers are caught up in the pattern of evangelical authority too: insofar as these teachers communicate the word of truth, they participate in the triune economy of light, as ministerial authorities (normed norms) who serve not their own agenda but Christ's.[70]

The Christian life is not one of solitary confinement but of life together, in community; similarly, interpreting Scripture is not the prerogative of lone exegetical rangers but of the gathered church, a creature of the word and

---

[68]John Calvin, letter to Edward Seymour, October 22, 1548 (cited in Scott M. Manetsch, *Calvin's Company of Pastors: Pastoral Care and the Emerging Reformed Church, 1536–1609* [Oxford: Oxford University Press, 2013], p. 266).

[69]John Calvin, *The Epistles of Paul the Apostle to the Galatians, Ephesians, Philippians, and Colossians*, Calvin's Commentaries, ed. David W. Torrance and Thomas F. Torrance (Grand Rapids: Eerdmans, 1965), p. 178.

[70]Cf. Allen and Swain: "The church's accredited teachers faithfully fulfill their ministries when they demonstrate that their teaching is nothing other than the teaching of the Holy Spirit speaking in the Scriptures" (*Reformed Catholicity*, p. 106).

hence an interpretive community. Lacking space here to develop a full-orbed ecclesiology, we can only call attention to central metaphors Scripture uses to describe the church: *body* of Christ, *people* of God, *fellowship* of the Holy Spirit. The church is a communion. Believers read Scripture and break bread *together* for the same reason: the gospel announces not a new route to heaven but a new root to a new humanity, in Christ through the Spirit. In light of this new communion, we demonstrate our love for God precisely by loving one another (1 Jn 4:20-21), so the Lord has ordained that we teach and learn from one another: "The Lord nourishes his body and causes it to grow by means of the body's own proper agency and work."[71]

Councils: Corporate dogmatic judgments. The church incorporates men and women into the domain of Christ, where the Spirit edifies and governs by ministering the word of God written to hearts and minds. As the Spirit uses varieties of gifts to build up the church (1 Cor 12:4), so the Spirit uses its many members to grant unifying insights into gospel truth. Acts 15 provides "a paradigmatic model of ecclesial authority exercised in the form of a church council."[72] Of particular relevance is how the Spirit brings to James' mind the prophecy from Amos 9:11-12 concerning God's calling the Gentiles, thus allowing him to reason canonically (in light of Peter's experience of the Gentiles too receiving the Spirit) that the Gentiles are not bound by the old covenant sign of circumcision. This "judgment" won unanimous consent from the elders and apostles who comprised the Jerusalem Council: "It seemed good to the Holy Spirit and to us."

We must not skim over this accomplishment. Consensus is often difficult, and never more than when it involves overturning centuries-old tradition: "Church dogma . . . is a sign of Christ's victory, accomplished through Word and Spirit, within the common mind of the church."[73] Moreover, in this case the tradition had centuries-old biblical roots, so that its overturning required a new pattern of biblical reasoning in the light of Christ. Just as significant was the manner in which the council's judgment was then made known: Paul and Timothy took the news to various cities and "delivered to them for observance the decisions [τὰ δόγματα] that had been reached by

---

[71]Ibid., p. 100.
[72]Ibid., p. 74.
[73]Ibid., p. 112.

the apostles and elders who were in Jerusalem" (Acts 16:4). Of special interest is the term δόγματα, meaning "authoritative judgment," and from which theology gets the term *dogma*—a summary statement of biblical truth in the church's own language that everyone in the church is obligated to believe.[74]

Martin Luther appealed to the Jerusalem Council as a template for subsequent church councils. He saw no necessary conflict between *sola Scriptura* and church councils issuing dogmatic decrees, provided that they do not add materially to the faith once received: "A council has no power to establish new articles of faith, even though the Holy Spirit is present."[75] Stated in terms of the present work: the Protestant Reformers acknowledged valid ministerial authority for church councils and their decrees, provided that the latter reflected what was already implicit or explicit in the mirror of Scripture.

One particular postapostolic council stands out for producing a *dogma* of particular importance, a judgment that has become a standard of Christian orthodoxy. The Council of Nicaea (325), after long debate, decided that the Son was not a creature but *homoousios* ("of the same nature") as God. *Homoousios* is not in the Bible, but faithfully renders what is implied by passages such as Philippians 2:6, which speaks of the Son's "equality with God" (ἴσος θεός). The Council of Nicaea said what virtually amounts to the *same* thing: they rendered the same *judgment* as Paul though with different *concepts*.[76] The technical, ontological concept *homoousios* expresses a nonidentical equivalence to Paul's ἴσος θεός. The orthodox doctrine of the Trinity achieved dogmatic status when the Council of Constantinople agreed in 381 with Basil of Caesarea's biblical reasoning that the Spirit too is *homoousios*.[77] Again, the integrity of the gospel

[74]See Bavinck's discussion in *Prolegomena*, pp. 28-34. Cf. Tom Greggs: "*sola scriptura* is a doctrine concerning the *church's* relationship to the sovereignty of Scripture over it *before* it is a doctrine of the *individual's* relationship to Scripture" ("Biblical Hermeneutics and *Relational* Responsibility," in *The Future of Biblical Interpretation: Responsible Plurality in Biblical Hermeneutics*, ed. Stanley E. Porter and Matthew R. Malcolm [Downers Grove, IL: InterVarsity Press, 2013], p. 128, emphasis original).

[75]Martin Luther, *On the Councils and the Church*, in *Church and Ministry III*, ed. Eric W. Gritsch, Luther's Works 41 (Philadelphia: Fortress, 1966), p. 123.

[76]I here follow David Yeago's analysis, and his conclusion that "the same judgment can be rendered in a variety of conceptual terms" ("The New Testament and the Nicene Dogma: A Contribution to the Recovery of Theological Exegesis," in *The Theological Interpretation of Scripture: Classic and Contemporary Readings*, ed. Stephen Fowl [Oxford: Blackwell, 1997], p. 93).

[77]See Basil of Caesarea, *On the Holy Spirit*, trans. Stephen Hildebrand (Crestwood, NY: St. Vladimir's Seminary Press, 2011).

is at stake: if neither the Son nor the Spirit were fully God, then the good news of believers being united to Christ by the Spirit for communion with God would be fatally compromised. That God is Father, Son and Spirit is a binding judgment on all Christians, then, as a faithful reflection of biblical truth. Notice that the church is not simply the gathering of those with common beliefs, but a means by which what is to be believed everywhere, at all times and by all is first discerned.

Catholicity: Tradition in the economy of light. No one period, culture or denomination has a monopoly on the gospel, or on the label "evangelical." *Evangelical* names an ambition—to be conformed to the new reality in Christ—not an achievement. No single glance at the mirror of Scripture sees all that is there. Even the Council of Nicaea, though seeing correctly, did not see everything about the identity and significance of Jesus Christ. Yet we should no more despise *homoousios* simply because it was discovered at a particular place and time than we should relativize Newton's Second Law of Motion just because he was a seventeenth-century Englishman. A valid insight into the ontology implied by the biblical texts remains a valid insight. It follows that the church should deliver to others for observance these Nicene decisions (δόγματα) too (cf. Acts 16:14).

Tradition is the means by which the church "hands down" beliefs and practices from one generation to the next. This passing on (*transmissio*) is an aspect not only of the church's mission but also of the Spirit's mission to build up the church in the unity of truth. "Catholicity" (Gk. καθ᾽ ὅλου = "referring to the whole") refers to the *whole* church, the people of God spread out over space, across cultures and through time. *Evangelical* and *catholic* belong together. *Catholic* qualifies *evangelical*, for the gospel gathers the church, while *catholicity* designates the scope of the gospel's reception. To speak of *catholic* evangelical theology adds a crucial qualifier that *prohibits* any particular way of receiving the gospel from becoming too paramount while requiring all particular receptions of the gospel to be cognizant of what all other believers everywhere and at all times confess.[78]

Mere evangelical theology regards catholic tradition as a ministerial authority. Twenty-first-century evangelicals cannot answer the question "Who

---

[78]Protestants understand the catholicity of the church to be a function not of institutional but rather of doctrinal continuity.

is Jesus Christ for us today?" as if they were the first to do so. There is a long tradition of faithful wrestling with Scripture over this matter; at stake in the ancient rule of faith and the Apostles' Creed is an understanding of salvation. Each is a summary of the biblical drama of redemption, a secondary mirror of the economy of salvation, and thus a helpful guide to reading Scripture.[79] Christians who peer into the mirror of Scripture to see "fairest Lord Jesus" do well to be aware of what others, especially the early ecumenical councils, have seen. The Council of Chalcedon in 451 too, in declaring Jesus Christ to be "one [person] in two natures, without confusion, without change, without division, without separation," reflects biblical truth.[80] Yet, while the formula speaks the truth and nothing but the truth, it does not speak the *whole* truth. While it may have represented the "whole" church at its time, even then it could not exhaust the truth, let alone addressing every important question or context since. Nevertheless, the early creedal statements enjoy ministerial authority for churches in every context insofar as they provide valid insights into the coherence of the biblical narratives and the *what* of Jesus' *who*.[81] As such their scriptural anchorings are welcome instruments for maintaining the unity of the church across times and places.

The tradition of orthodoxy is not a merely human achievement, to be described in immanent historical-sociological terms alone, but a work of the Spirit. It is part of what it means to confess, "We believe in the church": we believe that the risen Christ has deployed his Spirit to gather a people, a community of the new covenant whose members have Christ's word etched on their hearts (Jer 31:33; 2 Cor 3:3). If the "whole" church carries epistemic authority, this authority is not a function of a Pew Research Center poll, but rather the πνεῦμα of truth guiding Christ's disciples ("you") into all truth (Jn 16:13—the "you" is a second person *plural*). Further, what is authoritative in the rule of faith and ancient creeds are not the individual concepts so much as the judgments—the wisdom—rendered by these concepts: what is

---

[79]For an extended defense of "ruled reading," see Allen and Swain, *Reformed Catholicity*, chap. 4.

[80]Translation from Henry Bettenson, *Documents of the Christian Church* (Oxford: Oxford University Press, 1947), p. 73.

[81]The Nicene-Constantinopolitan Creed (381) is of particular significance as the product of the First and Second Ecumenical (i.e., "whole" catholic church) Councils. Note that it summarizes both the gospel events and the triune economy of redemption, which we have identified as the material principles of mere evangelical theology.

crucial is affirming that Jesus Christ is fully human and fully divine, not necessarily using the concepts *hypostasis* and *homoousios*, however necessary they may originally have been.[82]

Mere evangelical theology is both catholic and apostolic. To say *apostolic* affirms the supreme authority of the commissioned testimony from the prophets and apostles—those "sent" to extend in writing Christ's self-communication. *Apostolic* thus signifies the inspired human writings borne along by the Holy Spirit, who "speaks only what he hears" in bearing witness to the Word incarnate, Jesus Christ. To say *apostolic* identifies what anchors both faith and theology: the canonical gospel. To say *catholic* explains what is "mere" about evangelical theology's focus, namely, what it believes *with the whole church* about the gospel of God and the God of the gospel.

Neither catholicity nor tradition need contradict *sola Scriptura*. To be sure, there is no place for supplanting divine revelation with merely human tradition (Mk 7:8)—beliefs and practices that have no basis in Scripture—in the pattern of theological authority. But this is the only one of eight senses of tradition that Martin Chemnitz, the Lutheran Reformer, saw fit to reject.[83] By contrast, Protestants who affirm *sola Scriptura* ought also to affirm catholic tradition as *a Spirit-guided embodiment of right biblical understanding*. With this thought we expand Luther's observation: "God's word cannot be without God's people, and conversely, God's people cannot be without God's word."[84] *Sola Scriptura* would be an empty slogan without a people living under Scripture's authority. To assert the Bible's supreme authority without at all specifying its meaning generates not an anchored but an *empty* set. What the catholic tradition "hands on" from one generation to the next is a pattern of *orthodoxy* ("right opinion"). If apostolicity provides the anchor, then catholicity is the rope that connects it to the ship of the faithful.

Catholicity—the consensus tradition passed down through the centuries—helps to address pervasive interpretive pluralism. Recall the problem: *sola Scriptura* as a rallying cry does not adequately delimit the range of ac-

---

[82]Of course, if one *does* use these concepts, it is important to remain in continuity with their usage in the early creeds, as they are now part of the church's catholic wisdom.

[83]See Martin Chemnitz, *Examination of the Council of Trent*, trans. Fred Kramer (St. Louis: Concordia, 1971), p. 277.

[84]Martin Luther, *On the Councils and the Church*, in Gritsch, *Church and Ministry III*, p. 150.

ceptable interpretations, or even true from false teaching: most heretics in the early church were known for their "biblicism." George Lindbeck is right: "The Protestant, beginning with the *sola scriptura*, needs to interpret the *sola* in such a way as not to exclude the development of doctrinal traditions possessing some degree of effective authority."[85] The catholic tradition, viewed theologically as woven by the Spirit into the pattern of ecclesial authority, reflects the process of right dogmatic development. As such, it is an element in the economy of light, that on which the "children of light" agree (Eph 5:8; 1 Thess 5:5). The church is a creature of the word, and its life is an embodiment of the word rightly received. Tradition plays the role of moon to Scripture's sun: what light (and authority) tradition bears is derivative, ministerial, a true if dim reflection of the light of Christ that shines forth from the canon that cradles him.

WHAT IS IN CHRIST: HOW THE CHURCH GROWS INTO THE FULL STATURE OF CHRIST

The Lord hath more truth and light yet to
break forth from His holy word.
JOHN ROBINSON, "FAREWELL SERMON" (JULY 1620)

Evangelical theology is anchored in Christ's self-publication through the prophets and apostles, and tethered to this anchor by the rope of catholic tradition. To complete this model, however, we also must consider the ship of faith on the water's surface, namely, the church's present cultural context. To be anchored is not the same as being rigidly fixed to only one point. An anchored set resembles an inverted cone, with its greatest latitude at the surface, at the mouth of the cone. This too is catholicity: extension not simply through time (continuity: the same rope) but also over space (discontinuity: different locations).

Intrinsic to evangelical theology is the impulse to share the good news. Mission is part of the evangelical heritage reaching back to the New Tes-

---

[85]George Lindbeck, "The Problem of Doctrinal Development and Contemporary Protestant Theology," in *Man as Man and Believer*, ed. Edward Schillebeeckx and Boniface Willems (New York: Paulist, 1967), p. 135.

tament itself, a means of coming to deeper understanding of the gospel and hence of doing theology. As the best way to learn is to teach, so one of the best ways to deepen Christian faith is to share it with others. Mere evangelical theology is catholic by being tethered to tradition, but also by being committed to extending the gospel into new contexts, and not merely by repeating earlier formulas identically. The one gospel elicits many cultural receptions. What initially looks like more interpretive pluralism can disclose, on closer inspection, the ecumenical plurality that should be one of the great strengths of evangelical theology: its ability to preserve healthy tension between unity and diversity, tension that gets expressed concretely in fellowship that is as transdenominational as it is transnational.

Evangelistic: Mission as crosscultural communication. According to Luke–Acts, the explosive force of the gospel does not diminish but intensifies the further it travels. Luke highlights Jesus' maturity ("Jesus increased in wisdom and stature"—Lk 2:52); Acts traces the progress of God's word from Jerusalem to Rome, making a special point that it "increased" and "multiplied" along the way (Acts 6:7; 12:24; 19:20). The word of God continues to increase—not only in the number of adherents but in the depth of understanding—as it penetrates further into new cultures and new contexts. The doctrine of the Trinity exemplified not the "Hellenization" of the gospel but rather the *evangelization* of Hellenism, the triumph of distinctly Christian grammar and logic in Greco-Roman language.

Andrew Walls contends that the history of Christian mission is a series of translations of the gospel into the languages, thought forms and practices of other cultures.[86] Christian mission is lived theology: the attempt to "mirror" Scripture in new contexts, via translations both literally of the Bible and figuratively of its good news. What ultimately gets translated in Christian mission is the mind of Christ. The church evangelizes by taking every thought and practice captive to Christ, demonstrating in the process what discipleship (and thus the lordship of Christ) means in specific situations. To examine the history of Christian mission is to discover the inadequacy of monolithic sameness that would require all Christians to use the same conceptual systems or follow the same cultural practices. The gospel plays

---

[86]Andrew Walls, *The Missionary Movement in Christian History: Studies in the Transmission of Faith* (Maryknoll, NY: Orbis, 1996).

no favorites with culture: no one reception exhausts the fullness of Jesus Christ, even if many contextual receptions, like Nicaea's, add to the church's permanent treasure of wisdom.

As in Acts, any subsequent success stems not from human methods but from the illumination of the Holy Spirit. Each crosscultural contextualization results in net conceptual gain, a firmer and fuller grasp on the purchase of the gospel. Calvin says that the word of God grows in two ways: when converts come to faith, and when those who are already disciples "go forward therein."[87] The very process of communicating crossculturally—the process of thinking biblically with new materials—became a means not merely to tell others about Christ, but to deepen the church's own understanding: "The process was hugely enriching; it proved to be a discovery of the Christ. . . . It is as though Christ himself actually grows through the work of mission."[88]

Dialogic: The difference between pervasive pluralism and Pentecostal plurality. Yes, it is as though Christ "grows" through the work of mission— and theology. As we have seen, theology is the attempt to set forth in speech (and eventually in individual and corporate life) *what is in Christ.* There is true deity (*homoousios*); there is the forgiveness of sins (atonement); there is true humanity (the *imago Dei*). There is much else besides, so much so that no one denomination or theological system exhausts everything there is to be said. One may speak the truth, and perhaps nothing but the truth, but not the *whole* truth (we use the singular purposely). To speak the *whole* truth, we need the *whole* (catholic) church.

History—the passing of time—need not erode truth, especially if the church is faithful in handing down the apostolic deposit. Time is God's gift to the church: an opportunity for growth and mission. It took time for Jesus' disciples to realize who he was ("What I am doing you do not understand now, but afterward you will understand"—Jn 13:7). It took time in dialogue with Jesus for the two disciples on the road to Emmaus to reach the point where they could recognize him (Lk 24:13-32).[89]

---

[87]Calvin, *Commentary upon the Acts of the Apostles* (Edinburgh: Calvin Translation Society, 1844), 1:239.

[88]Walls, *Missionary Movement in Christian History*, p. xvii.

[89]The actual moment of recognition took place when they were at table with Jesus, but the dialogue was instrumental: "Did not our hearts burn within us while he talked to us on the road,

Like those disciples, mere evangelical theologians are often found "talking with each other about all these things that had happened [to Jesus at Jerusalem]" (Lk 24:14). The most interesting, and perhaps challenging, discussions are either crosscultural or global: Ought Majority World theologians understand the gospel in terms of the ancient creeds? How can they when their languages lack close equivalents to concepts like *hypostasis*? What does Nicaea have to do with Nigeria, Chalcedon with China?[90] The requirement to minister the *same* gospel (what is in Christ) to *different* contexts suggests that mere evangelical theology must be both faithful and free: faithful to the "faith . . . once for all delivered" (Jude 3), free to "become all things" (and to use all concepts) to communicate to all. We believe that Mikhail Bakhtin's model of creative understanding provides helpful categories with which to understand the Spirit's ministry of "increasing" the word of the gospel through crosscultural mission (contextual theology).

Bakhtin's account of how textual understanding grows is perhaps the hermeneutical equivalent of Walls's account of the history of Christian mission. Both agree that cultural distance is not an obstacle to, but rather the very condition of deeper understanding. Bakhtin's central idea is that dialogue is not simply a conflict of interpretations but a means of appreciating a text's full meaning potential. In a genuine dialogue, neither conversation partner is absorbed into the other. "Meaning potential" is the operative concept: subsequent dialogue about the text—whether in the context of doctrinal development or crosscultural mission (which are often equivalent)—does not *add* new material to the text but rather discovers for the first time what was already there, though hidden from monocultural view. We need *outsideness*—different languages, concepts and cultural locations—to mine the treasures buried in Scripture: "It is only in the eyes of *another* culture that foreign culture reveals itself fully and profoundly."[91]

Crosscultural mission is itself an exercise in doctrinal development. Once again, Bakhtin provides hermeneutical reinforcement of Walls's missiological observations: "Semantic phenomena can exist in concealed form,

---

while he opened to us the Scriptures?" (Lk 24:32).

[90]For further exploration of such issues, see Gene L. Green, Stephen T. Pardue and K. K. Yeo, eds., *Jesus Without Borders: Christology in the Majority World* (Grand Rapids: Eerdmans, 2014).

[91]Mikhail Bakhtin, "Response to a Question from the *Novy Mir* Staff," in *Speech Genres and Other Late Essays* (Austin: University of Texas Press, 1986), p. 7.

potentially, and be revealed only in semantic cultural contexts of subsequent epochs that are favorable for such disclosure."[92] Mission—setting forth in word, deed and presence what is in Christ—becomes an exercise in doctrinal development whenever a different language, whether of a different culture, social class or even ecclesial tradition, is involved. Every attempt to cross cultural borders requires theological wisdom: the ability to go on in the same Way of Jesus Christ in new situations.[93]

The Spirit of truth has been leading the church into the truth, "further up and further in," for centuries.[94] Dialogue takes time. To freeze the discussion at one time only (e.g., Nicaea) is to enclose understanding within its own epoch, thus reducing its reach to what Bakhtin calls "small time." However, the word of God "increases" over time: the canon is closed, of course, but not so the process of the church's increase in understanding. Understanding increases not when we simply replicate the past, but when we try to translate it into the present. This is "creative" faithfulness: to continue the same apostolic tradition in new ways fit for different contexts. This was Nicaea's achievement with *homoousios*: the council practiced *sola Scriptura* by saying the same biblical thing in new theological ways. But such dialogue takes time—what Bakhtin calls "great time"—time for wisdom to follow the Spirit's guidance, if understanding is to be both creative and faithful.

All the treasures of wisdom are in Jesus Christ. However, just as it took four Gospels to set forth his narrative identity in speech, so it may take many interpretations—communicated and lived—to embody the wisdom potential that is in Christ. Mere evangelical theology does not result in a cacophony of conflicting interpretations—that way lies pervasive interpretive pluralism—but rather in a distinct "Pentecostal" plurality. As many members with different gifts make up the one body of Christ (Rom 12:4; 1 Cor 12:12), so many anchored (apostolic) readings make up the fullness (catholicity) of evangelical theology. Scripture is sufficient, yet it takes four Evangelists to tell the story of Jesus Christ. In similar fashion, could it not take a number of different voices (denominations, cultures, even eras) to articulate all the

---

[92]Ibid., p. 5.

[93]See further Vanhoozer's attempt to explain this "going on in the same way" in terms of theatrical improvisation in *Faith Speaking Understanding*, pp. 188-204.

[94]The reference is to C. S. Lewis's Narnia (from *The Last Battle*) and the idea that we will never be able exhaustively to assimilate the domain of Jesus Christ.

wisdom and blessings that are in Christ? Pentecostal plurality is the miracle of different voices speaking the same thing in different languages *and* the increase of understanding in which hearing this diversity results.

The temptation, of course, is to prefer what is familiar—especially one's own voice. It is also tempting to want to control the dialogue. Limitations there must be (hence the anchor!), but ultimately pastors and theologians are but servants and stewards in the Master's house. We have a share in the treasures of wisdom in Christ, not full possession. Once again: evangelical theology is an aspiration, not an achievement.

Walls's term for two people from different cultures coming together to learn Christ is "the Ephesian moment."[95] Here is how Walls describes the process: "We need each other's vision to correct, enlarge, and focus our own; only together are we complete in Christ."[96] It takes time for the church to plumb the depths of God's authoritative word. It takes time for individuals to attain "the measure of the stature of the fullness of Christ" (Eph 4:13). It takes *great* time for the church to grow men and women who can exhibit *great understanding* of the gospel, the unity of the faith, and the diversity of discipleship.

The last word on the matter belongs to Walls: "It is a delightful paradox that the more Christ is translated into the various thought forms and life systems which form our various national identities, the richer all of us will be in our common Christian identity."[97] This delightful paradox is none other than the promise of mere evangelical theology.

MERE EVANGELICAL THEOLOGY: "THE WISDOM TO KNOW THE DIFFERENCE"

Does an appeal to "Pentecostal plurality" solve or exacerbate our second presenting problem, the apparently self-destructive evangelical practice of ascribing supreme authority to Scripture alone but then failing to locate interpretive authority, with the result that every reader does what is right in his or her own eyes? Words matter, and "plurality" (the state of being plural)

---

[95]The reference is to the most radical doctrinal development of all in the early church, namely, the insight that the gospel was for Gentiles as well as Jews (Eph 2:11-21).
[96]Andrew F. Walls, *The Cross-Cultural Process in Christian History* (Maryknoll, NY: Orbis, 2002), p. 79.
[97]Walls, *Missionary Movement in Christian History*, p. 54.

is not "pluralism," if that implies never ruling out any interpretations or discerning between them.

Reinhold Niebuhr's "Serenity Prayer" asks for "the wisdom to know the difference" between things that can and cannot change.[98] *Mere evangelical theology likewise needs wisdom to know the difference between courageously preserving the truths of the gospel that cannot change and charitably acknowledging the interpretive diversity of nonessential truths.* The material principles, the substance, of mere evangelical theology are strong Trinitarianism and strong crucicentrism, each focusing on *what is in Christ.* Lending credence to these material principles are the formal principles that run in tandem: the magisterial authority of the canonical Scriptures and the ministerial authority of the catholic tradition. We conclude this chapter with a preliminary discussion—to be revisited in part two—of how these formal principles indicate what is essential for mere evangelical theology.

First, *apostolicity, the magisterial authority of canonical judgments*: There is "not . . . another [gospel]" than that announced by the prophets and apostles (Gal 1:6-7). It is a love story that turns on the ups and downs of covenantal relationships. The Bible recounts, in various literary genres, a unified story with a beginning, middle and end, in which the God who creates is the same as the Father who raises Jesus from the dead by the Spirit. Right understanding depends on being able rightly to identify the characters in the story and rightly to connect the canonical dots. Mere evangelical theologians agree that the Bible recounts the world's true story. We are all literally on the same authoritative page: *sacra doctrina* is accountable to *sacra pagina*. We agree on who the main characters are ("who was conceived by the Holy Ghost"), what happened ("he was crucified, dead, and buried") and what happened as a result ("the forgiveness of sins; the resurrection of the body, and the life everlasting"). The rule of faith and the ecumenical creeds acknowledge the authority of these events depicted in Scripture.

Christ is our salvation because of who he is and what he did. What makes someone a disciple is being incorporated into Christ's person and work. Strictly speaking, we don't believe in doctrines but in the reality they indicate. C. S. Lewis put it well to his friend Arthur Greeves: "The

---

[98]The Serenity Prayer has been adopted by Alcoholics Anonymous, among other organizations.

'doctrines' we get *out* of the true myth are of course *less* true: they are translations into our *concepts* and *ideas* of wh. [*sic*] God has already expressed in language more adequate, namely the actual incarnation, crucifixion, and resurrection."[99] Of first evangelical theological importance is getting the story right. One need not have an advanced degree in Trinitarian theology to trust in Christ: we have only to be like children to enter the kingdom of heaven (Mt 18:3; Mk 10:15; Lk 18:17), and that means being able to follow God's story.

To preserve the integrity of the gospel one need not arrive at a fixed interpretation of every detail. There is a difference between getting the story of salvation essentially right on the one hand and interpretive going "further up and farther in" on the other. Mere evangelical theology, as Trinity-centric and crucicentric, insists that Jesus was God in the flesh and died on the cross for our sins. So far, so central. One cannot deny that Jesus came in the flesh or was raised from the dead and preserve the integrity of the gospel. Other questions one can ask about the story are equally legitimate, but their answers may not require universal assent. While it is essential to insist that Jesus died "for us . . . for the forgiveness of sins," it is perhaps less essential to say *how*. There are many atonement theories, several of which have strong biblical warrant. We tentatively suggest that, while the *that* of atonement is essential (a doctrine of the first order), the *how* of atonement may belong on a different level. There are many other examples.

Evangelicals who affirm *sola Scriptura* must be prepared to live with some degree of doctrinal diversity concerning such nonessentials. We have suggested that one way of determining what the essentials are is to ask what would preserve the integrity of the story of salvation. If Jesus' death on the cross were not sufficient to take away the sins of the world, the story would implode: it would no longer be gospel, but tragedy. But preserving the story logic is only our first criterion.

Second, *catholicity, the ministerial authority of the scope of the Spirit's illumination*: To invoke catholicity as a second criterion acknowledges the importance of doing theology in communion with the saints—the

---

[99]Letter to Arthur Greeves (October 18, 1931), in Walter Hooper, *The Collected Letters of C. S. Lewis*, vol. 1, *Family Letters 1905–1931* (New York: HarperCollins, 2004), p. 977 (emphasis original).

scope of the gospel's faithful recipients. By studying earlier creedal formulations and cultural contextualizations, the church today gains precious insight into the gospel of God and the God of the gospel. Early creedal formulations in particular command respect because Christians for centuries, despite diverse contexts, have found these creeds to be faithful mirrors of Scripture.

Catholic sensibility—the awareness of what the whole church does or does not believe—also affords us a practical gauge for distinguishing between levels of doctrine. Indeed, only catholicity allows evangelicals to maintain healthy tension between unity (on essentials) and diversity (on nonessentials). In particular, catholicity helps us to distinguish three different levels of dogmatic rank, for which chapter five explores the biblical basis in more detail.

A first-level doctrine—one that identifies the persons of the triune God on whom the gospel's integrity depends—is one in which the communion of the saints has already formed a consensus. Level-one doctrines represent the agreed universal judgments of the church: what Christians at all times and places must confess in order to preserve the gospel's intelligibility (the material principle) and partake of the fellowship of the saints (the formal principle). These first-level doctrines are *dogmas*, teachings for which the Spirit has seen fit to illuminate the whole church. To deny a dogma is tantamount to apostasy or heresy.

Level-two doctrines treat events (e.g., atonement, resurrection) and aspects of salvation history (e.g., image of God, sin, justification) that must be affirmed, though there is some scope for different interpretations. Many level-two doctrines are answers to the *how* questions mentioned above (e.g., different atonement theories). These secondary doctrines lack full catholicity: they are the doctrines on which evangelicals who affirm *sola Scriptura* have not reached agreement. Many level-two doctrines arose at times when a vital truth seemed to be in danger of getting lost. Whereas level-one doctrines are theologically *essential*, however, level-two doctrines are best understood as theologically *expedient*. Disagreements about level-two doctrines do not disqualify one from the fellowship of the saints, though they often represent points of significant "regional" difference—points important enough to require for membership and shared ministry within a church or denomination, yet without impeding all translocal co-operation between evangelicals.[100]

Finally, level-three doctrines, enjoying even less catholicity than the first two kinds, allow for considerable freedom of opinion without fostering congregational division. For differences over them are not damaging to the gospel or debilitating for shared mission. That Jesus will return to judge the living and the dead is first order, the nature of the millennium is second order and the exact sequence of events pertaining to the millennium is probably third order.

While Scripture alone is the norming norm, catholicity—the scope of agreement about what Scripture teaches—is a helpful secondary normed norm insofar as it draws on the lived, Spirit-guided wisdom of the communion of saints, the whole people of God "from every tribe and language and people and nation" (Rev 5:9).

Third, *wisdom, increasing in (apostolic) word and (catholic) Spirit*: The church is relevant to recognizing the evangelical essentials in one final respect: it is the place where believers learn the mind of Christ. We can offer no mere panacea to the problem of pervasive interpretive pluralism, no easy method to "apply" for resolving such disagreements. A method is only as profitable as its users are proficient. Mere evangelical theology is not a method but rather a call to canon sense, catholic sensibility, contextual sensitivity and, above all, to maturity in Christ.

It takes wisdom to agree to disagree about nonessentials; it takes maturity and humility to acknowledge that one's own list of the essentials may not line up with the rest of the church—or, for that matter, with Scripture. At its best, mere evangelical theology is a way of exercising scriptural responsibility in the face of interpretive pluralism by encouraging charitable dialogue across denominational traditions and cultural contexts.

Mere (catholic) evangelicals stand united in agreement on the essentials, and united in their agreement to disagree about the nonessentials, and to

---

[100]For a broadly similar treatment of dogmatic rank, see Stanley J. Grenz and Roger Olson, *Who Needs Theology? An Invitation to the Study of God* (Downers Grove, IL: InterVarsity Press, 1996), pp. 73-77. See also David S. Dockery: "The great confessional tradition, though not the final authoritative word, can serve as a tremendously helpful resource for us in distinguishing primary from secondary issues" (*Southern Baptist Consensus and Renewal: A Biblical, Historical, and Theological Proposal* [Nashville: B&H, 2008], p. 36.

speak the truth in love whatever the level of doctrine under discussion. Mere evangelicals are well placed historically and globally to demonstrate the translocal, transdenominational unity for which Jesus prayed: "That they may be one" (Jn 17:11). And mere evangelicals are well placed to learn from one another as they seek to set forth in the conceptual and concrete idioms of their respective contexts the wonders of *what is in Christ*. Mere evangelicals are well placed globally to go "further up and further in" the mirror of the text, actualizing Scripture's meaning potential in pursuit of great understanding: "Great indeed, we confess, is the mystery of godliness" (1 Tim 3:16). But we are not there yet.

Part Two

THE ANALYSIS

The Practice of Evangelical Theology

Chapter Three

In Search of Wisdom

PART ONE PROPOSED MATERIAL and formal principles of truly evangelical theology—a theological ontology and epistemology reflecting reality in Christ. When evangelical churches appear in the theological mirror, they ought to reflect grace, not a lack of doctrinal backbone, and truth, not pervasive interpretive pluralism. Now part two proceeds to sketch more specific contours of this design: What implications for theological practice follow from this evangelical framework? If part one introduces an agenda for "mere" evangelical theology, then part two engages in more extensive analysis of how that agenda would reshape "evangelical" theology's current forms.

To begin that analysis, chapter three chronicles and critiques how recent evangelical theology has gone "in search of wisdom," ultimately arguing that more daring pursuit of wisdom is necessary. The focus of the present chapter is therefore on the *end* of mirroring Scripture, *what* such "theology" must aspire to be in order to transcend chasms between theory and practice. Chapter four follows by arguing that evangelical theology is "in need of theological exegesis" to avoid strictly two-step hermeneutical moves from theory to practice. The focus of this section's second chapter is therefore on the *manner* of mirroring Scripture, *in what* basic practice the wisdom of authentically "evangelical" theology fundamentally consists. Chapter five then asks more specifically what it means to do evangelical theology "in fellowship with the saints," not only relating the academy and the congregation but also negotiating relationships between various congregations, parachurch organizations, denominational churches and even ecumenical communions. The focus of this section's third chapter is therefore on the *agents* mirroring Scripture, *who* participates in the drama that comprises evangelical theological discourse. Finally in part two, chapter six goes "in pursuit of scholarly excellence," exploring how theological exegesis might fit within and foster authentically evangelical academic theology. The focus of this section's fourth chapter is therefore on the *intellectual practice* of mirroring Scripture, *how* evangelical "theologians" should engage their scholarly discipline(s).

The fourfold movement proposed in these chapters of part two—from searching for wisdom more biblically and holistically, to needing theological interpretation of Scripture, to enhancing theological fellowship with all the saints, to pursuing scholarly excellence—unfolds in ongoing dialogue with 1 Corinthians. Each chapter begins with reflections on how Paul's epistle addresses its subject. Appealing to 1 Corinthians goes beyond merely putting hermeneutical theory into practice. The letter poignantly addresses the pluralistic, philosophically posturing, theologically chaotic, morally disordered context of late modernity. While these scriptural reflections may not generate new exegetical claims, it is helpful to "read" the contemporary evangelical situation in light of analogous dynamics from the Corinthian context. Biblical guideposts make clearer the signs of the times. Scripture shapes wise theology's self-understanding along the way, in addition to its final judgments.

CORINTHIAN REFLECTIONS: THE MIND OF CHRIST

If any scriptural book presents daunting challenges to appeals for wisdom, 1 Corinthians is a leading candidate. Thus the present chapter must address 1 Corinthians 1–2 if its call for wisdom is not to ring hollow. Similarly, the final chapter must relate scholarly excellence to 1 Corinthians 8–9; 13 if claims about theological knowledge are to ring true. In between, 1 Corinthians 3–4; 10 illuminate the redemptive history shaping theological exegesis, while 1 Corinthians 5–7; 11–12 have implications for saintly fellowship. The opportunities and threats of the contemporary evangelical situation need the voice of this ancient epistle, since our strengths and weaknesses echo aspects of the Corinthian chaos.

Protestant catholicity: Gospel grace calls the church (1 Cor 1:1-3). Paul's greeting in 1 Corinthians 1:1-3 already resonates with evangelical concerns. Paul's apostleship is Christ-centered (1 Cor 1:1): he communicates with the

Corinthians on behalf of Jesus Christ and about Jesus Christ. God chooses to send Paul on this mission by a mysterious communicative act. This "calling" is personal, not merely private; indeed, Sosthenes, brother in Christ, though not an apostle, joins Paul in communicating what follows.

The addressees (1 Cor 1:2) similarly share in the give and take of calling. Their status as "holy people," set apart by God, comes by divine calling. This shared sainthood means newfound vocation: saints are those who call on the name of our Lord Jesus Christ. This distributes sainthood unexpectedly: it is true of all, in every place, who thus call on the name. Sainthood is particularized too: it is true of all, in every place, who call on Jesus Christ as Lord. This name reflects his divine identity as Yʜwʜ, which the Greek "Lord" (κύριος) translates, and in contrast to Caesar, the κύριος of the wider Greco-Roman world. Calling returns personal commitment, naming Christ as "our" Lord, identifying faith in terms of worship: prayer is the posture by which faith receives and then responds to God's call.

The content of the initial greeting (1 Cor 1:3) further underscores the gospel's precedence over the church's response: divine favor ("grace") promotes human flourishing ("peace"). Similarly, the Corinthians are the church of God, the community gathered in Christ, as a result of prior divine initiative; they have been "sanctified," set apart for service. Even Paul's apostolic communication stems from "the will of God." The Trinitarian character of this divine grace is not fully explicit, but it is incipient. Though "God" in these New Testament contexts often properly names the Father, there is movement toward identifying Jesus Christ as divine via κύριος. Here Paul apparently specifies the way "God" functions as a particular name by referring explicitly to "our Father." The Holy Spirit is not named, yet the rest of the epistle more than makes up for that. Christ's preeminence must be established first in light of Corinthian tendencies to overemphasize the Spirit and treat his work independently.

The gospel precedes and evokes the church's gathering in response to Christ's call. Evangelical Protestants rightly emphasize divine grace. Yet a corollary emphasis is present, easily neglected: Grace works in the whole church. Saints respond, calling on Christ together as church, not just separately or privately. Saints share *shalom*, not just peace as absence of war but the anticipation of eschatological flourishing, the fellowship of "all" who are in Christ. Evangelical theologians must still recognize that the gospel precedes the church, while their gospel begins more fully to *include* the church, as a reconciling reality that God's grace calls into existence. The church receives and responds to the gospel, as a creation of the grace it communicates. A Protestant principle is present along with catholic priorities.

Evangelical perseverance: Even misused spiritual gifts enrich the church (1 Cor 1:4-9). Succeeding verses, 1 Corinthians 1:4-9, extend Paul's gratitude for this grace and its specific work among the Corinthians (1 Cor 1:4). Beyond forgiveness, redeeming grace persistently communicates the means of fellowship (1 Cor 1:9)—enriching saints in Christ for all speech and knowledge, thereby confirming the gospel's testimony (1 Cor 1:5-6). Thus the Corinthian community lacks no spiritual gift for the present (1 Cor 1:7a), anticipating the full realization of their sanctification. Receiving the full revelation of Christ, they will finally realize the blameless response to God for which they long (1 Cor 1:7b-8).

Here the contemporary evangelical parallels are even more explicit. The gospel's preceding the church confirms classic evangelical commitment, though the church's participation in the gospel confronts evangelical neglect of ecclesiology. More concretely, Anglo-American evangelicals can find their proper place in God's economy when juxtaposing Paul's gratitude for Corinthian gifts with the rest of the letter. We may richly possess divine gifts in the church while simultaneously being impoverished through their (mis)use. It might be true both that evangelical theology should consult the faithful and that many churches, or at least many people in them, have no place for truth.[1] Corinthian chaos cannot drown out the good news: Paul retains hope for the saints' ultimate destiny, remaining thankful for the gifts God has abundantly showered on them, because the priority of grace makes perseverance possible.

Evangelical unity: Baptism calls the church to one mind (1 Cor 1:10-17). Accordingly, in 1 Corinthians 1:10-17 Paul sets the stage for his letter's most fundamental exhortation. The Corinthians ought to avoid divisions, agreeing to pursue the same viewpoint (1 Cor 1:10). Their present quarrels (1 Cor 1:11)

[1]Richard J. Mouw, *Consulting the Faithful: What Christian Intellectuals Can Learn from Popular Religion* (Grand Rapids: Eerdmans, 1994); David F. Wells, *No Place for Truth: Or, Whatever Happened to Evangelical Theology?* (Grand Rapids: Eerdmans, 1993).

bear remarkable resemblance to our own, being dominated by allegiances to theological or ministerial celebrities (1 Cor 1:12). Even those who appeal for getting along by simply loving Jesus cannot get off the hook, for such a rallying cry may itself be quarrelsome. Paul appeals to the one, whole Christ, thus pointing to a theology of the cross, since that central redemptive act is unique (1 Cor 1:13). Paul gladly escapes mistaken allegiances to the human baptizers through whom God calls people into the church (1 Cor 1:14-16). Even baptism, the vital point of entrance into the church as a human community, involves the Word, since it transpires "in the name" of Christ and no other. The gospel message is self-effacing for everyone, because its cross-centered character puts to death the pretensions of our clever speech (1 Cor 1:17). Baptism ordains every saint to priestly ministry.[2] Instead of merely inviting people to join the theological party of one spiritual leader or another, baptism obligates each and every member of Christ's body to follow the same mindset, the way of the cross. The judgment of the cross is nullified, rather than shared, if human leaders separate Christians from each other and thereby from Christ.

Evangelical scandal: The wisdom of Christ seems foolish to this world (1 Cor 1:18–2:5). Paul expands on this theme in 1 Corinthians 1:18-25 by contrasting two effects of gospel proclamation that reflect the character of its Word. Those who reject the gospel and continue "perishing" treat the cross as foolishness. Jewish scorn asks for a sign—some concrete intervention that one can take to be undoubtedly divine. John 6 confirms and deepens Paul's point: one can see numerous miracles yet stumble further into unbelief. Gentile scorn seeks apparent wisdom by way of impressive rhetoric. But a crucified criminal never seems philosophically sophisticated no matter how well-spoken his messenger. Those who believe the gospel and enjoy the new reality of "being saved" bear testimony to God's power, not only in the message but even in their opportunity to receive it as wisdom rather than folly.

This point gets further consideration in 1 Corinthians 1:26–2:5, with divine calling again the initial theme. In 1 Corinthians 1:26-31 Paul establishes the power and wisdom of divine calling in terms of Corinthian status. Their status was lowly; God's choice makes them what they are—sharers in

---

[2]As established in Peter J. Leithart, *The Priesthood of the Plebs: A Theology of Baptism* (Eugene, OR: Wipf & Stock, 2003).

all that Christ is. Hence they have no room for boasting.[3] Neither, according to 1 Corinthians 2:1-5, does Paul: he is simply a witness to Christ. Aware of the Corinthian penchant for wisdom rhetoric, Paul focuses particularly on the cross, effacing techniques of human persuasion and avoiding any basis for their faith besides divine power.

Again there are parallels on the contemporary evangelical scene. Preoccupation with celebrity leaders easily grows out of attachment to their ministries in people's lives, often stemming from genuine divine gifts. How quickly attention shifts from the gospel to the preacher, though, and the preacher's attention from the cross to crowning achievements! Soon Christians fall back into the very folly from which the gospel delivers, forgetting their former status and attributing current significance to themselves. Contemporary theologians must be vigilant against this foolish transference. Self-interested appeals to wisdom are tempting not only for "postmodern" culture in general but also in evangelical subcultures reengaging academic life.

It is therefore no accident that Paul waits until 1 Corinthians 2:4 to mention the Holy Spirit, having firmly established Christ-centeredness. No doubt the church sometimes marginalizes the Spirit inappropriately, as much evangelical theology is guilty of doing. If, however, pneumatology is a typical intersection of the gospel with cultural engagement, churchly gifts and personal subjectivity, then Paul's cruciform strategy is well taken. Beginning quasi-independently with the Spirit would only exacerbate Corinthian folly. The Spirit gives freedom for responding to divine power and wisdom in Christ.

All the same, it is possible to overextend 1 Corinthians 2:1-5 in ways that ignore 1 Corinthians 2:6-16. A ready example comes from the once-popular notion that Paul's Corinthian practice repudiated his Athenian strategy.[4] On this reading, the cultural engagement reflected in Acts 17:16-34, making

---

[3]For poignant implications of this text, see Amos Yong, *The Bible, Disability, and the Church: A New Vision of the People of God* (Grand Rapids: Eerdmans, 2011), pp. 96-103.

[4]A view apparently popularized by William Ramsey, *St. Paul the Traveller, and Roman Citizen* (London: Hodder and Stoughton, 1898), pp. 249-52, also influencing F. F. Bruce, *Paul: The Apostle of the Heart Set Free* (Grand Rapids: Eerdmans, 1977), p. 246. In opposing this reading, we make no particular assumptions about Paul's Athenian use of cultural "points of contact."

points of contact with Greek philosophy, was a mistake. Paul soon realized this and took another course in Corinth. The ministry practices emerging from such a reading include suspicion of seminary education, neglect of sermon preparation, celebration of backward simplicity and the like, in favor of more spontaneous speech "from the heart" as the proper mode of experiencing the Spirit's power. Ironically, in the name of Christ-centeredness it becomes easy to rely on oneself.

An anti-intellectual reading is historically dubious, to begin with, since the passage makes no explicit reference to a Pauline repudiation or change. A policy tailored to Corinth is emphasized, but not in contrast with policy for any other place, and certainly not in contrast with previous mistakes. The historically dubious nature of such a reading is also manifest via subtle uses of rhetoric throughout Paul's writings—many of these apparently later than 1 Corinthians—and not least in this letter itself, even in this passage. Avoiding words of worldly wisdom that might persuade foolish Corinthians did not entail spurning written argument.

This glance at the rest of Paul's writing, especially in 1 Corinthians, sheds light on what is theologically dubious in such a "spiritual" reading of 1 Corinthians 2:1-5. Paul does not avoid talking about the Holy Spirit, but he avoids associating the Spirit merely with human inwardness or spontaneity or passivity. If anything, alternative "aw shucks," overly spiritualized approaches to ministry would actually foster the quasignostic practices that Paul opposes.[5] For such Corinthian parallels would denigrate time, body, community and so forth—as succeeding chapters of the epistle make clear. Paul does not equate Christ-centeredness with anti-intellectualism. Neither does Paul avoid talking about wisdom, or simply use the term negatively, in the following verses.

The evangelical mind: The wisdom of Christ provides spiritual understanding (1 Cor 2:6-16). The focus of 1 Corinthians 2:6-16 is the counter-wisdom Paul promotes as both the beginning and end of Christian maturity. That such wisdom involves cognition is evident in 1 Corinthians 2:6, since the wisdom is spoken. The difference between Christian wisdom and its pagan counterfeit is not cognition but the end of its animating

---

[5]For a broadside against modern American "gnosticism" see Philip J. Lee, *Against the Protestant Gnostics* (Oxford: Oxford University Press, 1987).

principle. The pagan counterfeit is the wisdom of secular power(s), doomed to pass away. Christian wisdom endures, taking the time required for speaking and hearing among those who pursue maturity. Christians can take this time trusting that the cross of Jesus Christ is not a passing fashion; the God revealed there may never be in fashion, but the gospel is no weaker for that.

Paul narrates this God's redemptive history beginning in 1 Corinthians 2:7. Christian wisdom involves mystery, but again not in the Corinthian sense. Its aura of mystery is not esoteric, eliciting merely human philosophizing or religion of a sort that resulted in crucifying Christ, the true divine revelation (1 Cor 2:8). Instead, the mystery's hiddenness stems from God's lordship over history (1 Cor 2:9), which leaves humans waiting for the Holy Spirit to connect them with divine self-revelation (1 Cor 2:10-12). Despite the spiritual nature of the speaking and hearing involved, true understanding remains human activity involving cognition: the Spirit teaches, using words (1 Cor 2:13); discerning judgments involve both cognition and volition (1 Cor 2:14). The Spirit is essential to attaining this wisdom, as the Spirit of freedom— calling saints out of enslavement under the judgments of other, merely human power(s) (1 Cor 2:15). The Spirit can give this freedom because of sharing in divine self-knowledge, but free agency does not make the Spirit an independent contractor: the end of this wisdom is our sharing in the mind of Christ (1 Cor 2:16).

Referring to the mind of Christ raises a theological question of subsequent significance for our project: Is this νοῦς divine, human or both? Isaiah 40:13 poses a rhetorical question: the answer is that no merely human thinker, naturally foolish without God's Spirit, can know the mind of YHWH. But there is "double intent"[6]: the quotation not only puts down the pretensions of those with whom the Corinthians are enamored, but it also prepares an invitation to pursue true wisdom. Double entendre comes into play because Paul's use of a Greek (LXX) translation relates νοῦς to the Hebrew רוּחַ, "spirit": "Given the whole context, it is evident that Paul understands the terms 'mind' and 'spirit' to be synonymous. Because he also understands 'the Lord' to be Jesus, and because Christians have received

---

[6]Gordon D. Fee, *The First Epistle to the Corinthians*, NICNT (Grand Rapids: Eerdmans, 1987), p. 119.

the Spirit, he can move forward to his final audacious claim: 'We have the mind (=spirit) of Christ.'"[7] This "we"—at least identifying Paul and his co-author, and potentially including right-headed Corinthians who embrace the apparent foolishness of the cross—indicates that the Spirit makes the understanding accessible at a human level. While there for the receiving and not the taking, authentically human understanding is involved. Like φρόνησις vocabulary elsewhere, νοῦς here designates a "mode of thought" or "mindset," in which a set of beliefs guides judgment and action.[8] One might say that this νοῦς confronts both the scandal of the evangelical mind and that of the evangelical conscience—in this case, with the latter rooted in the former.

Likewise the shift from Κύριος to Χριστός moves in two directions. On one hand, speaking specifically of Christ evokes the letter's consistent associations of that name with the cross. The Corinthians have no room for reinstating pursuit of spiritual elitism through the back door of Paul's words. On the other hand, we hear another divine identification of Christ. There is no need to claim that Paul consciously holds a developed two-natures Christology.[9] The simpler point will do, that the logic of divine self-disclosure in this text depends on Christ's mediation of the divine mind to human beings by his Spirit. The Protestant orthodox formula of archetypal and ectypal theology fits this pattern well. The divine Son, the second Person of the Triune God, enjoys the most intimate personal knowledge of the Father, the archetype for any true knowledge of God and God's works. As the Son took on human life, he gained this knowledge in the preeminent ectypal form, an appropriate creaturely analogue shareable by the ever-wise Holy Spirit.[10]

---

[7]Richard B. Hays, *First Corinthians*, Interpretation (Louisville: Westminster John Knox, 1997), p. 47.

[8]See Anthony C. Thiselton, *The First Epistle to the Corinthians*, NIGTC (Grand Rapids: Eerdmans, 2000), p. 275, citing Robert Jewett, *Paul's Anthropological Terms* (Leiden: Brill, 1971), pp. 361-62. Margaret M. Mitchell, in *Paul, the Corinthians and the Birth of Christian Hermeneutics* (Cambridge: Cambridge University Press, 2010), e.g., p. 52, demonstrates its hermeneutical significance in that Origen took the word to have a sense roughly akin to "meaning." Thiselton's helpful, brief history of interpretation even refers to φρόνησις, in the context of Thomas Aquinas's approach (p. 283).

[9]Likewise Basil of Caesarea (c. 330–379) and others find in 1 Corinthians 2:10-11 the divinity of the Holy Spirit, along with his distinction from the Father, in a pastoral Trinitarian theology entailing both the Spirit's personal agency (rather than merely instrumental function) and intimate relatedness to the Father and Son (so Thiselton, *First Epistle to the Corinthians*, pp. 280-81).

[10]On archetypal and ectypal theology see Richard A. Muller, *Post-Reformation Reformed Dogmatics: The Rise and Development of Reformed Orthodoxy, ca. 1520 to ca. 1725*, vol. 1, *Prolegomena to*

The μίμησις—the imitation of behavior and representation of reality that are both ingredient to mirroring in a theological sense—for which authentically evangelical theology ought to strive involves creaturely correspondence to divine self-knowledge. Philosophically speaking, to define and pursue natural correspondence between human minds and worldly reality often seems to be virtually impossible. Yet the spiritual participation of saintly minds in Christ apportions this unspeakable gift. Such correspondence cannot solely involve propositional truth claims abstracted from life contexts, given the rich concept of *mindset* in this passage and others. Neither can such correspondence be reduced to noncognitive, moral or spiritual, imitation of Christ, given the preponderance of cognitive elements in the same passage noted above.

This reading of 1 Corinthians 1–2 began with a Protestant version of catholic principle: both the gospel's precedence for the church and the church's participation in the gospel. The fact of church leadership gets tacit acknowledgment along with properly evangelical appraisal: leaders are gifts to the saints insofar as they keep the cross of Christ central to their proclamation. Theological wisdom is for all the saints, while pursuit of elite sophistication and status is fraught with worldly peril. Yet the saints inhabit religious and philosophical cultures with characteristic pathologies of foolishness, so one cannot simply champion populism over elitism. Theological wisdom is spiritual by depending on the Holy Spirit of Christ. The Spirit directs our words to the Word. His redemptive work in history elicits further speech and hearing, implicating human bodies in time and communal space. The Spirit can work against or despite our frail cognitive and communicative powers; often, though, he chooses to accomplish divine purposes in and through them. In short, it is appropriate, even preferable, to speak of theology in terms of *wisdom*, involving personal knowledge. Without speaking of Christian theological wisdom we leave room for counterfeit pagan forms, whether esoteric spirituality or elite abstraction. The proper form of representation for the evangelical mind involves correspondence to Christ. In subsequent chapters we explore more fully what that christological reference point means for how theology mirrors Scripture.

Theology, 2nd ed. (Grand Rapids: Baker Academic, 2003), especially pp. 229-38.

BIBLICAL WISDOM

This initial defense of defining Christian theology via wisdom gains further credence from the rest of Scripture. Biblical wisdom has potential to heal one of evangelical theology's deepest wounds: the pathological split between head and heart. At a more academic level this pathology creates perennial tensions between Protestant orthodoxy and evangelical pietism. This widespread two-party historiography does explain some features of evangelical theology while conveniently supporting the agendas animating different constituencies. If this propositionalism versus pietism narrative is not to become a self-fulfilling prophecy, however, then evangelical theology requires a framework acknowledging both concerns—and not just the head or heart but the hands as well. First Corinthians 1–2 has already offered a taste of wisdom's medicine: wisdom dynamically holds together Word and Spirit, finality of revelation's content in Christ and freedom for its reception by the Spirit, use of words and need for spiritual life, gospel and church—rather than statically privileging one over the other. Dichotomous tendencies in these areas are human theological folly, putting asunder what biblical wisdom has joined together.[11]

In a wider biblical theology of wisdom the starting point is Genesis 3:1 as a cautionary tale: wisdom terminology appears early in Scripture, when the serpent is described as crafty. Sometimes when speaking of wisdom, the Bible refers to cleverness or instrumental skill, or to human moral judgment not necessarily directed by God. Hence we hear bracing critiques of worldly wisdom in texts such as James 3:13-18. From the beginning temptation lured humans into the pursuit of moral autonomy, the knowledge of good and evil—living apart from God rather than acknowledging God's gifts. That wisdom promotes boasting in human strength and worldly riches, as condemned in Jeremiah 9:23-24. First Corinthians reiterates this critique against any so-called wisdom that relies on weak, sinful humanity apart from Jesus Christ. James further connects genuine wisdom to Christ-like gentleness, unlike worldly wisdom that promotes arrogance and selfish ambition, resulting in communal evil.

---

[11]The following biblical overview gets more extensive treatment in Daniel J. Treier, *Virtue and the Voice of God: Toward Theology as Wisdom* (Grand Rapids: Eerdmans, 2006), especially chap. 2, as well as a terse summary in idem, "Wisdom," *DTIB*, pp. 844-47.

A cautionary tale might not seem to be a promising start for thinking about the nature of theology. However, without biblical wisdom terminology referring to a demonic alternative, modern theologians might be altogether too optimistic about human resources for knowing God and teaching the church. Given the deadly consequences of crafty, worldly wisdom right from the beginning, evangelicals must not characterize wisdom in a glib or vague fashion, as some "postmodern" epistemologies might tempt theologians to do.

For all the dangers, though, Scripture remains committed to the way of wisdom. The tree of the knowledge of good and evil from the Genesis fall gives way to wisdom as a tree of life in Proverbs 3:18, and the identification of wisdom with the Creator in Proverbs 3:19-20 soon becomes even stronger in Proverbs 8:22-36. Whatever one's conclusions about certain historical-critical debates, wisdom literature in the Old Testament was not pursuing a reality alien to the ordinary Israelite. Instead sages personalized the doctrine of creation for everyday life. The Pentateuchal narratives have sapiential motifs, while Proverbs and even Ecclesiastes have creation language from Genesis and covenant language related to Deuteronomy. The theme of wisdom literature involves pursuing the character necessary to discern and obey God's law in particular circumstances. The various wisdom books explore the possibilities and pitfalls of relating good character to human flourishing. They presume that God created the cosmos to be orderly, and that the covenant community and human culture should continue reflecting such design to some degree, even after the fall. In short, wisdom in its fullness is knowledge of the Creator God shaping the character of ordinary lives in the covenant community—as manifest particularly in their communication.

New Testament wisdom teaching is more clearly salvation-historical in context and redemptive in focus. Jesus was partly a teacher of wisdom, as portrayed by Gospel records of his parables and aphorisms. John arguably presents Christ as Wisdom incarnate, while Matthew presents him as Wisdom's teacher. In 1 Corinthians 1-2, again, Jesus Christ both is our God-given wisdom and enables us to become wise by the Spirit. The Old Testament focus on wisdom as embodying Torah gives way to New Testament focus on Word and Spirit. The Son embodied the divine instruction to Israel in human form, suffered for Israel's failure on behalf of the world and now speaks as head of the church through his apostles. The Spirit who enabled

Jesus' obedience and emboldened the apostolic witness now enlivens the church's hearing of that testimony. Shaping the body to correspond to its head, the Spirit makes it possible for the church to mature in the mind of Christ. Philippians 2:5 famously commends Christ's φρόνησις—wisdom or practical reason—for our imitation. Pauline prayers are rife with pleas for the Holy Spirit to grant understanding or discernment regarding the divine will and what is best for particular situations.

To oversimplify, two terms depict this positive biblical wisdom: σοφία and φρόνησις. Σοφία for the Greeks pointed to an unchanging abstraction that humans contemplate—somewhat akin to theory, basically pure knowledge of reality. Paul criticized worldly wisdom using this term, pointing to Jesus Christ as our σοφία. In him people come to know unchanging truth, but this truth is profoundly personal, mediated by divine revelation rather than human abstraction. Φρόνησις for the Greeks involved how the good related to particular situations—in other words, prudence, minus excessive connotations of caution. This situation-specific discernment fits what Paul commended in Philippians 2:5 and prayed for on so many other occasions.

Having sketched biblical cautions alongside promotion of wisdom, how should evangelical theology proceed? That requires two more steps, surveying further territory: next, recent prolegomena on evangelical theological method, and, subsequently, recent debates on the nature of theology shaping theological education. The point of these two surveys is that evangelical theology undoubtedly pursues wisdom, but remains vulnerable to a misleading detour on the way.

EVANGELICAL PROLEGOMENA
A generation ago few evangelical theologians treated theological method, generally reserving prolegomena for large systematic theologies when they spoke of divine revelation. From 1976 to 1983 the various volumes of Carl Henry's *God, Revelation, and Authority* were published, embodying substantial evangelical thought during the era of the battle for the Bible.[12] Simultaneously, however, others challenged evangelical assumptions about

---

[12]Carl F. H. Henry, *God, Revelation, and Authority*, 6 vols. (Waco, TX: Word, 1976–1983).

how scriptural authority ought to shape theology: James Barr criticized concepts of biblical authority themselves, along with mistaken word studies; David Kelsey surveyed the apparently selective forms of authority behind theologians' actual appeals to the Bible; and Edward Farley insisted that the classic Protestant "house of authority" connecting God to Scripture had crumbled along with its royal doctrine of God.[13] In response, especially to Kelsey's challenge, Robert Johnston edited a 1985 volume entitled *The Use of the Bible in Theology: Evangelical Options*. It is not clear that the volume was widely influential, though an essay by Packer did use the phrase "theological exegesis."[14]

The early 1990s saw publication of several relevant volumes. Trinity Evangelical Divinity School faculty, in particular, continued the work they began in the prior decade.[15] These volumes reflected strong commitment to biblical inerrancy and the occasionally rationalistic tendencies of Henry. But they also provided thorough, mainstream evangelical engagement with broader academic theology and modern philosophical thought. Soon thereafter Stanley Grenz published his first manifesto, *Revisioning Evangelical Theology*, favoring more pietist and communal approaches to the theological task.[16] The same year Richard Lints published a densely crafted effort to place evangelical prolegomena within a broadly Reformed, redemptive-historical and biblical-theological, framework.[17]

Each of these trajectories persisted at the turn of the millennium, although discussions clustered around so-called postmodernism and herme-

---

[13]On word studies see James Barr, *The Semantics of Biblical Language* (London: Oxford University Press, 1961); otherwise see several works, including idem, *The Scope and Authority of the Bible* (Philadelphia: Westminster, 1980), which juxtaposes "historical reading" and "the theological interpretation of Scripture." See also David H. Kelsey, *The Uses of Scripture in Recent Theology* (Philadelphia: Fortress, 1975); Edward Farley, *Ecclesial Reflection: An Anatomy of Theological Method* (Philadelphia: Fortress, 1982).

[14]See J. I. Packer, "In Quest of Canonical Interpretation," in *The Use of the Bible in Theology: Evangelical Options*, ed. Robert K. Johnston (Atlanta: John Knox, 1985), pp. 35-55.

[15]John D. Woodbridge and Thomas Edward McComiskey, eds., *Doing Theology in Today's World: Essays in Honor of Kenneth Kantzer* (Grand Rapids: Zondervan, 1991). From earlier see D. A. Carson and John D. Woodbridge, eds., *Scripture and Truth* (Grand Rapids: Zondervan, 1983); idem, *Hermeneutics, Authority, and Canon* (Grand Rapids: Zondervan, 1986).

[16]Stanley J. Grenz, *Revisioning Evangelical Theology: A Fresh Agenda for the 21st Century* (Downers Grove, IL: InterVarsity Press, 1993).

[17]Richard Lints, *The Fabric of Theology: A Prolegomenon to Evangelical Theology* (Grand Rapids: Eerdmans, 1993).

neutics. In 2000 a Regent College (Vancouver) conference on theological method saw two essays expand into books.[18] One came from Grenz, who promoted a more "postmodern" and pietist version of "postconservative" evangelicalism.[19] More conservative and rationalist evangelicals responded with a vigorous 2004 critique of most "postconservative" approaches.[20] Another approach presented at Vancouver also labeled itself postconservative, yet received little conservative censure at this stage, perhaps due to obvious differences from Grenz.[21] Its focus on drama was friendly to Michael Horton's 2002 prolegomena volume in his larger series, which extended the trajectory of Lints's work.[22]

In most of those volumes, whether left, right or Reformed, wisdom vocabulary is largely absent. Undoubtedly all see the lived application of biblical knowledge as an essential outcome. For many, though, it has remained important to defend theology's "scientific" status in some fashion, typically tied to hermeneutics of authorial intention whether or not the larger epistemologies can meaningfully be called "foundationalist."[23] The laudable goal of biblical application must not come at the expense of responsible interpretation. On this view we protect Scripture's unique authority by thoroughly distinguishing the historical voices of its human authors from those of any readers. Others of a more pietist, communal bent may not protect scientific hermeneutics in the same way. But they continue to presuppose fairly strong principial, not just functional, distinctions between academic and ordinary

---

[18]John G. Stackhouse Jr., ed., *Evangelical Futures: A Conversation on Theological Method* (Grand Rapids: Baker, 2000); see especially the essays by Grenz, "Articulating the Christian Belief-Mosaic: Theological Method After the Demise of Foundationalism" (pp. 107-36) and Kevin J. Vanhoozer, "The Voice and the Actor: A Dramatic Proposal About the Ministry and Minstrelsy of Theology" (pp. 61-106).

[19]Stanley J. Grenz, *Renewing the Center: Evangelical Theology in a Post-Theological Era* (Grand Rapids: Baker, 2000); also Stanley J. Grenz and John R. Franke, *Beyond Foundationalism: Shaping Theology in a Postmodern Context* (Louisville: Westminster John Knox, 2001).

[20]Millard J. Erickson, Paul Kjoss Helseth and Justin Taylor, eds., *Reclaiming the Center: Confronting Evangelical Accommodation in Postmodern Times* (Wheaton, IL: Crossway, 2004).

[21]Kevin J. Vanhoozer, *The Drama of Doctrine: A Canonical-Linguistic Approach to Christian Theology* (Louisville: Westminster John Knox, 2005).

[22]Michael S. Horton, *Covenant and Eschatology: The Divine Drama* (Louisville: Westminster John Knox, 2002).

[23]See, emblematically, Walter C. Kaiser Jr., "The Nature and Criteria of Theological Scholarship: An Evangelical Critique and Plan," *Theological Education* 32, no. 1 (1995): 57-70, in relation to Walter C. Kaiser Jr. and Moisés Silva, *An Introduction to Biblical Hermeneutics: The Search for Meaning* (Grand Rapids: Zondervan, 1994).

theology. Oddly, then, wisdom has not been a key pietist concept either; it almost seems that postmodern reactions to more rationalist approaches talk enough of community that there is little to say about knowledge.

David Clark's thorough and excellent 2003 textbook offers only a partial recent exception.[24] While Clark's own tendencies remain helpfully conservative and arguably somewhat rationalistic, he has appreciative comments concerning wisdom. Plus he avoids some pitfalls of older scientific approaches—regarding conversion of Scripture into "principles," for example. Likewise, ongoing debates over going "beyond" the Bible (to theology) biblically manifest increasing recognition that principles may be part, but cannot be all, of the solution to questions of context.[25] Wisdom is necessary for integrating appeal to principles, awareness of redemptive history and assessment of how biblical contexts relate to eschatological ideals. Still, this is a rather limited acknowledgment and rational construal of wisdom, especially when more extensive appeals to φρόνησις generate balking or bewilderment.

Of course other evangelicals, too numerous to mention, have written on subjects relevant to theological method—postmodernism, the doctrine of Scripture, biblical hermeneutics and the like. Even so, these various evangelical prolegomena say relatively little about wisdom, tending instead to reflect polarized epistemological or hermeneutical concerns. When evangelical theologians do mention wisdom, they usually treat it as a desirable outcome, the product of the right intellectual input and proper processes of scholarly reasoning. Conversely, popular evangelicalism lauds the spiritual dimensions of wisdom much more readily than its cognitive components.

THEOLOGICAL EDUCATION

An early arena in which contemporary theologians appealed to wisdom—literature on theological education—contributes important perspective. Farley's 1983 book *Theologia* proposed a unifying focus on wisdom. Several complementary proposals ensued, from Charles Wood, Kelsey and others.[26]

---

[24]David K. Clark, *To Know and Love God*, FET (Wheaton, IL: Crossway, 2003).

[25]Gary T. Meadors, ed., *Four Views on Moving Beyond the Bible to Theology* (Grand Rapids: Zondervan, 2009).

[26]Edward Farley, *Theologia: The Fragmentation and Unity of Theological Education* (Philadelphia: Fortress, 1983); Charles M. Wood, *Vision and Discernment: An Orientation in Theological Study*, Studies in Religious and Theological Scholarship (Atlanta: Scholars Press, 1985); Barbara G.

Most of this literature emerged within mainline Protestantism, as concern grew over its dying seminaries and churches.[27] Evangelicals such as Richard Muller, Robert Banks and others eventually chimed in.[28] The common concern was fragmentation: How can a seminary student experience his or her education as a unified whole, successfully addressing personal identity and professional ministry formation? The theological curriculum is often experienced as a hodgepodge of courses that do not fit together, taught by faculty who do not agree with one another, from departments that do not understand or perhaps even value each other. The poor student is left to piece together how original language biblical exegesis coheres with the Christian theological tradition, let alone how either coheres with practical ministry approaches or the survival skills needed by graduates and desired by those who hire them.

Literature on theological education proposed wisdom as a motif that would unify the curriculum, thereby reconciling academy and church. Kelsey quickly challenged such proposals by analyzing the different notions of wisdom on offer in the classic Christian tradition, let alone the contemporary theological context. Concepts of wisdom variously prioritize "contemplation, discursive reasoning, the affections, and the actions that comprise a Christian's life."[29] One might hope that these elements could be integrated, at least within a range of permissible construals, in light of the scriptural centrality of wisdom for the knowledge of God. Regardless of that hope, Kelsey found seminaries to be caught between "Athens" and "Berlin": the more ancient Athens model expressed in contemplative, person-forming pedagogies; the modern Berlin model expressed in questioning, research-producing ideals.[30]

Wheeler and Edward Farley, eds., *Shifting Boundaries: Contextual Approaches to the Structure of Theological Education* (Louisville: Westminster John Knox, 1991); David H. Kelsey, *To Understand God Truly: What's Theological About a Theological School* (Louisville: Westminster John Knox, 1992).

[27]John H. Leith, *Crisis in the Church: The Plight of Theological Education* (Louisville: Westminster John Knox, 1997).

[28]Richard A. Muller, *The Study of Theology: From Biblical Interpretation to Contemporary Formulation*, Foundations of Contemporary Interpretation 7 (Grand Rapids: Zondervan, 1991); Robert Banks, *Reenvisioning Theological Education: Exploring a Missional Alternative to Current Models* (Grand Rapids: Eerdmans, 1999).

[29]Kelsey, *To Understand God Truly*, p. 34.

[30]David H. Kelsey, *Between Athens and Berlin: The Theological Education Debate* (Grand Rapids: Eerdmans, 1993).

This analysis of competing wisdom proposals remains pertinent for evangelical biblical and theological scholars, whose spiritual aims so frequently clash with their scientific sensibilities. Let us not fault these scholars too much: when church members and leaders so frequently disparage seminaries as cemeteries while insisting on knee-jerk, selective Scripture citations to serve felt needs, the desire to protect the integrity of the biblical message is quite understandable. The question is whether evangelicals' current hermeneutical approach offers the best form of protection, or only exacerbates the problem. Our answer to this quandary is a more holistic concept of how theology mirrors the mind of Christ in Scripture—neither rejecting that evangelical commitment, nor simply reasserting it without reform.

HISTORICAL HEALING

Much preliminary spadework is now done, making it possible to dig into the heart of this chapter's dilemma: good intentions to pursue wisdom as the outgrowth of evangelical scholarship may be thwarted by the inevitable tensions produced within modern forms of theological study. Thus bolder pursuit of wisdom requires a more unified notion of theory and practice than either evangelical saints or scholars tend to possess. That claim unfolds in three subpoints, each requiring evangelical theologians to renew our tradition by learning from others. First, Ellen Charry refines the nature of "theory" involved in Christian wisdom. Second, Alasdair MacIntyre refines the notion of "practice" that Christian wisdom aims to incorporate. Third, theological exegesis—introduced here and then more extensively in the next chapter—resists the apparent necessity of strict two-step, theory-to-practice, hermeneutics for preserving historical integrity.

Wise contemplation. In 1997 Charry published *By the Renewing of Your Minds: The Pastoral Function of Christian Doctrine.*[31] This deservedly praised book is frequently cited to highlight the virtue-producing potential of biblical teaching. But Charry demonstrates more specifically that classic theologians took the formation of virtue to signal what biblical teaching truly is. Readers of her book should no longer accept the widespread evan-

---

[31]Ellen T. Charry, *By the Renewing of Your Minds: The Pastoral Function of Christian Doctrine* (Oxford: Oxford University Press, 1997).

gelical tendency to treat theory and practice as having one-way, linear movement. Charry's case studies demonstrate that classic theologians discerned biblical truth partly by asking which theological interpretations would undergird Christian virtue. She routinely found "so that" phrases connecting their claims about truth to virtuous purposes or results, with the former taught as if they were integrally linked with the latter. Theology is like medicine: primarily an art of healing, learned by long apprenticeship to master practitioners. Within this craft, scientific developments have their place, but theoretical knowledge requires growth in careful, experienced discernment for right use.

A proper kind of "theory" is ingredient to Christian theology, but its contemplation is disinterested only in a particular sense. Purification from idolatrous self-interest directs us toward, and is directed by, contemplation of God and God's works. To contemplate who God is, finite creatures must contemplate what God has said and done. This contemplation is in our interest, but not as idolatrous, isolated selves; to contemplate God invites pondering and participating in God's work in the world. Human interest aligns with divine action, both for our own healing and thereby for helping others. Theoretical moments in theology focus on God, albeit never in total abstraction from the concrete concerns of the world God loves. Such contemplation accordingly is communicative activity; theologians easily forget that prayer is first theology.[32]

True praxis. Philosophical treatments of φρόνησις and of "practices" support this notion that, for theology to result in the wisdom Charry portrays, distinctions must not become separations perpetuating one-way, linear movement from theory to practice. Alasdair MacIntyre's work suggests that the ancients did not merely apply a vision of the good life to discernment in concrete situations; these challenges of practical reason led to sharper understanding of the good itself.[33] This refinement within practice resonates with many biblical journeys of discipleship in which revelation occurs progressively, one obedient step at a time. In Wood's terms,

---

[32]"If you are a theologian you will pray truly. If you pray truly, you are a theologian" (Evagrius of Pontus, *Chapters on Prayer*, no. 60, in *Evagrius of Pontus: The Greek Ascetic Corpus*, ed. and trans. Robert Sinkewicz, Oxford Early Christian Studies [Oxford: Oxford University Press, 2003], p. 199).

[33]Alasdair C. MacIntyre, *After Virtue: A Study in Moral Theory*, 2nd ed. (Notre Dame, IN: University of Notre Dame Press, 1984).

large-scale theoretical "vision" and local, practical "discernment" oscillate back and forth.

Hence the word *practical* should not merely designate application of theoretical means to external ends, as if there were interchangeable tools for obtaining desired results. The pragmatic orientation implicitly conveyed by such vocabulary creates false dichotomies between sainthood and scholarship. No, in classic practices the means involved standards of excellence that were internally defined by the ends.[34] Thus, for example, one could not properly choose between prayer, Bible study or church attendance, engaging in only one of these according to which practice seems to be most personally effective. The very goal of Christian spiritual formation requires complex integration of all these core practices, not as disconnected means but as integral elements of the end itself. The Lord's Supper is not a means of grace if and only if it works at a given moment for a given person or group. As means of grace such practices are theological in themselves, ingredient to full participation in the knowledge of God. Practices have notions of the good embedded within them, by which to learn the good.

The evangelical two-step? Saints in the pews—or multipurpose seats— may define what is practical in unhealthy terms, regarding immediately felt needs. Yet many really do want to know what the Bible says, and they want to trust scholarly help in hearing God speak. However, their desire to move from practical concerns through theoretical contemplation back to practical application is thwarted, whether by scholarly jargon or declining cultural literacy or academic refusal to address what matters most.

The widespread evangelical approach to biblical hermeneutics can exacerbate this problem. The core distinction, between exegesis of a text's one meaning and many applications of the resulting significance, tends to institutionalize a sharp dichotomy between theory and practice and a linear di-

---

[34]According to MacIntyre, a classic practice is "any coherent and complex form of socially established cooperative human activity through which goods internal to that form of activity are realized in the course of trying to achieve those standards of excellence which are appropriate to, and partially definitive of, that form of activity, with the result that human powers to achieve excellence, and human conceptions of the ends and goods involved, are systematically extended" (*After Virtue*, pp. 186-87). For theological appropriations of this concept, see especially James J. Buckley and David S. Yeago, eds., *Knowing the Triune God: The Work of the Spirit in the Practices of the Church* (Grand Rapids: Eerdmans, 2001); Miroslav Volf and Dorothy C. Bass, eds., *Practicing Theology: Beliefs and Practices in the Christian Life* (Grand Rapids: Eerdmans, 2002).

rection from the former to the latter. This dichotomy is unnecessary but, when theory or exegesis is treated as step one and practice or theology as step two, the result is a fracture of the integral connection between healing aims and contemplative actions. Virtues become aftereffects—rather than precursors, partners and pointers to sound scriptural interpretation.

Whether or not one holds author-oriented hermeneutics of some kind (as we do), the key lies in resisting problematic two-step versions in practice. When undertaking scholarly exegesis for certain venues, it makes sense to appeal to an ontological distinction between the text itself, with its range of potential meanings, and subsequent readings or contexts. But that is not the same as organizing most or all institutions, curricula, commentary formats and homiletical approaches around sequential two-step hermeneutics, in which the exegetical and theoretical stage is essentially completed without meaningful engagement in practical realms, similarly relegating theology to a postexegetical stage. When simplistic versions of such a model dominate biblical and theological cultures, the likely result is fragmentation between disciplines, between academy and church, and so forth—appearing as if, in that case, biblical scholars function as a new Protestant magisterium. What if a picture holds people captive? What if modern scholars assume that the only way to be historically responsible and biblically faithful is to specialize, so much that necessary divisions of labor turn into hard-and-fast separations of what God joins together? Appeals for theological exegesis face and try to rework this picture.

BOLDER INTEGRATION

Recovery of wisdom calls for boldness, to resist when unhealthy two-stage models fragment theological study. Discussions of wisdom in theological education and appeals to virtue in theological hermeneutics have important parallels deserving joint consideration.[35] It is important to inform these conversations with a biblical theology of theology as wisdom. Otherwise knowledge concepts get defined with whatever philosophical resources someone happens to prefer. The biblical framework sketched above should chasten some forms of both evangelical rationalism and

---

[35]Again, this approach is explored at more length in Treier, *Virtue and the Voice of God.*

evangelical postmodernism. On thinking about theology sapientially and about wisdom theologically, different doctrinal categories and operational distinctions gain prominence.

Doctrinal categories. Given the democratization of the Holy Spirit in Christ, a sapiential account of theology should incorporate the priesthood of all believers. Theology is fundamentally an every-member ministry of God's people. Of course we should not lose evangelical concern for biblical truth; both scholarly integrity and pastoral leadership are vital for teaching the people of God and engaging the public square. Evangelical concern for biblical truth, though, has always walked in tandem with commitment to active obedience. As Miroslav Volf insists, "To the extent that theology is able to shape broader society at all, it will be able to do so *largely to the degree that it is able to shape the life of Christian communities.*"[36] Our appeal to φρόνησις does justice to these concerns. Wisdom concretely speaks to and from the ordinary lives of the people of God, even their interactions with pagan culture(s). Wisdom also hears the voices of earlier traditions, present-day teachers and inquiring learners. One cannot help but notice that throughout the Pauline epistles, quite pervasively, wisdom is prayed for, sought as an ongoing gift from the Holy Spirit for all. Christian wisdom can incorporate sage collection and critical questioning, but these practices integrate with rather than ignore the spiritual practice of all the baptized and their local leaders.

Alongside the church's royal priesthood, another theological locus similarly gives wisdom both form and freedom. Trinitarian theology, with its doctrine of appropriation, delicately balances Word and Spirit. In Christ is the heart of any divine action the Father originates; in the Spirit, the feet bring the action to completion. Wisdom has christological fixity: Jesus is our wisdom (1 Cor 1:30). God's final Word addresses us in Jesus Christ and in the verbal testimony of the apostles and prophets regarding him, presented in Holy Scripture. Any true wisdom has a form that corresponds to Jesus Christ—to God's knowledge that only the Son can embody in perfectly human form. Yet wisdom involves pneumatological freedom as well as christological form. The same Spirit who inspired the Old Testament tes-

---

[36]Miroslav Volf, *Captive to the Word of God: Engaging the Scriptures for Contemporary Theological Reflection* (Grand Rapids: Eerdmans, 2010), p. 10, emphasis original.

timony to which the Son corresponds also empowered and directed his earthly vocation, to which Christians correspond when the truth sets us free and we pursue the mind of Christ. The Spirit's formation does not exceed the boundaries of the long shadow Jesus casts via Scripture; however, only as believers come closer to this form in concrete situations are we free to see its particular contours clearly. In this way Scripture makes us wise unto salvation (2 Tim 3:15). Of course, such particular spiritual formation only happens to and in the body of Christ. To reconcile saints and scholars requires recognizing the Trinitarian harmony of Word and Spirit.

Particular Christians pursuing wisdom do so in the context of the church and its divine providence. Romans 12:1-8 celebrates communal shaping of the self without minimizing its particular gifts and responsibilities. Perennial tensions between divine sovereignty and human responsibility do not allow us to minimize either or to treat them as simple competitors. Thus each Christian applies a particular measure of faith to pursue transformation and accordingly to practice φρόνησις in their self-offering to God for churchly service. Renewal of our minds, like reception of our spiritual gifts, comes via divine initiative. Saints can be tempted to evade their theological responsibility by appealing to divine sovereignty or clergy privilege. Scholars can be tempted to exaggerate their theological responsibility by appealing to method as a substitute for divine grace. In both cases, not only can there be over- or underemphasis on divine action; gifts are also misconstrued individualistically, so that Christians consider themselves piously wise without effort or else too cognitively weak to pursue and teach wisdom. The christological form of σοφία corresponds to divine revelatory initiative; the pneumatological freedom of φρόνησις incorporates various forms of human, churchly response. The Spirit liberates all believer-priests to understand the Word and to bless others, while calling particular teachers to guide that understanding and thereby to guard the church's freedom in Christ.

To return to a classic category, wisdom helps us to affirm robustly that knowledge of God and knowledge of self coinhere. To speak in more recent terms, dogmatics and ethics are inseparable. A wisdom paradigm engages Word and Spirit, divine sovereignty and human responsibility, self and community, within ongoing relationship rather than fixed hierarchies that privilege one side or the other. These relationships involve the dynamic movement of wisdom oscillating between tradition and inquiry, just as its Old Testament literary deposit leads us to expect. Of course distinctions are vital between the Word that we hear by the Spirit's divine initiative—which establishes our personal identity and freedom in coming to know God—and our individual experiences or communal traditions developed in response. Even so, wisdom therefore offers a theological paradigm that focuses on unfolding doctrinal relationships in relation to practice rather than fixing isolated concepts in theory alone.

Operational distinctions. Biblical wisdom seeks to perpetuate the best of classic traditions, precisely by having parents and trusted others pass them on in new contexts. Invariably traditions face tough questions and find fresh formulations. Viewed from the other side, inquiry requires something to question: critics must receive one or more traditions to chew on. Therefore, it is hardly a mark of wisdom to reject scholarly engagement out of hand, hunkering down in ecclesiastical or personal ghettos. Neither would it be wise to reject tradition out of hand, wholly embracing the latest scholarly fashions or hippest ecclesiastical trends. Wisdom is not just transfer of knowledge content or a set of skills, whether academic or churchly. Wisdom is the intersection of knowledge and practice, rooted in the virtue of good judgment—judgment only formed as Scripture (re)shapes how Christian communities live, as people improvise in the context of new challenges.

In place of a theory versus practice dichotomy, the better distinction is operational, between the process of reaching theological judgments and justifying those judgments. Theological discovery itself is distinct from verifying and communicating such discoveries. To be sure, the scholarly processes of verifying and communicating those discoveries can be occasions for fresh insight. Still, both saints and scholars—both informal Christian practices and formal scholarly methods—pertain to the process of theological judgment, the discovery of biblical truth. In principle, saints and scholars are accountable for the same *kind* of understanding. The intellectual advantages of scholars lie in the *degrees* of expertise and focus they pursue with extra time and training. Alternative advantages for saints may involve simplicity and directness in practices such as prayer, service and Scripture reading. Scholarly expertise and focus make it possible for clergy or interested laypersons at one level, for students and professors at other levels, to deliberate over theological proposals in ways that many believer-priests cannot. These measures of specialization will not generate unhealthy elitism if the people in question understand themselves as divine gifts to the church, sharing responsibilities with fellow members from whom they receive in return. If instead people behave like "God's gifts to the world," then God-given unity shatters.

Biblical and theological scholars do not stop being "ordinary" believer-priests when they study Scripture non-devotionally. In an important sense Scripture study is never non-devotional. It is perfectly appropriate to specialize in methods applied to a given text or problem for a time, and to communicate selectively for scholarly audiences. It is not appropriate, however, to wall off such occasions—or our classrooms—from the presence of the living Lord whose Word speaks in Scripture. In operational terms, then, a danger of scholarly method(s) lies in using them as a Pelagian form of self-salvation. For the ancients, ἐπιστήμη designated scientific knowledge, and τέχνη skill or technique. These forms of knowledge have their places, but only within a broader vision of the good, σοφία, and practical judgment about how to pursue the good concretely, φρόνησις. In other words, scholarly knowledge and academic skills are poorly used unless by divine grace they are properly integrated by people of good character and pursued for the common good.

Admittedly, a loose end remains within this sapiential account: Does speaking at such length of theology as wisdom, inviting all believer-priests to discern Scripture's teaching, result in a merely formal approach that lacks material commitments? Already, to begin with, part one of this book has contemplated reality "in Christ," specifying Trinitarian and crucicentric dimensions of gospel wisdom more fully. And, in fact, the present chapter has drawn materially on biblical theology and subsequent Christian doctrine: contrasting wisdom in Jesus Christ with worldly counterfeits; construing the work of Word and Spirit in Trinitarian terms; and calling for the church to embrace its theology of the cross, not only as a message about Christ but also as a mindset made possible in the Spirit. Thus attempting to embody evangelical wisdom, however modestly, we have not borrowed heavily from philosophy or made ourselves accountable to nontheological agendas. We have kept our focus on biblical material even in our account of theological prolegomena.

While more detailed proposals may appropriately use specific philo-sophical schemes, for the moment ensuing disputes over them are unlikely to sharpen the basic evangelical framework pursued by the current project. Such a biblically and theologically focused evangelical framework leaves room for later discernment about philosophical nuances fitting particular situations. Likewise, positive appeal to particular "methods" is scarce here, not because procedural rules of thumb are utterly inappropriate, but because the Word of Scripture must preside over any human wisdom. Moreover, appeal to method tends to reflect a very particular modern context.[37] Indeed, "Western" evangelical prolegomena tend to be inadequately shaped by the material of Christian dogmatics—perhaps from neglecting the theological prominence and ecclesiological shape of biblical wisdom. Evangelical theo-logians will be more convincing to biblical scholars and fellow saints alike if, while avoiding falsely scientific "proof-texting," they still make frequent recourse to scriptural materials. Theology is the art of fitting biblical texts together well—with each other and with our places in the drama of re-demption. This art must shape even how we begin and how we understand our task.

Art is indeed the preferable term, as John Webster explains: "By 'arts' I mean those excellencies of action which are the appropriate means to attain an end (the term is much to be preferred to the term 'method,' which sug-gests something more regular in its operations, and less alert to the varieties of ends)."[38] The form of exegesis that shapes evangelical theology must be theological in beginning with Christian presuppositions and prayerful prep-aration, and in aiming at virtuous ends. Furthermore, as the next chapter explores in more detail, this theological art of biblical exegesis requires in-teracting with God and the gospel throughout its entire process. Methods can contribute to the theological art, especially in relation to scholarly guilds. But sophisticated methods are not essential to reaching and teaching biblical

[37]In this respect, see the compelling anecdote in E. Randolph Richards and Brandon J. O'Brien, *Misreading Scripture with Western Eyes: Removing Cultural Blinders to Better Understand the Bible* (Downers Grove, IL: InterVarsity Press, 2012), p. 211, in which one of the authors recalls trying to distill concrete suggestions for culturally sensitive reading. A church member who came from a non-Western context challenged them regarding how characteristically American it would be to seek three easy steps for removing cultural presuppositions.
[38]John Webster, *The Domain of the Word: Scripture and Theological Reason* (London: T&T Clark, 2012), p. 28.

judgments. Instead, more modestly, methods as rules of thumb help to articulate desired starting points and difficult questions along the way. These rules of thumb emerge from apprenticeship more than theorizing, when engaging particular texts, traditions and problems with discernment.

Evangelical theologians need the wisdom to realize what scholarly arts—and methodological disputes over prolegomena—can and cannot do. Wisdom is not merely a formal notion but the material reality of participating in the Triune God's self-communication. More important than plumbing exegetical or theological method, then, is mining the treasures of Christian wisdom more deeply. Wisdom is the biblical *end* of mirroring Scripture, *what* best characterizes "theology" that is biblical and evangelical. Thus the next chapter explores how theological exegesis enriches authentically evangelical theology.

Chapter Four

IN NEED OF
THEOLOGICAL EXEGESIS

PROMOTING WISDOM AS theology's overarching concept may
seem to privilege evangelical piety and the priesthood of all believers
over concern for biblical truth and public persuasion. To avoid misunderstanding, therefore, the present chapter addresses biblical hermeneutics,
specifically the recent fascination with "theological interpretation of
Scripture" (hereafter TIS). By demonstrating that TIS upholds rather than
undermines properly evangelical historical inquiry, this chapter tackles potential concerns about appeals to wisdom, and actual concerns about theological exegesis. These concerns may be most common among biblical
scholars broadly, but they also arise among conservative evangelicals more
specifically. In response, this chapter addresses the *manner* of mirroring
Scripture, *in what* basic practice the wisdom of authentically "evangelical"
theology fundamentally consists. TIS fosters wisdom by attending not only
to the Bible's conceptual content but also to its redemptive-historical form.

Accordingly, the first section of the chapter sets theological parameters
for historical understanding in light of 1 Corinthians. The earthly history
leading to and from Jesus Christ crucially shapes how we mirror Scripture.
Yet we relate to this history not only through μίμησις—mental representation and sanctified imitation—but also through mysterious participation
in union with Christ. The second section introduces theological exegesis in
this light. The third section engages the ensuing complexities over hermeneutics vis-à-vis modern notions of "historical" inquiry. The fourth section
then develops the theological upshot of this chapter: evangelical biblicism,

in the best sense, challenges theology to reflect the forms and content of Scripture, yet theological exegesis challenges evangelical theology to do so without proof-texting or mere repetition. All the while, as 1 Corinthians establishes, Scripture's own embrace of redemptive-historical mystery challenges evangelical scholarship to be neither historicist nor ahistorical.

CORINTHIAN REFLECTIONS: MYSTERY AND MEANING

Modern polarizations between biblical and theological studies could easily degenerate into a struggle between "history" and "mystery."[1] Two important passages from 1 Corinthians, however, challenge evangelicals to resist such a dichotomy, to acknowledge the mysterious nature of redemptive history while also affirming the historical nature of Christ's mysterious self-revelation.

Spiritual stewardship of historical mysteries (1 Cor 3:1–4:21). The first passage, 1 Corinthians 3:1–4:21, addresses spiritual leadership. The Corinthians are fleshly, immature in their merely natural or human approach to leaders (1 Cor 3:1-3). Ironically they wind up looking childish in their desire to be sophisticated. The bridge of 1 Corinthians 3:4-5 leads to an extended treatment of spiritual leadership (1 Cor 3:6-15). Paul does not focus on apostolic distinctiveness but on missionary commonality. Human leaders are simply divine servants with providentially given opportunities. God rewards these laborers, but their task is to point away from themselves or any temporary, creaturely reality toward the one foundation Christians share. God will test whether each one's work is built to last. To destroy the church, God's dwelling place, by laying another foundation or using the wrong materials, is a severe error (1 Cor 3:16-17). Paul closes this section with another contrast between worldly folly and true wisdom, the latter giving everything to Christians because they belong to Christ (1 Cor 3:18-23).

This sets the table for Paul's brief mention of mysteries in 1 Corinthians 4:1-5, before he deepens the contrast between apostolic folly (in the world's eyes) and Corinthian fullness (1 Cor 4:6-13), and accordingly calls for them to imitate his humility (1 Cor 4:14-21). On the surface Paul's appeal to his

---

[1]See Daniel J. Treier, "Heaven on Earth? Evangelicals and Biblical Interpretation," *Books & Culture* online (January 2012): www.booksandculture.com/articles/webexclusives/2012/january/heaven onearth.html.

status as their father in the gospel might seem like a power play (1 Cor 4:14-
16), contradicting what he said about baptism earlier (1 Cor 1:14-17) and
locating the power of God's kingdom in words (contra 1 Cor 4:20). But Paul's
ways center in Christ (1 Cor 4:17), subject to the Lord's will (1 Cor 4:19), requiring the Spirit's power to overcome Corinthian perceptions of his apostolic folly. Crucial to Paul's hope of success is the brief theology of revelatory
stewardship at the beginning of 1 Corinthians 4. Stewards are accountable
to the one who entrusts something to them. Paul is so concerned with
serving God, and no one else, that he disregards not only Corinthian ex-
aminations but also his own. The Lord, whose wisdom far transcends Paul's,
will render the true verdict of acquittal or guilt. How to apply this text to
present-day—or even perennial—evangelical disputes is initially obvious.
Most important is trustworthy stewardship before God. Single-minded
service frees us to admonish each other without fear of what might result,
even from foolish responses. We even gain freedom to discern when others'
admonitions are mistaken rather than spiritually powerful.

What are these "mysteries," already introduced at 1 Corinthians 2:7?
While Paul may allude to the term's technical use in mystery religions, one
could hardly be certain that such quotation is involved.[2] In any case, the
overt claim of 1 Corinthians 2:7 opposes any spiritual elitism: "In the singular the term 'mystery' ordinarily refers to something formerly hidden in
God from *all* human eyes but now revealed in history through Christ and
made understandable to his people through the Spirit."[3] Its context is eschatological divine disclosure. The audience's spiritual perception is at
stake, not primarily that of prophets, whom God might use wittingly or
unwittingly. Prophetic stewards need the resolve to be faithful in trans-
mitting the message; at this moment the general Corinthian need is more
acute, involving the spiritual perception to receive Paul's message as divine
revelation. Mystery is not esoteric, but a matter of redemptive history's
revelation and reception.

The upshot of this first passage is that human spirituality matters a great

---

[2]Anthony C. Thiselton, *The First Epistle to the Corinthians*, NIGTC (Grand Rapids: Eerdmans,
2000), pp. 241-42.
[3]Gordon D. Fee, *The First Epistle to the Corinthians*, NICNT (Grand Rapids: Eerdmans, 1987), p.
105.

deal for truly evangelical theology, albeit only in a very particular way. Paul continues a withering attack against fixations on particularly charismatic human preachers. These obsessions demonstrate spiritual immaturity at best, destroying the congregation at their arrogant worst. For faithful theological stewards, according to 1 Corinthians 4:2 in Thiselton's words, "like a dispensing chemist who makes up a medical prescription prescribed by a doctor, the requirement is to do the job *as instructed*, and not to try to make self-devised 'improvements' of one's own."[4] In this sense truly evangelical theologians are not defined preeminently by creative insight. Still, they do need spiritual perception, as followers of Jesus seeking to receive—and transmit afresh—this mysterious revelation stewarded by Paul. Maintaining historical concern helps to check the spiritual pretensions of unduly creative theologians, keeping pursuit of glory oriented to God's redemptive history rather than human folly. Even so, historical concern must not be maintained by purely natural ways and means. Foolish academic allegiances could then easily fill the gap vacated by ecclesiastical hero worship or self-centered piety. The crucial point is not to pit history and mystery against each other: mystery gets defined redemptive-historically by Paul, while redemptive history is perceived spiritually and not just naturally.

Typological understanding of history as mysterious (1 Cor 10:1-11). The second relevant passage from 1 Corinthians concerns Paul's own interpretive practice in 1 Corinthians 10:1-11, again interweaving history and mystery. To engage the intricate and endlessly debated details of the passage would go well beyond our purview. Nevertheless Paul makes important statements about the mysterious spiritual connections shared across redemptive history.

In 1 Corinthians 10:6 Israel's historical events are "examples," τύποι, with a present-day spiritual purpose or result: "to keep us from setting our hearts on evil things as they did." Paul does not deny that Israel's earlier dealings with God matter in their own right. Τύποι involve correspondence between Old Testament persons, institutions or events and later ones with elevated significance, especially in the New Testament.[5] The correspondence depends

---

[4]Thiselton, *First Epistle to the Corinthians*, p. 336.
[5]Briefly, see Daniel J. Treier, "Typology," in *DTIB*, pp. 823-27; more expansively, see especially Richard M. Davidson, *Typology in Scripture: A Study of Hermeneutical τύπος Structures* (Berrien

on the presumed integrity of initial antetypes. In the present passage, definite statements are made about the Israelite forefathers' both being acted on (with implications for their status) and acting. They were providentially guided and blessed; they were redeemed; they were baptized; they received ongoing spiritual sustenance (1 Cor 10:1-4). They underwent divine judgment (1 Cor 10:5) because they craved evil, committed idolatry, acted immorally, tested the Lord and grumbled (1 Cor 10:6-10). Paul finds correspondence between God's actions among the forefathers and the divine gifts already enjoyed by the Corinthians. Thus Paul forestalls finalizing correspondence between the forefathers' disobedience, which resulted in judgment, and the Corinthians' current pattern. The disobedience of Paul's addressees threatens to become an antitype of Israel, resulting in judgment (1 Cor 10:12). Hope remains, though, precisely due to God's faithful provision of a way of escape, even in Paul's exhortation (1 Cor 10:13).

In 1 Corinthians 10:11 Paul reiterates that "these things happened to them as an example," this time focusing adverbially on the mode of occurrence. Happening typologically implies, for scriptural events, openness to—even need for—later redemptive-historical understanding. It is not enough to say that Paul gains access, by unusual divine inspiration, to typological patterns that were uniquely suited for an unusual Corinthian situation while his criteria of interpretation are normally inadmissible. Though true enough in themselves, claims about biblical inspiration are inadequate for unfolding the fullness of Paul's claims. Those claims amount to nothing less than a miniature theology of redemptive history, not just shaping but also shaped by his interpretation of Scripture. Trying to isolate Paul's claims from supposedly ancient and invalid hermeneutical criteria risks undermining not only his teaching but also his apostolic authority. Israel's story is ours; Christians share redeemed identity by way of initiatory events and ongoing participation. The experiences of earlier people of God are not only their own but also our patterns; past events count as present examples, by way of scriptural writings. Evangelical theology works with the matter of shared par-

---

Springs, MI: Andrews University Press, 1981). Many contemporary scholars see typological fulfillment occurring even within the Old Testament itself, for example in Israel's preliminary return from exile prior to the Christian era, although subsequent New Testament fulfillment is further heightened.

ticipation in the gospel in order to seek the appropriate form of response: correspondence to Christ, not the idolatrous responses of earlier generations from which he came to redeem us.

Because of Jesus, Paul's typological understanding of scriptural history is not solely about correspondence: There is also escalation. As those "on whom the end of the ages has come" (1 Cor 10:11), we are not doomed to repeat failed human history. To recognize the patterns linking Israel's Scriptures with the mysteries of the church's life in Christ requires both historical judgment and spiritual discernment. Not all theological exegesis will correspond specifically to typological patterns. But genuinely spiritual interpretation, like this prominent example of its innerbiblical practice, will incorporate historical integrity within the larger pursuit of the fullness of the churchly figure of Christ. Henri de Lubac alludes to the Apocalypse: the Lion must break open the seals of redemptive history's book.[6] Whatever else that might mean, not everything significant about biblical texts could readily be clear to human authorial consciousness. It is not that ancient exegetes, if alive today, would generally reject modern historical knowledge; speculation aside, their practice supports the opposite conclusion. Modern scholars find ancient exegetical moves strange due in part to the necessity and success of those moves in addressing their earlier contexts.[7] In some ways, the story of hermeneutical tension is hardly new, given the tensions between "Antiochene" and "Alexandrian" tendencies. Behind the present-day extent of the ensuing tensions, however, stand institutionalized forms of theological specialization.[8]

The terminology and institutional challenges of theological exegesis may come and go; the priority of recovering unity between history and mystery will not. Evangelical biblicism, though freshly under attack, retained aspects of that unity rejected elsewhere. Popular biblicist aberrations need little pretense of scholarly sophistication to document, even if they make for fun sport. To what degree these aberrations reflect poorly on classic evangelical commitments such as "the priesthood of all believers" is a matter for ongoing

---

[6]Henri de Lubac, *History and Spirit: The Understanding of Scripture According to Origen*, trans. Anne Englund Nash (San Francisco: Ignatius, 2007), p. 453.
[7]Ibid., pp. 429-31.
[8]Ibid., p. 473.

debate.[9] Earlier fundamentalist retreat undoubtedly exacerbated populist biblicism, and recent scholarly reengagement is helpful for eradicating churchly excesses. Yet such reengagement can encourage neglect of fully theological exegesis. Facets of TIS now need recovery, albeit in the post-fundamentalist, chastened fashion introduced by our prior discussion of critical evangelical biblicism.

In the last chapter, wisdom began to unveil new possibilities for μίμησις of biblical truth: the church's pursuit of the mind of Christ. In this chapter, the historical nature of God's self-revelation begins to shape how evangelical theology might mirror biblical teaching. Biblical theology is diverse in literary genres; historical settings of authors, texts and readers; redemptive-historical epochs; and word usage fostering theological concepts. However, this diversity calls for reworking rather than abandoning the evangelical commitment to mirroring a unified, scriptural theology. One resource for that reworking is theological exegesis, which offers more supple possibilities for encountering the fullness of biblical teaching. TIS prompts both theologians and biblical scholars, while acknowledging diversity in biblical theology, nevertheless to pursue conceptual unity as well.

THEOLOGICAL EXEGESIS: CANON, CREED AND CULTURE

Classic evangelicals such as F. F. Bruce and J. I. Packer occasionally used the adjective *theological* in the context of biblical interpretation. Others too, such as Peter Stuhlmacher and even critics of the concept, did so prior to recent discussion.[10] To some degree the concept owes its origins even earlier to Karl Barth and Dietrich Bonhoeffer. The most influential recent protago-

---

[9]For further response, especially to the critique of Christian Smith, *The Bible Made Impossible: Why Biblicism Is Not a Truly Evangelical Reading of Scripture* (Grand Rapids: Brazos, 2011) previously sketched, see Treier, "Heaven on Earth?" John M. Frame suggests that it is good to be accused of something close to biblicism every now and then, even if biblicism per se is inappropriate ("In Defense of Something Close to Biblicism: Reflections on *Sola Scriptura* and History in Theological Method," *Westminster Theological Journal* 59 [1997]: 269-91, esp. p. 275). Somewhat similarly (though perhaps surprisingly given his academic esteem), biblicism characterizes the "baptist vision" commended by James William McClendon Jr. (*Ethics*, vol. 1 of *Systematic Theology*, 2nd ed. [Nashville: Abingdon, 2002], especially pp. 28-35).

[10]F. F. Bruce and J. J. Scott Jr., "Interpretation of the Bible," in *Evangelical Dictionary of Theology*, 2nd ed., ed. Walter A. Elwell (Grand Rapids: Baker, 2001), pp. 612-13; Packer, "In Quest of Canonical Interpretation," pp. 45, 47; Peter Stuhlmacher, *Historical Criticism and Theological Interpretation of Scripture*, trans. Roy A. Harrisville (Philadelphia: Fortress, 1977).

nists have been Stephen Fowl, Kevin Vanhoozer and Francis Watson,[11] with others now enhancing the conversation.[12] Sorting through the maze brings three consistent priorities to the surface.

First, *canon* points to lack of shyness about relating particular passages to the larger context of the entire Bible. Theological exegetes should not ignore the historical development of words and concepts, or make simplistic connections. But neither should they be prisoners of academic guilds imposing alien standards, rejecting the unity of Scripture or relating passages only on the narrowest criteria. For instance, in a now-famous study, David Yeago defends the coherence of the christological judgments in John 1:1-18 and Philippians 2:5-11 despite their varied concepts. John 1 has the language of incarnation whereas Philippians 2 does not. However, James D. G. Dunn's substitution of a posited "Adam Christology" background for the incarna-

---

[11]Stephen E. Fowl, *Engaging Scripture: A Model of Theological Interpretation* (Oxford: Blackwell, 1998); Kevin J. Vanhoozer, "Introduction: What Is Theological Interpretation of the Bible?" in *DTIB*, pp. 19-25; Francis Watson, *Text, Church, and World: Biblical Interpretation in Theological Perspective* (Grand Rapids: Eerdmans, 1994); idem, *Text and Truth: Redefining Biblical Theology* (Grand Rapids: Eerdmans, 1997); all of these figures appear in A. K. M. Adam et al., *Reading Scripture with the Church: Toward a Hermeneutic for Theological Interpretation* (Grand Rapids: Baker Academic, 2006).

[12]Earlier, Stephen E. Fowl, ed., *The Theological Interpretation of Scripture: Classic and Contemporary Readings* (Oxford: Blackwell, 1997); more recently and briefly, Stephen E. Fowl, *Theological Interpretation of Scripture*, Cascade Companions (Eugene, OR: Cascade, 2009); for practitioners, J. Todd Billings, *The Word of God for the People of God: An Entryway to the Theological Interpretation of Scripture* (Grand Rapids: Eerdmans, 2010). See also the *Journal of Theological Interpretation* plus relevant commentary and monograph series. Miroslav Volf asserts that TIS is the most significant theological event of the last two decades (Volf, *Captive to the Word of God: Engaging the Scriptures for Contemporary Theological Reflection* [Grand Rapids: Eerdmans, 2010], p. 14).
Some of the following reflects the survey of Treier, *Introducing Theological Interpretation*. In addition to Karl Barth, treated there, Dietrich Bonhoeffer uses the terminology "theological exposition" in *Creation and Fall: A Theological Exposition of Genesis 1–3*, trans. Douglas Stephen Bax, ed. John W. de Gruchy, Dietrich Bonhoeffer Works English Edition 3 (Minneapolis: Fortress, 1997), pp. 22-23. *Introducing Theological Interpretation* does not usually promote programmatic views or engage thinkers whose relation to TIS terminology is only indirect (e.g., Richard B. Hays, recently pilloried on such grounds in Joachim Schaper, "Historical Criticism, 'Theological Exegesis,' and Theology Amongst the Humanities," in *Theology, University, Humanities: Initium Sapientiae Timor Domini*, ed. Christopher Craig Brittain and Francesca Aran Murphy [Eugene, OR: Cascade, 2011], pp. 75-90). One flaw of *Introducing Theological Interpretation* is neglect of Jewish exegesis manifesting the theological nature of biblical scholarship. Another potential flaw is unscientific labeling of TIS as a "movement," perhaps overstating its coherence. On these points see Markus Bockmuehl, "Bible Versus Theology: Is 'Theological Interpretation' the Answer?" *Nova et Vetera* 9, no. 1 (2011): 27-47; and R. W. L. Moberly, "What Is Theological Interpretation of Scripture?" *Journal of Theological Interpretation* 3, no. 2 (2009): 161-78, although for a partial response see Daniel J. Treier, "What Is Theological Interpretation? An Ecclesial Reduction," *International Journal of Systematic Theology* 12, no. 2 (April 2010): 144-61.

tional Christology of the hymn collides with its narrative logic, which apparently parallels John 1. This logic is buttressed by the appeal of Philippians 2 to Isaiah 45:21-24, applying a strongly monotheistic text to proclaim Jesus' identity with ΥΗWΗ/Κύριος, Israel's God—regarding which Yeago relies on N. T. Wright's analysis.[13]

Second, *creed* highlights the rule of faith as another crucial context for the church's engagement with Scripture. Narrowly speaking, this entails reading the Bible in light of the Trinitarian and christological heritage of the early church that became formalized in symbols such as the Nicene Creed. Subordinate to Scripture in principle, in practice this rule of faith summarizes its core teaching about the divine identity. More broadly, "ruled reading" approaches Scripture within living tradition(s), practices and habits of mind that earlier Christians passed on. Furthermore, subsequent confessions or other dogmatic symbols may extend the regulative and renewing function of doctrine into particular churchly contexts. Most broadly for classic Protestantism, this becomes interwoven with commitment to canon through application of the "analogy of faith."[14] Rules of faith may not determine exegetical decisions, but creedal context prompts questions about the biblical texts, and may suggest portions of answers, that readers would otherwise miss. Yeago's essay again illustrates the point. He not only demonstrates the coherence between John 1 and Philippians 2 given the appeal to Isaiah 45; he also defends their contributions to patristic orthodoxy. Interminable debates over whether or not Pauline word usage is directly ontological can give way instead to recognition of common patterns between the creedal and the canonical judgments. The creeds provoke questions that the scriptural canon helpfully answers.

Third, *culture* involves not only historical awareness of how social contexts influence the church's reading of Scripture, both well and poorly, but also acknowledgment of present-day hermeneutical locations. Presupposi-

---

[13]David S. Yeago, "The New Testament and the Nicene Dogma," *Pro Ecclesia* 3, no. 2 (Spring 1994): 152-64. More extensive treatment than the summary here appears in Daniel J. Treier, "Christology and Commentaries: Examining and Enhancing Theological Exegesis," in *On the Writing of New Testament Commentaries: Festschrift for Grant R. Osborne on the Occasion of his 70th Birthday*, ed. Stanley E. Porter and Eckhard J. Schnabel (Leiden: Brill, 2012), pp. 299-316.
[14]Still helpful is Henri Blocher, "The 'Analogy of Faith' in the Study of Scripture: In Search of Justification and Guidelines," *Scottish Bulletin of Evangelical Theology* 5, no. 1 (Spring 1987): 17-38.

tions often have a bad name in biblical studies; when they are acknowledged, the admission comes grudgingly. Presuppositions are "baggage" to set aside as much as humanly possible in a quest for "objectivity." This metaphor actually suggests an alternative: baggage mostly carries what is essential, not extraneous or dangerous. What if presuppositions are not always threats to objectivity but frequently aid in preserving it? Indeed, presuppositions can preserve perspectives from outside our own time and place and personal subjectivity. Of course, preunderstanding is unhealthy if it prevents Scripture from reforming human ideas; attention to detail in biblical texts fosters their correction of current perspectives. Even so, presuppositions provide essential points of connection to Scripture's subject matter, which various lenses help to display more fully.

The metaphor of lenses puts interpretive difference and change in fresh perspective. Some interpretations are surely wrong, others more or less right. But that is not the nature of every difference. Perspectives might be complementary rather than contradictory, with various lenses providing (epistemological) access to dimensions of the one (ontological) truth. Suitably chastened, diverse methods too function as helpful perspectives. In cases when differences do involve contradiction, still interpretations may not be entirely right or wrong even if some elements require choosing one or the other.[15] God's Spirit may bless and lead the church even through mistaken use of its gifts or merely partial understanding. After all, if 1 Corinthians is any indication, then the Holy Spirit typically works in and through the messiness of human nature when pouring out divine grace.

---

[15]For an example see Treier, *Introducing Theological Interpretation*, pp. 203-4, regarding Martin Luther, "Preface to the Complete Edition of Luther's Latin Works" (1545), in *Career of the Reformer IV*, Luther's Works 34, ed. and trans. Helmut L. Lehmann and Lewis W. Spitz (Minneapolis: Fortress, 1960), p. 337. This example is criticized by Stanley E. Porter, "What Exactly Is Theological Interpretation of Scripture, and Is It Hermeneutically Robust Enough for the Task to Which It Has Been Appointed?" in *Horizons in Hermeneutics: A Festschrift in Honor of Anthony C. Thiselton*, ed. Stanley E. Porter and Matthew R. Malcolm (Grand Rapids: Eerdmans, 2013), pp. 234-67, at p. 266. Numerous characterizations of TIS in Porter's essay are open to challenge, despite his laudable concerns—sometimes because he confuses description of others' views with positive assertions. In the present example, we never deny the possibility of arriving at the meaning of Romans 1:17—just the opposite. At issue is the degree of technical precision necessary for claiming to have done so. Given the unending proliferation of technical disagreements, it seems impossible to claim that we only arrive at a biblical text's meaning exhaustively or else not at all. More broadly, Porter's criticism that TIS is not hermeneutically robust never includes clarity about which hermeneutical claims or resources would render TIS adequate.

Reflecting on the activity of God in, behind and before the church's reading is at the heart of TIS. Volf suggests thinking of texts neither as agents nor as things, but in terms of social relations.[16] With "culture," then, we name a focus that could also be dubbed "church" or "community": how the church's mission in varied social contexts properly informs our questions about biblical texts. Internal disagreements remain among TIS proponents over how to address biblical theology as a discipline, how to appropriate general hermeneutics and how to engage contemporary global Christianity. When it comes to canon, creed and culture, though, TIS advocates share a commitment to reading the whole of Scripture in the presence of the Triune God for the health of the church's witness in the world.[17]

BIBLICAL HOLISM: HISTORY AND HERMENEUTICS

Most TIS advocates do not reject critical methods, ignore historical concerns, adopt relativist pluralism or refuse to interact with scholarly guilds and assumptions of religious others. Rather, theological exegesis can incorporate the best of "historical-critical" or "grammatical-historical" tools within a more basic vocational framework. In fact, TIS initially seemed to offer hermeneutical language supporting evangelical biblical scholarship, since historical criticism per se is not its fundamental vocation.[18]

For analytical simplicity, let us distinguish between the beginning, the middle and the end of interpretation. When evangelical scholars *begin* with acknowledged presuppositions or doctrinal convictions, and with prayer, anticipating the grace of the Holy Spirit working in and through natural talents and labors, this is an aspect of "theological" exegesis. When these scholars direct their service to churchly *ends*—preaching, teaching, translating; when resulting commentaries address pastoral and lay readers instead of solely pursuing academic notoriety; and when canonical "biblical

---

[16]Volf, *Captive to the Word of God*, p. 28.

[17]Previously acknowledged, in this regard Jewish exegesis raises the wider issue of religious pluralism, whereas the present book addresses Christian TIS. Other religious traditions should correspondingly be free to pursue their own versions of TIS both inside and outside university contexts. Christian TIS should be open to learning from alternative versions, perhaps via "scriptural reasoning" as well as other practices.

[18]*Historical criticism* is notoriously slippery terminology, as acknowledged in Richard E. Burnett, "Historical Criticism," in *DTIB*, pp. 290-93. Despite narrower technical uses, though, the term can refer more generally to a vocational paradigm or dominant set of scholarly interests.

theology" is an outcome, the orienting vocation could be called "theological" exegesis. The muddle lies in the *middle*, from which instrumental approaches to wisdom and pathological versions of two-step hermeneutics sometimes exclude canon, creed and culture.

TIS language could further legitimate evangelical biblical scholarship, widening its audience. As a leavening influence, TIS could make academic space for theologians to engage Scripture and pursue the riches of biblical studies more robustly. TIS could then embolden biblical scholars to engage canon, creed and culture more centrally and creatively in the exegetical process. In short, the goal would be iron sharpening iron between biblical studies and theology (Prov 27:17)—their disciplinary integrity generating occasional friction, their practitioners' Christian vocations making that friction productive in the context of friendship.

If instead TIS terminology produces even more fragmentation of Scripture and theology, then it may be better off abandoned. Before that happens, however, it is worth examining whether useful disagreements are surfacing, or apparent disagreements are needless misunderstandings. What needs clarification, at least among evangelicals, is not primarily the beginning or the end(s), but rather the middle—the appropriate practices and criteria of scriptural interpretation itself. We can address some representative concerns and objections[19] in the form of five questions, with the answers being our own and not necessarily belonging to other TIS advocates.

First, naming: Does TIS unfairly claim high ground by implicitly defining historical exegesis as nontheological?[20] Without quarreling about words, somehow we need to analyze the relevant disagreements. TIS insists that *all* exegesis is broadly theological—invoking God's presence or absence whether exegetes acknowledge this or not—so adherents are not trying to win a debate simply by choosing a clever name, but instead being intentional

---

[19]Beyond the critical literature cited below, see the survey of Mark W. Elliott, *The Heart of Biblical Theology: Providence Experienced* (Burlington, VT: Ashgate, 2012), chap. 2, and Stanley E. Porter, "Biblical Interpretation and Theological Responsibility," in *The Future of Biblical Interpretation: Responsible Plurality in Biblical Hermeneutics*, ed. Stanley E. Porter and Matthew R. Malcolm (Downers Grove, IL: InterVarsity Press, 2013), pp. 29-50.

[20]John C. Poirier, "'Theological Interpretation' and Its Contradistinctions," *Tyndale Bulletin* 61, no. 1 (2010): 105-18, at p. 107.

about exegesis without presuppositions being impossible.[21] We need to deploy the right set of presuppositions in the right ways at the right times.

Second, respecting authorial history: Does TIS disregard study of textual origins?[22] No; the root disagreement involves the middle of exegesis, as already noted, plus the norms for the church's reading of Scripture. Historical study of human authors can be important without being exclusively normative. Some TIS challenges to the two-step sequential model abandon authorial intention—but not all. Even strong versions of TIS allow for ongoing historical work. Plus weaker versions are possible, distinguishing processes of discovery from justification and communication of results. Grammatical-historical exegetes could still allow canon, creed and culture to serve as interpretive inputs, even when their output adopts restricted language for their guilds. Ironically, many leading historians today reject authorial intention hermeneutics as such.[23] Moreover, a well-known hermeneutical defender of authors these days is an advocate of TIS.[24] So the two are not mutually exclusive.

Third, making confessionalism the root issue: Does TIS provide a convenient new mask with which conservative Reformed presuppositions may infiltrate the mainstream academy?[25] Again ironically, the strongest versions do not fit this pattern, coming from nonevangelicals without appeal

---

[21]See especially Mark Alan Bowald, *Rendering the Word in Theological Hermeneutics: Mapping Divine and Human Agency* (Aldershot, UK: Ashgate, 2007).

[22]Poirier, "'Theological Interpretation,'" e.g., p. 109.

[23]See e.g. David C. Steinmetz, a renowned historian who sees his careful practice to be consistent with much broader hermeneutics famously advocated in "The Superiority of Pre-Critical Exegesis," reprinted in *Theological Interpretation of Scripture*, pp. 26-38, and defended in idem, "Appendix: Footnotes to an Old Complaint," in his *Taking the Long View: Christian Theology in Historical Perspective* (Oxford: Oxford University Press, 2011), pp. 161-67.

[24]Poirier, "'Theological Interpretation,'" p. 110n13, equates reading historically with using intentionalist hermeneutics, contra "nearly every recent proponent of 'theological interpretation,'" a point falsified for instance by the authorially focused hermeneutics of Vanhoozer's *Is There a Meaning in This Text?* On the intentionalist influence of E. D. Hirsch Jr., *Validity in Interpretation* (New Haven, CT: Yale University Press, 1967)—which, by the way, is of much more recent vintage than classic evangelical doctrines of Scripture or primary interest in biblical authors, while frequently seen as quaint in the wider humanities—see Roger Lundin, "Intentional Ironies," in *From Nature to Experience: The American Search for Cultural Authority* (Lanham, MD: Rowman & Littlefield, 2005), pp. 153-75. In this regard B. H. McLean (*Biblical Interpretation and Philosophical Hermeneutics* [Cambridge: Cambridge University Press, 2012], p. 7) critiques biblical scholarship for lingering historical positivism, rooted in nihilism.

[25]Poirier, "'Theological Interpretation,'" especially pp. 109, 113, 117.

to verbal, plenary inspiration of Scripture.[26] Evangelical TIS proponents are simultaneously attacked by biblical scholars, including fellow evangelicals, for being too theological or not historical enough—and by other advocates of theological exegesis, for being too conservatively or historically devoted to human authors. A related misunderstanding behind this anti-"confessional" objection stems from sole focus on the beginnings and end(s) of exegesis— having interpretive results match doctrinal presuppositions. To the contrary, much TIS has primary interest in the middle of exegesis—in churchly practices by which God forms the reader(s). There is nothing antihistorical about these practices offering a larger context within which to employ scholarly skills and rules. TIS addresses the historicity of interpreters along with texts—only opposing hegemonic, academic understandings of history that hinder churchly hearing of the divine Word.[27]

Fourth, by contrast and more conservatively, maintaining evangelical commitment: Does TIS diminish the historical and propositional character of biblical truth? Agreeing with the aforementioned complaint that history is "often . . . made out to be the villain" by TIS, D. A. Carson rightly asserts (with particular reference to New Testament treatment of the Old) that *"historical* reading is [properly] determinative for a great deal of *theological* interpretation."[28] He also rightly insists on acknowledging differences between Catholic and evangelical Protestant appeals to Christian doctrine alongside similarities of "historic confessional Christianity"; on remaining open to the church's need for iconoclastic challengers and to the nuances of "the Enlightenment"; on being God- rather than church- or subjectivity-centered; and therefore on addressing all the biblical narrative's major plot elements, including divine judgment.[29] Yet a biblical approach to redemptive

[26]It is surprising for Poirier's evangelical journal (*Tyndale Bulletin*) article to cast James Barr as hero, crusading against TIS proponents whose nonevangelical doctrines of Scripture actually match Barr's in some respects. Those proponents are most critical of authorial intention hermeneutics, defended by Vanhoozer—whose traditional doctrine of Scripture concerns Poirier.

[27]The relative methodological disarray in biblical studies is a significant theme of Markus Bockmuehl, *Seeing the Word: Refocusing New Testament Study*, Studies in Theological Interpretation (Grand Rapids: Baker Academic, 2006).

[28]D. A. Carson, "Theological Interpretation of Scripture: Yes, But . . . ," in *Theological Commentary: Evangelical Perspectives*, ed. R. Michael Allen (London: T & T Clark, 2011), pp. 187-207, at pp. 189, 190.

[29]Carson, "Yes, But . . . ," pp. 194, 197, 200-203, 206. Mention of "some sort of hegemonic view of TIS" (p. 196) may be ironic, since TIS proponents themselves acknowledge internal differ-

history needs clarifying: However confessional he might be, Carson seems wary of classic Christian doctrine when he accuses TIS of "undigested proposals" concerning Trinitarian theology as a key hermeneutical lens, raising the paradigmatic question of whether it is a dangerous fad.[30] The answer lies in the very criterion of God-centeredness offered as a critique: Trinitarian doctrine clarifies who speaks in the pages of the Bible, whom to worship if we would avoid the biblical-theological critique of idolatry, whether to read the Old and New Testaments together as one scriptural canon—affecting all the priorities animating this concern. The significance and plausibility of Jesus' resurrection, the nature of the gospel, the structure of the story now coming to its consummation, the meaning of Christ being the ultimate Word—all these "concepts" of biblical theology relate to the identity of Israel's God as Father, Son and Holy Spirit. To be sure, Trinitarian theology has become a zone of some unhealthy speculation, but in TIS this is much less popular than in generic evangelicalism, precisely due to classic Christian doctrine. It seems difficult to conclude that prioritizing the Trinitarian identity of the Bible's God makes an undigested imposition on Christian interpretation of scriptural texts.

The real challenge concerns how much modern academic history-writing tends toward naturalism, affecting biblical theology's treatment of historical

---

ences quite directly. The allegation of prioritizing narrative over propositions is accompanied by no cited evidence, and only some TIS literature may be guilty. The fact that what is valuable in TIS is typically not new (p. 207), and that confessional evangelicals have preserved many of these values (p. 202), again has been acknowledged by some TIS proponents (e.g., Treier, *Introducing*, pp. 11-38).

[30]Carson, "Yes, But . . . ," p. 205. Somewhat similarly, Charlie Trimm, "Evangelicals, Theology, and Biblical Interpretation: Reflections on the Theological Interpretation of Scripture," *Bulletin for Biblical Research* 20, no. 3 (2010): 311-30, worries that theology obscures biblical particularities. His spectrum of theologically opposed—open—curious—focused approaches sees the last as fundamentally dangerous. Whether or not the spectrum positions are correctly distributed, the terminology labels exonerated evangelical theologians (like the present authors) with a word—"curious"—that is weak on one hand, yet on the other hand considered a vice by the church fathers. The typology aside, Trimm does not carefully explain why "history" is privileged over "theology" in relation to "text." Such privilege is not self-evident from a classic Protestant doctrine of Scripture. Why assume that background studies are closer to the text than theology (as the Institute for Biblical Research likewise assumes when it defines various forms of ancient Near East and Greco-Roman background study as "cognate" disciplines while theology does not qualify)? Might theological focus in fact possess or promote literary savvy or historical sophistication? These questions become all the more important when Trimm correlates answers with (un)faithfulness to biblical authority.

texts and events.[31] Many but not all TIS advocates, likewise concerned about naturalism, are less optimistic than many evangelical biblical scholars about the success of conservative historiography in response. Such assessments affect how readily one expects to make historical or literary arguments about Christian readings of the Old Testament, the historical Jesus and the Christ of faith and the like. Beyond these prudential disagreements about the state of the academy, theological differences come into play too. Carson's approach reflects providentialist historiography, more Reformed in nature, studying events according to the possibility of divine, not just creaturely, action. An illustrative contrast can be found in Catholic Matthew Levering's "participationist" approach, attracting some TIS Protestants.[32] The providentialist focus often becomes epistemological, hoping for redemptive transformation of academic *history-writing.* The participationist hope is sacramental, focusing on churchly transformation stemming from *historical events* themselves stretching redemptively across time, with perhaps history-writing itself participating in such events by extension. The providentialist approach is concerned primarily with evaluating biblical theology's proposals themselves, the participationist approach with using critical historiographies secondarily in churchly theological exegesis.

These historiographical complexities are important, though a range of theological assessments seem to be legitimately debatable. To be sure, certain viewpoints within the broad TIS conversation might be inappropriate for many evangelicals, and the aforementioned concerns can help evangelical TIS advocates to clarify their commitments.[33] More clearly reaffirming the

---

[31]Evangelical biblical scholars such as Iain W. Provan, V. Philips Long and Tremper Longman III, "History, Historiography, and the Bible," part one in *A Biblical History of Israel* (Louisville: Westminster John Knox, 2003), pp. 3-104; and Craig Blomberg, *The Historical Reliability of the Gospels,* 2nd ed. (Downers Grove, IL: InterVarsity Press, 2007), have capably applied philosophy of history to some contested cases. Carson himself, concerned about naturalism (e.g., on p. 201 of "Yes, But . . ."), highlights different reference points for "history"—event versus communication (pp. 189-90). But there has been less evangelical engagement with philosophy of history when it comes to acknowledging challenges to "objectivity" or addressing general hermeneutics theologically.

[32]Matthew Levering, *Participatory Biblical Exegesis: A Theology of Biblical Interpretation* (Notre Dame, IN: University of Notre Dame Press, 2008). For Protestant embrace of this perspective, see, e.g., Hans Boersma, *Heavenly Participation: The Weaving of a Sacramental Tapestry* (Grand Rapids: Eerdmans, 2011), and in response Daniel J. Treier, *"Heavenly Participation: The Weaving of a Sacramental Tapestry—*A Review Essay" (with a response from Hans Boersma), *Christian Scholar's Review* 41, no. 1 (Fall 2011): 67-71.

[33]Another sample clarification: Carson writes, "In his support for TIS, Treier, as we have seen,

significance of history in every genuine sense of that word, celebrating the accomplishments of evangelical biblical scholarship, and avoiding unnecessarily stark TIS juxtapositions (with biblical theology, for instance) could be fruitful results of these critiques.

Fifth, however, concern still lingers over pursuing evangelical theology's academic (re)entry: Does TIS variety, with its inclusion of nonevangelicals and friendliness toward more "catholic" approaches, fail to protect evangelical identity?[34] In what sense should biblical scholarship be preeminent in evangelical scriptural exegesis and theological practice?[35] Conversely, might not evangelical identity and the integrity of biblical scholarship be fundamentally distinct? TIS advocates probably are guilty of overstating the compromises of evangelical biblical scholars with historical criticism. All the same, evangelical biblical scholars are sometimes more scrupulous in return about critiquing theologians' ecumenical forays into TIS than evaluating their own academic reentry via biblical theology. In both cases it is easy for protecting disciplinary turf to get confused with policing doctrinal fidelity. One can readily grant that TIS discourse has its dangers, including faddishness. TIS may remain "frustratingly disparate"—like evangelical theology and biblical scholarship generally, not to mention biblical theology—standing shoulder to shoulder with unlikely or partial allies because core commitments come under frequent attack, even from friendly fire.[36] TIS affords opportunities for

---

includes allegorical readings of Scripture among the approaches he is willing to support" ("Yes, But . . . ," p. 198). However, the quotation apparently referred to (on pp. 196-97: from Treier, *Introducing*, p. 40) is merely descriptive regarding a commentary series, puts "allegorical" in scare quotes, and never says what Treier does or does not support in particular.

[34]See, e.g., Carson, "Yes, But . . . ," p. 204, although as he mentions at least four TIS subgroups he helpfully grants their distinctiveness (rather than unfairly lumping in confessional evangelicals with Barthians, for example).

[35]Carson, "Yes, But . . . ," p. 207, seemingly limits the framing work of systematic theology to what one should "indulge . . . only with the greatest caution, and only after the writer has done a lot of work on the first three levels." The present evangelical defense of TIS, agreeing about the other three levels (local exegesis, broader biblical theology and appeal to the analogy of faith), disagrees about relegating the fourth level (systematic framing) to cautious indulgence (contra too a theologian's presentation of similar "orders of discourse" in Graham A. Cole, "The Perils of a 'Historyless' Systematic Theology," in *Do Historical Matters Matter to Faith? A Critical Appraisal of Modern and Postmodern Approaches to Scripture*, ed. James K. Hoffmeier and Dennis R. Magary [Wheaton, IL: Crossway, 2012], pp. 55-69).

[36]Carson, "Yes, But . . . ," p. 204. For a chronicle of unhealthy perceptions to overcome on both sides, see Kevin J. Vanhoozer, "Interpreting Scripture Between the Rock of Biblical Studies and the Hard Place of Systematic Theology: The State of the Evangelical (dis)Union," in *Renewing the Evangelical Mission*, ed. Richard Lints (Grand Rapids: Eerdmans, 2013), pp. 201-25; for an

evangelical theologians to undertake more sustained biblical exegesis as a scholarly contribution. Like biblical theology a generation ago, planting those seeds might bear lasting fruit, even if some weeds are inevitable.

To conclude the argument: Scripture does require historical integrity in its interpretation. The redemptive nature of its history, though, requires spiritual perception, to discern the revelation of its mystery in earlier textual patterns. Evangelical biblicism needs reform and renewal to escape unhealthy proof-texting, but preserves a noble, classic commitment to the unity of scriptural teaching. Canon, creed and culture name not just beginning presuppositions or laudable ends, but even central practices of reading Scripture. Scripture's authority is magisterial, making the canonical lens dominant; the church's authority, adding perspective variously through creedal and cultural lenses, is ministerial. Beyond highlighting this evangelical commitment, the present understanding of TIS can address other widespread concerns among biblical scholars—as we summarize with the following denials alongside key affirmations.

(1) TIS does not demonize opponents through clever naming, but rather insists that all biblical interpretation is actually theological. (2) Theological exegesis does not automatically reject author-centered hermeneutics or historical concerns, but rather addresses the frequent tendency of so-called historical criticism to go beyond offering helpful tools and to function as an antitheological research program. (3) Theological exegesis is not simply or even primarily "confessional," since the inputs of interest go far beyond confessional statements to involve various church practices and interdisciplinary interactions. Thus, (4) TIS need not weaken evangelical commitments to historical truth, but rather surfaces important descriptive and prescriptive questions about the nature of "history" in the contemporary academy—about which disagreements are important but not automatically definitive for evangelical fidelity or intellectual integrity. Finally, (5) TIS need not weaken evangelical identity any more than biblical theology.[37]

---

account of unexpected academic fellowship, see Treier, "What Is Theological Interpretation?"

[37]On the parallels and interrelationships between biblical theology and TIS see Edward W. Klink III and Darian R. Lockett, *Understanding Biblical Theology: A Comparison of Theory and Practice* (Grand Rapids: Zondervan, 2012), especially their BT5, and the earlier fivefold typology of Daniel J. Treier, "Biblical Theology and/or Theological Interpretation of Scripture?" *Scottish Journal of Theology* 61 (2008): 16-31.

Therefore the next component of our evangelical account involves greater specificity about the contribution of doctrinal judgment(s) within theological exegesis. Proof-texting is the derogatory concept typically used in criticizing biblicist evangelical aspirations to represent with one system the form and content of Scripture. To be sure, a text without a context is a pretext for proof texts. Examples of unhealthy proof-texting abound, and not just at the popular level; evangelical systematic theologies frequently contain them too. Still, one can defend aspects of biblicism, even having broad parallels to proof-texting, without which it would be hard to imagine meaningfully "evangelical" theology—namely, practices of appealing to Scripture as the primary source of support for claims about Christian doctrine.[38] Hence our primary goal: retaining the impulses behind, yet refining the implementation of, evangelical theology mirroring Scripture. Once reformed, the aspiration is right to seek biblical support for Christian doctrine—not only bringing exegesis to bear on doctrinal judgment(s), but also bringing such possible judgment(s) to bear in proposing interpretations of Scripture.

DOCTRINAL JUDGMENT(S): CONCEPTS AND CONTEXTS

This argument about theological judgment(s) proceeds in a series of steps, appropriately beginning with biblical uses of mirroring imagery. Although theological exegesis involves more than just reciting such texts, wrestling with them provides a ladder to climb toward greater understanding. Biblical images underscore the eschatological indirectness and ethical wholeness of theological knowledge: the people of God, growing in true charity by the Holy Spirit, increasingly reflect the glory of Christ revealed in Scripture as they see themselves reflected in that mirror. Disciplined scrutiny intersects with these eschatological and ethical dimensions through the concept of judgment.

In our final chapter, such judgment gets another look, in terms of the scholarly discipline of theology as such: appreciating the variety of literary material in the Bible, the significance of drama as a master concept for theology and the moods that shape its dialogue; attending to the propriety and nature of theological systems; and assessing the contributions of biblical

---

[38]Beyond materials mentioned earlier see Daniel J. Treier, "Proof Text," in *DTIB*, pp. 622-24; R. Michael Allen and Scott R. Swain, "In Defense of Proof-texting," *JETS* 54, no. 3 (2011): 589-606.

theology as a scholarly discipline. Here we focus on theological exegesis as such, in terms of how doctrinal judgment(s) inform and are informed by biblical interpretation itself. Given the eschatological and ethical context of mirroring images in the Bible, a sapiential context ought to shape the concepts with which we move between exegesis and theological judgment(s). Pursuing such wisdom frees us to develop theological concepts that maintain various forms of narrative coherence with the world(s) in Scripture itself.

Mirror images in eschatological and ethical context. First Corinthians 13 is a starting point for biblical mirror imagery, with its meaning as murky as "seeing through a glass darkly" suggests! One reason behind Paul's use of the image may be the mirror industry thriving at Corinth.[39] The Greek idiom, seeing "through," seems strange to English ears, focusing on the unique nature of the reflection—directing attention away from the image reflected to its content revealed.[40] The chief exegetical dilemma concerns whether the reflection is merely indirect or actually indistinct, distorted: ἐν αἰνίγματι enigmatically, shall we say, qualifies the seeing. "Darkly," suggesting distortion, may sell short the Corinthian mirrors.[41] Furthermore, the contrast with "face to face," combined with the eschatological context, suggests that Paul has in mind indirect or incomplete vision, not dark or distorted understanding. Finally, a Platonic contrast between indirect perception of images and direct apprehension of ideas may hover in the background.[42] Now Christians know "in part," but "know" they do. The contrast runs not between distorted error and future knowledge but between partial present knowledge, with ongoing growth needed in charity and the fullness of relational knowledge that comes with perfect charity.

Emphasizing wholeness coheres with connecting wisdom and charity. Old Testament wisdom literature is concerned with integrity of character, with consistency between head, heart and hands—consistency expressed especially via money and the mouth.[43] Such wholeness can only be

---

[39]Richard B. Hays, *First Corinthians*, Interpretation (Louisville: Westminster John Knox, 1997), p. 230.

[40]Fee, *First Epistle to the Corinthians*, p. 647 n. 41.

[41]Ibid., p. 648.

[42]Thiselton, *First Epistle to the Corinthians*, p. 1069.

[43]For more technical accounts, see William P. Brown, *Character in Crisis: A Fresh Approach to the Wisdom Literature of the Old Testament* (Grand Rapids: Eerdmans, 1996); idem, *The Ethos of the Cosmos: The Genesis of Moral Imagination in the Bible* (Grand Rapids: Eerdmans, 1999). For

completely ours in Christ, when he is all in all (1 Cor 15:28) and we are fully known (1 Cor 13:12). In the here and now, pursuing the mind of Christ follows the "more excellent way" (1 Cor 12:31) of love. Christ should be in the mirror of theological knowledge, then, and this signals that theology's mirroring of Scripture cannot solely consist of corresponding beliefs. Ultimately we correspond to Christ in love—loving hearts, loving speech, loving practices. Yet wisdom's pursuit of the mind of Christ is ingredient within true charity; theology seeks after partial knowledge that, however partial, does correspond to knowledge of Christ in both the subjective and objective senses. Theological knowledge is not impossible, but it is integrative and therefore dialectical: we know in part because in this era we love in part.

Another mirroring image appears in 2 Corinthians 3:18: "And we all, with unveiled face, beholding the glory of the Lord, are being transformed into the same image from one degree of glory to another. For this comes from the Lord who is the Spirit." Margaret Mitchell shows that this passage regularly appears with 1 Corinthians 13 in patristic hermeneutics: "The tension between the hidden and the revealed, between clarity and obscurity—clear eye and obscure object, occluded eye and clear object—runs as a fault line down the Corinthian correspondence, and from it into the stream of Christian hermeneutics."[44] The mirror image, focused on indirectness in 1 Corinthians 13, focuses here on transformative revelation: "In Paul, as in his interpreters, the two [mirror and veil] can be tactically employed to emphasize the partial access they afford or the occlusion they maintain."[45] First Corinthians 13 eschatologically defers; 2 Corinthians 3 proleptically brings forward a glimpse of the anticipated face-to-face encounter. Of course, the passage is notoriously difficult:

> Unfortunately, 2 Corinthians 3, though squeezed and prodded by generations
> of interpreters, has remained one of the more inscrutable reflections of a man
> who had already gained the reputation among his near-contemporaries for

---

theological expansion of such themes, see Daniel J. Treier, *Proverbs and Ecclesiastes*, Brazos Theological Commentary on the Bible (Grand Rapids: Brazos, 2011).

[44]See Margaret M. Mitchell, in *Paul, the Corinthians and the Birth of Christian Hermeneutics* (Cambridge: Cambridge University Press, 2010), chap. 4, pp. 58-78: "The Mirror and the Veil: Hermeneutics of Occlusion," here quoting p. 58.

[45]Ibid., p. 59.

writing letters that were "hard to understand" (2 Peter 3:16). It is hard to escape the impression that, to this day, when 2 Corinthians 3 is read a veil lies over our minds.[46]

Mitchell presses further, though, suggesting that Paul's inscrutability was not simply a problem arising later or elsewhere; it is the animating situation behind the argument of this passage itself.[47]

Whatever one makes of the passage overall, the veil and image make its chief contribution to our larger argument. The veil more clearly, so to speak, reveals the present-day dialectic stemming from the eschatological deferral. The veil is portable—not, in fact, hiding Paul's meaning but blinding Corinthian minds.[48] For Origen, then, the veil can signify the shameful sin that keeps people hiding from God, rather than coming into the light so that they can understand.[49] The image of Christ appearing once again demonstrates the hermeneutical significance of spiritual sight. Beholding the Lord's glory transforms us into his image. That people become what they worship is not just negatively but also positively true.[50] Those whose understanding mirrors the mind of Christ reflect his image in glorious living. Precisely for that reason, their understanding can only be partial and always in process, until their transformation is complete.

In a third mirror passage James adds a new element to our collage of images: hearing.

> Anyone who listens to the word but does not do what it says is like someone who looks at his face in a mirror and, after looking at himself, goes away and immediately forgets what he looks like. But whoever looks intently into the perfect law that gives freedom, and continues in it—not forgetting what they have heard, but doing it—they will be blessed in what they do. (Jas 1:23-25 NIV)

Shifting metaphors signal that in this era of redemptive history Christians do not actually gaze at God in Christ. In an important respect, the eschatological dialectic mentioned above entails hearing God while seeing our-

---

[46]Richard B. Hays, *Echoes of Scripture in the Letters of Paul* (New Haven, CT: Yale University Press, 1989), p. 123.
[47]Mitchell, *Paul, the Corinthians and the Birth of Christian Hermeneutics*, p. 70.
[48]Ibid., p. 72.
[49]Ibid., pp. 74-75.
[50]G. K. Beale, *We Become What We Worship: A Biblical Theology of Idolatry* (Downers Grove, IL: InterVarsity Press, 2008), especially reflecting Psalm 115.

selves. Hearing is the epistemologically primary metaphor for the present, despite divine discourse being textually mediated, requiring some vision for its reading.[51] Seeing is a secondary trope for how faith affects believers—not all of whom are readers themselves. The Pauline veil addresses the authorized spiritual reading of Torah and its transformative hearing by the rest of the people.

These mirror images, however varied in their original contexts, together bring to focus some biblical-theological reflections on the knowledge of God. James's mirror reflects Christians—whether or not we display the free obedience for which God newly creates us. Paul's mirrors both reflect and eschatologically deflect knowledge of the God heard in Scripture. Paul's mirrors tether true theology to growth in spiritual transformation; James's mirror warns against the kind of theological knowledge that can be gained without such transformation. Together these mirrors display the image of God: the Word of the Son, by the Spirit, helping people to grow into filial freedom reflecting the Father's own life. It is appropriate to speak of "eschatological" realism, signaling that apprehension of the truth is partial, holistically integrated with life practices, involving growth in Christian community over time.[52] However, it is necessary to speak of eschatological "realism" in ways that strive for disciplined intellectual responsibility, not settling for endless deferral of actual truth claims.[53]

---

[51]Peter J. Leithart, *Deep Exegesis: The Mystery of Reading Scripture* (Waco, TX: Baylor University Press, 2009), p. 193, notes that despite the enlightenment motif in John's Gospel, especially John 1, even John is not an "oracularcentric" theologian; the Light is the Word.

[52]In Stanley J. Grenz and John R. Franke, *Beyond Foundationalism: Shaping Theology in a Postmodern Context* (Louisville: Westminster John Knox, 2001), especially pp. 266-73, Grenz and Franke advocate "eschatological realism," trying to account for these concerns. It remains unclear at best, however, whether they are claiming some form of critical realism or not—whether the eschatological "world" is the only objective one and, if so, how that world could bear on adjudicating present truth claims. A better, less confusing account—to an extent because of what it does not say—is Merold Westphal, "Hermeneutics and Holiness," in *Analytic Theology: New Essays in the Philosophy of Theology*, ed. Oliver D. Crisp and Michael C. Rea (Oxford: Oxford University Press, 2009), pp. 265-79.

[53]In an indelicately worded essay, Randal Rauser poignantly raises this concern, applying it to the work of Grenz and Franke among others (see "Theology as a Bull Session," in Crisp and Rea, *Analytic Theology*, pp. 70-84). If Rauser is right about what we must attempt, Rowan Williams nevertheless reminds us about the spirit of the attempt: "The continuing labour of adjustment to what is believed to be the context in which life continues *shows* its obedience to and seriousness about an abiding and mind-independent reality in its willingness to go on testing what is said—intellectually, spiritually, and in terms of practice in general—with confidence and courage. It is a courage that includes the willingness to say of this or that formulation, 'This is our

Though partial, provisional and holistic, only attempted truth claims create reflections at which to look intently, assessing how well they reflect the biblical teaching that gives freedom. Mirrors both reflect and reverse ourselves.[54] The broader concept of theology as wisdom incorporates the witness of all God's people, verbal and nonverbal, from excellent to unwise, as a variety of Christian practices communicate views of God. These views are reflected in the biblical mirror of Christ whether or not they come to theoretical focus. A more particular concept of theology, as an intellectual discipline, explicitly and intentionally involves judgment(s): both φρόνησις— the capacity for reaching particular conclusions—and the truth claims themselves. To stay with our overarching metaphor, judgments in that disciplined sense involve moments of looking carefully in the mirror, not just causing a reflection. Yet judgments arise any time Christian believers speak and act before God and others about what we see. These judgments therefore implicitly or explicitly answer questions about the correspondence we do or do not see between ourselves and the biblical Christ—whether personally or communally, intellectually or practically. Theology remains at its roots a practice of prayerful scrutiny of Scripture before God: "This is the thankfull glasse, That mends the lookers eyes."[55]

Theological concepts in sapiential context. Sooner or later we must discern the relation between theological concepts and Scripture, let alone the world. This book's title apes an influential book by Richard Rorty: *Philosophy and the Mirror of Nature.*[56] Rorty's sharp pragmatic turn practically

---

best verbal "strategy" for responding to the current of God's action, and we may not be able to imagine any better; but we are not claiming that what is on offer is a simple descriptive summary.' Or, in slightly different terminology, exactly *how* such theological formulation refers is not something we can scrutinize; but the way in which the language operates, its points of strain or self-criticism, tells us that we cannot set aside the intention to refer, to tell a truth not reducible to an account of our own feeling or speculative play" ("Theology Among the Humanities," in *The Vocation of Theology Today: A Festschrift for David Ford*, ed. Tom Greggs, Rachel Muers and Simeon Zahl [Eugene, OR: Cascade, 2013], pp. 178-90, quoting p. 188).

[54]Alan Jacobs notes that W. H. Auden—appealing to the Hamlet quotation that introduces our final chapter—"uses the mirror as his key metaphor of what art does, . . . because it is not direct representation but, when done rightly, a Kierkegaardian 'indirect communication'" ("Textual Notes," in W. H. Auden, *For the Time Being: A Christmas Oratorio*, ed. Alan Jacobs [Princeton, NJ: Princeton University Press, 2013], p. 72n6).

[55]George Herbert, "The Holy Scriptures.I.," in *The Temple, Sacred Poems and Private Ejaculations* (Cambridge: Thomas Buck and Roger Daniel, 1633), lines 8-9.

[56]Richard Rorty, *Philosophy and the Mirror of Nature* (Princeton, NJ: Princeton University Press, 1979).

evacuates philosophy of any reason for being. He claims to reverse "the triumph of the quest for certainty over the quest for wisdom."[57] Assessing Rorty's historical narrative need not detain us for long. Whether or not it has been philosophy's self-conception to mirror nature, picturing knowledge "as an assemblage of accurate representations" while privileging certain representations as foundations certainly characterizes the aspiration of much evangelical theology.[58] On Rorty's account more generally, the ideal representations mirrored nature; among evangelicals, the foundations tried to mirror Scripture. Rorty's substitute claim about wisdom imposes a burden of clarity on contemporary theologians appealing to φρόνησις, concerning just how pragmatic they propose to be.

Rorty distinguishes sharply between epistemology and hermeneutics: epistemology assumes commensurable discourse between people as well as between their minds and reality, while hermeneutics denies having such "a set of rules which will tell us how rational agreement can be reached on what would settle the issue on every point where statements seem to conflict." Epistemology is about everyone doing their rational duties to find common ground, thus resolving conflicts or rendering leftover disagreements noncognitive, semantic or temporary.[59] Epistemology presumes familiarity that people wish to codify. Hermeneutics, by contrast, pertains "where we do not understand what is happening but are honest enough to admit it, rather than being *blatantly* 'Whiggish' about it."[60] Frequent dichotomies falsely attach epistemology to objectively mirroring nature and hermeneutics to subjectively being human.[61] Against juxtaposing hermeneutical "understanding" with more scientific "explanation" as distinct ways of knowing, Rorty proposes instead to hand "knowledge" over to the Kantian and Platonic traditions of philosophy, only to abandon their enterprise.[62]

Rorty complains about addiction to epistemology's focus on essences,

[57]Ibid., p. 61.
[58]Ibid., p. 163.
[59]Ibid., p. 316.
[60]Ibid., p. 321, emphasis original.
[61]Ibid., pp. 332-33, 342.
[62]Ibid., p. 356.

bite-sized basic elements that unify all discourse.[63] In contrast, Rorty calls for "edifying" rather than "systematic" philosophy. He rejects "the Platonic-Aristotelian view that the *only* way to be edified is to know what is out there (to reflect the facts accurately—to realize our essence by knowing essences)," suggesting instead "that the quest for truth is just one among many ways in which we might be edified."[64] Philosophy centered in epistemology is systematic, whereas properly edifying philosophy is suspicious about such pretensions.[65] Accordingly,

> One way of thinking of wisdom as something of which the love is not the same as that of argument, and of which the achievement does not consist in finding the correct vocabulary for representing essence, is to think of it as the practical wisdom necessary to participate in a conversation. One way to see edifying philosophy *as* the love of wisdom is to see it as the attempt to prevent conversation from degenerating into inquiry, into an exchange of views. Edifying philosophers can never end philosophy, but they can help prevent it from attaining the secure path of a science.[66]

Obvious challenges arise for Rorty's bracingly written position. First, why suppose that there must be "the" one correct vocabulary or else no interest in correctness at all; why not suppose that "a" correct vocabulary might be sought with more than one correct vocabulary allowed? Second, why suppose that a conversation will be perennially interesting or its participants wise without an "exchange of views," lacking intermittent "inquiry" taken to and from the conversation? Third, why suppose that only philosophy

---

[63]Ibid., p. 357.

[64]Ibid., p. 360.

[65]Ibid., p. 366. In numerous works, such as *Who's Afraid of Relativism? Community, Contingency, and Creaturehood*, The Church and Postmodern Culture (Grand Rapids: Baker Academic, 2014), James K. A. Smith defends pragmatic accounts against the charge that their nonrealism loses contact with Christian truth. He may well be correct about misreadings of some helpful accounts in the philosophical realm, but theologically we must be committed to a robust account of correspondence with scriptural truth—whatever the complexities—and Rorty's will not do. Even if Robert Brandom is correct (*Perspectives on Pragmatism: Classical, Recent, and Contemporary* [Cambridge, MA: Harvard University Press, 2011]—with thanks to Stephen Scheidell for the reference) that Rorty primarily breaks the tie between the world and beliefs with respect to justifying them, nevertheless the associated demotion of authority from the divine to the worldly sphere produces a theologically inadequate account of truth. If Jesus Christ is the Way, the Truth and the Life, then ectypal correspondence to God's knowledge becomes fundamental to a Christian account.

[66]Rorty, *Philosophy and the Mirror of Nature*, p. 372.

pursued with the security of a science would involve inquiry; has Rorty simply returned to the perennial contest between philosophers and poets, only to choose poetry and act as if it had no purchase on reality? Fourth, then, for someone supposedly interested in ordinary language, why suppose that the conversation must consist of only one type of speech act, or at least preclude certain other kinds? Why, in short, are views about truth excluded rather than expected to make the conversation lively?

Rorty's philosophical proposal announces the theological stakes for epistemological questions. Toward the end of his book he writes, "Epistemology is the attempt to see the patterns of justification within normal discourse as *more* than just such patterns. It is the attempt to see them as hooked on to something which demands moral commitment—Reality, Truth, Objectivity, Reason."[67] The attachment to truth retained by Christian wisdom is moral commitment indeed, involving evangelical theology in teleologically ordered conversation(s). Whether or not this truth-seeking gets expressed philosophically via "essences," humans are unique beings, created to mirror the character of God and the mind of Christ through the transforming power of the Spirit. We can take philosophy's pragmatic turn far enough to find freedom where earlier evangelical attachments to metaphysical essences and epistemological systems have misled.[68] Rorty helps to name the stereotypical animus against hermeneutical subjectivity that remains a problem among evangelicals. Yet he ironically reinforces an instrumental approach to wisdom—simply from the other, pragmatic rather than theoretical, side. The wisdom of the Christian gospel finds a properly "systematic" aspect of theology to be truly "edifying," even if the proof-texted pursuit of only one textbook system from the Bible must be left behind. For evangelical thought and speech, not just other kinds of action, must embrace the discipline of the gospel, and part of that discipline is conceptual.

From the perspective of Christian wisdom, a positive account of the Bible's informing theological concepts begins with the character of φρόνησις as a regulative virtue. As such Christian practical reason has both cognitive and habitual components, with language helping to tie these together. Ac-

---

[67]Ibid., p. 385.
[68]For a better philosophical account than Rorty's, again see Westphal, "Hermeneutics and Holiness."

counts of theology's "communicative praxis" can borrow from linguist and translator Kathleen Callow: A concept is "a mental correlate of words which is not language specific." Therefore concepts are "habitual events" acquired "by participation" in social activity, having "firm cores" of meaning along with vast amounts of detail. Hence "concepts are not what we think about; they are what we think with," accessing particular core aspects or details on any given occasion.[69] For this reason one can speak of "looking along" rather than just "at" biblical texts.[70]

A complementary, more philosophical account of concepts emphasizes that, instead of solitary minds seeking essences that mirror external reality, knowledge involves everyday communal practice.[71] For Christian theology, then, the Holy Spirit's leading of churchly recognition defines the process by which doctrinal concepts arise. Distinct from yet closely tied to the words of particular languages, they serve as habits of disciplined thinking, even crossing cultures to some degree. A concept is "a predicate of a possible judgment." Judgments are "(explanatorily) basic to language use"; their content arises out of actual use, in which a speaker counts him- or herself as taking on a normative commitment.[72] Thought relates to speech through language, and speech counts as action. A doctrine is a communally normative expression of Christian piety, exhibited as "'a product of the past and a kernel of the future'—that is, as carrying on the normative trajectory implicit in a series of recognized precedents and as exerting normative constraint on future candidates for currency."[73] Doctrinal concepts thus imply commitments to ongoing patterns of language use: they express and facil-

---

[69]See Kathleen Callow's *Man and Message: A Guide to Meaning-Based Text Analysis* (Lanham, MD: Summer Institute of Linguistics/University Press of America, 1998), addressed in Daniel J. Treier, *Virtue and the Voice of God: Toward Theology as Wisdom* (Grand Rapids: Eerdmans, 2006), especially pp. 94-95.

[70]Kevin J. Vanhoozer, "First Theology: Meditations in a Postmodern Toolshed," in *First Theology: God, Scripture, and Hermeneutics* (Downers Grove, IL: InterVarsity Press, 2002), pp. 15-44, borrowing the image from C. S. Lewis and then developing the hermeneutical, theological point (see especially pp. 17-19 and 36-40).

[71]Kevin W. Hector, *Theology Without Metaphysics: God, Language, and the Spirit of Recognition*, Current Issues in Theology (Cambridge: Cambridge University Press, 2011).

[72]Ibid., pp. 48-49. For an apparently complementary theological account, Anthony C. Thiselton, *The Hermeneutics of Doctrine* (Grand Rapids: Eerdmans, 2007), appeals to dispositional accounts of belief: "Confessions *declare a content*, but they *also* serve *to nail the speaker's colors to the mast* as an act of first-person testimony and commitment" (p. 13).

[73]Hector, *Theology Without Metaphysics*, p. 84.

itate theological judgment(s), with their meaning continually changing in small ways while remaining relatively stable at a broader level.[74] Whereas evangelical theologies have typically tied concepts to unchanging essences, fearing cultural relativism, in fact concepts can facilitate connections to reality without the indirectness of inferential use. Given their immediacy in ordinary language use, their perpetual change need not diminish relatively stable knowledge of biblical truth.[75] What theology should learn from pragmatism is that languages are "perspectival instruments"; far from panicking about this, evangelicals should therefore learn to "situate the propositional within the practical."[76]

Such an account of concepts draws crucially on a pneumatological commitment to tradition, refusing to leave individual knowers bereft of contact with reality unless concepts reveal essences. Instead, the Spirit takes up Christian social practice and enmeshes concept usage within its "ordinary" contact with reality.[77] As theologians appropriate recent philosophical work on the meaning of concepts, pneumatology and ecclesiology come to the fore. Nevertheless, although meaning lies in language use, and making judgments about truth does too, we should not reduce truth itself to a mere function of human language use. The challenge of an account that emphasizes the ordinary practice of Christian traditioning lies in promoting "expressive freedom": if one adopts communal practices to carry on as one's own, this expression of freedom needs to provide adequate variety in a community's mutual recognition.[78] The corresponding concern is "emancipatory critique," how to address lack of communal variety or loss of self-expressive freedom. In fact, far from being impossible because of communal constraints, contrary speech can exhibit implicit, although neglected or even suppressed, communal norms. In theological contexts, liberating critique

---

[74]Ibid., pp. 103-47.

[75]It may be reassuring that at least one reviewer criticizes Hector's account from the other side, for being too epistemologically stable; see George Pattison, review of Kevin Hector, *Theology Without Metaphysics*, *Reviews in Religion and Theology* 19, no. 3 (July 2012): 318-24.

[76]Adonis Vidu, *Theology After Neo-Pragmatism*, Paternoster Theological Monographs (Carlisle, UK: Paternoster, 2008), pp. 266, 293.

[77]At this point Hector's account seems to be theologically compatible with that of Reinhard Hütter, *Suffering Divine Things: Theology as Church Practice*, trans. Doug Stott (Grand Rapids: Eerdmans, 2000), on which see also Treier, *Virtue and the Voice of God*, chap. 3.

[78]Hector, *Theology Without Metaphysics*, p. 266.

can arise from within the church or be appropriated from without, as long as it displays standards that proper Christian concept use ought to meet. Church members might be provoked to discover within their tradition(s) possibilities for reform.[79]

To bring these conceptual threads together for evangelical theology: engagement with pragmatism addresses the meaning of concepts by highlighting pneumatological commitments and ecclesiological concerns. The truth of theological judgments need not be lost in such an approach, but can actually be protected from unnecessary and unrelenting epistemological vulnerability. Pragmatic approaches remain philosophically awkward at points of dissonance, though: Is focusing on ordinary communal use sufficient to foster liberating social orders? Such philosophical dilemmas aside, evangelical theologians further face more specific and ultimate questions of gospel freedom—not least from intellectual bondage to noetic effects of sin.[80] On one hand, then, pragmatic accounts appear to require deeper consideration of ideological critique. On the other hand, evangelical commitments to biblical authority require appreciation for Christian tradition: the divine truth of Scripture, though not our (mis)interpretations, does not count as merely human ideology. Some faith that the church maintains a measure of contact with that scriptural truth is what makes ideological critique of theology to be worth the bother.[81] Theologians cannot be so hamstrung over worries about ideology that we refuse to account for relatively stable concepts as one form of divine grace: God ordinarily enables Christian communities to transmit biblical convictions over time and across places.[82] There are plenty of exceptions, of course, due to churchly sin, cultural blindness, systemic oppression, mysterious providence and even radical divine intervention (visible or invisible). Even so, a pragmatically informed pneumatological ecclesiology tells part of theology's sapiential story.

---

[79]Ibid., p. 290.
[80]On these effects see Merold Westphal, "Taking St. Paul Seriously: Sin as an Epistemological Category," in *Christian Philosophy*, ed. Thomas P. Flint (Notre Dame, IN: University of Notre Dame Press, 1990), pp. 200-226.
[81]Robert W. Jenson asserts that to some degree the church must presume concordance between its dogmatic teaching and Scripture, or else there is no church and "Scripture" is a misnomer (*Systematic Theology*, vol. 2, *The Works of God* [Oxford: Oxford University Press, 1999], p. 281).
[82]See also the discussion of relative adequacy vis-à-vis the work of Bernard Lonergan and David Tracy, in Treier, *Virtue and the Voice of God*, pp. 91-94.

Yet not the whole story: according to Hector's account, "one counts as going on in the same way as Christ just in case one's performances are recognizable as carrying on the normative trajectory implicit in a series of precedents which not only includes Scripture, but which itself recognizes the authority of Scripture. . . . Scripture does not replace the Spirit's work, in other words; it is taken up into it."[83] Helpful as this claim is for philosophical ground-clearing over the development and operation of concepts, it makes only a start toward shoring up their theological foundations and maintaining their scriptural integrity. When it comes to continuity between the concept use of the apostles and prophets in Scripture and that of subsequent Christians, the *idem* identity of exact numerical sameness would be impossible between "then" and "now." The cells in the body of Christ necessarily change over time, so to speak. Instead, therefore, maintaining the *ipse* identity of narrative continuity—of a self or community maturing through time—is the correct aspiration.[84] Exact conceptual sameness is impossible between first-century biblical statements in Greek and twenty-first-century evangelical English, or among sinners of any and every age. Recognizable continuity, however, stems from God re-creating one new humanity that grows into the mind of Christ by the Spirit. It is appropriate to transpose Paul Ricoeur's concept of *ipse* identity into this doctrinal realm because discerning, living and teaching biblical concepts involves human activity, shaped by communal narrative(s) with identities under constant negotiation. The living Christ, divine and human, is the preeminent personal agent behind the conceptual habits we strive to learn, passing them on to his apostles and prophets by the Holy Spirit in order to start the proper chain of recognition.

Maintaining scriptural discipline requires properly recognizing the identity of theological concepts. Strongly pneumatological accounts offer some virtues with which evangelicals might overcome their essentialist and correspondentist past. Instead of accounting theologically for realities on the ground, sometimes we have been mired in rationalistic epistemological

---

[83]Hector, *Theology Without Metaphysics*, p. 233n35.

[84]Appealing to Paul Ricoeur, *Oneself as Another*, trans. Kathleen McLaughlin Blamey (Chicago: University of Chicago Press, 1992); see Treier, *Virtue and the Voice of God*, pp. 58-60, and Kevin J. Vanhoozer, *Biblical Narrative in the Philosophy of Paul Ricoeur* (Cambridge: Cambridge University Press, 1990).

generalities. Nevertheless, for all their helpfulness, ecclesiologically prag-matic accounts need greater christological vigilance regarding the reve-latory priority and authority of the divine Logos. The mind of Christ is not merely human: sharing in the divine archetype, Christ's patterns uniquely norm that to which our lives should finitely correspond. Archetypal the-ology is "the eternal or divine pattern for the perfect truth of supernatural revelation."[85] Ectypal theology embraces all finite knowledge of God: that of angels; that of humans, before the fall, after the fall yet shaped by grace, and in heaven at the end of pilgrimage; and, most importantly, that of Jesus Christ.[86] Merely apophatic awareness that the finite cannot contain the in-finite easily devolves into skepticism concerning knowledge of God. By contrast, Jesus Christ as divine self-revelation decisively overcomes this potential chasm between humans and God, providing Scripture as his on-going form of self-testimony.

The personal and redemptive nature of this revelation necessarily shapes how we receive the scriptural wisdom unto salvation. God graciously gives testimony about and from Jesus Christ that inculcates habits of proper re-sponse, involves finite proportions possible to receive and incorporates our freedom to communicate its blessing to others. Integrally connected to union with Christ throughout, the freedom involved in theological knowledge always receives his priestly benefits and responds to his kingly authority, listening to his delegates—the apostles and prophets of Holy Scripture—before claiming any prophetic ministry of its own. Therefore, evangelical theological freedom involves undergoing scriptural discipline and appropriating biblical concepts.[87] Theological exegesis engages

---

[85]Richard A. Muller, *Post-Reformation Reformed Dogmatics: The Rise and Development of Reformed Orthodoxy, ca. 1520 to ca. 1725*, vol. 1, *Prolegomena to Theology*, 2nd ed. (Grand Rapids: Baker Academic, 2003), p. 234. Muller indicates variety about whether this archetypal theology des-ignates God's infinite, necessary self-knowledge or, more restrictively, the eternal basis for the ectypal theology (without including, say, the divine knowledge of possibilities not made actual). The former definition tended to see theology as both speculative and practical, while the latter, narrower definition tended to treat theology as practical, focused on salvation.

[86]Ibid., 1:235.

[87]At its best, Protestant orthodoxy was far from an arrogant effort to put God in a dogmatic box; it was "essentially soteriological," a pursuit of rescued pilgrims (so Muller, *Post-Reformation Re-formed Dogmatics*, 1:268). Precisely this aspect of soteriological pilgrimage requires the view that theological concepts will change to some degree. It also suggests that in theology the contempla-tive and the practical are uniquely unified (Muller, *Post-Reformation Reformed Dogmatics*, 1:352).

Scripture and practices biblical scholarship as an opportunity for evangelical grace rather than a merely natural, and thus oppressively fallen, operation.

As we have already suggested, evangelical theology's coherence as an intellectual tradition prioritizes clear representation of biblical truth. Evangelical theologians have typically aspired to mirror Scripture's own teaching in content, and even in structure to some degree. Aberrant forms aside, much evangelical biblicism does not whimsically appeal to isolated proof texts but plausibly arranges coherent patterns of teaching. Tradition, reason and experience influence this activity, without garnering equally authoritative attention. Seeking to depict a unified system of scriptural truth, many evangelical theologians pursued increasingly close harmony with historically oriented biblical theology, and support for particular doctrinal claims from as many different passages as possible. Alternatively, among those who doubt the systemic unity of Scripture, historically oriented biblical scholarship unleashes increasing theological freedom from the constraining assumption that Scripture provides a coherent witness to redemptive history. In such antibiblicist cases, not just acontextualized prooftexting but nearly all efforts to reach doctrinal judgment(s) with scriptural support can seem arbitrary.

However, the evangelical aspiration to mirror Scripture is not altogether original but in some respects longstanding throughout Christian theological history. If our pursuit of this aspiration sometimes goes in vicious circles, then such vices lie at the extremes of otherwise virtuous practices: either paying so much attention to the content of biblical claims that we neglect formal creativity, or else paying so much attention to the form of biblical concepts themselves that we negate any material freedom for synthetic judgment. In the latter case, despairing of adequately representing biblical diversity within an evangelical unity, we abandon systematic theology for lack of imaginative coherence. The present evangelical account of TIS, in response, understands doctrinal judgment as a practice, and hence doctrinal judgments as potential presuppositions and products of scriptural exegesis, for the sake of the eschatological and ethical aspiration to mirror Scripture. Through wise acquisition of conceptual habits shaped by the Spirit, we exercise God-given freedom to foster the canonical imagination, that the church may reflect the fullness of Christ's image.

Accordingly the next chapter addresses the types of Christian fellowship and scholarly friendship that should be characteristic of truly evangelical theology. This present chapter has sharpened the focus of evangelical engagement with Scripture—accounting for the church's apostolicity before we examine its catholicity. Greater openness to canon, creed and culture throughout the process of interpreting Scripture need not threaten historical integrity; to the contrary, theological exegesis can reconnect the Bible and the church by recovering the God-centered focus of each. The next chapter, then, explores evangelical theology's service to the church more fully. Its focus lies on the *agents* mirroring Scripture, *who* participates in the drama of evangelical theological discourse. Evangelical theology is communal as well as personal, churchly as well as academic, and ecclesial as well as congregational. Part of the recovery of TIS underscores the divine harmony of history and mystery with implications, fittingly, for church unity and gospel truth. Indeed, an evangelical theology of shared redemptive-historical participation started to surface earlier in 1 Corinthians 10, pointing toward the Lord's Table. Ecclesiastical fellowship remains a pressing concern for rightly apprehending the mysteries of redemptive history. To that we now turn.

Chapter Five

In Fellowship
with the Saints

H AVING COMMENDED TO evangelical theology a search for
wisdom by way of theological exegesis, our proposal now addresses
how church and academy fit more specifically into that framework. Since
wisdom involves personal responses in communal life, we must account for
the fellowship of evangelical theology. Our focus will rest on the *agents* mirroring Scripture, *who* participates in the drama of evangelical theological
discourse. The multiple forms of evangelical fellowship relate particular
theologians—amateur and professional—to others inside and outside the
church, with different levels and kinds of pastoral authority or institutional
influence; to their own congregations and perhaps denominations; as well
as to parachurch organizations, other churches (denominational or not) and
academic environments. The present chapter sets forth a theological
framework for such fellowship.

This theological framework emerges from particular biblical passages
plus larger motifs related to gospel identity and church division. Its first
component is an account of theological scholarship as an activity of Christian
love, serving both church and world in ways framed by 1 Corinthians 9 and
following. The second component is an account of churchly division as a
possible necessity of Christian love, sometimes surprisingly preserving fellowship while multiplying ministry. The broad structure of this framework
distinguishes between gospel versus heresy and ministry versus ministry
levels of differences, plus a further level at which potential division must give
way to a united congregational mind. Specific application of this rubric re-

quires φρόνησις, not only to recognize how ecclesial situations correspond to one or more of the three levels but also to realize particular vocations of scholarly and churchly service. Evangelical wisdom can actually foster unity and fellowship in gospel truth, taking dynamic missional rather than just static institutional forms. The third component of this chapter's framework is therefore an attempt to understand evangelical theology as a particular intellectual tradition.

CORINTHIAN REFLECTIONS: LOVING SAINTS, CHURCHLY SCHOLARSHIP

The awkward balancing act between church and academy is certainly not envisioned directly in Scripture. Nevertheless it has important ramifications for contemporary "theological" discourse(s). In the broadest sense everyone is a theologian; all believer-priests teach each other, at least informally, and bear Christian witness. The work of all Christian scholars, then, has a theological dimension. Narrower still, the speech of biblical and theological scholars is intentionally and pervasively God-referring. Of particular concern in the context of this chapter, though, are the relationships of academic theologians to and on behalf of the church. Once again, 1 Corinthians offers relevant material for adjudicating these relationships.

Theologians and the academy (1 Cor 9–10). Relationships with the academy in general and with particular non-Christian scholars call to mind 1 Corinthians 9. Paul defends apostolic freedom and commends his own example, at least implicitly, to command Corinthian self-discipline for the sake of the gospel. Theologians should consider what it means to imitate Paul in offering the gospel without charge, not making full use of rights (1 Cor 9:1-18). In a sense, of course, *theologian* names a modern profession, to which a salary, meager royalties, tenure and the like might attach, yet these are secondary rewards compared to opportunities for promoting the gospel. Paul makes this more relationally concrete in 1 Corinthians 9:19-23. The Christian is paradoxically free from all and slave to all (1 Cor 9:19). Accountable to God and set free by the gospel, theologians need not pursue worldly fame or fashions of counterfeit wisdom. They are thereby free to pursue friendship with fellow scholars. Paul does not call Christians to flee earthly society (1 Cor 5:10), even if the effects of friendship call for caution

(1 Cor 15:33). Friendly relationships serve fellow scholars' need for the gospel, hoping to win them over for salvation (1 Cor 9:20-22). Evangelical theologians do not seek to persuade others of their own excellence or Christianity's worldly ideals—promoting instead the imperishable value of the gospel (1 Cor 9:24-27).

Evangelical theologians are accordingly free to engage not just particular scholars but the academy in general. We should be neither naive nor overly suspicious regarding fellow scholars' influence on our character. Instead, our focus should rest on the freedom of the gospel, which cures enslavement to both our own fancies and the fashions of others. Christ frees us to contextualize theological work prudently for the sake of gospel mission. Hence Christ also frees us to pursue God-honoring excellence, as 1 Corinthians 10:30-33 suggests. Academic engagement is not for our own sake, but for the salvation of many; that is the primary reason for putting no unnecessary stumbling blocks in others' way. Nevertheless, there is another reason for doing good academic work: scholarship is creaturely activity in which evangelical theologians are free to participate with gratitude, and thus do everything to glorify God.

Theologians and the congregation (1 Cor 11–14). These considerations in 1 Corinthians 9–10 have implications for serving within the church as well as outside. In the first-century context of pertinent biblical texts, the complexities of Jew-Gentile relationships blur some boundaries between church and world. Then, as now, the church could not wall off its membership from broader religious currents but needed discernment, dialogue and debate, whether the interlocutors were Jewish brothers and sisters, proto-Gnostic claimants or still others. The New Testament and early Christian literature manifest more permeable boundaries than present-day evangelicals sometimes reckon with, a factor to notice when applying texts about churchly particularity. Prudential freedom is necessary in any event, to serve Christ by communicating winsomely with fellow humans, and to glorify the Creator by gratefully enjoying cultural gifts. Beyond scholarly friends and academic guilds, likewise this key concept of creaturely freedom ought to shape how theologians serve fellow church members and their congregations.

Following the call of 1 Corinthians 10:31 to do everything for God's glory, 1 Corinthians 11 then places the churchly service of theologians within a twofold context: shared apostolic practices of ordered relations (1 Cor 11:1-16) and eucharistic fellowship (1 Cor 11:17-34). Whether ordained to the ministry of Word and sacrament or not, as baptized members theologians are accountable within and to their congregations. They dare not stand aloof, falling into academic tendencies of class warfare directed both higher and lower, thereby failing to discern the body of Christ (1 Cor 11:29). Intellectuals particularly tend to exonerate ourselves, so theologians should cultivate ecclesiastical accountability, to receive discipline from the Lord without needing the extraordinary measures to which this passage refers. First Corinthians 13 reinforces the primacy of charity, and 1 Corinthians 14 of edifying order, in setting forth a context for authentically evangelical theology.

According to the theology of 1 Corinthians 12, membership in Christ's body and reception of spiritual gifts ought to evoke not only humility from theologians, but also churchly freedom for them. Theologians are not free to betray the gospel with appeals to the Holy Spirit, whose genuine work promotes the lordship of Christ (1 Cor 12:3). The one God of the one gospel, though, gives many different gifts (1 Cor 12:4-11); the many members of Christ's one body share in receiving the gift-giving Holy Spirit (1 Cor 12:12-13), therefore needing all the gifts of other members (1 Cor 12:14-27). The church must promote legitimate freedom for theologians to exercise their gifts in its service. Such freedom is not limitless, but neither may the church enslave theologians to its current fashions, preventing their being all things to all people for the gospel's sake. Freedom to advance the gospel may even require freedom to admonish the church. Theologians should neither assess their gifts as the greatest, striving uncharitably for ecclesiastical prominence (1 Cor 12:31), nor accede to mistreatment as dishonorable members, accepting disregard in the name of charity.

Theologians are not directly listed among the redemptive-historical divine appointments in 1 Corinthians 12:28-30. However, several factors suggest that the church's spiritual gifts should not be limited to explicit references within biblical lists. For one, at least original apostleship and possibly other God-given offices have passed from the scene. So too has whatever level of institutional singularity pertained in early Christianity. Another factor is the tendency of New Testament church polities to emphasize freedom and function over singular and strict forms.[1] Sometimes the spiritual gift lists name people, other times activities. Their aim is not to provide restrictive accounts of either, but rather to portray a generous God— who gives each congregation all it needs, and each member all they need to bless the church.

Treating theologians, and theological reflection, as spiritual gifts therefore involves another appeal to wisdom. The church needs authentic biblical wisdom and hence theological reflection. Whether or not this activity necessarily or effectively operates within the academy, so that the church needs theologians in the professional sense, is a matter for ongoing discernment in particular contexts.[2] Certain times or places, even particular ecclesiastical traditions, may favor formal academic engagement more than others. The heart of the argument here concerns the freedom the gospel gives for φρόνησις, and correspondingly its orientation toward promoting the gospel both inside and outside the church.

Confirmation of this emphasis comes from another Pauline text addressing spiritual gifts: Romans 12. Famously clarifying the need for theological activity in light of the gospel is Romans 12:1-2: God's mercies elicit whole-personed self-offering as grateful worship. This self-offering seeks divine transformation, with renewal of the mind resulting in conformity to God's will rather than worldly fashion. Realistic self-appraisal becomes possible in that context, regarding gifts God has given to the church (Rom 12:3-8). No surprise: the vocabulary of wisdom, φρόνησις, appears. The freedom of the gospel fosters in theologians and their congregations wisdom for truly spiritual interaction and mutual edification—beyond simply appealing to chapter and verse for ironclad proofs or else having nothing to say. Theology's content shapes its form.

CHRISTIAN DIVISIONS: CHARITABLE NECESSITIES, POSSIBLE COMMUNION

Theological fellowship involves more than discerning freedom for academic

---

[1]See, e.g., the time-tested argument of Gordon D. Fee, "Reflections on Church Order in the Pastoral Epistles, with Further Reflection on the Hermeneutics of Ad Hoc Documents," *JETS* 28, no. 2 (June 1985): 141-51.

[2]Daniel J. Treier, *Virtue and the Voice of God: Toward Theology as Wisdom* (Grand Rapids: Eerdmans, 2006), especially chap. 7.

engagement as a form of churchly service. Fellowship in between these two poles runs along a wide spectrum of church and world relationships. The apostolic concern of biblical fidelity intersects with the catholic concern of ecclesial fraternity. The exhortation to be of the same mind (of Christ) seems to be in tension with academic life, which thrives on disagreement and novel developments. But of course the Bible confronts churchly division as a frequent occurrence that arises for reasons far beyond philosophizing. For all the proliferation of academic disagreements and novelties, the church too has more than its share of factions. How then should we approach the inevitability of theological division? First Corinthians again provides a point of departure.

Early on Paul castigates his addressees' factiousness and its fleshly origin. So 1 Corinthians 11:19 might initially surprise: "There must be factions among you in order that those who are genuine among you may be recognized." This sobering assertion puts necessary divisions within an apocalyptic context: they reveal divine approval and/or disapproval of those being tested.[3] "Factions" is a rendering of αἱρέσεις, used elsewhere by Paul only among the vices at Galatians 5:20. While here roughly synonymous with the σχίσματα ("divisions") of the preceding verse, this term hints at the severity of the test imposed on the church.[4] The necessity involved—δεῖ, "have to be"—is apparently of divine providence.

Contemplating the Corinthian factions, it becomes clear that New Testament fellowship puts both orthodoxy and orthopraxy at stake. Orthopraxy is at stake in the social stratification of the Corinthian Lord's Supper. Whereas the divisions of 1 Corinthians 1:10-12 run between house groups, now the divisions cut across classes of social advantage or disadvantage within the Corinthian congregation(s) as a whole.[5] Perceived tension between this passage and surrounding calls for unity should not entail attributing 1 Corinthians 11:19 to Corinthian opponents.[6] Instead, regrettably,

---

[3]Richard B. Hays, *First Corinthians*, Interpretation (Louisville: Westminster John Knox, 1997), p. 195.

[4]Gordon D. Fee, *The First Epistle to the Corinthians*, NICNT (Grand Rapids: Eerdmans, 1987), p. 538n34.

[5]Anthony C. Thiselton, *The First Epistle to the Corinthians*, NIGTC (Grand Rapids: Eerdmans, 2000), p. 857.

[6]Contra ibid., pp. 859-60.

church members may so severely resist Christlike love that they elicit divine judgment, precisely to protect and promote authentic gospel fellowship. In other words, divisions necessarily evoke discernment concerning when and how to resist them; sometimes discerning resistance results in ongoing or further division.[7] That is especially true when the gospel itself is at stake, as the following analysis of dogmatic rank makes clear.

Gospel versus heresy: Discerning dialogue. As we hinted early on, the New Testament contains a first level of Christian doctrine on which agreement is necessary for gospel fidelity. The beginning of 1 Corinthians puts the spotlight on Christ crucified; toward the end, in 1 Corinthians 15, the resurrection takes the leading role. Closest to a gospel summary in this epistle is 1 Corinthians 15:3-4, putting Jesus' death, burial and resurrection (along with its vindicating appearances) center stage. The drama of gospel doctrine in the rest of the New Testament is composed of similar or complementary plotlines. One could confirm this crux by studying explicit "gospel" texts, apparent summaries of the church's basic verbal proclamation and exhortations opposed to false teaching. Such "evangelical" Scripture passages both identify the gospel and clarify proper means of its preservation and promotion.

Without detailing all that work in this space, a summary of gospel fidelity in the other Pauline epistles similarly focuses on the Jesus narrative—notably his death, burial and resurrection—along with adherence to Christlike charity. Beyond a kerygmatic Christ narrative, the requirements imposed on potential Jesus followers also affect gospel fidelity. Without resolving the dilemmas faced by contemporary Pauline scholarship, one can suggest that the church's teaching about "staying in" the sphere of salvation must be consistent with its message about "getting in."[8] If salvation means

---

[7]It is true but misleading for Stephen E. Fowl to assert that all church divisions are failures of charity (see his *Theological Interpretation of Scripture,* Cascade Companions [Eugene, OR: Cascade, 2009], pp. 65-66, and "Scripture," in *The Oxford Handbook of Systematic Theology,* ed. John Webster, Kathryn Tanner and Iain Torrance [Oxford: Oxford University Press, 2007], pp. 345-46). It is true because Christian love rejoices with the truth (1 Cor 13:6). It is therefore misleading because sometimes opponents of truth within the church must be resisted to the point of exclusion from fellowship, as 1 Corinthians 5 makes clear. Such cases involve a kind of division, but the failure of charity may be entirely one-sided and the division therefore charitably necessary.

[8]For enduring insight on this relationship see Robert H. Gundry, "Grace, Works, and Staying Saved in Paul," *Biblica* 66, no. 1 (1985): 1-38.

knowing Christ, then how Christians stay in that loving relation must also ring true of the gracious lordship of Israel's God.

The other major section of this book already sketched the gospel's portrayal of reality in Christ. For now, the rest of the New Testament shades in two kinds of detail: first, illustrating the legitimate variety of "my" gospel proclamation, as Paul puts it, namely contingent contextualization; second, limiting that variety within orthodox identification of Jesus Christ. The material upshot of "catholic" writings like Hebrews, James, 1 Peter and Revelation is to uphold suffering or faltering Christians with the good news of ultimate vindication. The formal upshot is to illustrate the variety of conceptual frameworks with which the church can bear authentic gospel witness. Particular contextual emphases are not only doctrinally legitimate but also pastorally helpful. It further bears repeating that the New Testament gives us a fourfold Gospel.

The pastoral Christology of such gospel depictions consistently appears in nearly all New Testament writings. Beyond the Gospels (with Acts) and the Pauline epistles, other writings likewise focus the kerygma on Jesus. The Johannine epistles interweave light and life, truth and love, protecting the community from christological deviation precisely to promote true charity. Jude and 2 Peter protect against vice and promote virtue, as a way to proclaim the saving lordship of Jesus: evangelicals often lack such a proper eschatological orientation, failing either to manifest the gospel's promotion of moral excellence or else to extend God's mercy and patience.[9] Jude 20-23 clarifies how evangelical theology can contend for the faith without being wrongly contentious: first edifying rather than just opposing others; then being devoted to prayer in the Holy Spirit; remaining in the love of God with a keen eye on our future hope; and exercising pastoral discernment.

---

[9]As the discussion of Jude in Peter H. Davids, *The Letters of 2 Peter and Jude*, PNTC (Grand Rapids: Eerdmans, 2006), pp. 43-46, reflects, some scholars see the false teachers' error in doctrinal terms that elicit moral condemnation due to the Old Testament association of idolatry and immorality. Davids rightly counters that the error is moral according to the text itself, with denial of Christ's lordship not necessarily stemming from heresy that would be easy to spot. Instead, the immorality of the false teachers is tantamount to refusal of Christ's authority. Nevertheless, Jude's indication of their move from outside to inside this congregation, plus use of theological language and a holistically doctrinal approach in his response, reaffirms the appellation "false teachers." These are not simply people of bad behavior but those whose promotion of ethical license puts other congregants at risk.

Doctrinal controversy, John Webster reiterates, is a work of charity, of common discernment, of peaceful order.[10] We maintain unity of will despite diversity of judgment out of openness to the catholicity of the church as Christ's body. Still, some divergences are "not conflicts *within* the church so much as *about* the church," lying beyond the possibility of present concord, "there being no common object of love." In those cases we must pursue conversion.[11]

No doubt the ecclesiastical situation has changed drastically since New Testament times. Today some church structures may be more formally unified and institutionally systematized than those of the early Christian period. Given the very plurality of these structures or "churches," doctrinal discipline operates differently—not least in the absence of any original apostles. To propose specific ecclesiastical mechanisms for handling gospel-level doctrinal division would largely reveal our own context as authors. That said, however, for the mode of evangelical catholicity in which this book is operating, the foregoing New Testament survey entails two summary implications.

First, *identifying* the gospel. As good news its heart is announcement of God's glorious, saving and self-communicating deeds. The ultimate revelation comes in Jesus Christ fulfilling the mission he received from the Father in the power of the Holy Spirit. The human story behind these deeds is that of Israel and its divinely chosen vocation to bless the world.[12] Like an arch, the gospel has both a center and framing comprehensiveness. Its announcement embraces all that God accomplishes in redeeming cursed creation—cosmos and not just human chaos. The gospel confronts systems and not just individual sins or sinners. Yet, though comprehensive in its coverage, the good news conveys a central focus. Its story definitively iden-

---

[10]John Webster, *The Domain of the Word: Scripture and Theological Reason* (London: T&T Clark, 2012), p. 166.

[11]Ibid., p. 169.

[12]This approach to the gospel is largely compatible with Scot McKnight, *The King Jesus Gospel: The Original Good News Revisited* (Grand Rapids: Zondervan, 2011), and much from N. T. Wright (e.g., *How God Became King: The Forgotten Story of the Gospels* [New York: HarperOne, 2012]), although the latter's affirmations are typically wiser than his critiques and denials (see Kevin J. Vanhoozer, "Wrighting the Wrongs of the Reformation? The State of the Union with Christ in St. Paul and Protestant Soteriology," in *Jesus, Paul and the People of God: A Theological Dialogue with N. T. Wright*, ed. Nicholas Perrin and Richard B. Hays [Downers Grove, IL: InterVarsity Press, 2011], pp. 235-58). McKnight correctly studies gospel terminology in Scripture—albeit as one aspect of its contemporary theological delineation—and both thinkers helpfully discern the priority this places on the story of Jesus vis-à-vis Israel.

tifies Israel's God in Jesus Christ, so what became "orthodox" Christology is its animating New Testament principle. Denying Jesus' fully divine or human identity is tantamount to denying the gospel. Accordingly, the gospel insists that nothing supplant Christ's lordship in accomplishing salvation—neither in directing how the church lives throughout her sanctification nor in determining Christians' status at the initial point when they enter into God's justification. Romans and Galatians in particular define the gospel with reference to justification by faith alone, not because that is all the gospel contains but because its celebration of divine glory and grace among Jews and Gentiles would be nullified if clarity on this point were lost. Union with Christ is the more embracing category, of clearer first-order dogmatic rank. Still, the sanctification of the church and the redemption of the cosmos must be consistent with Christ's justification of God and sinners.

Thus, second, *preserving* the gospel. Multiple conceptual frameworks may be used for proclamation since the Bible itself does that. Positive use of core confessional formulae, combined with protective use of certain boundary markers, actually preserves rather than destroys this contextual freedom. We easily forget that the Pauline defense of justification by faith alone against any alternative gospel welcomes Gentiles into Christian liberty—unleashing the true gospel in new contexts. Similarly Johannine defenses of christological integrity, along with Petrine and other defenses of Christ's ethical authority, promote authentic charity—protecting Christians from schismatic counterfeits. The twin foci of gospel-level doctrine in the New Testament, then, are Christology—his person and work, inextricably linked—and ethics, promoting love and proscribing licentiousness. Losing these foci shrouds the light in darkness, spurning life in favor of death.

To be sure, the New Testament knows nothing of modern academic debate or ecumenical dialogue. Its priority is churchly preservation of gospel truth in a pluralistic context of imperious threats. This preservation does not, however, preclude dialogue with non- or heretical Christians; it simply prescribes the mode of that dialogue. Authentic gospel dialogue is missional, seeking to promote the truth and persuade others. Authentic dialogue is gentle, conforming our words and deeds to the love of Christ we commend (1 Pet 3:15-16). Authentic dialogue is evangelical, maintaining relational clarity about the truth and forms of life that do not conform to it.

Ministry and ministry: Maintaining fellowship. First Corinthians hints at a second level of Christian division and dogmatic rank by mentioning allegiances to various leaders such as Apollos, Cephas and Paul. At this level, the integrity of the gospel is not threatened; Christian fellowship remains, even if ministry is pursued separately. One way to provide brief treatment of this level is to focus on a crucial narrative of disagreement between Paul and Barnabas about whether to take John Mark along on another missionary journey. The story appears in a striking context, Acts 15:36-41, shortly after the happy resolution of the Jerusalem Council concerning inclusion of Gentile converts. In that case a common framework emerged from new understanding of Old Testament hopes, prompted by narratives of prophetic fulfillment among the early Christians. The common framework did not mandate uniformity of either mission or reception, making space for freedom within appropriate limits.[13]

The disagreement between Paul and Barnabas was admittedly "sharp," παροξυσμός, perhaps involving anger.[14] Barnabas headed to his homeland, Cyprus (Acts 15:39), while Acts explicitly records only Paul's churchly commendation (Acts 15:40). However, other factors mitigate any judgment against Barnabas and simply in favor of Paul. Barnabas, the son of encouragement (Acts 4:36), was later vindicated in his rehabilitation of Mark—by no less than Paul himself, with Luke present (2 Tim 4:11). In fact Paul's commendation may need to be explicit since Barnabas was the senior partner and more believers may have sided with him.[15] Barnabas was actually accomplishing part of the planned mission, returning to the first scenes of the earlier missionary journey, prior to Mark's point of desertion (Acts 13:4-13). Neither Paul nor Barnabas is clearly favored in the narrative.

Regrettable as aspects of this case may seem, then, at worst God brings good out of tragedy. Any tinge of sadness gives way to celebrating divine resourcefulness, as earlier when the gospel extended beyond Jerusalem to Judea and Samaria via persecution (Acts 8:1). In the present case, collabo-

---

[13]Appealing to Timothy Wiarda, "The Jerusalem Council and the Theological Task," *JETS* 46, no. 2 (2003): 233-48, David G. Peterson (*The Acts of the Apostles*, PNTC [Grand Rapids: Eerdmans, 2009], pp. 442-46) emphasizes that the focus of the narrative lies not on commending a decision-making process but on communicating doctrinal provision for the Gentiles.
[14]Peterson, *Acts*, pp. 447-48.
[15]Ibid., p. 449.

ration becomes impossible, yet waiting for agreement is counterproductive. Hence the minimal goal should be maintaining fellowship, even when a mission endeavor cannot be shared. God can use such situations to multiply ministry when necessary. Not every doctrinal or denominational division fits this paradigm. Gospel-level differences cannot; neither, at a third level, do many intracongregation differences treated below. All the same, the present case remains doctrinally relevant despite its surface concern over a ministry decision. Paul and Barnabas undoubtedly could have appealed to theological principle(s) in support of their positions even if personal gifts and tendencies may have played their part too.[16] Sometimes apparently competing principles encourage different practices without threatening the integrity of the gospel. Likewise doctrinal disagreements frequently transcend divergent biblical exegesis—about which views may be right or wrong, or better than others—to express alternative theological emphases or arrangements of principles. Fellowship need not be broken even though collaboration may prove impossible.

What does fellowship mean in such contexts? Luke's narrative gives no indication that Paul and Barnabas stopped recognizing each other as brothers in Christ or broke eucharistic communion. What a breach of fellowship might entail appears in 1 Corinthians 5, where discipline would involve no sharing of the Lord's Supper, no further acknowledgment of shared church life and even no signaling (through table fellowship) of shared identity in Christ. By positive contrast, fellowship means finding each other to belong to Christ, to have membership together in his body the church (whether of the same local gathering or not) and therefore—from a Protestant perspective—to be welcome communicants in the sacred meal celebrating such common life. On that basis further expressions of Christian fellowship can ensue.

On this account the very point of evangelical theology is to celebrate provision for ongoing doctrinal debate and divergent practices together with pursuit of whatever Christian fellowship and even collaboration remain

---

[16]It is a bit speculative, though plausible, to propose that Barnabas's gift of encouragement made him helpful to Mark but unduly pliant in the episode of Galatians 2:13, while noting Paul's more resolute tendencies, as in F. F. Bruce, *The Book of the Acts*, rev. ed., NICNT (Grand Rapids: Eerdmans, 1988), p. 302.

possible. Of course the original context of Acts 15:36-41 did not contain fundamentally distinct denominations or separated churches. Just so, its paradigm cannot today authorize or identify one purportedly right structure alone, or apply directly therein. Neither can it fully mitigate interecclesiastical differences, at least those stemming from precisely the situation this text depicts, when the issue is not preserving Christian fellowship but pursuing incompatible ministry decisions. Often, not to decide is to decide, and sooner or later mission must proceed separately. Acts 15:36-41 does not apply purely and simply to evangelical theology, but it does offer a partial rationale and a suggestive paradigm for proper Protestant ecumenism.

The same mind: Pursuing collaboration. Beyond gospel-level, necessary divisions (in which dialogue may be cautiously pursued) and ministry-ministry divisions (in which fellowship is vital to preserve), there are also intracongregation differences, of lowest dogmatic rank. This third level, at which ongoing collaboration is obligatory despite disagreement, is evident from Romans 14–15. Leaving aside endless debates over its precise historical context, the text's crucial issue is not just which theological principle is right, but how clearly biblical principle is even at stake. God allots to each a measure of faith (Rom 12:3). This faith ought to result in full conviction (Rom 14:5) about how to live gratefully unto the Lord (Rom 14:6-9), and mutual acceptance of others' accountability before the Lord (Rom 14:1, 12) instead of judgmental contempt for their perceived weakness (Rom 14:3-4, 10). Hence Christians ought not put stumbling blocks before others but rather walk in love (Rom 14:13-15). Serving Christ by sometimes sacrificing ourselves to pursue peace and edification, Christians actually protect even the reputation of that which others might regard as evil (Rom 14:16-20).

Paul is clear that God's kingdom is about the fruit of the Spirit rather than certain kinds of regulations (Rom 14:17). Paul does not contradict what he says elsewhere by allowing for ethical license here. Instead, we may disagree about the ongoing force of possible regulations, given a different eschatological context, or even about the propriety of certain ways of life. These ethical matters entail broader doctrinal accounts, of ecclesiology and eschatology, for example. Blessed, on the one hand, is the person not condemned by what they approve; faithful, on the other hand, is the person who lives out their conviction before God. The freedom of the gospel entails neither ignoring the needs of others nor becoming servile to their whims (Rom 14:22-23). Paul does not preclude theological admonition and debate over these ἀδιάφορα, but he does prioritize Christlike love—without neglecting either personal freedom or accountability.

The historical context behind another relevant conflict, in Philippians, is likewise debatable. But similar features pertain. Paul prays that love would abound in discernment, testing to discover what is truly excellent (Phil 1:9-10). The Philippians need to learn the same mind, that of Christ in his humility and regard for others (Phil 2:1-11). Timothy and Epaphroditus provide concrete examples of prioritizing Christ's interests, and therefore others over themselves (Phil 2:19-30). Paul so prioritizes proclaiming Christ that he rejoices when it happens, whatever the motives (Phil 1:18). By contrast the Philippians must beware of those who promote circumcision in place of Christ as the way of attaining life (Phil 3:1-16). Ironically, circumcision would stem from fleshly confidence that really leads to indulgence instead of obedience (Phil 3:17-21). In that context Paul addresses apparent conflict between Euodia and Syntyche (Phil 4:2-3), who need help to share the same mind. Paul does not explicitly specify the right answer to embrace, whether or not the theology of Philippians 3 is germane to the dispute. As members of the same congregation (and sharers in Paul's gospel struggle), what the women need is not primarily an answer but the right mindset, focused on following Christ.[17]

Returning finally to 1 Corinthians, Paul similarly pleads for sharing a common congregational mind—the mind of Christ—imitating Jesus in the very way Christians deal with one another. The central, ethical portion of the letter is therefore no surprise. On the one hand, Paul is resolute against sexual immorality. The Corinthian Christians are wrong to tolerate immorality that even pagans find disgraceful (1 Cor 5). They wrongly use freedom in Christ as license for immorality that does not build up their body, both personally and corporately (1 Cor 6). Ironically, they risk vulnerability to wrongful passions by promoting false ideals of abstinence (1 Cor 7). So too, when it comes to meat sacrificed to idols, they wrongly focus on surface scruples over the divine commands truly at stake—avoiding idolatry and

---

[17]In several books, such as *Cruciformity: Paul's Narrative Spirituality of the Cross* (Grand Rapids: Eerdmans, 2001), Michael Gorman has written compellingly on the crucial theme.

embracing the advance of the gospel (1 Cor 8–10). Knowledge can help—clarifying that an idol is nothing—but it can also hurt, if its claimants pridefully disregard the needs of brothers and sisters. The love celebrated in 1 Corinthians 13 and the New Testament gospel itself is not without ethical boundaries—being shaped by the cross contrary to self-centered, contemporary fashions.

Neither doctrinal convictions nor ethical boundaries are simplistically set aside by this third category. Its larger context includes the other two levels: the Christ-defined gospel and collaboration in its mission. Within the boundaries of the former, the latter invites freedom. The Christian leaders mentioned by 1 Corinthians are free to pursue diverse ministries. The Corinthians are not free to divide over these. In this era before the end, yet after centuries of division, we may need the freedom to remain in fellowship though ministries remain apart. Within particular congregations, we frequently must remain in eucharistic and missional fellowship despite principled differences. We do so by acknowledging others' ultimate accountability before God, and the differing levels of clarity that various issues present. Fellow congregants in particular and Christians in general simultaneously need to dialogue with and even admonish one another (Rom 15:14) while pursuing peace and the self-effacing mind of Christ (Rom 15:17-19).

As the next major section of this chapter makes even clearer, it is not just that prospective divisions are of different kinds—concerning the gospel, its ministry and personal conflicts or even disputed principles—but so too are their contexts. In New Testament passages with the gospel at stake, the apostles typically confront and correct false teaching that has infiltrated a congregation or city. In passages like Acts 15, the cases involve recognition of and collaboration in ministries that transcend a given church body, whether geographically on the large scale or interpersonally on a smaller scale. In passages with injunctions to pursue the same mind and avoid disturbing the peace, we return to the congregational level, addressing relationships within which unity is essential: these are situations for discerning how to maintain a common mind even without uniformity of principle or practice.[18] So what about our drastically different contemporary context, in

---

[18]It is necessary to keep in mind the ambiguity of "the church" in a New Testament epistle, when both household congregations and citywide structure(s) may be involved.

which the original apostles are no longer present, except through writings whose interpretation is now precisely the issue; in which, for Protestants, congregation-transcending ministries now lack a Jerusalem-type center around which to pursue definitive consensus; and in which congregational discipline addressing conflicts is low in frequency partly because it has little cultural effect? Now, as perhaps at the earliest, people can divide only to conquer somewhere else. Beyond the categories of divisions just provided, then, discernment becomes necessary to assess the contexts for different kinds of relationships. Evangelical theologians must particularize such discernment for rendering churchly service not just in scholarly guilds but also in ecumenical engagements.

EVANGELICAL ECUMENISM: CONTESTED TRADITION(S)

This framework of dogmatic rank for theological ecumenism, distinguishing between gospel-level dialogue, ministry-level fellowship and congregation-level collaboration, should fit evangelical theology quite comfortably. That claim may be counterintuitive at first glance, given the surfeit of Protestant denominations and parachurch organizations claiming evangelical faith. If, however, biblical unity is not just institutionally monolithic but missionally active, then orthodox, pietist Protestant ecumenism might take eschatologically provisional and evangelically free forms. The purpose of this chapter's third section is to sustain that argument more deeply—to articulate a form of mere evangelical theology in principle that accounts for its inevitably (and properly to some degree) contested nature in practice.

Theological fellowship: Current evangelical alternatives. Major approaches to evangelical identity and fellowship are helpfully laid out in a recent collection we referenced earlier.[19] Exploring these four approaches in greater detail here will underscore nuances of our own. Particular sympathies are evident between Kevin Bauder's fundamentalism and Albert Mohler's confessional evangelicalism on the one hand, and John Stackhouse's generic evangelicalism and Roger Olson's postconservative evangelicalism on the other. Thus some suggest that there are really two basic

---

[19]Andrew David Naselli and Collin Hansen, eds., *Four Views on the Spectrum of Evangelicalism*, Counterpoints (Grand Rapids: Zondervan, 2011).

positions, a handy conclusion for many on both the left and the right.[20] Yet nuances of each position are worth exploring, and the two-party narrative oversimplifies the complexity of contemporary evangelical theology—especially since even these four views are not really exhaustive.[21]

The fundamentalist approach begins with commitment to "minimal" Christian fellowship rooted in the basic core of the gospel.[22] The church is ultimately an invisible reality but strives for a form of visible, evangelical unity on earth. People may not have to know explicitly all gospel truths in order to receive salvation, but denying a fundamental truth means implicitly denying the gospel. In pursuit of more maximal Christian fellowship, fundamentalists account for various levels tied to the importance of particular doctrines. Separation among Christians may be necessary, even secondarily among those who agree on gospel fundamentals. They may have different attitudes in approaching doctrinal and practical disagreements—with some demonstrating a lack of discernment by refusing to separate from non-Christians or compromised Christians. Bauder acknowledges that the fundamentalist movement languishes today: internal tensions are present due to inheriting anti-intellectualism from populist revivalism and failing to confront the parasite of hyperfundamentalism adequately. Nevertheless Bauder defends the biblical idea of fundamentalism and accordingly a chastened version of the movement, cautiously but more openly interacting with conservative evangelicals.

Confessional evangelicalism acknowledges that evangelical identity is essentially contested while continuing to insist that doctrinal criteria remain essential.[23] Evangelicalism assuredly lacks a magisterium, but merely phenomenal approaches provide no foundation for enduring coherence or credibility. Thus a confessional approach focuses on convictional continuity with the formulas of the Protestant Reformation, insisting that evangelicalism should acknowledge both centered and bounded sets. Proper theological

---

[20]Olson could take this as further evidence of his narrative about pietism versus Protestant orthodoxy, while Andrew David Naselli, "Conclusion," in *Four Views on the Spectrum of Evangelicalism*, reaches a similar suggestion on p. 214.

[21]David Bebbington, "About the Definition of Evangelicalism . . ." (Review of *Four Views on the Spectrum of Evangelicalism*), *Evangelical Studies Bulletin* 83 (Fall 2012): 1-6.

[22]Kevin T. Bauder, "Fundamentalism," in *Four Views*, pp. 19-49.

[23]R. Albert Mohler Jr., "Confessional Evangelicalism," in *Four Views*, pp. 68-96.

triage, then, distinguishes between first-level (i.e., Trinity, full deity and humanity of Christ, justification by faith alone, and authority of Scripture), second-level (e.g., meaning and mode of baptism) and third-level (e.g., eschatology) doctrines. Differences over the first level are fundamental, while at the second level they are church dividing but acceptable within evangelical cooperation. Third-level variety is possible within ongoing, close congregational fellowship. The goal should be to avoid the collapse of first-order doctrines and obsession or schism over third-order doctrines. Second-order doctrines are therefore the most difficult to discern and address. Ironically, Mohler's use of the term *confessional* despite a dearth of any specifically binding confessional documents increases the difficulty of defending these particular doctrinal distinctions.

Generic evangelicalism in a sense lacks a proper adjective, suggesting that alternatives share the same mistake: they provide definitions that fit themselves best, inadequately accounting for others.[24] The aspiration of evangelical theology, on this view, is simply to be Christian theology in tenets, affections and practices; evangelical theology stems from missional initiatives, pursuing church renewal on a different level than denominations or broader traditions. Evangelical theology is inherently radical, pursuing a return to basic roots and reform at particular times or places. The famous historical quadrilateral of evangelical characteristics—activism, biblicism, conversionism, crucicentrism—proposed by David Bebbington, augmented variously since, here gains an additional factor from Stackhouse: transdenominational cooperation.[25] Evangelicals are not simply conservative Protestants whom pollsters find holding certain beliefs; they pursue interaction across denominational lines with others who share doctrinal affirmations and renewing aspirations. These affirmations and aspirations function together as a set, making the whole

---

[24]John G. Stackhouse Jr., "Generic Evangelicalism," in *Four Views*, pp. 116-42.
[25]As in our introduction, see David W. Bebbington, *Evangelicalism in Modern Britain: A History from the 1730s to the 1980s* (London: Unwin Hyman, 1989), pp. 2-17. See also Timothy Larsen, "Defining and Locating Evangelicalism," in *The Cambridge Companion to Evangelical Theology*, ed. Larsen and Daniel J. Treier (Cambridge: Cambridge University Press, 2007), pp. 1-14, which highlights the originating historical context presumed by Bebbington and reworks the characteristics so as to stress the personal work of the Holy Spirit. Bebbington's review of the four-views volume challenges Stackhouse's proposal, suggesting that his additional factor fails to account for contradictory historical evidence such as Church of England–only evangelicals ("About the Definition of Evangelicalism . . . ," p. 5).

more than simply the sum of its parts. Orthopraxy, not just orthodoxy, is at issue. On Stackhouse's view, the more important question is not the historical or definitional one of recognizing authentic evangelicalism; instead, our priority should be discerning the propriety of cooperation with or among certain people or groups. Institutions, particularly in America, may generate definitional dilemmas that some evangelicals need to face, but these quandaries do not globally put the gospel itself at risk.

Olson's postconservative evangelicalism, even more overtly than the others, reflects his personal approach; the term *postconservative* has covered alternative standpoints elsewhere.[26] Olson's version begins and ends with anecdotes, continuing to reflect his frequent assertions about tensions between pietism and Protestant orthodoxy, carrying along in tow the aforementioned two-party evangelical debate between traditionalists and reformists. Olson's account claims that evangelicalism has no defined boundaries but is only a centered set. To distinguish between evangelical organizations and the evangelical movement, the latter has a common core while the former need not. Asking rhetorically (with a null answer) the question behind this present section, Olson writes, "What is 'evangelical theology' but theology done by evangelicals?"[27] Conversionism does not just identify evangelicals based on their location within a set of boundaries. It is also interested in the direction of their current movements toward or away from a center. *Sola Scriptura* means that evangelicals reserve the right to reform historic Christian orthodoxy even if they respect it. Because active piety remains his primary consideration, Olson categorizes some groups that formally reject creedal Christology as evangelical, while other, more officially "orthodox" groups fall afoul of orthopraxy criteria and count as nonevangelical.

---

[26]Roger E. Olson, "Postconservative Evangelicalism," in *Four Views*, pp. 161-87. For instance, as noted earlier, this term is used by Kevin J. Vanhoozer, "The Voice and the Actor: A Dramatic Proposal About the Ministry and Minstrelsy of Theology," in *Evangelical Futures: A Conversation on Theological Method*, ed. John G. Stackhouse Jr. (Grand Rapids: Baker, 2000), p. 76, largely exempted from the critiques of Grenz found in Millard J. Erickson, Paul Kjoss Helseth and Justin Taylor, eds., *Reclaiming the Center: Confronting Evangelical Accommodation in Postmodern Times* (Wheaton, IL: Crossway, 2004), p. 17. Vanhoozer interacts with Grenz's legacy in "Three (or More) Ways of Triangulating Theology: On the Very Idea of a Trinitarian System," in *Revisioning, Renewing, and Rediscovering the Triune Center*, ed. Derek Tidball, Brian Harris and Jason Sexton (Eugene, OR: Cascade, 2014).

[27]Olson, "Postconservative Evangelicalism," p. 165.

The four essays and subsequent responses contain mixtures of historical, sociological and theological criteria. Despite many insights, consistently missing are overtly scriptural accounts of apostolicity and catholicity, of how evangelical fellowship might reflect and contribute to the biblical fidelity and wholeness of the church(es). Bauder comes closest in one respect, trying to distinguish gospel doctrines from others while providing an account of how division and levels of fellowship between Christians should relate to each. Interestingly enough, he is the only contributor who makes substantial, overt reference to Scripture. Mohler provides a three-level distinction between various doctrines, a superficial parallel to the structure we proposed above. But Mohler does not develop deeply biblical or confessionally informed criteria for either the category scheme or its use.[28] Olson does not provide for division over doctrine apart from divergent pieties. Stackhouse focuses basically on two categories: doctrines that unite evangelicals as a subset of all Christians, and those that indicate when certain evangelicals are aberrant yet still evangelical since they are still Christian.

An ongoing ecclesiological deficit therefore remains. The four views above tend to accept the fact of evangelical cooperation (to some degree) without arguing for its value. In a broad sense our appeal for "mere" evangelicalism may seem to have the greatest affinity with Stackhouse's "generic" category. However, we neither make transdenominational cooperation historically or theologically definitive in the same sense as he does, nor do we take self-identifications or aspirations quite as seriously in our approach. For at stake are Trinitarian and crucicentric verities that may make recognizing authentic evangelical theology more essential for certain institutions or relationships than a generic approach allows. Moreover, we attempt here to clarify the value, not just appeal to the fact, of evangelical cooperation—a deficit that this chapter's sketch of properly Protestant theological fellowship starts to remedy. We now provide a further supplement to that sketch by pondering whether evangelical theology can be more than just the sum of

---

[28]Similarly the helpful treatment of catechesis by J. I. Packer with Gary A. Parrett, "The Return to Catechesis: Lessons from the Great Tradition," in *Renewing the Evangelical Mission*, pp. 111-33, distinguishes four catechetical levels: Christian consensus, evangelical essentials, denominational distinctives, congregational commitments (pp. 129-30). The several broad parallels such as this provide basic confirmation of our approach, while still indicating the need for careful biblical delineation of the categories and a theology of discernment concerning their deployment.

its parts—more than just the theology done by particular evangelicals.

Conservative Protestants and ecumenical theology. Theologians interact professionally and missionally with the academy and non-Christian scholars, spiritually and vocationally with their congregations. Twenty centuries after the apostolic era, in the wake of a divided Christendom, the Scriptures give no easy answers to the ecclesiological questions affecting theological vocations, whether about ordination or whatever else. Different evangelical traditions respond in varied polities, so "mere evangelicalism" cannot promote a uniformly specific approach. Instead evangelical theologians can and must exercise discernment, pursuing ecumenical engagement appropriate for their confessional and vocational circumstances.

The multilevel framework above provides a clarifying biblical rubric for that discernment, as well as a broader rationale for the pursuit of evangelical theology. At the gospel level, theologians pursue mission to those outside the faith and fellowship with those inside the church, alongside various possibilities of dialogue and friendship in each sphere. At the ministry level, varieties of Christian friendship and collaboration remain possible and vital despite forms of ecclesiastical separation. At the congregational level, eucharistic fellowship nurtures pursuit of a common mind even if disagreements remain over ἀδιάφορα. From missional presence to dialogue, friendship, fellowship and collaboration—discerning how to navigate these spheres of ascending influence and mutual accountability leaves no substitute for evangelical φρόνησις, emplotting particular circumstances within Christ-shaped biblical narrative(s). The changes in historical context mentioned earlier may entail that wise responses to doctrinal differences are sometimes ἀδιάφορα themselves. For instance, one evangelical theologian discerns a call to remain within their mainline Protestant denomination; another discerns a need to depart for the sake of their own or a family's spiritual growth.[29] These decisions depend on wisely exercising personal freedom for churchly service, albeit while articulating how the biblical analogy of faith is their

---

[29]For a recent example of the former, see Thomas C. Oden, "Do Not Rashly Tear Asunder: Why the Beleaguered Faithful Should Stay and Reform Their Churches," *First Things* (April 2012): 40-44. The latter is a common occurrence, as noted by William J. Abraham, "Inclusivism, Idolatry and the Survival of the (Fittest) Faithful," in *The Community of the Word: Toward an Evangelical Ecclesiology*, ed. Mark Husbands and Daniel J. Treier (Downers Grove, IL: InterVarsity Press, 2005), pp. 131-45, especially pp. 142-43.

impetus. More broadly, by nature evangelical theology promotes communion and collaboration between those whose actions in such cases—and
ecclesiological rationales—may differ.

Beyond informing wise exercise of particular spiritual gifts, 1 Corinthians
issues a profound challenge to an increasingly postdenominational, supposedly postmodern and possibly postliberal epoch. First Corinthians 15
makes clear that Christ's resurrection is a watershed issue. Sharing this
gospel crux explains why evangelical theology increasingly finds fellowship
and common cause with much Catholic and Orthodox theology as well as
some (so-called) postliberal Protestantism.[30] Yet, at the same time, tensions
have emerged within postliberal circles over apologetics and history, as well
as sexual ethics. First Corinthians 5 and 6 make clear the watershed significance of the latter—still another reason why postliberal, and intraevangelical,
conversations can be fraught with complexity. Christology and even ethics,
after all, can raise issues of gospel-level dogmatic rank. Contemporary debates over sexual ethics sometimes take inappropriate prominence over
Christological orthodoxy. However, as noted in the biblical-theological
sketch above, promotion of immorality contradicts Christ's lordship, affecting the integrity of gospel witness. Disagreeing over sexual ethics means
differing, to some degree, over the story of Jesus.[31] Assessing the ecclesiological significance of that connection will test evangelical Protestant ecumenical φρόνησις for the foreseeable future.

In this context the concerns of 1 Corinthians hint at the potentially unique

---

[30]For different sets of doubts about the coherent existence of postliberal theology, see George
Hunsinger, "Postliberal Theology," in *The Cambridge Companion to Postmodern Theology*, ed.
Kevin J. Vanhoozer (Cambridge: Cambridge University Press, 2003), pp. 42-57, and Paul J.
DeHart, *The Trial of Witnesses: The Rise and Decline of Postliberal Theology*, Challenges in Con-
temporary Theology (Malden, MA: Blackwell, 2006). Both are insightful; nevertheless, consider
the linkage between whatever *postliberal* might mean and the language of TIS in Daniel J. Treier,
"What Is Theological Interpretation? An Ecclesial Reduction," *International Journal of Systematic
Theology* 12, no. 2 (April 2010): 144-61. Consider also George Lindbeck's earlier remark about
evangelicals offering the best possibility of realizing the postliberal agenda: "I will also say that
if the sort of research program represented by postliberalism has a real future as a communal
enterprise for the church, it's more likely to be carried on by evangelicals than anyone else" ("A
Panel Discussion," in *The Nature of Confession: Evangelicals and Postliberals in Conversation*, ed.
Timothy R. Phillips and Dennis L. Okholm [Downers Grove, IL: InterVarsity Press, 1996], pp.
252-53).

[31]For one account of such divergence, see Kathryn Greene-McCreight, "The Logic of the Interpretation of Scripture and the Church's Debate over Sexual Ethics," in *Homosexuality, Science, and
the "Plain Sense" of Scripture*, ed. David L. Balch (Grand Rapids: Eerdmans, 2000), pp. 242-60.

contribution of evangelical theology: gospel-level christological and ethical fidelity to Scripture, freedom for ministry-level diversity and fellowship. Yet some historical and sociological accounts of evangelical theology already challenge its past coherence, and two-party theological accounts highlight basic incompatibilities going forward—most notably, between Protestant orthodox traditionalists and pietists more open to certain reforms. Without claiming to address all these practical complexities, the account offered here tries to defend the possible coherence of evangelical theology as an intellectual tradition—precisely by underscoring the unique kind of tradition it could be in principle. This defense of an evangelical tradition incorporates a series of distinctions.

First, Olson's distinction between the evangelical movement and an evangelical ethos points to a related distinction: *between theologies written by particular theologians secondarily sharing the evangelical ethos and the doctrinal conversation (broadly) or consensus (narrowly) of those primarily identified in terms of the "evangelical" movement.* So, for instance, Herman Bavinck's theology may be evangelical in European senses having to do with ethos, and it has been influential within some Anglo-American sectors. All the same, Bavinck's is a self-consciously Dutch Reformed theology, not primarily identifiable in terms of the evangelical movement even though it is secondarily amenable to evangelical ethos and influence. Likewise, one might dub Missouri Synod Lutheran theology evangelical in this secondary sense; fitting within the evangelical movement's theological tradition is not its primary goal. By contrast, figures as diverse as Carl Henry and Donald Bloesch, whether strongly affiliated with a particular Protestant denomination (Bloesch) or not (Henry), had "evangelical" as their primary theological identifier. In between, boundary cases such as Michael Horton position some works primarily within narrower ecclesial circles, with others seeking a wider evangelical audience.[32] In short, these examples begin to address the distinction between evangelical theology and theology done by

---

[32]Horton's four-volume dogmatics comes from the mainline Presbyterian publisher Westminster John Knox. His one-volume shorter dogmatics textbook comes from the evangelical publisher Zondervan. As interest in the Reformed tradition increases among younger evangelicals, Horton can be an exception proving the rule: addressing not just broader academic but also generically evangelical audiences with self-consciously Reformed writing—and interacting generously without compromise.

evangelicals—without functionally denying the former, defending the diversity of the latter.

Second, deepening this distinction is a related difference *between elite or formal and popular discourse(s)*. Again particular evangelical strengths and weaknesses obtain. So many publications in evangelical theology have taken textbook form that truly elite discourse has been comparatively lacking, while much formal discourse has been more intraevangelical and pedagogical than broadly academic or ecumenical. When characterizing an evangelical theological tradition, then, should focus rest on popular tendencies or more formal alignments? The present book has no particular stake in legislating how historical or sociological work on evangelical identity ought to be done, as long as any conceptual analysis is doctrinally astute. Our burden instead concerns evangelical theology as an intellectual discipline—not necessarily depending on the vagaries of academic guilds, but pursuing carefully ordered reflection. In principle this task is open to all evangelicals, professional theologians or not, ordained or not. In practice, though, much of its teaching and writing will come from those having specialized privileges and responsibilities. "Evangelical theology" as a fuzzy characterization of mainstream tendencies may reflect more unified popular trends than outliers and academic nitpickers would suggest: a doctrine like substitutionary atonement may be widespread across subtraditions though disputed especially among their elites. Academic "evangelical theology," though, generates written evidence that is easier to access and to analyze, sometimes making evangelical variety more apparent than unity.

Third, one can add a useful distinction *between coherence and comprehensive agreement (or even consensus) within a tradition*. Many act as if evangelical theology, to be coherent, must have debate come to an end. The idea seems to be that asserting theological boundaries should be enough to banish violators from the field, or conversely that providing historical and sociological counterexamples should be enough to banish claims about consensus boundaries. Missing from both of these sides, though, is adequate understanding of how a tradition works. As Alasdair MacIntyre suggests, humans are bearers of tradition as historical beings, requiring narratively shaped self-understanding:

For all reasoning takes place within the context of some traditional mode of thought, transcending through criticism and invention the limitations of what had hitherto been reasoned in that tradition; this is as true of modern physics as of medieval logic. Moreover when a tradition is in good order it is always partially constituted by an argument about the goods the pursuit of which gives to that tradition its particular point and purpose.

More pointedly, "Traditions, when vital, embody continuities of conflict. . . . A living tradition then is an historically extended, socially embodied argument, and an argument precisely in part about the goods which constitute that tradition."[33] On this account, what makes a tradition is not a set of uniform answers but common practices and arguments. Ecumenical efforts at mirroring Scripture among orthodox, pietist Protestants, for good and ill, define an evangelical theological tradition whose expectation is to generate those extended arguments.[34]

Fourth, within this tradition—distinct, not separate, from theology done by evangelicals—one must distinguish *between normative and prescriptive accounts.* The difficulties faced by descriptive accounts simply have to be acknowledged, largely left in historical and sociological hands (even to the degree that they involve theology). A normative account involves some description, characterizing the generally pertinent norms of a tradition while expecting exceptions (otherwise it would not be interesting to try specifying norms). A prescriptive account involves claims about what should be, not in the first instance what is. Now of course a prescriptive account implies description too; totally ignoring current reality would be utopian and perhaps useless. And a normative account intertwines description with prescriptive implications, intentionally or unintentionally. Nevertheless, applying the normative-prescriptive distinction to the goods animating the evangelical theological tradition helps to clarify and even justify its essentially contested character. Alternative prescriptions are not automatic evidence that norms are nonexistent or impossible to generate. Alternative prescriptions are actually part of the norm, given the particular kind of tra-

---

[33]Alasdair C. MacIntyre, *After Virtue: A Study in Moral Theory*, 2nd ed. (Notre Dame, IN: University of Notre Dame Press, 1984), p. 222.
[34]William J. Abraham bluntly insists that if the term *evangelical* went missing tomorrow, we would have to invent it ("Church and Churches," in *The Oxford Handbook of Evangelical Theology*, ed. Gerald R. McDermott [Oxford: Oxford University Press, 2010], pp. 296-309, at p. 303).

dition evangelical theology is; at the same time, evangelical prescriptions inevitably assume that the Bible functions in a normative fashion.

Thus, fifth and finally, we return to *the distinct but not separate "evangelical theology" and theology done by evangelicals*, with special attention to confessional integrity. Indisputably the evangelical movement has no magisterium or particularly effective mechanisms of formal doctrinal discipline—a point Olson celebrates, Mohler concedes and Horton in a sense champions when prioritizing his confessional tradition.[35] Yes, evangelicalism is like C. S. Lewis's hallway or a village green. Churches are the rooms within which actually to live, rendering the hallway or village green secondary. The proposal of this chapter is basically amenable to that perspective, with this amendment: the absence of formal churchly mechanisms for doctrinal discipline does not preclude the existence or importance of an evangelical tradition, a tradition of a different (and ecumenical) kind. Indeed, a hallway and a village green are quite different: a hallway lies within a shared household, whereas a village green is public, visited occasionally by those of separate households. Preference for the latter approach to evangelical theology could be revealing about the legitimacy (or lack thereof) a theologian grants to other churches. Even within the hallway approach, confessional (or nonconfessional, pietist) theologians are free to focus on the integrity of particular traditions so long as they do not gainsay the pursuit of fellowship and measures of collaboration that the evangelical theological tradition—however undisciplined—makes possible.

Just to the degree that evangelical theology is less formally defined, selective involvement or even principled withdrawal becomes possible. If one publishes with a generic evangelical press for a wider audience, simultaneously counteracting certain materials from that press within or on behalf of one's own church, then evangelical principle is unharmed—whether or not Anglo-American culture increasingly thwarts this approach. No law requires collaboration with all "evangelicals" or else none; the tradition is inherently one of agonistic fellowship and sporadic collaboration. The evangelical

---

[35]Beyond the prior discussion of these figures, it is worth noting Horton's legitimate insistence that J. Gresham Machen–era Presbyterian battles not be interpreted primarily through a fundamentalism-modernism lens but rather in terms of intraconfessional identity (Old versus New School Presbyterianism) as well. Charles Finney's soteriology in important respects was closer to the Council of Trent than the magisterial Protestant Reformers.

ethos entails a patchwork consensus, ever fragile and difficult to define, overly influenced by particular figures, institutions and relationships. The goods involved are precisely those of trans- or nondenominational Protestant ecumenism, so the churchly histories to which theologians appeal for self-understanding already comprise conflict. After all, some theological traditions once tried to martyr others.

Attempts to construe evangelical history are always already theological, at least implicitly: norms are partly prescriptive. Similarly, historical norms intrude on contemporary prescriptions: No attempt to address evangelical theological identity can spell out its concepts in a vacuum. Even so, the issues faced by a living tradition change over time; no set of norms will adequately settle identity questions except by informing new prescriptions. The patient both matures and declines: in this case, part of the presenting problem lies in the difficulty of discerning what counts as a malady and what counts as vigor, or which malady to prioritize.

The present distinctions establish that institutionally diverse forms of discipline and historically diffuse norms do not preclude a coherent evangelical theological tradition; they may simply define it. Similar complexities attend other theological traditions about which we regularly speak—not least "ecumenical," "Reformed," "holiness" and "Pentecostal" theologies, to name a few. Divergent norms for doctrinal discipline are among the goods evangelical theology argues about. Its particular subtraditions differ even in their relative amounts and appreciation of written academic discourse. This unique character of the evangelical tradition is worth celebrating, not just criticizing: against the idea that variety precludes unity, there is a core commitment of evangelical catholicity—namely that gospel unity welcomes some variety and accommodates still more. As a tradition of Protestant ecumenical engagement within parameters of informally recognized, shared piety, having distinctive commitment to involving laypersons and less formal discourse, evangelical theology is inevitably agonistic—agonistic about the shared aspiration to be biblical.

"Evangelical theology" therefore designates broadly and narrowly. Broadly, evangelical theology comprises in principle all the theology done in the evangelical movement, with discernment required in practice to distinguish between exceptional and typical cases. Narrowly, evangelical theology coheres as an ecumenical Protestant tradition of orthodox, pietist, biblical reflection. That construal of its narrower sense is essentially contestable, of course: a proposal about what the theological ethos of the evangelical movement should be—not what it is, or can be or comprehensively has been. On this account, evangelical theology's particular eclecticism is not just historically accidental but ecclesiologically principled—it is the flawed genius of what other theological traditions cannot do. It has limitations, to be sure—precisely why eclectic plundering of other traditions is pervasive in practice. Evangelical theology could excel if it used these other resources to address the deficits of its biblical representation, while treasuring that tradition enough to share it humbly and generously.

The multilevel framework provided in this chapter enables particular laypeople, pastors, theologians and churches to maintain Christian fellowship in the gospel, to minister together when possible, and to make space for doctrinal dialogue and disagreement, within whatever freedom of theological φρόνησις God works in them. Two-party advocates may be increasingly correct about historical realities on much of the ground; confessional purists may be ecclesiologically correct, from their perspective, to relegate evangelical engagement to a secondary priority; pietists may be spiritually correct, from their perspective, not to focus on technical precision when defining ecumenical relationships. *Protestant* may almost come to mean nothing more than denial of Orthodox or Catholic claims and affiliation. Some Catholic and Orthodox Christians will share the evangelical ethos despite their churches defining them outside the evangelical movement in principle. None of these points can gainsay the propriety of biblically obedient, christologically orthodox, ecumenical Protestants perceiving and acting on a shared identity. The proposal here could only be falsified *historically* if an orthodox, pietist Protestant discourse coherently characterized by a certain "biblicist" aspiration could never be found. Present-day variety, perhaps even to the point of incoherence by *sociological* measures, we simply have to concede. The core of this proposal is *theological*, to be evaluated in terms of scriptural doctrine, not its likely acceptance or rejection by any contemporary "evangelicals" or interested others. Whether or not this proposal ideally characterizes the movement in the past, or encompasses fully its ethos in the present, it extends the argument about its proper future—celebrating the potential of orthodox, pietist Protestant ecumenism in principle.

Evangelical catholicity pursues whatever level of ecumenical progress is possible in the gospel we share; whatever level of fellowship is possible, both personally and communally, in that light; and whatever level of collaboration is possible despite ongoing differences, in the freedom of the gospel to use our spiritual gifts. Pursuing theological wisdom, evangelical catholicity flowers differently in various traditions, polities and even scholarly vocations. It should not surprise that some orthodox, pietist Protestant theologians are more transdenominationally active than others: varied personal and vocational discernment should only dismay us when either the basic truth of the gospel or its gift of fellowship seems to be fundamentally diminished.

For all that varied discernment of personal callings, nevertheless this chapter has offered a theological framework for evangelical catholicity. The focus has been on the *agents* of mirroring Scripture, *who* participates in the drama of theological discourse. To answer that question in a manner consistent with the theological end of wisdom, and the theological and historical manner of biblical exegesis, requires an evangelical account of catholicity—addressing how academic theologians may serve the church not only in particular congregations but also in broader church and parachurch institutions, ecumenical relationships and missional dialogue. Having thus established some incentives for intentionally "evangelical" theological work, we must now develop a more detailed framework for evangelical "theology" as an intellectual discipline. In the final chapter, we explore in further detail how scholarly theological excellence contributes to mirroring Scripture.

Chapter Six

IN PURSUIT OF
SCHOLARLY EXCELLENCE

> *The purpose of playing, whose end, both at the first and now,*
> *was and is, to hold, as 'twere the mirror up to nature—to show*
> *virtue her own feature, scorn her own image, and the*
> *very age and body of time his form and pressure.*
>
> HAMLET, ACT III, SCENE 2, LINES 20-24

OUR PROPOSAL TURNS, finally, to the *intellectual practice* of mirroring Scripture, *how* evangelical "theologians" should engage their scholarly discipline(s). Yet academic theology perennially vexes evangelicals: alongside the general risks of intellectual aspiration and arrogance come the more specific risks of proof-texting on the one side and extrabiblical abstraction on the other. A new account of evangelical theology mirroring Scripture should make appropriate space for its full potential of scholarly engagement, believing that true intellectual excellence can actually deepen biblical fidelity and spiritual vitality. To defend that claim requires, first, focusing on spiritual vitality: distinguishing between the Corinthian arrogance Paul condemned and the scholarly aspirations this chapter commends. Then, second, detailing the claim requires focusing further on biblical fidelity: delineating how, by way of φρόνησις, the form and content of doctrinal judgment(s) mirror Scripture—not just from the perspective of theological exegesis (as in chapter four) but also in disciplined constructive and dogmatic reflection (here). Third and finally, developing these claims

THEOLOGY AND THE MIRROR OF SCRIPTURE

about theology's intellectual excellence requires focusing on academic creativity: depicting the shapes that evangelical scholarly contributions might take. Deepening intellectual excellence need not result in elitist arrogance or mere abstraction. Instead, genuine intellectual excellence may enhance evangelical theology's missional appeal. More fully digging into the treasures of wisdom hidden in Christ will display the gospel's beauty before church and world alike.

CORINTHIAN REFLECTIONS: LOVE'S TRUE KNOWLEDGE

So, first, the risks of intellectual aspiration and arrogance: Much of the evangelical network, retaining culturally separatist tendencies, remains suspicious of elite discourse.[1] Preceding chapters should begin to reduce—not eliminate—these suspicions biblically. First Corinthians 1–2 affirms true wisdom in Christ over against worldly folly—neither rejecting all "wisdom" pure and simple, nor accepting self-promotion and status envy. First Corinthians 9–10 frees us to enjoy all created goods for God's glory, and to engage all human cultures—including the academy—with the gospel. Still, concerns over intellectual elitism come to further expression through 1 Corinthians 8 and 13.

The words of 1 Corinthians 8:1 are well known: "'Knowledge' puffs up, but love builds up." Lest this slogan mislead, however, it needs context. The issue is not the rejection of knowledge but its proper use. Paul concedes the crucial points that Corinthians claim to know: there is only one true God, idols therefore are nothing, and even food per se is nothing one way or the other (1 Cor 8:4, 7-13). So knowledge as such is not the problem; Paul bases his own position on that knowledge. Moreover Paul places this knowledge within a deeper, more authentically Christian, theological framework in his succeeding chapters.

The challenge is not simply to affirm the oneness of the Creator but to

---

[1]Not all of these suspicions are unfounded, with a distinction between folk and popular (as mass) culture providing helpful nuance in treating evangelical hesitations about scholarship; so Dale M. Coulter, "Evangelicals, Pop Culture, and Mass Culture," *First Things*, February 11, 2014, www.firstthings.com/blogs/firstthoughts/2014/02/evangelicals-pop-culture-and-mass-culture. Elite appeals to aspects of folk culture in Nazi Germany, however, provide a case that further muddies these waters. Appreciating the evangelical populism stemming from the priesthood of all believers, and accommodating its messiness, does not entail avoiding elite intellectual culture as a pervasive plague.

appropriate that truth, which the Corinthians had not adequately done. Really grasping the truth of Christian monotheism would breed intellectual humility rather than arrogance.[2] In addition, humbly grasping truth means edifying others the Creator loves, not serving oneself (1 Cor 8:1-2). True knowledge means loving God, acknowledging that God's love embraces us first (1 Cor 8:3).[3]

This dismantling of Corinthian pretensions depicts theological knowledge in terms quite favorable to true wisdom. On the one hand, such knowledge in itself is not a human achievement; it can easily turn Christians away from the humility needed to love God and others. On the other hand, the key is not knowing less but knowing rightly, even (in one respect) knowing more. The point is not to settle for knowledge but to seek true wisdom, inextricably linked to charity. Nothing in 1 Corinthians 8 actually makes academic endeavors more dangerous than church life; we must not forget that this passage addresses an ecclesiastical context. Pretensions to philosophical elitism were a Corinthian problem, as indeed they could be for Christians today. All the same, though, 1 Corinthians 8 opposes misuse of theological knowledge, not careful pursuit of doctrinal wisdom itself. Evangelicals should not assume that their theologians have only "made it" as scholars once secular academic guilds warmly embrace them. But neither does the opposite assumption hold true, that the praise of an academic guild automatically renders a theologian's humility or biblical fidelity suspect.[4]

---

[2]As Anthony C. Thiselton, *The First Epistle to the Corinthians*, NIGTC (Grand Rapids: Eerdmans, 2000), p. 624, notes, the contrasting verbs of 1 Corinthians 8:2 highlight process: some Corinthians claim to have achieved knowledge (perfect infinitive), whereas they have not yet come to know (ingressive aorist). This note of process should foster humility, especially in light of the eschatological note to come in 1 Corinthians 13.

[3]The textual problem in 1 Corinthians 8:2 puts classic principles of textual criticism at odds. Fee, *First Epistle to the Corinthians*, pp. 367-68, opts for the shorter reading, which then removes direct reference to knowing or being known by God, as in, "If anyone thinks he has arrived at knowledge, he does not yet know as he ought to know; *but* if anyone loves, this one truly knows (or, is known)" (emphasis his). To the contrary, given the broader Pauline theology that Fee acknowledges, divine knowledge must hover in the background of any assertions about rightly used, truly charitable, human knowledge. It also seems odd, given the immediate context, to suggest that the Corinthian claim does not refer to knowing God. Plus, given the larger context, it seems odd to suggest that being known refers to divine love in 1 Corinthians 13 but not here.

[4]A recent example of such debates appears in Jay Green, "Making It," *Books & Culture* (May/June 2012): 33, reviewing Randall J. Stephens and Karl W. Giberson, *The Anointed: Evangelical Truth in a Secular Age* (Cambridge, MA: Harvard University Press, 2011). Green rightly worries that the book in question capitulates to the former principle, as if evangelicals are inherently anti-

First Corinthians 13 continues the theme: Having all divine knowledge, however esoteric, means nothing without charity (1 Cor 13:2). Such charity is not arrogant or self-seeking (1 Cor 13:4-5), thus avoiding a trap into which theological scholars surely fall. Yet love rejoices with the truth (1 Cor 13:6), seeking mature, not childish thought (1 Cor 13:11). What 1 Corinthians 13 adds to the challenge from 1 Corinthians 8 is an eschatological context. Human knowledge per se is partial and instrumental (1 Cor 13:8-10). As an aspect of divine love, wisdom—active, relational knowledge—will remain eternally (1 Cor 13:13). For now, earthly knowledge can still support growth toward Christian maturity, even though ultimately it will give way to the immediacy of perfect love.[5] Genuine theological knowledge is relational, a matter of being divinely known more than knowing (1 Cor 13:12).

Our current labors are meaningful in light of the certainty, given Christ's resurrection, that one day we will enjoy this genuine knowledge (1 Cor 15:58). Simultaneously this very certainty restrains potential hubris. Evangelical theology cannot grasp any certainty apart from the gospel, and divine revelation does not grant comprehensive knowledge in this era of redemptive history. Scripture can mirror only partially the fullness one might long to know, and theology can mirror only partially the teaching of Scripture itself. Only in the context of charity, with eschatologically informed humility, do we claim theological knowledge. Important implications follow from this point for our next subject, the way in which evangelical theology should aspire to mirror biblical teaching in forms of disciplined reflection.

THEOLOGICAL DISCIPLINE(S): WISDOM'S FULL REFLECTION

In chapter four we incorporated the formation of doctrinal judgment and

---

intellectual unless popular among elites. But the corollary is dangerous too: It is easy to slide into the idea that lack of popularity—in either realm—is required to be faithful. Popular tides ebb and flow, reaching different places at different times.

[5]Fee, *First Epistle to the Corinthians*, p. 647, understands the analogy of 1 Corinthians 13:11 not to condemn childish behavior but simply to deepen the surrounding contrast between two ages. For at least two reasons, though, it seems better to see the analogy having multifaceted significance, including an allusion to Corinthian immaturity. For one, childishness is at issue elsewhere (1 Cor 3:1), and such echoes would be hard to keep at bay; Paul's language need not perform only one act. For another reason, the crucial contrast between the two ages consists in the perfect charity Christians come to share: the contrast concerns maturity versus immaturity. The Corinthians ironically thwart their growth toward perfection by claiming to possess "knowledge" as such instead of pursuing its proper end, love.

interaction with particular judgments into our account of theological exegesis. The concept of judgment placed theology's disciplined scrutiny within the eschatological and ethical context of wisdom. The context of wisdom promoted an account of concepts as habits, which we are free to develop in various forms of narrative coherence with the world(s) of Scripture itself—forms through which our judgments can correspond to its reflection of God's self-communication in Jesus Christ. Wisdom has the cognitive component of judgment aspiring to correspond with truth, while the understanding and communication of judgments have their meaning affected by contexts of practice.

If this account satisfies certain evangelical concerns, especially those of biblical scholars regarding historical integrity, still another dimension lingers from the larger concern over proof-texting. The concerns of theologians come from another direction, namely that TIS might reduce evangelical theology to restating biblical theology, with little attention to other sources or contexts. Indeed, some evangelical theologies are now period pieces, reflecting undue modern optimism about the possibilities of systematizing biblical truth. Some of these biblicist theologies largely ignore extrabiblical sources; their minimal appeals to reason accomplish little besides constricting biblical interpretation through wooden propositionalism. Such theologies claim to read Scripture as objectively or even alone as possible, yet tradition and experience exert unacknowledged pressure through mental and institutional back doors. Although such theologies have their virtues, particularly in serving laypersons well, the worst-case scenario is that their proof texts reflect ironically traditional and inadequately contextual readings. It would be understandable for other evangelical theologians to worry that TIS working closely with biblical theology only exacerbates these vices.

This state of affairs elicits two increasing reactions. Many non-Reformed theologians resist the objectivity implied in such systems, adverting to a more pietistic or progressive heritage and acknowledging the perceived impossibility of representing a conceptually unified biblical theology. Many Reformed or epistemologically conservative theologians realize that optimism about scriptural objectivity is only tenable if they can establish a strong relationship between biblical and systematic theology. The progress and pitfalls of biblical theology in the twentieth century make clear that representing an internal scriptural unity must involve historical framing, not just conceptual patterns. To focus solely on concepts would surely degenerate into mere proof-texting—or further skepticism. The pressing question, of course, concerns how to address the historical framing alongside the conceptual patterns, without rendering systematic theology impossible or at best subservient to biblical studies. Furthermore, it is easy for historical interests to obscure the need for conceptual analysis amid the tasks of biblical theology, especially if its focus concerns redemptive-historical progression.

To address this set of concerns, the present chapter's reflection on theological discipline(s) supplements the earlier account of doctrinal judgment(s) and biblical exegesis in three ways. First, focusing on theology's *constructive* aspect: the literary variety within Scripture and the drama of doctrinal development fund a properly dialogical imagination—affecting judgments concerning not only theological content but also form, even the very concepts to use. Second, focusing on theology's *systematic* aspect: a revised account of this aspiration sustains a pursuit of coherence grounded in, rather than opposed to, contemplation—accounting for sources beyond Scripture. Tradition, reason and experience integrate biblical faith and practice with the whole of God's revealing and redeeming work. Third, focusing on theology's *dogmatic* aspect: placing Scripture's regulative role in these sapiential contexts suggests a rubric for engaging biblical theology as an academic discipline—appreciating its aid while requiring its interaction with the broader disciplines of Christian doctrine. Supplemented by these accounts, the earlier picture of wise doctrinal judgment looks more appealing, enabling us finally to appreciate the full array of scholarly shapes for evangelical theology to take.

Constructively: Scriptural drama and dialogical imagination. Theological judgment(s) mirroring Scripture must incorporate the eschatological and ethical dimensions introduced earlier. To these dimensions we now add the wide literary range of biblical material, as we discussed briefly in chapter two and as David F. Ford recently emphasizes. Together these eschatological, ethical and literary dimensions commend a dramatic model for doctrinal development. Ford sees Job as epitomizing the dramatic cries for God appearing in Scripture: "New, overwhelming challenges require fresh wrestling with God and reality together."[6] Too often theology has been tantalized by epic modes of thought, pursuing detached and comprehensive coherence. Ford recognizes that lyric alternatives could easily be trapped in subjective interiority, so he calls for dramatic modes of thought to embrace both epic and lyric, and for figural interpretation of Scripture along the lines of New Testament use of the Old.[7] He further calls for theology to free itself from the tyranny of the indicative mood, suggesting that in Scripture narrative is most basic—hosting interplay of all the other moods:

> The biblical theodrama . . . is an unfinished story; final affirmations cannot be made yet; all are provisional until the consummation. The promises embedded in biblical testimonies kindle the desire for God's future, and this openness is reflected in a theology led by this desire and alert for possibilities and surprises. So the optative of desire and longing repeatedly challenges both the neat packages, which already have past, present, and future wrapped up, and the opposite tendencies toward lack of definiteness and direction.[8]

Dramatic interplay between biblical moods sounds very appealing. Ford notes that intensive conversation is a crucial factor in intellectual creativity, according to a major, long-term sociological study of philosophy.[9] Theology needs, therefore, "civil wisdom" when it comes to public and especially academic conversation between various religions, with special focus on their scriptures.[10] One more pillar in this support for a drama of biblical conversation is the accompanying theme of "boldness" (παρρησία, in New Testament terms), by which theology's intimacy with God flows into free communication that truly blesses others.[11] Indeed, Ford's call for dialogically

---

[6]David F. Ford, *The Future of Christian Theology*, Blackwell Manifestos (Malden, MA: Wiley-Blackwell, 2011), p. 3.

[7]Ibid., pp. 26, 37. Matthew Milliner highlights the visual arts as a crucial, perennial mode of the church's TIS in "Anchors Aweigh: The Neglected Art of Theological Interpretation," *Comment* (Fall 2012): 82-91. Milliner's examples should provoke new thought about the meaning of "figures" in figural reading.

[8]Ford, *Future*, p. 72.

[9]Ibid., p. 98.

[10]Ibid., p. 147. Brian W. Hughes (*Saving Wisdom: Theology in the Christian University* [Eugene, OR: Pickwick, 2011]) helpfully analyzes appeals to wisdom in four major figures: Friedrich Schleiermacher, John Henry Newman, Avery Cardinal Dulles and Edward Farley. He concludes that a distinction between exclusive and inclusive soteriologies (in this case, the two liberal Protestants holding the latter, the two Catholics holding the former to some degree) affects how proposals play out regarding the sapiential character of theology in a university context.

[11]Ford, *Future*, p. 180. See p. 223n5 for a clever example of how theology can help the university

engaging the fullness of dramatic material in the Bible should challenge
evangelicals:

> Those who, for example, take the Bible as a set of propositions, that can be
> grasped without attending to their literary forms and contexts, are likely to
> think and write theology very differently from those who do not. The whole
> mindset of theologians who take the Bible seriously will be affected by their
> level of sensitivity to its forms of expression. . . . Theologians who read
> scripture mainly as a source for assertions and commands, missing its direct
> and indirect encouragement of questioning, exploring, and, above all, de-
> siring God's as yet unrealized future, are unlikely to write in ways that en-
> courage their readers to question, explore, or desire.

On this basis Ford concludes that "narrative and poetry (which often
overlap) are perhaps the two basic literary forms for Christian theology."[12]

Evangelical theologians need to heed this challenge, yet without simply
abandoning their tradition. Absolutely prioritizing narrative and poetry
could confuse a necessary distinction between forms in the Bible itself and
forms theology can or should take. Insisting on one-to-one correspondence
between these forms could turn theology into mere repetition of biblical
material. Since Ford cannot mean that, the more charitable and contextual
reading is a claim of narrative and poetic primacy within the Bible itself,
with implications for broader theological practice. More specifically, the
practice of theological judgment must work wisely, giving narrative and
poetry (etc.) their due but also recognizing that doctrinal judgments typically are propositional in character. Nonpropositional materials shape and
supplement such judgments, rather than replacing them. Even within narrative and poetry one nevertheless finds truth judgments—both expressed
and implied—that can be treated in propositional form. Even within less
assertive theological moods one still finds it necessary to speak using embedded assertions. Theological discourse communicates and complements
instead of supplanting or competing with biblical materials. In a delicate

---

to fulfill its calling: Ford draws an analogy between economic study expecting economists still
to involve themselves in economic activity, and religious study—which on that basis can legitimately incorporate its scholars' spiritual practices or theological perspectives without automatically jeopardizing its integrity.

[12]Ibid., p. 202.

balancing act, theology must clarify the meaning and significance of biblical revelation to be useful at all, without substituting its clarified content for Scripture itself. Hence theology must use communicative forms both similar to and different from the biblical materials. If theology's forms focus only on similarity to the Bible, approaching exact sameness, then theology is actually at much greater risk of supplanting Scripture. People would then have greater difficulty distinguishing between theological frameworks and the biblical foundations on which they build.[13]

Like Ford, regarding drama's eschatological orientation Darren Sarisky learns from Rowan Williams: God makes time for our learning. Even ectypal theological knowledge is not ours all at once; in this life it never will be fully ours, and this can serve as a doctrinally potent critical principle.[14] De Lubac intriguingly suggested long ago that what is most controversial about the spiritual sense of Scripture is its commitment to the progress of spiritual life in the church.[15] The Word of God is not a spotlight but a torch, guiding our next steps as we journey rather than blinding us with everything immediately.[16] Theological judgment is something learned; doctrinal judgments are contingently made and expressed as the drama of redemptive history—and its understanding—unfolds. There is a script, but learning to

---

[13]In a related vein, Peter J. Leithart (*Deep Exegesis: The Mystery of Reading Scripture* [Waco, TX: Baylor University Press, 2009], p. 55) champions taking time with texts in order for them to transform us into God's image. Scripture is not designed to contain theological kernels that can be extracted from their textual husks. Still, Leithart's is only one side of the story: meaning takes time, but its understanding takes different form. A measure of fresh expression, if not extraction, is the result.

There is plenty to criticize about translation of biblical concepts as a model for doing theology; most famously, perhaps, see David H. Kelsey, *Proving Doctrine: The Uses of Scripture in Modern Theology* (Harrisburg, PA: Trinity Press International, 1999). But the model can be used metaphorically here to establish two basic points. One is the necessity for some difference between biblical and theological idioms: only if theology's forms are similar enough to connect with the Bible in all its variety, yet also different enough to clarify aspects of its teaching, can theology remain properly secondary—leaving room for Scripture to communicate in its own way while enjoying the freedom to help communicate that Word in contemporary contexts. A second point is the legitimacy or even necessity of variety: different translations are stronger at some tasks, weaker at others. The advantages of having a culturally dominant translation such as the Vulgate or the Authorized Version cannot be gainsaid, but also come at a price.

[14]Darren Sarisky, *Scriptural Interpretation: A Theological Exploration*, Challenges in Contemporary Theology (Malden, MA: Wiley-Blackwell, 2013), p. 203.

[15]Henri de Lubac, *History and Spirit: The Understanding of Scripture According to Origen*, trans. Anne Englund Nash (San Francisco: Ignatius, 2007), p. 505.

[16]Ibid., p. 449n59.

read its internal dialogue well is part of its ongoing performance.[17]

Beyond a dialogical imagination nurtured over time by the literary variety within Scripture itself, the drama of doctrine involves the whole of life. Our next subsection explores the implications of this point regarding extrabiblical sources; for now we must further address the very character of theological understanding and hence the vital supporting role played by imagination itself. As Kelsey suggests, understanding involves a set of capacities for action in relations—consistent with our earlier practical notion of concepts as habits.[18] Aspiring to have integrity between our thinking and living, to attain wholeness, involves finding and reflecting on patterns. The synthetic faculty of imagination recognizes internal relations across the diverse but splendid array of scriptural texts, and external relations between biblical patterns and other aspects of our thinking and living. Imagination perceptively recognizes constitutive patterns that are more than any part or sum of their parts, and it further helps us to appropriate those patterns in thought, word and deed. In other words, imagination addresses both initial perception and subsequent performance interpretation.[19] Biblical interpretation and imaginative theological construction are mutually reinforcing; the more fully we aspire to bring patterns from each realm into meaningful interaction, the more fruitfully coherent will be the perception and the interpretation that inform our theological judgment.

Systematically: Coherent thinking and extrabiblical sources. So far, then, evangelical theology's drama of mirroring Scripture commends greater eschatological reserve and dialogical imagination. When it comes next to matters of coherent structure, A. N. Williams likens theology "to a jigsaw puzzle: even if one does not have all the pieces, the shape of any one of them reflects its orientation towards others as parts of a larger pattern. When there are enough such pieces to hand, a complete picture forms, but even in the absence of a whole, unified image, a solitary piece displays by its very

---

[17]For prior evangelical appropriations of drama, see Michael S. Horton, *Covenant and Eschatology: The Divine Drama* (Louisville: Westminster John Knox, 2002); Kevin J. Vanhoozer, *The Drama of Doctrine: A Canonical-Linguistic Approach to Christian Theology* (Louisville: Westminster John Knox, 2005).

[18]David H. Kelsey, *To Understand God Truly: What's Theological About a Theological School* (Louisville: Westminster John Knox, 1992), pp. 123-29.

[19]See David H. Kelsey, *Imagining Redemption* (Louisville: Westminster John Knox, 2005), pp. 100-101, drawing on the work of Garrett Green.

shape its trajectory towards linkage." Most enduring Christian theology does not appear in the genre of a one- or multivolume comprehensive system.[20] To the contrary, influential treatments of particular loci, often rather implicitly, presume "an *oikonomia*, a providentially ordered creation intended for harmony with its maker and therefore, for harmony within itself," on which their *ratio*—their rational ordering—is based.[21] Accordingly, the nature of Christian theological material itself—the Triune God and God's created works—impels latent drive toward systematic coherence.[22]

Interesting claims follow about "reason" as a theological "source" in relation to Scripture. Reason rarely serves as a source of direct evidence or doctrinal warrant. Yet, surfacing in the latent drive for doctrinal coherence, though "not legitimate as a theological norm," reason is "not merely an indispensable theological tool, but *the* tool."[23] Neither reason nor tradition nor experience can provide freestanding theological warrant,[24] although they impinge on the reading of Scripture. From a Protestant perspective, Scripture may still be distinguished from tradition, reason and experience as the final court of hermeneutical appeal at the same time that we acknowledge reason as the distinctive instrument of its reading. The other "sources" besides the Bible impinge on, but do not determine, theological judgments finally made: Scripture needs interpretation while ultimately serving as its own interpreter.

The aspiration behind such an account of *sola Scriptura* depends on a network of other Protestant claims: that all baptized believers have priestly access to God, which is not the exclusive provenance of a magisterial class; that Scripture's saving wisdom is clearly accessible with "a due use of the ordinary means" (*Westminster Confession of Faith* I.7); that many difficulties of understanding have to do with human finitude and/or fallenness, not the

---

[20]A. N. Williams, *The Architecture of Theology: Structure, System, and Ratio* (Oxford: Oxford University Press, 2011), p. 1.

[21]Ibid., p. 2.

[22]Ibid., p. 4. Webster speaks of a sense in which there is only one Christian doctrine, the Trinity, regarding God's inward and outward movements (*The Domain of the Word: Scripture and Theological Reason* [London: T&T Clark, 2012], p. 145).

[23]Williams, *Architecture*, pp. 6, 10 (emphasis original).

[24]Neither can Scripture, for Williams, who brushes aside *sola Scriptura*. In response, without descending into technical arguments about what the Protestant Reformers said and meant, evangelical academic theology now routinely avoids the fallacy that a text could be "read apart from readers" (contra ibid., p. 94).

(lack of) clarity of the biblical texts themselves; that other difficulties may be addressed in light of Scripture's central message and clearer passages; and that, beyond what is clearly binding for salvation, difficulties of understanding lie within realms of evangelical freedom.[25] Freedom is also part of the Protestant aspiration: creeds and confessions should minimally specify what is binding for salvation and churchly holiness before confessions and catechisms nourish particular congregations in gospel liberty and ministry. Freedom further emerges when we acknowledge that Scripture has theological riches to explore beyond its explicit meaning, in its presuppositions, implications and entailments.[26] These riches both fund and guide our journeys; they require stewardship yet foster generosity. All of these Protestant claims stem from a particular understanding of God and the gospel, of how God graciously communicates by Word and Spirit. The magisterial Reformers may not have fully lived up to their own ideals, with for instance (Williams insists) Luther's doctrine of justification coming to function as an ironically (and overly) systematic principle.[27] But one can appreciate the basic drift of Williams's practical treatment of warrant while embracing a more nuanced Protestant principle: Scripture has primacy in adjudicating doctrinal claims despite not operating in a vacuum, since other "sources" comprise its interpretive contexts.

Scripture and tradition, then, are distinct as theology's "generative principles," with the latter depending on the former. Reason and experience, respectively, comprise tools and environments within which the generative reading unfolds.[28] As N. T. Wright puts it, these sources "are not so much

---

[25]Recent treatments of the clarity of Scripture include James Callahan, *The Clarity of Scripture: History, Theology and Contemporary Literary Studies* (Downers Grove, IL: InterVarsity Press, 2001), which provides helpful historical detail but seems somewhat theologically confusing; better theologically are Mark D. Thompson, *A Clear and Present Word: The Clarity of Scripture*, NSBT (Downers Grove, IL: InterVarsity Press, 2006) and (with special respect to the ways in which struggles over clarity are, and are not, about authority) John Webster, "On the Clarity of Holy Scripture," in *Confessing God: Essays in Christian Dogmatics II* (London: T&T Clark, 2005), pp. 33-67.

[26]This is language borrowed from J. L. Austin's speech-act theory in *How to Do Things with Words* (Oxford: Oxford University Press, 1962), pp. 47-48, which is handy for expressing a commitment as old as Protestant orthodoxy.

[27]Williams, *Architecture*, p. 96.

[28]Ibid., p. 108. The recent *Analytic Theology* volume edited by Oliver D. Crisp and Michael C. Rea (*Analytic Theology: New Essays in the Philosophy of Theology* [Oxford: Oxford University Press, 2009]) strikingly offers chapters on reason and experience, but not tradition, as sources: the

like apples, pears and oranges as like apples, elephants and screwdrivers. . . . Scripture is the bookshelf; tradition is the memory of what people in the house have read and understood (or perhaps misunderstood) from that shelf; and reason is the set of spectacles people wear in order to make sense of what they read," while experience deals with the effects of that reading.[29] In this way, notes Williams, "Theology never rests: the conjectures and solutions of one generation become the questions and disputes of another."[30] Contributing starting points for reflection as opposed to "definitive settlements," these traditioning sources count as warrants, not direct authorities— eliciting the nebulous, initially descriptive but implicitly somewhat normative, discipline of historical theology.[31]

As Ford and others already suggested, figurative language complicates the Bible's theological function. The very richness of trope is "a productive ambiguity," making theological reflection possible. This richness is volatile, making theological reflection necessary: "The fact that in this life, theology's surest ground, the Bible, gives us access to this knowledge only through the veil of human language, with its approximations of the immaterial in material images, means all theology in this life is provisional, awaiting both correction and fulfillment in the Age to Come."[32] Hence the eschatological and literary contexts that previously surfaced now shape the architecture of theological argument. Evangelical theology must give up trying to distill one and only one true and finally complete theological system supposedly provided in Scripture—without relinquishing the latent systematic drive of Christian doctrine itself or the traditions it has spawned.

Attending to contemplation prevents the eschatological and literary pressures from distorting theology's structural integrity. Contemplation integrates spiritual and doctrinal pursuit of coherence. As "the silent form" of giving praise to God, contemplation is "the point at which the voiced human

---

relevant section is entitled "ON THE DATA FOR THEOLOGY: SCRIPTURE, REASON, AND EXPERIENCE"! This may be both a lacuna of that specific volume and a general manifestation of the fact that tradition has a different theological role from Scripture, yet a more generative role than reason or experience.

[29]N. T. Wright, *The Last Word: Scripture and the Authority of God—Getting Beyond the Bible Wars* (San Francisco: HarperOne, 2006), pp. 100-105, quoting p. 101.

[30]Williams, *Architecture*, p. 110.

[31]Ibid., p. 111.

[32]Ibid., pp. 118, 120, 126.

response has yielded to sheer awe," representing "not the antithesis to intellectual inquiry, but its culmination: its sabbath from restless questioning,
when there is nothing left but to repose in the enjoyment of truth and its
triune source." This more classic sense of theology's true end and proximate
means can nudge evangelical theologians toward seeing "formal meditation"
as but "a means of keeping the restless mind fixed on God": "The mind's
impulse to rove faith's terrain eventually subsides into stillness; the busy
work of forging connections yields to the calm gaze that takes in the whole
and rests in adoration; just so theology," even if in "ephemeral glimpses" that
only "gesture towards the eternal."[33]

In this way the systematic dimensions of theology embrace its spiritual
dynamic. Gesturing toward contemplation as theology's restful end is consistent with knowledge's eschatological reserve and wisdom's wholeness.
Theology tries to discern the divine *ratio* in itself and then in the world as
an expression of God's love.[34] Here it is worth noting how often early Protestant authors apply mirror images to the created order. Calvin, for instance,
speaks of the created order as a mirror for contemplating God.[35] Though
subordinate to Scripture as the final court of appeal, the book of nature too
communicates a form of divine self-revelation. Evangelical debates about
the hermeneutical authority of Scripture often pay inadequate attention to
"general" revelation, misunderstanding the sufficiency of Scripture to entail
that it must furnish direct proof texts for every issue.[36] Part of theology's
contemplative drive toward systematic coherence, then, involves reflection
on all the truth of God's Word mirrored throughout God's world.

Systematic theology is accordingly "a form of mimesis: not an original, but
a reflection and echo." As a response to revelation, theology "genuinely reflects
human desire and not only divine intellect." Theology's systems represent de-

---

[33]Ibid., pp. 21, 22, 226.
[34]Ibid., pp. 15-17.
[35]John Calvin, *Institutes of the Christian Religion*, trans. Ford Lewis Battles, ed. John T. McNeill,
   Library of Christian Classics (Philadelphia: Westminster Press, 1960), 1.5.1.
[36]For some of the worst popular instances of this misunderstanding, as discussed previously, see
   Christian Smith, *The Bible Made Impossible: Why Biblicism Is Not a Truly Evangelical Reading of
   Scripture* (Grand Rapids: Brazos, 2011); for brief treatment of more academic instances and their
   consequences, see Al Wolters, "A Reflection by Al Wolters," in *Four Views on Moving Beyond the
   Bible to Theology*, ed. Gary T. Meadors, Counterpoints (Grand Rapids: Zondervan, 2009), pp.
   299-319, especially p. 317.

sired growth in μίμησις, doubly so: pursuing the knowledge of God, first—knowledge to which humans aspire, second, as divine image-bearers.[37] This double μίμησις integrates different kinds or aspects of Christian belief: (1) beliefs about how God relates to all situations, such as doctrines of providence, might be theorized in ways that are necessarily impossible for (2) situations that are unique in principle, such as narratives of creation *ex nihilo* or the incarnation. (3) Systematic and pastoral theology then blur elements of universality with uniqueness, such as redemption applying once-for-all atonement to particular lives: neither strictly theoretical nor strictly narrative analysis can be pursued in isolation. Accordingly, different ways of being systematic are possible: systematic theology might involve step-by-step procedure gaining in complexity; or it may involve grammatical exploration of interconnections; or it may even involve a technical, theoretically coherent schematic proposal.[38] The aspiration behind appropriate systematic constructions is not removing all mystery, but attaining a measure of clarity, along with wholeness—integrity within and between our thinking and living.[39]

Now evangelicals have perhaps distinctively recognized that theology is not just contemplative but apostolic as well.[40] For this reason they have comparatively excelled at providing clear, textbook-level instruction in the biblical content of Protestant faith. Such excellence can come at an unnecessary cost, though: threatening to lose the eschatological reserve, ethical holism, literary variety and contemplative embrace of properly systematic thinking. When striving to mirror the teaching of Scripture, the evangelical theologian therefore pursues the mind of Christ via spiritual scholarship. The intellectual mirroring to pursue is not representing one and only one complete system of biblical truth, but at minimum being consistent with, and at maximum communicating clearly, segments of scriptural teaching. The proper goal is to be free of evident contradiction from either biblical texts or internal incoherence.

---

[37]Williams, *Architecture*, pp. 18, 19, 185.

[38]Kelsey, *Imagining Redemption*, pp. 90-91, 87.

[39]Referencing Kelsey's work in a special roundtable on analytic theology, Jesse Couenhoven, "Fodge-ogs and HedgeOxes," *Journal of the American Academy of Religion* 81, no. 3 (September 2013): 586-91, at p. 589: there are types of mystery susceptible to some analysis, while metaphor can be used carefully in ways whose aptness we can assess.

[40]To borrow categories from Webster, *Domain of the Word*, p. 151.

If the eschatological, ethical and literary dimensions have a constructive focus, and the contemplative dimension has a systematic focus, then a dogmatic focus will complete the theological picture: personal contemplation and creativity are vital, but ecclesial communion and nurture are ultimate. The traditioned and practical character of concepts in chapter four sketched some background for church dogmatics; here the disciplined character of biblical theology fills in additional contours of theological judgment's doctrinal dimension—its character as Christian teaching.

Dogmatically: Biblical theology and doctrinal discipline. The character of biblical theology is quite complex: Should we emphasize its potential as an academic discipline (a bridge, perhaps, between critical exegesis and classic or contemporary theology) or its perennial churchly practice?[41] The earlier treatment of theological exegesis in chapter four already has implications for answering this question. To recap, there we established the need for evangelical theology's conceptual patterns to find narrative coherence with the world(s) of Scripture. Undergirding this possible coherence is Yeago's distinction between biblical judgments and the conceptual terms that render them.[42] Theological judgment(s) appeal to the Bible in very diverse ways, as Kelsey further establishes by appropriating Stephen Toulmin's architecture for arguments.[43] Not all biblical materials lend themselves readily to conceptual redescription, yet all should somehow inform theological judgments.[44] The purpose of the present section is to add further scholarly precision regarding the interface between academic biblical theology and dogmatic reflection.

In terms of *material* precision, we can build further on Ford's general

---

[41]Charles H. H. Scobie, *The Ways of Our God: An Approach to Biblical Theology* (Grand Rapids: Eerdmans, 2003), narrates the history of biblical theology in terms of the church's "integrated" premodern approach preceding the rise of the "independent" modern academic discipline.

[42]David S. Yeago, "The New Testament and the Nicene Dogma," *Pro Ecclesia* 3, no. 2 (Spring 1994): 152-64.

[43]Kelsey, *Proving Doctrine*, especially pp. 125-34, 144.

[44]Recognizing this years earlier was Kevin J. Vanhoozer, "The Semantics of Biblical Literature: Truth and Scripture's Diverse Literary Forms," in *Hermeneutics, Authority, and Canon*, ed. D. A. Carson and John D. Woodbridge (Grand Rapids: Zondervan, 1986), pp. 53-104. For a more detailed set of categories concerning how scriptural variety tends to shape different theological emphases, see Kevin J. Vanhoozer, "Scripture and Theology: On Proving Doctrine Biblically," in *The Routledge Companion to the Practice of Christian Theology*, ed. Mike Higton and Jim Fodor (New York: Routledge, 2015).

expansion of literary modes and theological moods. Literary emphases in biblical theology obviously demand that we pay greater attention to expressive genres—such as psalms, lament and apocalyptic. These expressive elements ought to mold poetic and spiritual approaches to performing in redemption's drama, since all biblical genres uniquely map theological aspects of reality in Christ.[45] For instance, alongside the typically dominant epistolary literature, prophetic and wisdom writings can also communicate doctrinal truths, even if they are most adept at questioning idolatrous ones. Or lament psalms, while they do not focus on conveying technical dogmatic judgments, nevertheless foster God's people learning to practice a doctrine of providence—via prayer. One could go on to itemize a wide range of possibilities. Narrative form, of course, has garnered the most biblical-theological attention for nearly a generation. For all the biblical diversity emphasized today and necessarily acknowledged, the canonical presentation of a coherent redemptive-historical drama remains basic to evangelical dogmatics—providing a framework within which various genres embody and encourage more particular theological vision(s).[46]

Beyond attending more fully to literary genres in applying biblical theology to dogmatic judgments at a broad level, we can add precision at a more detailed level regarding literary particulars and theological concepts. Most directly influencing biblical concept formation will be indicatives and imperatives, which are prominently blended in New Testament epistles. In appropriating these indicatives and imperatives, though, an analogy holds with earlier Torah and wisdom: as divine instruction, Torah provides conceptual narration and moral formation; wisdom must condition and question how such instruction becomes contextually particular. Even biblical indicatives and imperatives, therefore—the New Testament teaching equivalent of Torah—require theological φρόνησις to appropriate. Some dogmatic or pastoral contexts call for a deep, Pauline *ordo salutis*, others for a broad, Lukan apologetic narrative, or still others for Gospel kerygma that also fosters the *imitatio Christi*. And so on.

---

[45]Vanhoozer, *Drama of Doctrine*, pp. 295-97.
[46]The notion of such a "framework" is developed for evangelicals by Richard Lints, *The Fabric of Theology: A Prolegomenon to Evangelical Theology* (Grand Rapids: Eerdmans, 1993). The meaning of *metanarrative* is sufficiently contested that it is better off avoided these days.

Our emphasis on φρόνησις applies to not only material but also *methodological* precision regarding biblical theology. It would be inappropriate and impossible to specify all the rules of engagement in advance, particularly since biblical theology as an academic discipline remains contextually situated and historically evolving. A broad parallel applies between the "ad hoc" use of philosophy advocated in "postliberal" theological circles and the proper approach to academic biblical theology. Philosophy poses challenging questions to theology and provides potential resources for its conceptual analysis, but philosophy's role remains ministerial rather than magisterial. Likewise the considerable variety of academic biblical theology frees us from following one and only one approach or conceptual scheme in order to be scripturally faithful. Evangelical theology may engage the challenging questions posed by various biblical-theological approaches while appropriating select resources—with the integrity that comes from allowing for some inevitable tensions between theological exegesis and historically oriented biblical theology.[47] The resulting canonically engaged readings of Scripture count as material claims about "biblical theology" whatever their precise method(s). Accordingly, biblical theology pursued as an academic discipline, even with allowance for periodic material or methodological tensions that may arise, can make important ad hoc contributions. We detail five categories of those biblical-theological contributions next, in roughly ascending order of the evangelical freedom with which they foster scriptural dogmatics.[48]

---

[47]Beginning to suggest the parallel uses of biblical theology and philosophy is Daniel J. Treier, "Biblical Theology and/or Theological Interpretation of Scripture?" *Scottish Journal of Theology* 61 (2008): 16-31 (drawing on Colin E. Gunton, "Indispensable Opponent: The Relations of Systematic Theology and Philosophy of Religion," *Neue Zeitschrift für Systematische Theologie und Religionsphilosophie* 38, no. 3 [1996]: 298-306, as symptomatic of broader ad hoc appeals to philosophy). Gunton sees philosophy as theology's indispensable opponent in the current epoch of redemptive history—provoking theology to pursue intellectual responsibility, for which it must steal philosophy's weapons and use them in a counterattack. The parallel proposed for biblical theology vis-à-vis theological exegesis needs one additional nuance, namely that the former tends to privilege historical methods while the latter sometimes prefers literary ones. For surveys of the variety of "biblical theology," see Edward W. Klink III and Darian R. Lockett, *Understanding Biblical Theology: A Comparison of Theory and Practice* (Grand Rapids: Zondervan, 2012), and James K. Mead, *Biblical Theology: Issues, Methods, and Themes* (Louisville: Westminster John Knox, 2007).

[48]Broad parallels should be evident between the following criteria and those outlined by Kelsey, *Proving Doctrine*, pp. 196-97, despite different assumptions about the nature of Scripture's canonical authority.

First, at one end of the spectrum, biblical theology can *rule out* theological proposals that contradict scriptural judgments or cohere awkwardly with other biblical concepts. As an extreme example, it is hard to imagine evangelical theology defending the morality of adultery. Second, at the other end of the spectrum, biblical theology can *require* doctrinal proposals (or aspects thereof) that are clear and central in Scripture. For an easy example on this other side, it is hard to imagine an evangelical doctrine of God lacking holiness as a divine perfection. Of course these opposite ends of the spectrum will operate tacitly, almost intuitively, if catechesis does its proper work. What counts in either category will quickly become debatable in practice once we encounter Christians of different traditions or those of other cultures. Nevertheless, these ends of the spectrum establish important aspirational parameters in principle, even if the gradations in between prove to be where the action usually is.

Third, then, biblical theology can *permit* doctrinal proposals that do not contradict Scripture. In this respect we must remember that (so-called) tradition, reason, experience and general revelation properly function as secondary theological sources. Scripture is the primary Protestant theological source because it is the final dogmatic authority. But Scripture is not an exclusive source, because other, secondary norms exercise derived hermeneutical authority and offer extrabiblical access to the fullness of God's truth. Scripture is evangelically sufficient but not epistemologically exhaustive. Scripture is accordingly the final arbiter but not the only source to which dogmatics may appeal: such is what we might call the "external" form of doctrinal permission that Scripture gives.

Yet there is also a more "internal" form of theological permission from Scripture, with a well-known example illustrating this additional freedom that biblical theology provides. Longstanding tension between Romans 4 and James 2 over justification by faith demonstrates that we cannot proof-text theological concepts from biblical words. Paul uses *justification* and *faith* positively, with *justification* signifying a redemptive divine verdict and faith "alone" being credited as righteousness. James uses *justification* positively, though perhaps differently from Paul if human judgment is also in view. In any case, James uses *faith* negatively, explicitly rejecting "faith alone" (Jas 2:24) as if "without deeds." The full range of complexities aside, different conceptual patterns behind such common word usage preclude any direct correspondence between biblical and contemporary theological terms. From a broadly evangelical perspective concerning scriptural unity, Paul and James do not straightforwardly contradict each other; their overlapping words somehow convey complementary judgments through different concepts. Thus permission is granted here for a range of theological word and concept usage, as well as any judgments that do not contradict those of Romans or James.

Fourth, though, interrogating this example still more carefully, biblical theology can also *resource* doctrinal proposals that are made in this freedom it authorizes. Biblical theology can not only license creativity that does not contradict Scripture but also champion concepts whose positive use in biblical judgments commends them for contemporary theological use. In this case, from Paul a positive concept of faith, as whole-person trust in the divine Word, flowers ultimately in charity. His primary way to speak of gospel forgiveness, justification, has become a dominant Protestant concept. At least Matthew and perhaps James use that term differently, so theologians should variously account for their concepts of operative and visible righteousness. Still, Paul provides the most biblically prominent conceptual habit for conveying a crucial theological judgment. From James, a negative concept of faith, as mere mental assent to truth claims, warns against spiritual death. Far from contradicting the way a dogmatic theologian might speak of faith in view of Paul, James's warning confronts temptations of cheap grace. All too often we retain the Pauline *alone* but jettison its rich companion *faith*: James's conceptual warning has healthy spiritual consequences. In this way biblical theology regulates the judgments and resources the concepts of systematic theology, without unduly restricting its word usage, creative range or pastoral relevance.

Another example quickly buttresses the point.[49] David Peterson has dem-

---

[49]D. A. Carson helpfully highlighted this example in "The Vindication of Imputation: On Fields of Discourse and Semantic Fields," in *Justification: What's at Stake in the Current Debates*, ed. Mark Husbands and Daniel J. Treier (Downers Grove, IL: InterVarsity Press, 2004), pp. 48-49. Vern S. Poythress, *Symphonic Theology: The Validity of Multiple Perspectives in Theology* (repr., Phillipsburg, NJ: P&R, 2001), pp. 62-63, is so concerned to avoid improper usage of biblical words that he winds up with an exegete's ironic modesty about how Scripture can(not) inform theological concepts and judgments (terminology with which he could fruitfully deepen his account). The unfortunate result of this modesty is a nearly blanket admission that there are

onstrated that the New Testament speaks of "sanctification" not primarily as a process but instead as a status.[50] Sanctification in biblical theology, with its cultic background, designates God's setting apart people for service. Therefore sanctification deals more with the implications of initial conversion than subsequent growth, renewal or transformation—the terms the Bible most commonly uses to speak (in passive or middle voice) of postconversion spiritual progress. However, given a longstanding theological tradition of using *sanctification* progressively (with or without particular stages), it would be difficult and unduly restrictive to mandate that dogmatic theology simply alter its terminology to match the biblical theology concept. We have freedom to use words differently than biblical texts do, as long as our judgments are consistent with the scriptural message. All the same, this negative point about regulative freedom from restrictive constraints must not overwhelm the positive corollary about theological resources. The judgment(s) expressed in the biblical-theological concept of sanctification should chasten the dogmatic theological—and pastoral—tendency to overemphasize human cooperation while underemphasizing divine initiative. Furthermore, such biblical theology chastens our attendant preoccupation with individual effort to the neglect of communal context. Theologians are free to use "biblical" words in different ways. Such conceptual freedom is actually essential even for biblical theologians to analyze the content of scriptural texts. Yet the conceptual habits on offer in biblical texts help theologians to guard and share the treasures of Christian wisdom.

Robert W. Jenson proposes,

Finally, a *system* of theology . . . is tested against Scripture by its success or failure as a hermeneutical principle for Scripture taken as a whole, as one great text with a very complex internal structure. . . . Modern biblicisms . . . have supposed that for Scripture to be one text it must be epistemically homogeneous. Any text, however, no matter how short or long, works as discourse precisely by its inner differentiations, and a chief test of a hermeneutical prin-

---

almost no technical biblical terms for systematic theologies. This modesty sets theologians free in a way that easily generates a subsequent backlash: criticisms of theologians' arbitrariness, inattention to Scripture and so forth justify biblicists relegating Christian doctrine to an abstract afterthought.

[50]David Peterson, *Possessed by God: A New Testament Theology of Sanctification and Holiness*, NSBT (Grand Rapids: Eerdmans, 1995).

ciple for that text will be its ability to find and follow that structure.

Internal biblical proof . . . can therefore only be the system itself as it presents itself in the role of a general hermeneutical principle for Scripture taken as a single complex text, that is, as it marshals the structured whole of the Bible to its own systematic and argumentative purposes and just thereby displays or fails to display the coherent sense that the Bible itself is antecedently presumed to make. Individual biblical citations can only mark points in the mapping of the one structure on the other. Moreover, this internal testing is penultimate; final scriptural verification of a theological system occurs outside the system, as it proves or fails to prove itself as a hermeneutical principle for the church's general use of Scripture.[51]

In many respects Jenson is correct, properly chastening the biblicist pretensions and proof-texting practices of bygone evangelical days. Nevertheless, biblical theology can insightfully contribute to the internal testing he mentions. Particular scriptural citations can buttress the plausibility of a theological proposal. While citations in themselves cannot prove a claim or determine a system, surely the frequency, priority or strategic placement of biblical themes and concepts could assist in constructing and communicating one's case.

Still another example indicates the unsung virtue of evangelical interest in biblical theology. Many so celebrate the plurality within Scripture that they rarely emphasize or refuse to acknowledge its unity. Thus even relatively conservative theologians quickly highlight the fourfold nature of the Gospels as a relevant model, and earlier we showed that we agree about this relevance.[52] Less emphasized or even acknowledged, however, are the propriety and value of bringing together the Gospel witness in unified salvation nar-

---

[51]Robert W. Jenson, *Systematic Theology*, vol. 1, *The Triune God* (Oxford: Oxford University Press, 1997), p. 33.
[52]See, e.g., John R. Franke, *Manifold Witness: The Plurality of Truth*, Living Theology (Nashville: Abingdon, 2009), which sounds many correct notes but mutes biblical and theological unity, claiming on pp. 86-87 that the fourfold witness "indicates the irreducibility of the gospel of Jesus Christ to a single, universal account. Attempts to do this are inappropriate in the face of the canonical witness. A true harmony of the gospels is neither attainable nor desirable." In one sense these sentiments are true, but the final sentences are misleading: we do not face a stark dilemma of either false harmonization or else no unified teaching. Not coincidentally, perhaps, Franke's more academic proposal, *The Character of Theology: An Introduction to Its Nature, Task, and Purpose* (Grand Rapids: Baker Academic, 2005), laudably calls for always returning to Scripture, but interacts very little (if at all) with biblical theology, providing little discussion of how (if at all) scriptural criteria might operate in adjudicating theological claims.

ratives. The fourfold nature of the Gospels is a relevant but not exhaustive model. So, while we cannot and should not render "the life of Christ in stereo," conversely the church did not resist creating harmonies of the Gospels. Harmony arose at minimum in the rule of faith, and more maximally in various occasions of preaching, teaching, catechizing and so on. When appraising biblical-theological frameworks and their import for dogmatic coherence, evangelical theologians may require more flexible criteria than those of past proof-texting or present biblical theology. Yet surely the Bible itself—assumed ultimately to be not just a source but the final norm of unified Christian teaching—must play an adjudicating role. That role involves regulating and resourcing: our point is that sufficient unity of teaching exists for artful citations and combinations of Scripture texts—in all their variety—to increase the plausibility of theological proposals.

A fifth contribution of biblical theology identifies a final unsung virtue of evangelical theology's interest in mirroring Scripture: its linguistic connections with pastors and laypeople. Biblical theology can *relate* theological systems to church life through familiar scriptural language making Christian doctrine pastorally approachable. Not only language use but also textual citation can facilitate this evangelical priesthood of all believers. In light of the discussion above, it should be clear that this appropriation of biblical theology is a matter of wise judgment, not legalistic requirement. The Bible itself does not contain a monolithic conceptual scheme, so it would be impossible to mirror its theological language in one comprehensive system today. Additionally, the secondary literature of academic biblical theology can sometimes distract from the primary sources it describes. This fifth contribution stems from artful excellence in appropriating biblical theology, not slavish adherence to its academic guild(s). Even so, the more touch points between a theological system and scriptural texts, the more interesting, compelling, memorable and applicable its teaching will be for church life. The textbook nature of most evangelical theology admittedly has weaknesses to acknowledge and overcome. However, the alternative is not to abandon such communication entirely in favor of elite abstraction, especially since populist parts of the evangelical tradition have still erred on the side of rationalism anyway. Avoiding biblical idioms would offer no guarantees of reducing unhealthy proof-texting. The better path is to recognize how biblical concepts free theologians to explore doctrinal territory, generating multiple maps for various purposes. The effort to mirror scriptural judgments prevents getting lost, with TIS pointing toward this path of evangelical freedom.

SCHOLARLY SHAPES: THEOLOGY'S EVANGELICAL FREEDOM

The best-case scenario for TIS in evangelical theology, then, involves the deep redemptive-historical and wide literary contours of biblical theology informing thick descriptions and imaginative appropriations of scriptural texts—bringing theologians into closer interaction with their primary source and inviting them to help the church discern when biblical scholarship sheds light on Holy Scripture. Particular biblical scholars, while pursuing this wisdom holistically as saints, contribute special forms of expertise; all evangelical theological scholars should call on this expertise and acquaint themselves with its best practice. Evangelical teachers in both guilds communicate not only particular judgments but also the process of theological judgment. As publishing scholars, they enjoy the privilege and responsibility of undertaking distinctive research and prudentially communicating its results. No scholarly communication requires including the entire process—whether presuppositions, methods or results—related to every judgment; given the persuasive nature of academic publication, we inevitably design and selectively highlight original arguments and their necessary background. Caught between Athens and Berlin, pursuing both παιδεία and *Wissenschaft* so to speak, all evangelical theologians encounter biblical theology in their practice of theological judgment. Yet "biblical theology" now owes as much to Berlin as to Athens, and is not necessarily worse off for that. We plunder both Germans and Greeks, catering to neither.

Evangelical theologians should not worry that theological exegesis thereby restricts their scholarly options, as if they could only explore Berlin's biblical theology sector. To the contrary, TIS reopens the possibility for theologians to exegete the Bible as a form of scholarship that matters in their own precincts. This possibility may dissipate, but for the time being opportunities expand rather than contract. At the same time, richer forms of canonical, creedal and cultural engagement enliven the theological judgment involved in interpreting Scripture. To extend the metaphor almost to the breaking point, this Athenian citizenship of theological practice prepares for more delightful and strategic journeys to various sectors of Berlin.

If prolegomena address not just doctrinal judgment in general, but also scholarly expertise in particular, then finally evangelical theologians need a framework for discerning the appropriate range of academic contributions to pursue. The following typology sketches eight promising evangelical "shapes" for published theological scholarship to take and for doctrinal judgment to appropriate. These shapes most basically guide particular articles or books; more expansively they characterize a given dogmatics or a theologian's overall gifts and tendencies. Particular shapes are likely most fitting for particular doctrines, at certain times and places anyway. Speaking metaphorically of shapes fits our focus on mirroring Scripture: these scholarly contributions guide the theological imagination, helping us to see further aspects of the biblical truth in Christ, and to recognize how fully our understanding does or does not correspond.

Hermeneutics. Naturally, a first shape for evangelical scholarly contributions to take involves theology as hermeneutics. Or, instead of using the connector *as*, one could speak of theology being "primarily engaged with" hermeneutical understanding.[53] As exemplified in much of Kevin Vanhoozer's earlier work, this type particularly explores how a doctrine is affected by, and affects, biblical interpretation.[54] Because biblical hermeneutics can be a microcosm of broader cultural patterns, philosophers and literary critics are dialogue partners, not just biblical scholars and other theologians. How, for example, do cultural assumptions shape approaches to atonement metaphors?[55] While quite wide ranging as a form of faith seeking understanding, this approach sticks closely to Scripture by interrogating what it means for theologians to be biblical.

Integrative biblical theology. Second, evangelical theological scholarship can take the shape of integrative biblical theology, as for instance in

---

[53]The shorter form, theology "as," should not be taken restrictively but expansively: the point is to imply primary engagement, not exclusivity. For instance, hermeneutical and integrative biblical-theological foci are not mutually exclusive.

[54]In this regard see both the original preface and the preface to the tenth-anniversary edition of Vanhoozer, *Is There a Meaning in This Text?*

[55]E.g., Kevin J. Vanhoozer, "The Atonement in Postmodernity: Guilt, Goats, and Gifts," in *The Glory of the Atonement: Biblical, Theological, and Practical Perspectives*, ed. Charles E. Hill and Frank A. James III (Downers Grove, IL: InterVarsity Press, 2004), pp. 367-404.

the work of Henri Blocher. This type especially explores a doctrine's development in Scripture's redemptive-historical, progressive revelation. Being integrative in its use of biblical theology, this form of theology does not simply "translate" scriptural material into a monolithic system (as critiqued above). For it also engages critically reflective questions regarding the material (or assumed, traditional interpretations) from contemporary vantage points. As one case of this broader engagement, Blocher's creative treatment of original sin focally exegetes Romans 5 in the context of biblical theology, yet the book also incorporates psychology and other elements from modern culture; so too does Blocher's earlier treatment of the doctrine of creation in light of Genesis 1–3.[56]

Stewardship of the Great Tradition. Third, working gradually outward from most direct interaction with particular biblical texts, evangelical theology can take shape as stewardship of the Great Tradition. Here the prototype, in a robust sense, is the work of Thomas Oden.[57] This shape explores the doctrinal consensus reflected in the ecumenical creeds and the theological environment that gave rise to them. Such focus on the Great Tradition promotes Protestant appropriation of a Vincentian canon—"what is believed everywhere, always, and by everyone." Direct scriptural exegesis may be less prominent than in hermeneutical or biblical-theological approaches, but the Bible remains quite influential, not least via the idiom of the church fathers.

Church dogmatics. Fourth, evangelical theology as church dogmatics especially explores doctrinal development according to a particular church and/or confessional tradition. While open to asking new questions, in the hands of someone like John Webster this approach strives to respect classic categories and concerns. For Protestants, of course, there is no commitment merely to perpetuate institutional stability. Dogma must always stand under the judgment of the biblical gospel it serves, and someone like Bruce McCormack emphasizes this more critical sensibility.[58] In the background of

---

[56]Henri Blocher, *Original Sin: Illuminating the Riddle*, NSBT (Grand Rapids: Eerdmans, 1999); idem, *In the Beginning: The Opening Chapters of Genesis*, trans. David G. Preston (Downers Grove, IL: InterVarsity Press, 1984).
[57]See Thomas C. Oden, *Systematic Theology*, 3 vols. (San Francisco: Harper & Row, 1987–1992), and of course the Ancient Christian materials he spawned with InterVarsity Press.
[58]For a recent manifestation of differences between Webster and McCormack, see their ap-

this shape hovers the contested legacy of Barth along with, farther back, the scholastic legacies he contested at points. For various reasons, current practitioners have proliferated essays about the formal task of dogmatics, alongside more occasional glimpses of promising material outcomes. The relative lack of recent large-scale dogmatics may stem from certain cultural backgrounds and trends, since for instance the favored genre in British theology has long been the essay.[59] It is worth pondering A. N. Williams's point about the relative historical paucity of influential large-scale theologies, so that their publication should not be the only measure of vibrant dogmatic activity. Regardless, in principle the dogmatic theologian moves beyond direct scriptural statements toward implicit frameworks of what must be the case given what the Bible explicitly says. Properly undertaken, dogmatics avoids undue speculation and affords categories resistant to cultural faddishness. We may hope that enthusiasm over the recovery of Protestant dogmatics soon gives way to even more results.

Intellectual history. A fifth paradigm comes to mind when reading Colin Gunton, some of whose work also fit a dogmatic shape. Gunton explored strengths and weaknesses of doctrinal formulations in relation to intellectual history—for example, pursuing Trinitarian theology in relation to modern concepts of personhood and the history of science.[60] Gunton was not directly part of the British evangelical subculture. Still, though not using the label in print, Gunton trained many evangelical theologians while having affinities with others so labeled—not only Webster, but others like T. F. Torrance and Alister McGrath, who likewise fit this prototype given their special interest (and unique competence) in the sciences.

proaches to Hebrews 1: Webster in "One Who Is Son: Theological Reflections on the Exordium to the Epistle to the Hebrews," in *The Epistle to the Hebrews and Christian Theology*, ed. Richard Bauckham et al. (Grand Rapids: Eerdmans, 2009), pp. 69-94; and McCormack's critical response in "The Identity of the Son: Karl Barth's Exegesis of Hebrews 1:1-4 (and Similar Passages)," in *Christology, Hermeneutics, and Hebrews: Profiles from the History of Interpretation*, Library of New Testament Studies 423, ed. Jon C. Laansma and Daniel J. Treier (London: T&T Clark, 2012), pp. 155-72.

[59] As evident in the three-part portrayal of British theology from David Ford: "Theological Wisdom, British Style," *Christian Century* 117, no. 11 (April 5, 2000): 388-91; "British Theology After a Trauma: Divisions and Conversations," *Christian Century* 117, no. 12 (April 12, 2000): 425-31; "British Theology: Movements and Churches," *Christian Century* 117, no. 13 (April 19-26, 2000): 467-73.

[60] See, e.g., Gunton's extraordinarily thought-provoking *The One, the Three, and the Many: God, Creation, and the Culture of Modernity* (Cambridge: Cambridge University Press, 1993).

Analytic theism. These shapes proposed for evangelical theological scholarship have gradually been moving outward from direct, frequent engagement with scriptural texts toward more focused interaction with other sources. Simultaneously, they have been moving forward in time, from comparing biblical contexts with our own, to tracing conceptual development within and between biblical contexts, to focusing on the early Christian centuries, to engaging in a particular Protestant tradition, to wrestling with intellectual history and especially early modernity. Now the last three shapes grapple with the present day in particular. The sixth, theology as analytic theism, seeks conceptual, logical clarification, resulting in doctrinal dialogue with analytic philosophy of religion. In the work of someone like John Feinberg, references to biblical texts remain quite frequent and detailed.[61] Scriptural propositions are the primary subject matter on which logical tools are deployed. In the work of someone like Oliver Crisp, overt biblical exegesis is less prominent than treatment of the dogmatic tradition itself.[62] Analytic philosophy of course has ancient and medieval scholastic roots, from which have grown its earlier modern features. So while, on the one hand, this style of theology engages contemporary culture, it tends, on the other hand, to do so through relatively modern as opposed to "postmodern" lenses.

Living witness. The seventh shape, by contrast, appears to fit better into so-called postmodernity. Theology as primarily engaged with church witness and missional living is exemplified by Lesslie Newbigin and David Ford, among others. This type especially explores the Christ-centered, cross-cultural and perhaps countercultural analysis required for the church to be "a hermeneutic of the Gospel."[63] A key focus concerns how to understand and communicate the Christian faith for the sake of nonbelievers even in a church's native culture, and amid university life, not just in contexts of international mission. The former, native culture, was Newbigin's preoccupation, coming to expression in the missional church movement. The latter,

---

[61]See, e.g., John S. Feinberg, *No One Like Him: The Doctrine of God*, FET (Wheaton, IL: Crossway, 2001).

[62]See, e.g., Oliver D. Crisp, *Divinity and Humanity: The Incarnation Reconsidered*, Current Issues in Theology (Cambridge: Cambridge University Press, 2007).

[63]See especially Lesslie Newbigin, *The Gospel in a Pluralist Society* (Grand Rapids: Eerdmans, 1989), chap. 18 ("The Congregation as Hermeneutic of the Gospel"), where this phrase appears.

university life, is Ford's preoccupation at Cambridge and in his writings on wisdom, where interreligious dialogue is a primary commitment.[64] Ford's work on selfhood and spirituality speaks to and for Christians amid these cultural engagements, whereas Newbigin fundamentally challenged Western churches to recognize their post-Christendom status.[65] Neither of these theologians comes from the evangelical subculture, yet in each case British Protestants have again broadened evangelical horizons.

Healing resistance. A final shape for evangelical scholarly contributions moving forward concerns healing resistance to cultural trends of church and world. Examples of this type are understandably diverse, maybe even diffuse. One possibility comes from J. Kameron Carter in his *Race: A Theological Account.*[66] The movement most strongly informing Carter's work seems to be "radical orthodoxy," according to which he renarrates features of modernity theologically. Weaving together classic treatments of Christology with contemporary literature, he connects the death imposed on black persons with the Jesus of history and not just faith. Other exemplars of mining classic doctrines of Christology and Trinity for healing and liberation include Sarah Coakley, Kathryn Tanner and Ellen Charry.[67] For evangelicals such modes of theological work, though not mainstream, deserve prayerful attention and cautious imitation—precisely for the sake of obedience to the whole counsel of God.

Not every aspect of these eight shapes is healthy, and neither does any

---

[64]Beyond Ford's book referenced above, see his *Christian Wisdom: Desiring God and Learning in Love,* CSCD (Cambridge: Cambridge University Press, 2007); the early agenda in David F. Ford, *A Long Rumour of Wisdom: Redescribing Theology* (Cambridge: Cambridge University Press, 1992); plus *Fields of Faith: Theology and Religious Studies for the Twenty-First Century,* ed. David F. Ford, Ben Quash and Janet Martin Soskice (Cambridge: Cambridge University Press, 2005).

[65]David F. Ford, *The Shape of Living: Spiritual Directions for Everyday Life* (Grand Rapids: Baker, 1998); idem, *Self and Salvation: Being Transformed,* CSCD (Cambridge: Cambridge University Press, 1999).

[66]J. Kameron Carter, *Race: A Theological Account* (Oxford: Oxford University Press, 2008). Carter contributes "Race and the Experience of Death: Theologically Reappraising American Evangelicalism," in Larsen and Treier, *Cambridge Companion to Evangelical Theology,* pp. 177-98.

[67]See, e.g., Sarah Coakley, "*Kenōsis* and Subversion: On the Repression of 'Vulnerability' in Christian Feminist Writing," in *Powers and Submissions: Spirituality, Philosophy and Gender,* Challenges in Contemporary Theology (Oxford: Blackwell, 2002), pp. 3-39. For Coakley dialogue partners include feminism, gender theory and Christian spirituality; Tanner likewise interacts with a wide range of subjects such as economics. Charry's book, profiled in a previous chapter, embodies a more personal form of such resistance; trained in social work, she has healing of damaged selves at heart.

author's work take only one shape. The broad contours parallel the famous quadrilateral of Scripture, tradition, reason and experience as theological "sources"—specifying more concretely the kinds of scholarly engagement these sources can elicit.[68] The triad of canon, creed and culture fits that broad pattern too; thus in many respects TIS simply examines the full theological picture when exegeting particular biblical texts. By no means are all of the theologians just profiled active in conversation about TIS. Most of them, however, engage or influence advocates of theological exegesis, as well as evangelical theologians in general. For these scholarly shapes fill out the various forms that Christian theological wisdom may take as it emerges from hearing the Triune God speak in Scripture.

EVANGELICAL FORMATION: WISDOM'S THEOLOGICAL FORMS

Having sketched a design for evangelical theology's scholarly excellence in terms of spiritual vitality, biblical fidelity and academic creativity, we conclude by briefly situating this pursuit in our recent historical context. Earlier evangelical academic theologies have excelled primarily at integrative biblical theology and analytic theism. There are evangelical exemplars for other shapes, but fewer and farther between—frequently residing outside the American mainstream, typically being influenced by Barth and/or British theology. Hence the evangelical movement needs to expand its theological toolkit. Our academic theology has tended toward journalism, mediating textbook versions of broader ideas inside our own household, scarcely being heard in the intellectual public square. While the university realm may not listen to evangelical theologians' voices in the same way as sectors of historically oriented biblical studies, and a churchly ministry of teaching remains a vital priority, still we ought to foster contributions taking the neglected shapes—for the good of our own precincts whatever the reaction of the public square. Enhancing our capacities for rendering theological judgments in light of variegated scholarship would actually broaden and deepen our fidelity to Scripture.

---

[68]The shapes also indicate the ways in which reason and experience intertwine vis-à-vis "culture," as pointed out by Gabriel Fackre, *The Doctrine of Revelation: A Narrative Interpretation* (Grand Rapids: Eerdmans, 1997), pp. 13-14. Different facets of culture need correspondingly diverse scholarly treatment.

Formal evangelical theology helps to shepherd the wandering (in both senses of the term) people of God on their way. Its central challenges concern creativity and fidelity—finding nourishment and providing protection for the sheep—thus fitting the wisdom dialectic of tradition and inquiry.[69] Creative fidelity stems from scripturally formed imagination—a synthetic faculty of wisdom recognizing theological patterns within the biblical texts while relating Scripture and culture. Thus *theological* interpretation of *Scripture* fosters not only scholarly excellence but also saintly mirroring of the "mind" of Christ. Though only time will tell, the conversational trend of TIS provides fellowship and vocational focus for evangelical and other Christian scholars who may be neither well received in their local churches nor fully at home in their academic guilds. At a crucial juncture in the post-Christian West, what biblical faithfulness means ecclesiologically and vocationally seems less clear than ever. Evangelical scholars need fellowship, even with new conversation partners, to sustain our pursuit of biblical integrity and shape our theological identity in ever-changing contexts.[70]

Wisdom's perennial character requires attention to form and formation. Thus our guiding question: If the formation and reflection of biblical wisdom is the essence of Christian theology, then what forms of churchly practice and scholarly communication should evangelicals pursue? Evangelical theology has too often generated mere proof-texting as a churchly practice and boring propositional textbooks as scholarly communication. These well-intended byproducts stem from our commitment to ministering the message of the whole Bible for the whole people of God.[71] Without abandoning such commitment or its communicative strengths, we must deepen evangelical theology's catholic scriptural formation and widen its array of scholarly forms. Theological interpretation of Scripture can help to foster the wisdom

[69]For more reflection on this pastoral dimension, see Daniel J. Treier and Uche Anizor, "Theological Interpretation and Evangelical Systematic Theology: Iron Sharpening Iron?" *Southern Baptist Journal of Theology* 14, no. 2 (Summer 2010): 4-17; and the more accessible version of *Drama of Doctrine* in Kevin J. Vanhoozer, *Faith Speaking Understanding: Performing the Drama of Doctrine* (Louisville: Westminster John Knox, 2014).
[70]This suggestion about the providence behind TIS is developed at greater length in Daniel J. Treier, "What Is Theological Interpretation? An Ecclesial Reduction," *International Journal of Systematic Theology* 12, no. 2 (April 2010): 144-61.
[71]On democratization as an evangelical distinctive, see further Daniel J. Treier, "Pursuing Wisdom: (Back) Toward Evangelical Spiritual Exegesis," *Crux* 48, no. 2 (Summer 2012): 17-26.

each of us needs to contribute our respective gifts in that effort: while TIS may be a focus of scholarly publication for only a few, it needs to inform the practice of doctrinal judgment for all.

Evangelical theology by nature depends on other traditions and internal subtraditions. Its distinctive effort to mirror Scripture should help others in Christ's body as they pursue the fullness of theological wisdom. There will inevitably be a distinction between evangelical theology and theology done by evangelicals, with the contours of the former remaining appropriately more nebulous.[72] Those fuzzy contours will generate internal arguments and even fractures among those who nevertheless share the definitive aspiration: mirroring Scripture. The goal of our proposal is to restate this aspiration in biblically faithful, theologically fruitful and intellectually and pastorally winsome ways. By God's grace evangelical theology might realize this aspiration more fully, even enhancing its appeal for those outside the conservative Protestant subculture(s).

To that end, in this chapter first the *eschatological* context of theological knowledge came into focus. The appropriate mixture of eschatological reserve with biblical conviction is *ethically* indexed to growth in true charity. Second, since we come to mirror the "mind" of Christ as we see ourselves—even our knowledge of God—truly in the biblical mirror, it is necessary to appreciate the *dramatic richness* of biblical literature and aspire to theological *coherence* as a human share in divine wisdom. Biblical theology further helps both to regulate and to resource *disciplined* doctrinal reflection. Third, then, evangelical theology's possible *scholarly contributions* came into view. The resulting sketch of these eight particular shapes provided new

---

[72]Ross Douthat, *Bad Religion: How We Became a Nation of Heretics* (New York: Free Press, 2012), p. 287, references the Lewis hallway/room analogy to emphasize that we dare not neglect particular confessional rooms in favor of hallway conversation: "A conversation has to reach conclusions in order to actually stand for something; a community has to define itself theologically in order to be able to sustain itself across the generations. In an age of institutional weakness and doctrinal drift, American Christianity has much more to gain from a robust Catholicism and a robust Calvinism than it does from even the most fruitful Catholic-Calvinist dialogue." True enough, at the congregational level anyway (Douthat appeals to Timothy Keller's ministry as an illustration). However, one might suggest that in place of lowest-common-denominator church life we find some remaining value in common-denominator theology. Apart from mutual support among those in the hallway who share in the gospel, rooms may lack sufficient heat and light for robust life. Thus we need both (particular) theology done by evangelicals and others, as well as (general) evangelical theology, lest each church simply do what is right in its own eyes.

ways of envisioning the distinctive emphases and movements among theological sources. The sketch also throws into relief the pastoral work necessary to overcome unhealthy proof-texting: evangelical theology needs to develop biblically imaginative φρόνησις. Such pursuit of wisdom can make discerning use of the trend toward "theological interpretation of Scripture," aspiring to mirror the mind of Christ more fully and faithfully.

A City of Light

The Reality *in Front of* the Mirror

> *Men are mirrors, or "carriers" of Christ to other men. . . .*
> *That is why the Church, the whole body of Christians*
> *showing Him to one another, is so important.*
>
> C. S. Lewis, *Mere Christianity*

THE ULTIMATE PURPOSE of theology is to help the church glorify and enjoy God forever. The end result of theology is not theories about God but godliness: lives renewed and directed once again to image God. Evangelical theology formulates doctrine—sets forth in speech what is in Christ—in order to conform disciples to Christ. Scripture alone gives us the authoritative insight we need into this reality, but the study of Scripture is not an end in itself. Therefore it is only fitting that we conclude our case for mere evangelical theology by indicating what we hope our manifesto might accomplish in the church.

The Mirror of Nurture: Becoming What We Are in Christ

Let us return to James's mirror image, where he likens seeing oneself in the mirror and then forgetting what one sees to hearing God's Word but not doing it (Jas 1:23-25). James refers to Scripture as "the perfect law, the law of liberty" and says that those who obey what they see and hear will be blessed. It is fitting that we conclude with James, a pastoral application of Jesus' teaching and perhaps the closest thing to wisdom literature in the New Testament.

Scripture is not only the perfect law but the perfect gospel that gives freedom. As gospel, Scripture tells of news than which nothing greater can be imagined, for it concerns a doing, and a suffering, than which nothing greater can be conceived. What we see in the mirror of Scripture is ourselves, not just as we actually are (sinners), but as we have been remade by virtue of our union with Christ (saints).[1] Wisdom is what we need when we find ourselves undergoing trials or in confusing situations, and nothing more guides Christian freedom than remembering who we are, and are becoming, in Christ Jesus.

Hence Scripture is less the mirror of nature—an accurate reflection of empirical reality—than it is the mirror of nurture: a true reflection of eschatological reality, and thus a source of encouragement, direction and hope. What we see when we peer intently into the mirror of Scripture is our new humanity in Christ: we see the image of our true selves, as creatures designed to image God. Scripture is the mirror of nurture, because it shows us Christ, and serves as means the Spirit uses to conform us to his image.

No other text is conducive to wisdom as Scripture is. Other texts can mirror empirical reality, but only the Bible sets forth in textual forms what was, is and will be in Jesus Christ. Wisdom in the Old Testament is largely a matter of understanding and participating rightly in the created order. In Christ, however, there is "a new creation" (2 Cor 5:17). Scripture nurtures wisdom for the eschatological reality in Christ, enabling saints to fit into the created and new created orders alike; for both center on and cohere in Christ, the One through whom everything that was made was made, and made new.

DOCTRINE IN THE ECONOMY OF LIGHT: THE PURPOSE OF EVANGELICAL THEOLOGY

God is the Father of lights, the Son is light from light, and the Spirit is the one who shines the light of the gospel of the glory of Christ on our unveiled faces as we peer intently into the eschatological reality that is "in Christ." Evangelical theology has a distinct role in this economy of light, namely,

---

[1]The Psalms were for Augustine "a mirror in which he examined his soul" (Michael Cameron, *Christ Meets Me Everywhere: Augustine's Early Figurative Exegesis* [Oxford: Oxford University Press, 2012], p. 166).

providing "secondary reflections"—interpretations of the light of the gospel—in the form of doctrines that set forth in speech what is in Christ: the gospel of God and the God of the gospel. Evangelical theology shares the good news in its own distinct way: by ministering understanding of God and God's Word. Evangelical theology thus has a dramatic role to play in the communication of the light of the gospel.

In setting forth what is in Christ, doctrine aims not only to describe but to exhort. Though the mood is indicative—a statement of *what is* (in Christ)—the implication is imperatival: become what you are. Evangelical theology is failing its vocation to the extent that it is only idling in textbooks. Whether we use visual or verbal imagery, the point of doctrine is to make disciples who can image or echo Jesus Christ, the true Light and Word. God's intent for human beings "is that we mirror for the sake of creation the nature of the Creator."[2] Disciples are to embody and reflect the wisdom (φρόνησις) and light (φῶς) in the mirror of Scripture.

To reflect the truth of God's word, then, disciples have to do more than think thoughts. Discipleship is having the right beliefs, yes, but also acting on them, demonstrating our understanding of Scripture by the shape of our lives. Wisdom is precisely this lived understanding of the Word of God in the power of the Spirit. In living out their knowledge of God, disciples demonstrate their understanding of the gospel by participating in the eschatological reality in front of the mirror.[3] To the extent that disciples do what they see in the mirror of Scripture, they reflect the kingdom of God on earth as it is in heaven.

Wisdom's Ecclesial Form: The Church as City of Light

Disciples are always particular persons, yet it is impossible for individual disciples on their own to display the most important aspects of what is in Christ. It takes at least two or three to demonstrate the forgiveness that is in Christ (Eph 4:32) and to "love one another" (Jn 13:34) as Christ has loved us. It takes a company of disciples—a church—to embody in concrete practices *what is in Christ.*

---

[2]Stanley J. Grenz, *Theology for the Community of God* (Grand Rapids: Eerdmans, 2000), p. 177.
[3]Kevin J. Vanhoozer calls this the "drama of discipleship" in *Faith Speaking Understanding: Performing the Drama of Doctrine* (Louisville: Westminster John Knox, 2014), chap. 5.

The mirror of Scripture reflects eschatological reality: it shows not only individuals but the church as it is in Christ. Jesus verbalizes this image for those who cannot visualize it: "You are the light of the world. A city set on a hill cannot be hidden" (Mt 5:14). The juxtaposition of images is telling. Augustine viewed the church as the city of God. A city set on a hill is visible for miles. Jesus here conceives the church as a city of light. Paul encourages the Christian community at Philippi to "be conducting yourselves as citizens [πολιτεύεσθε] worthily of the gospel" (Phil 1:27).[4] The local church is a city of light whose vocation is to "let your light shine before others" (Mt 5:16). Churches are cities of light whose citizens are children of light (1 Thess 5:5), who walk as children of light (Eph 5:8) in the kingdom of light (cf. Col 1:13). The vocation of the church is to put on brilliant display on earth every spiritual blessing in Christ with which we have been blessed in heaven (Eph 1:3).

The church makes known "the plan of the mystery hidden for ages in God" (Eph 3:9) not only by proclaiming the gospel but by embodying it. The church is the body of Christ, charged with making visible the eschatological reality of the new humanity created by the cross and resurrection (Eph 2:15). The church is both people and place: a company and a theater for bodily enacting the gospel.[5] Empowered by the Spirit and instructed by Scripture, the church enacts parables of the kingdom of God. Better: the church *is* a parable of the kingdom of God insofar as it exhibits the (eschatological) extraordinary in the midst of the (created) ordinary, the strange cruciform wisdom of God in the midst of the conventional wisdom of the market. It takes a company of the baptized to be a theater of reconciliation.

Evangelical theology exists to help citizens of the city of light live lives worthy of the gospel. It helps the church understand what it sees when it looks at itself—and at the living Christ—in the mirror of Scripture. To be a city of light set on a hill means letting the church's light, whose source is Christ, shine before others. The church witnesses to the light through its speech and action, in particular through works of love. The church is to embody both the mind and the heart of Christ, and this means being disposed to act like Christ. Evangelical churches are by nature both evangelistic and "cardiactivist"—ready to speak God's truth in love and enact God's love in truth. Of course, the church can embody and enact truth and love only if it first understands them in Jesus Christ, "full of grace and truth" (Jn 1:14).

The local congregation is the heart of the church. Each local church has to decide how it will speak and act the new reality that is in Christ in ways that are in continuity with other local bodies while appropriate to their own particular place and time. Evangelical theology helps churches fulfill their vocation to image Christ in local contexts. Evangelical theology, in setting forth what is in Christ, prepares the church to be a people and place of light, displaying the mind and heart of Jesus Christ in ways of wisdom that witness to the world.

The church is as essential to evangelical theology as evangelical theology is to the church. *Evangelical theology without the church is disembodied, a mere abstraction; the church without evangelical theology is absent-minded, an impressionable busybody.*[6] Without the church's concrete contextualization, evangelical theological interpretation of Scripture falls short of the goal: *lived practical knowledge*—wisdom. Without evangelical theology, the church becomes as weak as any other human institution, subject to sociological critique and the prevailing winds of cultural doctrine—*sola cultura.*[7] The church is no appendix to evangelical theology: on the contrary, the church is a theological entity, a theme, result, embodiment and agent of the gospel.[8]

Earlier we posed a series of questions: Is there an evangelical doctrine of God? Is there an evangelical theological method? Those questions have now been answered, but there remains another: Is there an evangelical doctrine of the church, a mere evangelical ecclesiology? There is, but it is not the kind that narrows into a specific confessional tradition or denomination. Evangelical ecclesiology does not issue in particular deliverances concerning such

---

[6]Cf. David F. Wells, who points out that evangelicals' emphasis on parachurch organizations eventually led, in the 1980s, to evangelicalism's thinking of itself "apart from the church" (*The Courage to Be Protestant: Truth-Lovers, Marketers, and Emergents in the Postmodern World* [Grand Rapids: Eerdmans, 2008], p. 10).

[7]Wells notes that the crucial issue is "whether evangelicals will build their churches *sola Scriptura* or *sola cultura*" (ibid., p. 4).

[8]See further Kevin J. Vanhoozer, "Evangelicalism and the Church: The Company of the Gospel," in *The Futures of Evangelicalism: Issues and Prospects,* ed. Craig Bartholomew, Robin Parry and Andrew West (Leicester, UK: Inter-Varsity Press, 2003), pp. 40-99, esp. pp. 71-77.

issues as church government, the mode of baptism or the nature of Christ's presence in the Lord's Supper. Yet this breadth does not mean that mere evangelical ecclesiology has nothing to contribute. Evangelical theology is a pro-ecclesial ethos rather than an argument for a particular confession or polity. It is pro-ecclesial because it is pro-evangel: as we have argued, the church plays a vital role in the economy of light. The church embodies the mind and heart of Christ in particular times and places and is thus "the only hermeneutic of the gospel."[9] Evangelical theology contributes to a gospel-centered ethos in the church (regardless of affiliation), while the church is a visible anticipation of the gospel-centered telos of theology.

THE OPEN TABLE: A SUMMA OF THE GOSPEL

There is one final mirror to consider. Believers have gathered together in churches at all times and places not only to hear the Word of God but also to undertake certain practices that the Lord has commanded, the most important of which is keeping his feast: "Do this in remembrance of me" (Lk 22:19; cf. 1 Cor 11:24-25). In celebrating the Lord's Supper, the church rehearses a climactic scene of the New Testament, one that recalled earlier covenant meals in Israel, foreshadowed Jesus' impending death and anticipates the future marriage supper of the Lamb of God (Rev 19:9). Its cup overflows with meaning.

There is continuing debate as to the nature of Christ's presence in the Supper, yet it is clear that by celebrating communion, the church rehearses the climax of the covenant and represents the body of Christ (1 Cor 10:17) in the sense of pointing to and participating in it. To celebrate the Lord's Supper is to celebrate the reconciliation with God and with one another there is in Christ. Paul says that when congregations celebrate the Lord's Supper, they *proclaim* the Lord's death (1 Cor 11:26). In this sense, communion is one of the most *evangelistic* practices of the church. In proclaiming the Lord's death, the church sets forth in speech *and action* the new life in Christ. To celebrate communion is to mirror what is in Christ—or rather, what was, is now and will ever be in Christ. The Lord's Supper is a complex theological act that commingles past, present and future: the church remembers, presently cel-

---

[9]Lesslie Newbigin, *The Gospel in a Pluralist Society* (Grand Rapids: Eerdmans, 1989), p. 227.

ebrates and anticipates ("until he comes"—1 Cor 11:26) the spiritual blessings that come from union with Christ. The Eucharist's enacted proclamation recapitulates the whole economy of salvation. It is therefore no exaggeration to suggest that what we see in the mirror of the Lord's Supper is the *summa* of evangelical theology—its summary statement and its summit: communion with God.

The Lord's Supper is also a symbol for mere evangelical theology, a concrete example of how fellowship in Christ can extend beyond confessional, denominational, geographical and contextual boundaries. The triune God of the gospel is our material principle, and *sola Scriptura* is our formal principle, but the open Table is our practical principle and anchoring practice. The Table is emblematic of the communion of the saints, and hence evangelical catholicity.

Closed communion is, on one level, a virtual contradiction in terms, restricting participation in the Lord's Supper to those who are members in good standing of a particular local church or denomination. In extreme cases, some churches have built actual fences to cordon off the communion table from the congregation, and only accredited members may enter.[10] To be sure, there must be self-examination and, when necessary, church discipline to ensure that we do not eat the break or drink the cup "in an unworthy manner" (1 Cor 11:27). But this biblical caution is altogether different from disallowing those who are not members of one's own church to partake. With apologies to Robert Frost, in this context good fences do *not* make good neighbors. For it is not a Baptist table or a truly Reformed table, an independent church's table or an Anglican table (even if they have the nicest table setting): it is the Lord's Table. All baptized Christians—all those who have made a public demonstration of the faith that unites one to Christ—are invited to be communicants, people who together share in their communion with Christ.[11]

---

[10]The phrase "fenced table" derives from the practice of closed communion in early Scottish Calvinism, where there were literal fences enclosing the communion table.

[11]Note: in some quarters, "open table" refers to the practice of letting unbaptized Christians take communion. That is not what we are advocating here. On the contrary, we believe the Great Commission clearly indicates that baptism is part and parcel of discipleship, and that in the economy of salvation, baptism—incorporation into Christ's body—ought to be prior to participating in communion, which presupposes that one is already a part of the one body. See further Charles Hefling, "Who Is Communion for? The Debate over the Open Table," *Christian Century* (Nov. 19, 2012).

Mere evangelicals need to take their celebrations of the Lord's Supper, and the open Table, with joyful seriousness and serious joy. Insofar as the Lord's Supper is a proclamation and *summa* of the gospel, it is one of the most *theological* practices for evangelicals to enjoy. Insofar as it is a practical demonstration of the communion the saints have in Christ, it is one of the most *evangelical* practices by which evangelicals, theologians and all, glorify God. Stated differently: that Protestants from one church or denomination can share the Lord's Supper with others is a public demonstration of mere evangelical theology. We may not agree on the nonessentials, but we agree that the gospel is the good news about the triune God and that all our dogmas, doctrines and opinions are under the supreme authority of Scripture. What disagreements remain are not such as to break our communion.

The local church is both mirror and *summa* of the gospel when evangelicals from east and west, Baptist and Presbyterian, Arminian and Calvinist, Puritan and Pentecostal share together in the Lord's Supper. In thus proclaiming the gospel of the Triune God, the open Table serves as both identity and mission statement for the evangelical city of light—a visible sign of the invisible grace of our transdenominational, multiethnic fellowship in Christ.

BIBLIOGRAPHY

Abraham, William J. "Church and Churches." In *The Oxford Handbook of Evangelical Theology*, edited by Gerald R. McDermott, pp. 296-309. Oxford: Oxford University Press, 2010.

———. *The Coming Great Revival: Recovering the Full Evangelical Tradition*. San Francisco: Harper & Row, 1984.

———. "Inclusivism, Idolatry and the Survival of the (Fittest) Faithful." In *The Community of the Word*, edited by Mark Husbands and Daniel J. Treier, pp. 131-45. Downers Grove, IL: IVP Academic, 2005.

Adam, A. K. M., Stephen E. Fowl, Kevin J. Vanhozer and Francis Watson, eds. *Reading Scripture with the Church: Toward a Hermeneutic for Theological Interpretation*. Grand Rapids: Baker Academic, 2006.

Adeyemo, Tokunboh, ed. *Africa Bible Commentary: A One-Volume Commentary Written by 70 African Scholars*. Grand Rapids: Zondervan, 2006.

Akers, John N., John N. Armstrong and John D. Woodbridge, eds. *This We Believe: The Good News of Jesus Christ for the World*. Grand Rapids: Zondervan, 2000.

Allen, R. Michael, ed. *Theological Commentary: Evangelical Perspectives*. London: T&T Clark, 2011.

Allen, R. Michael, and Scott R. Swain. "In Defense of Proof-texting." *JETS* 54, no. 3 (2011): 589-606.

———. *Reformed Catholicity: The Promise of Retrieval for Theology and Biblical Interpretation*. Grand Rapids: Baker Academic, 2015.

Antonio Domini. *De Republica Ecclesiastica* IV.

Austin, J. L. *How to Do Things with Words*. Oxford: Oxford University Press, 1962.

Bakhtin, Mikhail. *"Speech Genres" and Other Late Essays*. Austin: University of Texas Press, 1986.

Banks, Robert. *Reenvisioning Theological Education: Exploring a Missional Alternative to Current Models*. Grand Rapids: Eerdmans, 1999.

Barr, James. *The Scope and Authority of the Bible*. Philadelphia: Westminster, 1980.

———. *The Semantics of Biblical Language*. London: Oxford University Press, 1961.

Barth, Karl. *Church Dogmatics*. Edited by G. W. Bromiley and T. F. Torrance. Translated by G. W. Bromiley, G. T. Thomson et al. Four volumes in 13 parts. Edinburgh: T&T Clark, 1936-1977.

———. *Evangelical Theology*. Grand Rapids: Eerdmans, 1963.

———. *The Humanity of God*. Atlanta: John Knox, 1960.

Basil of Caesarea. *On the Holy Spirit*. Translated by Stephen Hildebrand. Crestwood, NY: St. Vladimir's Seminary Press, 2011.

Bauckham, Richard. *Jesus and the Eyewitnesses: The Gospels as Eyewitness Testimony*. Grand Rapids: Eerdmans, 2006.

———. "Where Is Wisdom to Be Found? Colossians 1:15-20 (2)." In *Reading Texts, Seeking Wisdom: Scripture and Theology*, edited by David F. Ford and Graham Stanton, pp. 129-38. Grand Rapids: Eerdmans, 2003.

Bauder, Kevin T. "Fundamentalism." In *Four Views on the Spectrum of Evangelicalism*, edited by Andrew David Naselli and Collin Hansen, pp. 19-49. Counterpoints. Grand Rapids: Zondervan, 2011.

Bavinck, Herman. *Prolegomena*. Vol. 1 of *Reformed Dogmatics*. Edited by John Bolt. Grand Rapids: Baker Academic, 2003.

Beale, G. K. *We Become What We Worship: A Biblical Theology of Idolatry*. Downers Grove, IL: IVP Academic, 2008.

Bebbington, David W. "About the Definition of Evangelicalism . . ." (review of *Four Views on the Spectrum of Evangelicalism*). *Evangelical Studies Bulletin* 83 (Fall 2012): 1-6.

———. *Evangelicalism in Modern Britain: A History from the 1730s to the 1980s*. London: Unwin Hyman, 1989.

Best, Ernest. *A Commentary on The First and Second Epistles to the Thessalonians*. London: Adam & Charles Black, 1977.

Bettenson, Henry. *Documents of the Christian Church*. Oxford: Oxford University Press, 1947.

Billings, J. Todd. *Union with Christ: Reframing Theology and Ministry for the Church*. Grand Rapids: Baker Academic, 2011.

———. *The Word of God for the People of God: An Entryway to the Theological Interpretation of Scripture*. Grand Rapids: Eerdmans, 2010.

Blake, William. "The Everlasting Gospel." In *The Oxford Book of English Mystical Verse*, edited by D. H. S. Nicholson and A. H. E. Lee. Oxford: Clarendon, 1917.

Blocher, Henri. "The 'Analogy of Faith' in the Study of Scripture: In Search of Justification and Guidelines." *Scottish Bulletin of Evangelical Theology* 5, no. 1 (Spring 1987): 17-38.

———. *In the Beginning: The Opening Chapters of Genesis*. Translated by David G. Preston. Downers Grove, IL: InterVarsity Press, 1984.

———. "John 1." In *Theological Commentary: Evangelical Perspectives*, edited by R. Michael Allen, pp. 115-28. New York: T&T Clark, 2011.

———. *Original Sin: Illuminating the Riddle*. NSBT. Grand Rapids: Eerdmans, 1999.

Block, Daniel I. *The Gospel According to Moses*. Eugene, OR: Cascade, 2012.

Blomberg, Craig. *The Historical Reliability of the Gospels*. 2nd ed. Downers Grove, IL: IVP Academic, 2007.

Blowers, Paul. *Drama of the Divine Economy: Creator and Creation in Early Christian Theology and Piety*. Oxford: Oxford University Press, 2012.

Bockmuehl, Markus. "Bible Versus Theology: Is 'Theological Interpretation' the Answer?" *Nova et Vetera* 9, no. 1 (2011): 27-47.

———. *Seeing the Word: Refocusing New Testament Study*. Studies in Theological Interpretation. Grand Rapids: Baker Academic, 2006.

Boersma, Hans. *Heavenly Participation: The Weaving of a Sacramental Tapestry*. Grand Rapids: Eerdmans, 2011.

Boesel, Chris. "Better News Hath No Evangelical Than This: Barth, Election, and the Recovery of the Gospel from Evangelicalism's Territorial Disputes." In *Karl Barth and the Future of Evangelical Theology*, edited by Christian T. Collins Winn and John L. Drury, pp. 162-90. Eugene, OR: Cascade, 2014.

Bonhoeffer, Dietrich. *Creation and Fall: A Theological Exposition of Genesis 1-3*. Translated by Douglas Stephen Bax. Edited by John W. de Gruchy. Dietrich Bonhoeffer Works English Edition 3. Minneapolis: Fortress, 1997.

Bowald, Mark Alan. *Rendering the Word in Theological Hermeneutics: Mapping Divine and Human Agency*. Aldershot, UK: Ashgate, 2007.

Brandom, Robert. *Perspectives on Pragmatism: Classical, Recent, and Contemporary*. Cambridge, MA: Harvard University Press, 2011.

Brown, William P. *Character in Crisis: A Fresh Approach to the Wisdom Literature of the Old Testament*. Grand Rapids: Eerdmans, 1996.

———. *The Ethos of the Cosmos: The Genesis of Moral Imagination in the Bible*. Grand Rapids: Eerdmans, 1999.

Bruce, F. F. *The Book of the Acts*. Rev. ed. NICNT. Grand Rapids: Eerdmans, 1988.

———. *Paul: The Apostle of the Heart Set Free*. Grand Rapids: Eerdmans, 1977.

———. *Philippians*. Grand Rapids: Baker, 1989.

Bruce, F. F., and J. J. Scott Jr. "Interpretation of the Bible." In *Evangelical Dictionary of Theology*, 2nd ed., edited by Walter A. Elwell, pp. 612-13. Grand Rapids: Baker, 2001.

Buckley, James J., and David S. Yeago, eds. *Knowing the Triune God: The Work of the Spirit in the Practices of the Church*. Grand Rapids: Eerdmans, 2001.

Burnett, Richard E. "Historical Criticism." In *Dictionary for Theological Interpretation of the Bible*, edited by Kevin Vanhoozer, pp. 290-93. Grand Rapids: Baker Academic, 2005.

Burney, C. F. "Christ as the ARXH of Creation." *Journal of Theological Studies* 27 (1926): 160-77.

Callahan, James. *The Clarity of Scripture: History, Theology and Contemporary Literary Studies*. Downers Grove, IL: InterVarsity Press, 2001.

Callow, Kathleen. *Man and Message: A Guide to Meaning-Based Text Analysis*. Lanham, MD: Summer Institute of Linguistics/University Press of America, 1998.

Calvin, John. *Commentary on the First Epistle to the Corinthians*. Edinburgh: Calvin Translation Society, 1848.

———. *Commentary upon the Acts of the Apostles*. Vol. 1. Edinburgh: Calvin Translation Society, 1844.

———. *The Epistle of Paul the Apostle to the Hebrews and the First and Second Epistles of Peter*. Grand Rapids: Eerdmans, 1994.

———. *The Epistles of Paul the Apostle to the Galatians, Ephesians, Philippians, and Colossians*. Calvin's Commentaries. Edited by David W. Torrance and Thomas F. Torrance. Grand Rapids: Eerdmans, 1965.

———. *The Gospel According to St. John 11-21 and The First Epistle of John*. Translated by T. H. L. Parker. Edited by David W. Torrance and Thomas F. Torrance. Grand Rapids: Eerdmans, 1961.

———. *Institutes of the Christian Religion*. Translated by Ford Lewis Battles. Edited by John T. McNeill. 2 vols. Library of Christian Classics. Philadelphia: Westminster Press, 1960.

———. *Sermons on the Epistle to the Ephesians*. Edinburgh: Banner of Truth, 1973.

Cameron, Michael. *Christ Meets Me Everywhere: Augustine's Early Figurative Exegesis*. Oxford: Oxford University Press, 2012.

Carpenter, Joel A. *Revive Us Again: The Reawakening of American Fundamentalism*. Oxford: Oxford University Press, 1997.

Carson, D. A. "Theological Interpretation of Scripture: Yes, But . . ." In *Theological Commentary: Evangelical Perspectives*, edited by R. Michael Allen, pp. 187-207. London: T&T Clark, 2011.

———. "The Vindication of Imputation: On Fields of Discourse and Semantic Fields." In *Justification: What's at Stake in the Current Debates*, edited by Mark Husbands and Daniel J. Treier, pp. 46-78. Downers Grove, IL: InterVarsity Press, 2004.

Carson, D. A., and John D. Woodbridge, eds. *Hermeneutics, Authority, and Canon*. Grand Rapids: Zondervan, 1986.

———. *Scripture and Truth*. Grand Rapids: Zondervan, 1983.

Carter, J. Kameron. *Race: A Theological Account*. Oxford: Oxford University Press, 2008.

———. "Race and the Experience of Death: Theologically Reappraising American Evangelicalism." In *The Cambridge Companion to Evangelical Theology*, edited by Timothy Larsen and Daniel J. Treier, pp. 177-98. Cambridge: Cambridge University Press, 2007.

Charry, Ellen T. *By the Renewing of Your Minds: The Pastoral Function of Christian Doctrine*. Oxford: Oxford University Press, 1997.

Chemnitz, Martin. *Examination of the Council of Trent*. Translated by Fred Kramer. St. Louis: Concordia, 1971.

Chillingworth, William. *The Religion of Protestants: A Safe Way to Salvation*. London: Henry G. Bohn, 1846.

Clapp, Rodney. "The Remaking of Evangelical Theology." *Books & Culture* 5 (May/June 1999): 25.

Clark, David K. *To Know and Love God*. FET. Wheaton, IL: Crossway, 2003.

Coady, C. A. J. *Testimony: A Philosophical Study*. Oxford: Clarendon, 1992.

Coakley, Sarah. *Powers and Submissions: Spirituality, Philosophy and Gender*. Challenges in Contemporary Theology. Oxford: Blackwell, 2002.

Cole, Graham A. *God the Peacemaker: How Atonement Brings Shalom*. Downers Grove, IL: InterVarsity Press, 2009.

———. "The Perils of a 'Historyless' Systematic Theology." In *Do Historical Matters Matter to Faith? A Critical Appraisal of Modern and Postmodern Approaches to Scripture*, edited by James K. Hoffmeier and Dennis R. Magary, pp. 55-69. Wheaton, IL: Crossway, 2012.

Couenhoven, Jesse. "Fodge-ogs and HedgeOxes." *Journal of the American Academy of Religion* 81, no. 3 (September 2013): 586-91.

Coulter, Dale M. "Evangelicals, Pop Culture, and Mass Culture." *First Things*,

February 11, 2014, www.firstthings.com/blogs/firstthoughts/2014/02/evangel
icals-pop-culture-and-mass-culture.

Crisp, Oliver D. *Divinity and Humanity: The Incarnation Reconsidered*. Current
Issues in Theology. Cambridge: Cambridge University Press, 2007.

Crisp, Oliver D., and Michael C. Rea. *Analytic Theology: New Essays in the Philosophy of Theology*. Oxford: Oxford University Press, 2009.

Davids, Peter H. *The Letters of 2 Peter and Jude*. PNTC. Grand Rapids: Eerdmans,
2006.

Davidson, Richard M. *Typology in Scripture: A Study of Hermeneutical* τύπος
Structures. Berrien Springs, MI: Andrews University Press, 1981.

Dayton, Donald W., and Robert K. Johnston, eds. *The Variety of American Evangelicalism*. Knoxville: University of Tennessee Press, 1991.

DeHart, Paul J. *The Trial of Witnesses: The Rise and Decline of Postliberal Theology*. Challenges in Contemporary Theology. Malden, MA: Blackwell, 2006.

Diller, Kevin. *Theology's Epistemological Dilemma: How Karl Barth and Alvin
Plantinga Provide a Unified Response*. Strategic Initiatives in Evangelical Theology. Downers Grove, IL: IVP Academic, 2014.

Dockery, David S. *Southern Baptist Consensus and Renewal: A Biblical, Historical, and Theological Proposal*. Nashville: B&H, 2008.

Dodd, C. H. *According to the Scriptures*. London: James Nisbet, 1952.

Douthat, Ross. *Bad Religion: How We Became a Nation of Heretics*. New York:
Free Press, 2012.

Dyrness, William A., and Veli-Matti Kärkkäinen, eds. *Global Dictionary of Theology*. Downers Grove, IL: IVP Academic, 2008.

Edwards, Jonathan. "Miscellany 332," in *Works of Jonathan Edwards*, vol. 13, p. 410.
New Haven, CT: Yale University Press, 1994.

———. *The Works of Jonathan Edwards*. 26 vols. New Haven, CT: Yale University
Press, 1957–2008.

Elliott, Mark W. *The Heart of Biblical Theology: Providence Experienced*. Burlington, VT: Ashgate, 2012.

Erickson, Millard J. *The Evangelical Left: Encountering Postconservative Evangelical Theology*. Grand Rapids: Baker, 1997.

———. *Postmodernizing the Faith: Evangelical Responses to the Challenge of Postmodernism*. Grand Rapids: Baker, 1998.

Erickson, Millard J., Paul Kjoss Helseth and Justin Taylor, eds. *Reclaiming the
Center: Confronting Evangelical Accommodation in Postmodern Times*.
Wheaton, IL: Crossway, 2004.

Evagrius of Pontus. *Chapters on Prayer*, no. 60. In *Evagrius of Pontus: The Greek Ascetic Corpus*, edited and translated by Robert Sinkewicz, pp. 183-209. Oxford Early Christian Studies. Oxford: Oxford University Press, 2003.

"Evangelicals and Catholics Together: The Gift of Salvation." *CT* 41, no. 15 (December 1997): 35-38.

Fackre, Gabriel. *The Doctrine of Revelation: A Narrative Interpretation*. Grand Rapids: Eerdmans, 1997.

Fairbairn, Donald. *Life in the Trinity: An Introduction to Theology with the Help of the Church Fathers*. Downers Grove, IL: IVP Academic, 2009.

Farley, Edward. *Ecclesial Reflection: An Anatomy of Theological Method*. Philadelphia: Fortress, 1982.

———. *Theologia: The Fragmentation and Unity of Theological Education*. Philadelphia: Fortress, 1983.

Fee, Gordon D. *The First Epistle to the Corinthians*. NICNT. Grand Rapids: Eerdmans, 1987.

———. "Reflections on Church Order in the Pastoral Epistles, with Further Reflection on the Hermeneutics of Ad Hoc Documents." *JETS* 28, no. 2 (June 1985): 141-51.

Feinberg, John S. *No One Like Him: The Doctrine of God*. FET. Wheaton, IL: Crossway, 2001.

Fergusson, David. "Theology Today—Currents and Directions." *Expository Times* 123, no. 3 (2011): 105-12.

Ford, David F. "British Theology After a Trauma: Divisions and Conversations." *Christian Century* 117, no. 12 (April 2000): 425-31.

———. "British Theology: Movements and Churches." *Christian Century* 117, no. 13 (April 2000): 467-73.

———. *Christian Wisdom: Desiring God and Learning in Love*. CSCD. Cambridge: Cambridge University Press, 2007.

———. *The Future of Christian Theology*. Blackwell Manifestos. Malden, MA: Wiley-Blackwell, 2011.

———. *A Long Rumour of Wisdom: Redescribing Theology*. Cambridge: Cambridge University Press, 1992.

———. *Self and Salvation: Being Transformed*. CSCD. Cambridge: Cambridge University Press, 1999.

———. *The Shape of Living: Spiritual Directions for Everyday Life*. Grand Rapids: Baker, 1998.

———. "Theological Wisdom, British Style." *Christian Century* 117, no. 11 (April 2000): 388-91.

Ford, David F., Ben Quash and Janet Martin Soskice, eds. *Fields of Faith: Theology and Religious Studies for the Twenty-First Century*. Cambridge: Cambridge University Press, 2005.

Fowl, Stephen E. *Engaging Scripture: A Model of Theological Interpretation*. Oxford: Blackwell, 1998.

———. "Scripture." In *The Oxford Handbook of Systematic Theology*, edited by John Webster, Kathryn Tanner and Iain Torrance, pp. 345-61. Oxford: Oxford University Press, 2007.

———. *Theological Interpretation of Scripture*. Cascade Companions. Eugene, OR: Cascade, 2009.

———, ed. *The Theological Interpretation of Scripture: Classic and Contemporary Readings*. Oxford: Blackwell, 1997.

Frame, John M. *The Doctrine of the Word of God*. Phillipsburg, NJ: P&R, 2010.

———. "In Defense of Something Close to Biblicism: Reflections on *Sola Scriptura* and History in Theological Method." *Westminster Theological Journal* 59 (1997): 269-91.

Franke, John R. *The Character of Theology: An Introduction to Its Nature, Task, and Purpose*. Grand Rapids: Baker Academic, 2005.

———. *Manifold Witness: The Plurality of Truth*. Living Theology. Nashville: Abingdon, 2009.

Garrett, James Leo. *Systematic Theology: Biblical, Historical, and Evangelical*. Vol. 1. Grand Rapids: Eerdmans, 1990.

Geisler, Norman L. "Methodological Unorthodoxy." *JETS* 26, no. 1 (March 1983): 87-94.

Gentry, Peter J., and Stephen J. Wellum. *Kingdom Through Covenant: A Biblical-Theological Understanding of the Covenants*. Wheaton, IL: Crossway, 2012.

George, Timothy. "Directions: If I'm an Evangelical, What Am I?" *CT* 43, no. 9 (August 1999): 62.

Gorman, Michael J. *Cruciformity: Paul's Narrative Spirituality of the Cross*. Grand Rapids: Eerdmans, 2001.

———. *Inhabiting the Cruciform God: Kenosis, Justification, and Theosis in Paul's Narrative Soteriology*. Grand Rapids: Eerdmans, 2009.

———. "Participation and Mission in Paul." *Cross Talk ~ crux probat omnia* (blog). December 12, 2011. www.michaeljgorman.net/2011/12/12/participation-and-mission-in-paul/.

"The Gospel of Jesus Christ: An Evangelical Affirmation." *CT* 43, no. 7 (June 1999): 51-56.

Green, Gene L., Stephen T. Pardue and K. K. Yeo, eds. *Jesus Without Borders: Christology in the Majority World*. Grand Rapids: Eerdmans, 2014.

Green, Jay. "Making It." *Books & Culture* 18, no. 3 (May/June 2012): p. 33.

Greene-McCreight, Kathryn. "The Logic of the Interpretation of Scripture and the Church's Debate over Sexual Ethics." In *Homosexuality, Science, and the "Plain Sense" of Scripture*, edited by David L. Balch, pp. 242-60. Grand Rapids: Eerdmans, 2000.

Greggs, Tom. "Biblical Hermeneutics and *Relational* Responsibility." In *The Future of Biblical Interpretation: Responsible Plurality in Biblical Hermeneutics*, edited by Stanley E. Porter and Matthew R. Malcolm, pp. 117-31. Downers Grove, IL: IVP Academic, 2013.

Grenz, Stanley J. *Renewing the Center: Evangelical Theology in a Post-Theological Era*. Grand Rapids: Baker, 2000.

———. *Revisioning Evangelical Theology: A Fresh Agenda for the 21st Century*. Downers Grove, IL: InterVarsity Press, 1983.

———. *Theology for the Community of God*. Grand Rapids: Eerdmans, 2000.

Grenz, Stanley J., and John R. Franke. *Beyond Foundationalism: Shaping Theology in a Postmodern Context*. Louisville: Westminster John Knox, 2001.

Grenz, Stanley J., and Roger Olson. *Who Needs Theology? An Invitation to the Study of God*. Downers Grove, IL: InterVarsity Press, 1996.

Gundry, Robert H. *Commentary on the New Testament: Verse-by-Verse Explanations with a Literal Translation*. Peabody, MA: Hendrickson, 2010.

———. "Grace, Works, and Staying Saved in Paul." *Biblica* 66, no. 1 (1985): 1-38.

———. *Matthew: A Commentary on His Literary and Theological Art*. Grand Rapids: Zondervan, 1982.

———. "Why I Didn't Endorse 'The Gospel of Jesus Christ: An Evangelical Celebration' . . . Even Though I Wasn't Asked to." *Books & Culture* 7, no. 1 (January/February 2001): 6-9.

Gunton, Colin E. "Indispensable Opponent: The Relations of Systematic Theology and Philosophy of Religion." *Neue Zeitschrift für Systematische Theologie und Religionsphilosophie* 38, no. 3 (1996): 298-306.

———. *The One, the Three, and the Many: God, Creation, and the Culture of Modernity*. Cambridge: Cambridge University Press, 1993.

Gushee, David P., ed. *A New Evangelical Manifesto: A Kingdom Vision for the Common Good*. St. Louis: Chalice, 2012.

Harnack, Adolf von. *History of Dogma*. Translated by Alexander Balmain Bruce. 7 vols. Boston: Roberts, 1896–1899.

272 THEOLOGY AND THE MIRROR OF SCRIPTURE

Harper, Brad, and Paul Louis Metzger. *Exploring Ecclesiology: An Evangelical and Ecumenical Introduction*. Grand Rapids: Brazos, 2009.

Hart, D. G. *Deconstructing Evangelicalism: Conservative Protestantism in the Age of Billy Graham*. Grand Rapids: Baker, 2004.

Hauerwas, Stanley. *Unleashing the Scripture: Freeing the Bible from Captivity to America*. Nashville: Abingdon, 1993.

Hauerwas, Stanley, and L. Gregory Jones, eds. *Why Narrative? Readings in Narrative Theology*. Grand Rapids: Eerdmans, 1989.

Hays, Richard B. *The Conversion of Imagination: Paul as Interpreter of Israel's Scripture*. Grand Rapids: Eerdmans, 2005.

———. *Echoes of Scripture in the Letters of Paul*. New Haven, CT: Yale University Press, 1989.

———. *First Corinthians*. Interpretation. Louisville: Westminster John Knox, 1997.

———. *Reading Backwards: Figural Christology and the Fourfold Gospel Witness*. Waco, TX: Baylor University Press, 2014.

Hector, Kevin W. *Theology Without Metaphysics: God, Language, and the Spirit of Recognition*. Current Issues in Theology. Cambridge: Cambridge University Press, 2011.

Hefling, Charles. "Who Is Communion for? The Debate over the Open Table." *Christian Century* 129, no. 24 (2012): 22-27.

Henry, Carl F. H. *God, Revelation, and Authority*. 6 vols. Waco, TX: Word, 1976–1983.

———. *The Uneasy Conscience of Modern Fundamentalism*. Grand Rapids: Eerdmans, 1947.

Herbert, George. "The Holy Scriptures I." In *The Temple, Sacred Poems and Private Ejaculations*. Cambridge: Thomas Buck and Roger Daniel, 1633.

Hirsch, E. D., Jr. *Validity in Interpretation*. New Haven, CT: Yale University Press, 1967.

"History." Evangelical Presbyterian Church. www.epc.org/history?

Hoekema, Anthony. *Saved by Grace*. Grand Rapids: Eerdmans, 1989.

Holmes, Stephen R. "Evangelical Doctrine: Basis for Unity or Cause for Division?" *Scottish Bulletin of Evangelical Theology* 30, no. 1 (2012).

Hooper, Walter. *The Collected Letters of C. S. Lewis*. Vol. 1, *Family Letters 1905–1931*. New York: HarperCollins, 2004.

Horton, Michael S., ed. "Are Charismatic-Inclined Pietists the True Evangelicals? And Have the Reformed Tried to Hijack the Movement? Interview with Donald Dayton." *Modern Reformation*. March/April 2001.

———. "The Battles over the Label 'Evangelical.'" *Modern Reformation*. March/
April 2001.

———. "The Church After Evangelicalism." In *Renewing the Evangelical Mission*,
edited by Richard Lints, pp. 134-60. Grand Rapids: Eerdmans, 2013.

———. *Covenant and Eschatology: The Divine Drama*. Louisville: Westminster
John Knox, 2002.

Hsu, Al. "Rene Padilla on the Cape Town Lausanne Congress." *The Suburban
Christian* (blog), November 10, 2010. http://thesuburbanchristian.blogspot
.com/2010/11/rene-padilla-on-cape-town-lausanne.html.

Hughes, Brian W. *Saving Wisdom: Theology in the Christian University*. Eugene,
OR: Pickwick, 2011.

Hunsinger, George. "Postliberal Theology." In *The Cambridge Companion to
Postmodern Theology*, edited by Kevin J. Vanhoozer, pp. 42-57. Cambridge:
Cambridge University Press, 2003.

Hunter, James Davison. *Evangelicalism: The Coming Generation*. Chicago: University of Chicago Press, 1987.

Husbands, Mark, and Daniel J. Treier, eds. *The Community of the Word: Toward
an Evangelical Ecclesiology*. Downers Grove, IL: IVP Academic, 2005.

Hütter, Reinhard. *Suffering Divine Things: Theology as Church Practice*. Translated by Doug Stott. Grand Rapids: Eerdmans, 2000.

Illich, Ivan. *In the Vineyard of the Text: A Commentary to Hugh's Didascalicon*.
Chicago: University of Chicago Press, 1996.

Jacobs, Alan. "Textual Notes." In W. H. Auden, *For the Time Being: A Christmas
Oratorio*, edited by Alan Jacobs. Princeton, NJ: Princeton University Press,
2013.

Jenson, Robert W. *The Triune God*. Vol. 1 of *Systematic Theology*. Oxford: Oxford
University Press, 1997.

———. *The Works of God*. Vol. 2 of *Systematic Theology*. Oxford: Oxford University Press, 1999.

Jewett, Robert. *Paul's Anthropological Terms*. Leiden: Brill, 1971.

Johnson, Luke Timothy. "Imagining the World Scripture Imagines." In *Theology
and Scriptural Imagination*, edited by L. Gregory Jones and James J. Buckley,
pp. 3-18. Oxford: Blackwell, 1998.

Johnson, Marcus Peter. *One with Christ: An Evangelical Theology of Salvation*.
Wheaton, IL: Crossway, 2013.

Kaiser, Walter C., Jr. "The Nature and Criteria of Theological Scholarship: An
Evangelical Critique and Plan." *Theological Education* 32, no. 1 (1995): 57-70.

Kaiser, Walter C., Jr., and Moisés Silva. *An Introduction to Biblical Hermeneutics: The Search for Meaning*. Grand Rapids: Zondervan, 1994.

Kelsey, David H. *Between Athens and Berlin: The Theological Education Debate*. Grand Rapids: Eerdmans, 1993.

———. *Imagining Redemption*. Louisville: Westminster John Knox, 2005.

———. *Proving Doctrine: The Use of Scripture in Modern Theology*. Harrisburg, PA: Trinity Press International, 1999.

———. *To Understand God Truly: What's Theological About a Theological School*. Louisville: Westminster John Knox, 1992.

———. *The Uses of Scripture in Recent Theology*. Philadelphia: Fortress, 1975.

Kierkegaard, Søren. *Without Authority*. Translated by Howard V. Hong and Edna H. Hong. Princeton, NJ: Princeton University Press, 1997.

Kilner, John. *Dignity and Destiny: Humanity in the Image of God*. Grand Rapids: Eerdmans, 2015.

Klink, Edward W., III, and Darian R. Lockett. *Understanding Biblical Theology: A Comparison of Theory and Practice*. Grand Rapids: Zondervan, 2012.

Kuyper, Abraham. *Encyclopedia of Sacred Theology: Its Principles*. New York: Charles Scribner's Sons, 1898.

Lamont, John. *Divine Faith*. Aldershot, UK: Ashgate, 2004.

Larsen, Timothy, and Daniel J. Treier, eds. *The Cambridge Companion to Evangelical Theology*. Cambridge: Cambridge University Press, 2007.

Lee, Philip J. *Against the Protestant Gnostics*. Oxford: Oxford University Press, 1987.

Leith, John H. *Crisis in the Church: The Plight of Theological Education*. Louisville: Westminster John Knox, 1997.

Leithart, Peter J. *Deep Exegesis: The Mystery of Reading Scripture*. Waco, TX: Baylor University Press, 2009.

———. *The Priesthood of the Plebs: A Theology of Baptism*. Eugene, OR: Wipf & Stock, 2003.

Levering, Matthew. *Participatory Biblical Exegesis: A Theology of Biblical Interpretation*. Notre Dame, IN: University of Notre Dame Press, 2008.

Lewis, C. S. *Introduction to Athanasius, On the Incarnation*. Crestwood, NY: St. Vladimir's Seminary Press, 1993.

———. *Mere Christianity*. San Francisco: HarperSanFrancisco, 2001.

Licona, Michael. *The Resurrection of Jesus: A New Historiographical Approach*. Downers Grove, IL: IVP Academic, 2010.

Lindbeck, George. "The Problem of Doctrinal Development and Contemporary

Protestant Theology." In *Man as Man and Believer*, edited by Edward Schillebeeckx and Boniface Willems, pp. 133-49. New York: Paulist, 1967.

Lindsell, Harold. *The Battle for the Bible*. Grand Rapids: Zondervan, 1976.

Lints, Richard. *The Fabric of Theology: A Prolegomenon to Evangelical Theology*. Grand Rapids: Eerdmans, 1993.

———, ed. *Renewing the Evangelical Mission*. Grand Rapids: Eerdmans, 2013.

Lubac, Henri de. *History and Spirit: The Understanding of Scripture According to Origen*. Translated by Anne Englund Nash. San Francisco: Ignatius, 2007.

Lundin, Roger. *From Nature to Experience: The American Search for Cultural Authority*. Lanham, MD: Rowman & Littlefield, 2005.

Luther, Martin. Large Catechism (1529).

———. "On the Councils and the Church." In *Church and Ministry III*, edited by Eric W. Gritsch, pp. 9-178. Luther's Works 41. Philadelphia: Fortress, 1966.

———. "Preface to the Complete Edition of Luther's Latin Works" (1545). In *Career of the Reformer IV*, Luther's Works 34, edited and translated by Helmut L. Lehmann and Lewis W. Spitz. Minneapolis: Fortress, 1960.

Luy, David. *Dominus Mortis: Martin Luther on the Incorruptibility of God in Christ*. Minneapolis: Fortress, 2014.

MacIntyre, Alasdair C. *After Virtue: A Study in Moral Theory*. 2nd ed. Notre Dame, IN: University of Notre Dame Press, 1984.

Manetsch, Scott M. *Calvin's Company of Pastors: Pastoral Care and the Emerging Reformed Church, 1536–1609*. Oxford: Oxford University Press, 2013.

Marion, Jean-Luc. *God Without Being*. Chicago: University of Chicago Press, 1991.

Marsden, George M. *Fundamentalism and American Culture: The Shaping of Twentieth-Century Evangelicalism 1870–1925*. Oxford: Oxford University Press, 1980.

———. *Reforming Fundamentalism: Fuller Seminary and the New Evangelicalism*. Grand Rapids: Eerdmans, 1987.

McCormack, Bruce L. "The Identity of the Son: Karl Barth's Exegesis of Hebrews 1:1-4 (and Similar Passages)." In *Christology, Hermeneutics, and Hebrews: Profiles from the History of Interpretation*, edited by Jon C. Laansma and Daniel J. Treier, pp. 155-72. Library of New Testament Studies 423. London: T&T Clark, 2012.

McClendon, James William, Jr. *Ethics*. Vol. 1 of *Systematic Theology*. 2nd ed. Nashville: Abingdon, 2002.

McDermott, Gerald R. "The Emerging Divide in Evangelical Theology." *JETS* 56, no. 2 (2013): 355-77.

————. "Evangelicals Divided: Gerald McDermott Describes the Battle Between Meliorists and Traditionalists to Define Evangelicalism." *First Things* 212 (2011): 45-50.

————, ed. *The Oxford Handbook of Evangelical Theology.* Oxford: Oxford University Press, 2010.

McFarland, Ian A. *The Divine Image: Envisioning the Invisible God.* Minneapolis: Augsburg Fortress, 2005.

McGrath, Alister. *Evangelicalism and the Future of Christianity.* Downers Grove, IL: InterVarsity Press, 1995.

————. "Faith and Tradition." In *The Oxford Handbook to Evangelical Theology*, ed. Gerald R. McDermott, pp. 81-95. Oxford: Oxford University Press, 2010.

————. *The Genesis of Doctrine: A Study in the Foundation of Doctrinal Criticism.* Oxford: Basil Blackwell, 1990.

McGuckin, John. *Saint Cyril of Alexandria and the Christological Controversy.* Crestwood, NY: St. Vladimir's Seminary Press, 2004.

McKnight, Scot. *The King Jesus Gospel: The Original Good News Revisited.* Grand Rapids: Zondervan, 2011.

McLean, B. H. *Biblical Interpretation and Philosophical Hermeneutics.* Cambridge: Cambridge University Press, 2012.

Mead, James K. *Biblical Theology: Issues, Methods, and Themes.* Louisville: Westminster John Knox, 2007.

Meadors, Gary T., ed. *Four Views on Moving Beyond the Bible to Theology.* Grand Rapids: Zondervan, 2009.

Millar, J. G. "People of God." In *New Dictionary of Biblical Theology*, edited by T. D. Alexander and Brian S. Rosner, pp. 684-87. Downers Grove, IL: InterVarsity Press, 2000.

Milliner, Matthew. "Anchors Aweigh: The Neglected Art of Theological Interpretation." *Comment* (Fall 2012): 82-91.

Mitchell, Margaret M. *Paul, the Corinthians and the Birth of Christian Hermeneutics.* Cambridge: Cambridge University Press, 2010.

Moberly, R. W. L. *The Bible, Theology, and Faith: A Study of Abraham and Jesus.* Cambridge: Cambridge University Press, 2000.

————. "What Is Theological Interpretation of Scripture?" *Journal of Theological Interpretation* 3, no. 2 (2009): 161-78.

Mohler, R. Albert, Jr. "Confessional Evangelicalism." In *Four Views on the Spectrum of Evangelicalism*, edited by Andrew David Naselli and Hansen Collin, pp. 68-96. Counterpoints. Grand Rapids: Zondervan, 2011.

Moo, Douglas J. *The Letters to the Colossians and to Philemon*. PNTC. Grand Rapids: Eerdmans, 2008.

———. "Matthew and Midrash: An Evaluation of Robert H. Gundry's Approach." *JETS* 26, no. 1 (March 1983): 31-39.

Moreau, A. Scott. *Contextualization in World Missions: Mapping and Assessing Evangelical Models*. Grand Rapids: Kregel, 2012.

Moule, C. F. D. "The Borderlands of Ontology in the New Testament." In *The Philosophical Frontiers of Christian Theology: Essays Presented to D. M. MacKinnon*, edited by Brian Hebblethwaite and Stewart Sutherland, pp. 1-11. Cambridge: Cambridge University Press, 1982.

Mouw, Richard J. *Consulting the Faithful: What Christian Intellectuals Can Learn From Popular Religion*. Grand Rapids: Eerdmans, 1994.

Muller, Richard A. "The Foundation of Calvin's Theology: Scripture as Revealing God's Word." *Duke Divinity School Review* 44, no. 1 (1979): 14-23.

———. *Post-Reformation Reformed Dogmatics: The Rise and Development of Reformed Orthodoxy, ca. 1520 to ca. 1725*. Vol. 1 of *Prolegomena to Theology*. 2nd ed. Grand Rapids: Baker Academic, 2003.

———. *The Study of Theology: From Biblical Interpretation to Contemporary Formulation*. Foundations of Contemporary Interpretation 7. Grand Rapids: Zondervan, 1991.

Murray, John. *Redemption, Accomplished and Applied*. Grand Rapids: Eerdmans, 1955.

Naselli, Andrew David, and Collin Hansen, eds. *Four Views on the Spectrum of Evangelicalism*. Counterpoints. Grand Rapids: Zondervan, 2011.

Newbigin, Lesslie. *The Gospel in a Pluralist Society*. Grand Rapids: Eerdmans, 1989.

Niebuhr, H. Richard. *The Kingdom of God in America*. New York: Harper & Row, 1959.

Noll, Mark A. *American Evangelical Christianity: An Introduction*. Oxford: Blackwell, 2001.

———. *Between Faith and Criticism: Evangelicals, Scholarship, and the Bible in America*. San Francisco: Harper & Row, 1986.

———. *The Civil War as a Theological Crisis*. Chapel Hill: University of North Carolina Press, 2006.

———. "Ecumenical Realities and Evangelical Theology." In *Renewing the Evangelical Mission*, edited by Richard Lints, pp. 51-68. Grand Rapids: Eerdmans, 2013.

———. *Jesus Christ and the Life of the Mind*. Grand Rapids: Eerdmans, 2011.

———. *The Scandal of the Evangelical Mind*. Grand Rapids: Eerdmans, 1994.

———. "What Is 'Evangelical'?" In *The Oxford Handbook of Evangelical Theology*, edited by Gerald R. McDermott, pp. 19-32. Oxford: Oxford University Press, 2010.

Oden, Thomas C. "Do Not Rashly Tear Asunder: Why the Beleaguered Faithful Should Stay and Reform Their Churches." *First Things* (April 2012): 40-44.

———. *Systematic Theology*. 3 vols. San Francisco: Harper & Row, 1987–1992.

O'Donovan, Oliver. *Self, World, and Time*. Vol. 1 of *Ethics as Theology*. Grand Rapids: Eerdmans, 2013.

Olson, Roger E. "The Future of Evangelical Theology: Roger Olson Argues That a Division Between Traditionalists and Reformists Threatens to End Our Theological Consensus." *CT* 42, no. 2 (February 1998): 40-48.

———. "My Letter to First Things (Responding to the McDermott Article)." *Roger E. Olson: My Evangelical Arminian Theologial Musings* (blog), March 23, 2011. www.patheos.com/blogs/rogereolson/2011/03/my-letter-to-first -things-responding-to-the-mcdermott-article/.

———. "Postconservative Evangelicalism." In *Four Views on the Spectrum of Evangelicalism*, edited by Andrew David Naselli and Collin Hansen, pp. 161-87. Counterpoints. Grand Rapids: Zondervan, 2011.

———. *The Westminster Handbook to Evangelical Theology*. Louisville: Westminster John Knox, 2004.

Packer, J. I. *God Has Spoken: Revelation and the Bible*. Grand Rapids: Baker, 1979.

———. "In Quest of Canonical Interpretation." In *The Use of the Bible in Theology: Evangelical Options*, edited by Robert K. Johnston, pp. 35-55. Atlanta: John Knox, 1985.

———. "Why I Signed It: The Recent Statement 'Evangelicals and Catholics Together' Recognizes an Important Truth: Those Who Love the Lord Must Stand Together." *CT* 38, no. 14 (December 1994): 34-37.

Packer, J. I., and Gary A. Parrett. "The Return to Catechesis: Lessons from the Great Tradition." In *Renewing the Evangelical Mission*, edited by Richard Lints, pp. 111-33. Grand Rapids: Eerdmans, 2013.

Packer, J. I., and Thomas C. Oden. *One Faith: The Evangelical Consensus*. Downers Grove, IL: InterVarsity Press, 2004.

"A Panel Discussion." In *The Nature of Confession: Evangelicals and Postliberals in Conversation*, edited by Timothy R. Phillips and Dennis L. Okholm, pp. 246-53. Downers Grove, IL: InterVarsity Press, 1996.

Pattison, George. "Theology Without Metaphysics: God, Language, and the Spirit of Recognition—by Kevin W. Hector." *Reviews in Religion & Theology* 19, no. 3 (July 2012): 318-24.

Pelikan, Jaroslav. *Jesus Through the Centuries: His Place in the History of Culture.* New Haven, CT: Yale University Press, 1999.

Peterson, David G. *The Acts of the Apostles.* PNTC. Grand Rapids: Eerdmans, 2009.

———. *Possessed by God: A New Testament Theology of Sanctification and Holiness.* NSBT. Grand Rapids: Eerdmans, 1995.

Peterson, Eugene. *Christ Plays in Ten Thousand Places: A Conversation in Spiritual Theology.* Grand Rapids: Eerdmans, 2005.

———. *A Long Obedience in the Same Direction: Discipleship in an Instant Society.* 2nd ed. Downers Grove, IL: InterVarsity Press, 2000.

Piper, John. *God Is the Gospel: Meditations on God's Love.* Wheaton, IL: Crossway, 2005.

Plato. *Timaeus.* Translated by R. G. Bury. Loeb Classical Library. Cambridge, MA: Harvard University Press, 1929.

Poirier, John C. "'Theological Interpretation' and Its Contradistinctions." *Tyndale Bulletin* 61, no. 1 (2010): 105-18.

Pope, William Burt. *A Compendium of Christian Theology.* Vol. 2. Rev. ed. New York: Hunt & Eaton, 1889.

Porter, Stanley E. "What Exactly Is Theological Interpretation of Scripture, and Is It Hermeneutically Robust Enough for the Task to Which It Has Been Appointed?" In *Horizons in Hermeneutics: A Festschrift in Honor of Anthony C. Thiselton,* edited by Stanley E. Porter and Matthew R. Malcolm, pp. 234-67. Grand Rapids: Eerdmans, 2013.

Porter, Stanley E., and Matthew R. Malcolm, eds. *The Future of Biblical Interpretation: Responsible Plurality in Biblical Hermeneutics.* Downers Grove, IL: IVP Academic, 2013.

Poythress, Vern S. *Symphonic Theology: The Validity of Multiple Perspectives in Theology.* Phillipsburg, NJ: P & R, 2001.

Provan, Iain W., V. Philips Long and Tremper Longman III. *A Biblical History of Israel.* Louisville: Westminster John Knox, 2003.

Ramm, Bernard L. *Evangelical Heritage.* Waco, TX: Word, 1973.

———. *The Pattern of Religious Authority.* Grand Rapids: Eerdmans, 1957.

———. *Special Revelation and the Word of God.* Grand Rapids: Eerdmans, 1961.

———. *The Witness of the Spirit: An Essay on the Contemporary Relevance of the Internal Witness of the Holy Spirit.* Grand Rapids: Eerdmans, 1959.

Ramsey, William. *St. Paul the Traveller, and Roman Citizen.* London: Hodder and Stoughton, 1898.

Rasmussen, Joshua. *Defending the Correspondence Theory of Truth.* Cambridge: Cambridge University Press, 2014.

Rauser, Randal. "Theology as a Bull Session." In *Analytic Theology: New Essays in the Philosophy of Theology*, edited by Oliver D. Crisp and Michael C. Rea, pp. 70-84. Oxford: Oxford University Press, 2009.

Reeves, Michael. *Delighting in the Trinity: An Introduction to the Christian Faith.* Downers Grove, IL: InterVarsity Press, 2012.

Reno, R. R. "Biblical Theology and Theological Exegesis." In *Out of Egypt: Biblical Theology and Biblical Interpretation*, edited by Craig Bartholomew, Mary Healy, Karl Möller and Robin Parry, pp. 385-408. Grand Rapids: Zondervan, 2004.

Richards, E. Randolph, and Brandon J. O'Brien. *Misreading Scripture with Western Eyes: Removing Cultural Blinders to Better Understand the Bible.* Downers Grove, IL: IVP Books, 2012.

Ricoeur, Paul. *Oneself as Another.* Translated by Kathleen McLaughlin Blamey. Chicago: University of Chicago Press, 1992.

Rogers, Jack Bartlett, and Donald K. McKim. *The Authority and Interpretation of the Bible: An Historical Approach.* San Francisco: Harper & Row, 1979.

Rorty, Richard. *Philosophy and the Mirror of Nature.* Princeton, NJ: Princeton University Press, 1979.

Sanders, Fred, *The Deep Things of God: How the Trinity Changes Everything.* Wheaton, IL: Crossway, 2010.

———. *The Image of the Immanent Trinity: Rahner's Rule and the Theological Interpretation of Scripture.* New York: Peter Lang, 2005.

Sarisky, Darren. *Scriptural Interpretation: A Theological Exploration.* Challenges in Contemporary Theology. Malden, MA: Wiley-Blackwell, 2013.

Schaper, Joachim. "Historical Criticism, 'Theological Exegesis,' and Theology Amongst the Humanities." In *Theology, University, Humanities: Initium Sapientiae Timor Domini*, edited by Christopher Craig Brittain and Francesca Aran Murphy, pp. 75-90. Eugene, OR: Cascade, 2011.

Scobie, Charles H. H. *The Ways of our God: An Approach to Biblical Theology.* Grand Rapids: Eerdmans, 2003.

Schwöbel, Christoph. "The Trinity." In *God's Advocates: Christian Thinkers in Conversation*, edited by Rupert Shortt, pp. 86-102. Grand Rapids: Eerdmans, 2005.

Seitz, Christopher R. *Colossians*. Brazos Theological Commentary on the Bible. Grand Rapids: Brazos, 2014.

Smedes, Lewis B. "Evangelicalism: A Fantasy." *Reformed Journal* 30, no. 2 (1980): 2-3.

Smith, Christian. *American Evangelicalism: Embattled and Thriving*. Chicago: University of Chicago Press, 1998.

———. *The Bible Made Impossible: Why Biblicism Is Not a Truly Evangelical Reading of Scripture*. Grand Rapids: Brazos, 2011.

Smith, Christian, and Patricia Snell. *Souls in Transition: The Religious and Spiritual Lives of Emerging Adults*. New York: Oxford University Press, 2009.

Smith, James K. A. *Who's Afraid of Relativism? Community, Contingency, and Creaturehood*. The Church and Postmodern Culture. Grand Rapids: Baker Academic, 2014.

Spawn, Kevin L., and Archie T. Wright, eds. *Spirit and Scripture: Exploring a Pneumatic Hermeneutic*. London: T & T Clark, 2012.

Stackhouse, John G., Jr., ed. *Evangelical Ecclesiology: Reality or Illusion?* Grand Rapids: Baker Academic, 2003.

———, ed. *Evangelical Futures: A Conversation on Theological Method*. Grand Rapids: Baker, 2000.

———. "Generic Evangelicalism." In *Four Views on the Spectrum of Evangelicalism*, edited by Andrew David Naselli and Collin Hansen, pp. 116-42. Counterpoints. Grand Rapids: Zondervan, 2011.

Steinmetz, David C. *Taking the Long View: Christian Theology in Historical Perspective*. Oxford: Oxford University Press, 2011.

Stephens, Randall J., and Karl W. Giberson. *The Anointed: Evangelical Truth in a Secular Age*. Cambridge, MA: Harvard University Press, 2011.

Stuhlmacher, Peter. *Historical Criticism and Theological Interpretation of Scripture*. Translated by Roy A. Harrisville. Philadelphia: Fortress, 1977.

Swain, Scott R. *The God of the Gospel: Robert Jenson's Trinitarian Theology*. Strategic Initiatives in Evangelical Theology. Downers Grove, IL: IVP Academic, 2013.

Sweeney, Douglas A. *The American Evangelical Story: A History of the Movement*. Grand Rapids: Baker, 2005.

Thate, Michael J., Constantine R. Campbell and Kevin J. Vanhoozer, eds. *"In Christ" in Paul*. Tübingen: Mohr Siebeck, 2014.

Thiselton, Anthony C. *The First Epistle to the Corinthians*. NIGTC. Grand Rapids: Eerdmans, 2000.

———. *The Hermeneutics of Doctrine*. Grand Rapids: Eerdmans, 2007.

Thompson, Marianne Meye. *Colossians & Philemon*. Two Horizons New Testament Commentary. Grand Rapids: Eerdmans, 2005.

Thompson, Mark D. *A Clear and Present Word: The Clarity of Scripture*. NSBT. Downers Grove, IL: InterVarsity Press, 2006.

Tiénou, Tite. "Renewing Evangelical Identity from the Margins." In *Renewing the Evangelical Mission*, edited by Richard Lints, pp. 31-50. Grand Rapids: Eerdmans, 2013.

Treat, Jeremy R. *The Crucified King: Atonement and Kingdom in Biblical and Systematic Theology*. Grand Rapids: Zondervan, 2014.

Treier, Daniel J. "Biblical Theology and/or Theological Interpretation of Scripture?" *Scottish Journal of Theology* 61 (2008): 16-31.

———. "Christology and Commentaries: Examining and Enhancing Theological Exegesis." In *On the Writing of New Testament Commentaries: Festschrift for Grant R. Osborne on the Occasion of his 70th Birthday*, edited by Stanley E. Porter and Eckhard J. Schnabel, pp. 299-316. Leiden: Brill, 2012.

———. "Heaven on Earth? Evangelicals and Biblical Interpretation." *Books & Culture* (January 2012). www.booksandculture.com/articles/webexclu sives/2012/january/heavenonearth.html.

———. *"Heavenly Participation: The Weaving of a Sacramental Tapestry*—a Review Essay." *Christian Scholar's Review* 41, no. 1 (Fall 2011): 67-71.

———. *Introducing Theological Interpretation of Scripture: Recovering a Christian Practice*. Grand Rapids: Baker Academic, 2008.

———. "Proof Text." In *Dictionary for Theological Interpretation of the Bible*, edited by Kevin J. Vanhoozer. pp. 622-24. Grand Rapids: Baker Academic, 2005.

———. *Proverbs and Ecclesiastes*. Brazos Theological Commentary on the Bible. Grand Rapids: Brazos, 2011.

———. "Pursuing Wisdom: (Back) Toward Evangelical Spiritual Exegesis." *Crux* 48, no. 2 (Summer 2012): 17-26.

———. "Typology." In *Dictionary for Theological Interpretation of the Bible*, edited by Kevin J. Vanhoozer, pp. 823-27. Grand Rapids: Baker Academic, 2005.

———. *Virtue and the Voice of God: Toward Theology as Wisdom*. Grand Rapids: Eerdmans, 2006.

———. "What Is Theological Interpretation? An Ecclesial Reduction." *International Journal of Systematic Theology* 12, no. 2 (April 2010): 144-61.

———. "Wisdom." In *Dictionary for Theological Interpretation of the Bible*, edited by Kevin J. Vanhoozer, pp. 844-47. Grand Rapids: Baker Academic, 2005.

Treier, Daniel J., and Uche Anizor. "Theological Interpretation and Evangelical Systematic Theology: Iron Sharpening Iron?" *Southern Baptist Journal of Theology* 14, no. 2 (Summer 2010): 4-17.

Trimm, Charlie. "Evangelicals, Theology, and Biblical Interpretation: Reflections on the Theological Interpretation of Scripture." *Bulletin for Biblical Research* 20, no. 3 (2010): 311-30.

Vanhoozer, Kevin. "The Apostolic Discourse and Its Developments." In *Scripture's Doctrine and Theology's Bible: How the New Testament Shapes Christian Dogmatics*, edited by Markus Bockmuehl and Alan J. Torrance, pp. 191-207. Grand Rapids: Baker, 2008.

———. "The Atonement in Postmodernity: Guilt, Goats, and Gifts." In *The Glory of the Atonement: Biblical, Theological, and Practical Perspectives*, edited by Charles E. Hill and Frank A. James III, pp. 367-404. Downers Grove, IL: InterVarsity Press, 2004.

———. "At Play in the Theodrama of the Lord: The Triune God of the Gospel." In *Theatrical Theology: Explorations in Performing the Faith*, edited by Wesley Vander Lugt and Trevor Hart, pp. 1-29. Eugene, OR: Cascade, 2014.

———. *Biblical Narrative in the Philosophy of Paul Ricoeur*. Cambridge: Cambridge University Press, 1990.

———. *The Drama of Doctrine: A Canonical-Linguistic Approach to Christian Theology*. Louisville: Westminster John Knox, 2005.

———. "Evangelicalism and the Church: The Company of the Gospel." In *The Futures of Evangelicalism: Issues and Prospects*, edited by Craig Bartholomew, Robin Parry and Andrew West, pp. 40-99. Leicester, UK: Inter-Varsity, 2003.

———. *Faith Speaking Understanding: Performing the Drama of Doctrine*. Louisville: Westminster John Knox, 2014.

———. *First Theology: Essays on God, Scripture, and Hermeneutics*. Downers Grove, IL: InterVarsity Press, 2002.

———. "Holy Scripture: Word of God; Word of Christ; Sword of the Spirit." In *Christian Dogmatics*, edited by R. Michael Allen and Scott R. Swain. Grand Rapids: Baker, forthcoming.

———. "Interpreting Scripture Between the Rock of Biblical Studies and the Hard Place of Systematic Theology: The State of the Evangelical (dis)Union." In *Renewing the Evangelical Mission*, edited by Richard Lints, pp. 201-25. Grand Rapids: Eerdmans, 2013.

———. "Introduction: What Is Theological Interpretation of the Bible?" In *Dictionary for Theological Interpretation of the Bible*, edited by Kevin Vanhoozer, pp. 19-25. Grand Rapids: Baker Academic, 2005.

———. *Is There a Meaning in This Text? The Bible, the Reader, and the Morality of Literary Knowledge*. 2nd ed. Grand Rapids: Zondervan, 2009.

———. "Love's Wisdom: The Authority of Scripture's Form and Content for Faith's Understanding and Theological Judgment." *Journal of Reformed Theology* 5 (2011): 247-75.

———. "May We Go Beyond What Is Written After All? The Pattern of Theological Authority and the Problem of Doctrinal Development." In *"My Words Will Never Pass Away": The Enduring Authority of the Christian Scriptures*, edited by D. A. Carson. Grand Rapids: Eerdmans, forthcoming.

———. "The Pattern of Evangelical Theology: Hommage à Ramm." In Bernard Ramm, *The Evangelical Heritage: A Study in Historical Theology*, pp. ix-xxvii. Grand Rapids: Baker, 2000.

———. *Remythologizing Theology: Divine Action, Passion, and Authorship*. CSCD. Cambridge: Cambridge University Press, 2010.

———. "Scripture and Theology: On Proving Doctrine Biblically." In *The Routledge Companion to the Practice of Christian Theology*, edited by Mike Higton and Jim Fodor, pp. 141-59. New York: Routledge, 2013.

———. "The Semantics of Biblical Literature: Truth and Scripture's Diverse Literary Forms." In *Hermeneutics, Authority, and Canon*, edited by D. A. Carson and John D. Woodbridge, pp. 53-104. Grand Rapids: Zondervan, 1986.

———. "The Spirit of Light After the Age of Enlightenment: Reforming/Renewing Pneumatic Hermeneutics via the Economy of Illumination." In *Spirit of God: Renewal in the Community of Faith*, edited by Jeffrey W. Barbeau and Beth Felker Jones, pp. 149-67. Downers Grove, IL: InterVarsity Press, 2015.

———. "Three (or More) Ways of Triangulating Theology: On the Very Idea of a Trinitarian System." In *Revisioning, Renewing, and Rediscovering the Triune Center*, edited by Derek Tidball, Brian Harris and Jason Sexton, pp. 31-58. Eugene, OR: Cascade, 2014.

———. "The Triune God of the Gospel." In *The Cambridge Companion to Evangelical Theology*, edited by Timothy Larsen and Daniel J. Treier, pp. 17-34. Cambridge: Cambridge University Press, 2007.

———. "The Voice and the Actor: A Dramatic Proposal About the Ministry and Minstrelsy of Theology." In *Evangelical Futures: A Conversation on Theological Method*, edited by John G. Stackhouse Jr., pp. 61-106. Grand Rapids: Baker, 2000.

———. "Wrighting the Wrongs of the Reformation? The State of the Union with

Christ in St. Paul and Protestant Soteriology." In *Jesus, Paul and the People of God: A Theological Dialogue with N. T. Wright*, edited by Nicholas Perrin and Richard B. Hays, pp. 235-58. Downers Grove, IL: IVP Academic, 2011.

Vidu, Adonis. *Theology After Neo-Pragmatism*. Paternoster Theological Monographs. Carlisle, UK: Paternoster, 2008.

Vincent of Lérins. *Commonitorium*.

Volf, Miroslav. *Captive to the Word of God: Engaging the Scriptures for Contemporary Theological Reflection*. Grand Rapids: Eerdmans, 2010.

Volf, Miroslav, and Dorothy C. Bass, eds. *Practicing Theology: Beliefs and Practices in the Christian Life*. Grand Rapids: Eerdmans, 2002.

Wahlberg, Mats. *Revelation as Testimony: A Philosophical-Theological Study*. Grand Rapids: Eerdmans, 2014.

Walls, Andrew F. *The Cross-Cultural Process in Christian History*. Maryknoll, NY: Orbis, 2002.

———. *The Missionary Movement in Christian History: Studies in the Transmission of Faith*. Maryknoll, NY: Orbis, 1996.

Ward, Timothy. *Words of Life: Scripture as the Living and Active Word of God*. Downers Grove, IL: IVP Academic, 2009.

Watson, Francis. *Gospel Writing: A Canonical Perspective*. Grand Rapids: Eerdmans, 2013.

———. *Text and Truth: Redefining Biblical Theology*. Grand Rapids: Eerdmans, 1997.

———. *Text, Church, and World: Biblical Interpretation in Theological Perspective*. Grand Rapids: Eerdmans, 1994.

Webster, John. *Confessing God: Essays in Christian Dogmatics II*. London: T&T Clark, 2005.

———. *The Domain of the Word: Scripture and Theological Reason*. London: T&T Clark International, 2012.

———. *Holy Scripture: A Dogmatic Sketch*. Cambridge: Cambridge University Press, 2006.

———. "Jesus Christ." In *The Cambridge Companion to Evangelical Theology*, edited by Timothy Larsen and Daniel J. Treier, pp. 51-64. Cambridge: Cambridge University Press, 2007.

———. "One Who Is Son: Theological Reflections on the Exordium to the Epistle to the Hebrews." In *The Epistle to the Hebrews and Christian Theology*, edited by Richard Bauckham, Daniel R. Driver, Trevor A. Hart and Nathan MacDonald, pp. 69-94. Grand Rapids: Eerdmans, 2009.

Weigel, George. *Evangelical Catholicism: Deep Reform in the 21st Century Church*. New York: Basic, 2013.

Wells, David F. *The Courage to Be Protestant: Truth-Lovers, Marketers, and Emergents in the Postmodern World*. Grand Rapids: Eerdmans, 2008.

———. *No Place For Truth: Or, Whatever Happened to Evangelical Theology?* Grand Rapids: Eerdmans, 1993.

Westcott, Brooke Foss. *The Gospel According to St. John*. Grand Rapids: Baker, 1980.

Westphal, Merold. "Hermeneutics and Holiness." In *Analytic Theology: New Essays in the Philosophy of Theology*, edited by Oliver D. Crisp and Michael C. Rea, pp. 265-79. Oxford: Oxford University Press, 2009.

———. "Taking St. Paul Seriously: Sin as an Epistemological Category." In *Christian Philosophy*, edited by Thomas P. Flint, pp. 200-226. Notre Dame, IN: University of Notre Dame Press, 1990.

"What's the Good News? Nine Evangelical Leaders Define the Gospel." *CT* 44, no. 2 (February 2000): 46-51.

Wheeler, Barbara G., and Edward Farley, eds. *Shifting Boundaries: Contextual Approaches to the Structure of Theological Education*. Louisville: Westminster John Knox, 1991.

Whidden, David L., III. *Christ the Light: The Theology of Light and Illumination in Thomas Aquinas*. Minneapolis: Fortress, 2015.

Wiarda, Timothy. "The Jerusalem Council and the Theological Task." *JETS* 46, no. 2 (2003): 233-48.

Williams, A. N. *The Architecture of Theology: Structure, System, and Ratio*. Oxford: Oxford University Press, 2011.

Williams, Rowan. "Theology Among the Humanities." In *The Vocation of Theology Today: A Festschrift for David Ford*, edited by Tom Greggs, Rachel Muers and Simeon Zahl, pp. 178-90. Eugene, OR: Cascade, 2013.

Wolters, Al. "A Reflection by Al Wolters." In *Four Views on Moving Beyond the Bible to Theology*, edited by Gary T. Meadors, pp. 299-319. Counterpoints. Grand Rapids: Zondervan, 2009.

Wood, Charles M. *Vision and Discernment: An Orientation in Theological Study*. Studies in Religious and Theological Scholarship. Atlanta: Scholars Press, 1985.

Woodbridge, John D. *Biblical Authority: A Critique of the Rogers/McKim Proposal*. Grand Rapids: Zondervan, 1982.

Woodbridge, John D., and Thomas Edward McComiskey, eds. *Doing Theology in Today's World: Essays in Honor of Kenneth Kantzer*. Grand Rapids: Zondervan, 1991.

Worthen, Molly. *Apostles of Reason: The Crisis of Authority in American Evangelicalism*. New York: Oxford University Press, 2013.

Wright, N. T. *How God Became King: The Forgotten Story of the Gospels*. New York: HarperOne, 2012.

———. *The Last Word: Scripture and the Authority of God—Getting Beyond the Bible Wars*. San Francisco: HarperOne, 2006.

———. *The New Testament and the People of God*. London: SPCK, 1993.

———. *Simply Good News: Why the Gospel Is News and What Makes it Good*. New York: HarperOne, 2015.

Yarnell, Malcolm B., III. *The Formation of Christian Doctrine*. Nashville: B&H Academic, 2007.

Yeago, David S. "The New Testament and the Nicene Dogma." *Pro Ecclesia* 3, no. 2 (Spring 1994): 152-64.

Yong, Amos. *The Bible, Disability, and the Church: A New Vision of the People of God*. Grand Rapids: Eerdmans, 2011.

Zagzebski, Linda Trinkhaus. *Epistemic Authority: A Theory of Trust, Authority, and Autonomy in Belief*. Oxford: Oxford University Press, 2012.

Name Index

Abraham, William J., 47-48, 216
Aquinas, Thomas, 89
Auden, W. H., 181
Augustine, 12, 49, 256
Austin, J. L., 232
Bakhtin, Mikhail, 120-21
Banks, Robert, 147
Barr, James, 144, 171
Barth, Karl, 34, 50, 73, 90, 92, 94-95, 164, 247, 250
Basil of Caesarea, 113, 139
Bauckham, Richard, 62
Bauder, Kevin, 207-8, 211
Bavinck, Herman, 97, 214
Baxter, Richard, 49
Bebbington, David W., 27, 31, 36, 46, 49, 52, 78, 209
Best, Ernest, 56
Blake, William, 84
Blocher, Henri, 246
Bloesch, Donald, 214
Blomberg, Craig, 173
Bockmuehl, Markus, 171
Boesel, Chris, 90
Bonhoeffer, Dietrich, 164-65
Brandom, Robert, 183
Bruce, F. F., 164, 203
Burney, C. F., 62
Callahan, James, 232
Callow, Kathleen, 185
Calvin, John, 59, 69-72, 75-76, 98, 110-11, 119, 234
Carson, D. A., 171-74
Carter, J. Kameron, 249
Charry, Ellen, 148-49, 249
Chemnitz, Martin, 116
Chillingworth, William, 109
Clark, David K., 146
Coady, C. A. J., 91
Coakley, Sarah, 249
Coulter, Dale M., 222
Crisp, Oliver D., 232-33, 248
Cyril of Alexandria, 108

Davids, Peter H., 199
Dayton, Donald W., 25, 28-29, 34, 48
Descartes, René, 12
Diller, Kevin, 92
Dockery, David S., 126
Dodd, C. H., 101
Dominis, Marco Antonio, 49
Dorrien, Gary, 34
Douthat, Ross, 252
Dunn, James D. G., 165-66
Dyrness, William A., 37
Edwards, Jonathan, 37, 67
Erickson, Millard J., 33-34
Evagrius of Pontus, 149
Fackre, Gabriel, 250
Farley, Edward, 144, 146
Fee, Gordon D., 223-24
Feinberg, John S., 248
Fergusson, David, 36-37
Feuerbach, Ludwig, 58, 60
Ford, David F., 226-29, 233, 247-49
Fowl, Stephen, 165, 198
Frame, John M., 164
Franke, John R., 180, 242
Frost, Robert, 261
Garrett, James Leo, 81
Geisler, Norman L., 33
George, Timothy, 29-30, 46
Gorman, Michael J., 205
Graham, Billy, 30
Green, Garrett, 230
Green, Jay, 223-24
Grenz, Stanley J., 33-34, 47, 144-45, 180, 210
Grudem, Wayne, 33-34
Gundry, Robert H., 30, 32-33
Gunton, Colin E., 238, 247
Harnack, Adolf von, 32
Hart, D. G., 48
Hauerwas, Stanley, 83, 85
Hays, Richard B., 101-2, 165, 178-79

Hector, Kevin W., 186, 188
Henry, Carl F. H., 24, 33-35, 143-44, 214
Hirsch, E. D., Jr., 170
Holmes, Stephen, 47, 49-50
Horton, Michael S., 28-29, 145, 214, 217
Hugh of St. Victor, 105
Hughes, Brian W., 227
Irenaeus, 54, 63
Jacobs, Alan, 181
Jenson, Robert W., 66, 187, 241-42
Johnston, Robert K., 25, 144
Kärkkäinen, Veli-Matti, 37
Kelsey, David H., 144, 146-47, 230, 236, 238
Kierkegaard, Søren, 87-88, 91
Kilner, John, 60-61
Kuyper, Abraham, 98-99
Larsen, Timothy, 36, 209
Leithart, Peter J., 180, 229
Levering, Matthew, 173
Lewis, C. S., 12, 21, 23, 123-24, 217, 255
Licona, Michael, 33
Lindbeck, George, 117, 213
Lindsell, Harold, 32
Lints, Richard, 23, 106, 144-45, 237
Long, V. Philips, 173
Longman, Tremper, III, 173
Lubac, Henri de, 163, 229
Lundin, Roger, 170
Luther, Martin, 70, 113, 116, 232
MacIntyre, Alasdair, 148-50, 215-16
Marion, Jean-Luc, 105
Marsden, George M., 25, 27-28
McClendon, James William, Jr., 164
McCormack, Bruce, 246-47

SUBJECT INDEX

academic engagement
  as churchly service,
    194-97, 207, 220
  and friendship, 193-94
  and method(s), 154-57
  and mission, 193-94
  more robust among
    evangelicals, 24, 35-36,
    41, 147-48, 164, 174, 193,
    215, 221-53
  opposed by evangelicals,
    33, 137, 208, 222-24
apostle, 87, 89, 111
  contrast with genius, 88,
    91
archetypal theology, 139, 189
atonement, 31, 124
authority
  biblical, 82-85, 103
  magisterial, 123
  ministerial, 111, 114, 124
  pattern of, 13, 103-4
baptism, 134-35, 160, 162
battle for the Bible, 32
Berlin (versus Athens), 147,
  244-45
biblical theology, 164, 172,
  174-75, 190, 225-26, 236-46
biblicism, 33, 42, 46, 162-64,
  175-76, 225, 241-42
  naïve vs. critical, 85, 106
  and problem of pervasive
    interpretive pluralism,
    83, 86, 116
calling, 132-35
canon sense, 42, 165, 238
catechism, 110-11
charity, 177-78, 192, 195,
  198-201, 204-6, 222-24
Christ. *See* Jesus Christ
Christianity Today, 28, 30
Christus Victor, 55
church
  apostolicity of, 37, 39, 197,

211, 235
  catholicity of, 19, 35-39,
    41-42, 119, 132-33, 140,
    197, 200, 211, 218, 220,
    251
  as city of light, 257-58
  as context of doctrine, 19,
    186-88
  councils, 112-13
  division, 192, 197-209
  as event in drama of
    redemption, 76
  as God's family/
    household, 21-23
  hermeneutic of the gospel,
    260
  led by Spirit, 121
  local as mirror of
    universal, 77
  necessity of, 75
  as our mother, 23
  as part of the gospel, 76,
    110, 134, 140, 259
  place in economy of light,
    110
  structure(s), 200, 206
  unity, 134-35, 206-7, 218
coherence. *See* narrative;
  systematic theology
concepts, 38, 165, 181-90,
  229-30, 236-41, 243-44
constructive theology. *See*
  systematic theology
contemplation, 143, 148-50,
  233-35
context
  cultural, 42, 156, 166, 168,
    199, 206, 248-50
  and debates regarding
    contextualization, 25,
    136-37, 201
  and principles, 146
Creator/creation distinction,
  66

creed. *See* rule of faith
crucicentrism, 46
  strong vs. weak, 78-79
dialogue, 194, 198, 201, 206,
  212, 219, 227-28, 230, 249
difference(s), 167, 202-7, 209,
  212, 218-20, 229, 237, 241-42
disciples, discipleship, 45, 257
discipline, doctrinal, 28,
  199-201, 216-18, 236-44
diversity, biblical. *See*
  Scripture, unity of
doctrine
  development of, 107-8
  first-order vs. second-
    order, 49-50, 125
  sets forth what is in
    Christ, 106, 257
  sound, 94, 107
dogmatic theology. *See*
  systematic theology
drama, 27, 145, 156, 198,
  226-30, 237, 252
economy, divine, 64-68
  See also light, economy of
ectypal theology, 139, 183, 189,
  229
ecumenism, orthodox and
  pietist Protestant, 19, 24,
  204, 207, 218-20
elitism, 139-41, 148, 155, 160,
  195, 221-24, 243
emergent Christianity/culture,
  25-26
eschatological context, 176-81,
  224, 226, 229-30, 233-35, 252
ethical context, 176-81, 204-6,
  213, 224, 226, 235, 252
Eucharist. *See* Lord's Supper
Evangelical Theological
  Society, 31-33
evangelical theology
  as anchored in the gospel,
    78

as aspiration and
  ambition, 45, 114
as canonical reasoning,
  100
challenges to address,
  24-26, 35, 82-83
disputed doctrinal core of,
  46-48, 77
in economy of light, 256-57
and evangelicalism, 23, 27,
  215
intellectual tradition, 190,
  193, 214-19, 250
Lord's Supper as symbolic
  of, 261
material and formal
  principles of, 52, 78
"mere," 11, 45, 50-51, 57,
  78-80
Pentecostal plurality and,
  121
promise of, 122
as setting forth what is
  "in Christ," 86
and "theology done by
  evangelicals," 10, 26, 210,
  214-15, 217, 252
Trinity-centric, 52, 78-79,
  124
evangelicalism
  Achilles' heel of, 110
  and Anabaptists, 31
  as anchored set, 21, 40,
    51-52, 58, 117
  Anglo-American context,
    20, 27-29, 34-38, 134-36,
    210, 217, 250
  approaches to identity,
    26-29, 39, 145, 207-9,
    214-19
  and Arminians, 30-31
  and Baptists, 25, 30
  as bounded set, 48, 208,
    210
  British/European context,
    37-38, 248-50
  catholic, 114, 116-18
  center/consensus, 20,
    26-29, 34, 208, 210, 215
  as centered set, 48
  charismatic leaders, 28,
    134-36, 140, 159-61

and Dispensationalists, 34
doctrine of God, 31-32
ecclesiology, 19, 21, 27-28,
  36, 39-40, 212-13, 219
as ethos, 214, 219
fragmentation, especially
  into two parties, 20,
  26-27, 33-34, 36, 141, 208,
  210
historiography, 23, 27, 141
and Holiness Christianity,
  25, 28
as movement/subculture,
  11, 41, 214, 219
parachurch dominance, 28
and Pentecostal
  Christianity, 25, 39
and pietism, 20, 47, 141,
  145-46, 158, 208, 210, 214,
  217, 219, 225
as Protestant, 22, 29, 39,
  133-34, 140
recent changes, 24-26
and Reformed
  Christianity, 25, 28, 30,
  34-35, 145, 170, 214, 225
sociological realities, 23
theological method, 32-39,
  126, 143-46, 150-51, 156-57
exegesis
  Jewish, 165, 168
  of one meaning, 150-51
  original language, 147
  "theological," 144, 151, 156,
    164, 168-69, 238
experience. See context;
  sources, theological
faith, 90
false teaching, 93
fellowship, 20, 40-42, 133-34,
  191-220, 251
figural interpretation, 101, 227
first theology, 12-13
fragmentation
  healed by wisdom, 141,
    148-57
  of knowledge and life, 177,
    230, 234-35
  of Scripture and theology,
    169
  of theological education,
    146-48, 151

freedom, 136-38, 152-53, 160,
  186, 189, 193-96, 201-2,
  204-6, 232, 238-41, 244
gender, 37, 39, 249
general revelation, 234, 239
gifts, spiritual, 134, 195-96
global Christianity, increased
  evangelical interest in, 25,
  37-39, 248-49
God. See triune God
gospel, 29-31, 50, 53-58, 64,
  133-34, 198-201
  as ingredient in economy
    of light, 88, 92
  light of, 93
  narrative report of, 57
  proclaimed in Lord's
    Supper, 262
  subject and substance of,
    69-70
  as taught and told, 87
  unintelligible apart from
    the Trinity, 56-57, 64-65
  as what is "in Christ," 70-72
grace, 133-34, 150, 153
Great Christian tradition,
  increased evangelical
  awareness of, 24, 38-39, 246
Hellenization thesis, 32
hermeneutics
  against epistemology,
    182-84
  authorial intention, 145,
    151, 163, 170-71
  as a form of theological
    scholarship, 245
  two-step, 148, 150-51,
    169-70
historical integrity, 148, 150-51,
  158, 161-63, 168, 170-75, 191
Holy Spirit
  and church councils, 113
  illumination of the, 22, 59,
    119, 124, 186-88
  relation to nature and
    grace, 167-68
  role in economy of light,
    89-90
  unites to Christ, 72
homoousios, 113, 119, 121
imagination, 38, 102, 226, 230,
  245, 251

Scripture Index

THE STUDIES IN CHRISTIAN DOCTRINE AND SCRIPTURE SERIES

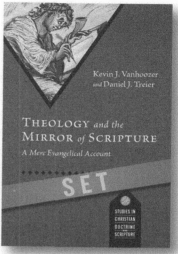

Kevin J. Vanhoozer
and Daniel J. Treier

THEOLOGY *and the*
MIRROR *of* SCRIPTURE
A Mere Evangelical Account

SET

STUDIES IN
CHRISTIAN
DOCTRINE
SCRIPTURE

Studies in Christian Doctrine and Scripture promotes evangelical contributions to systematic theology, seeking fresh understanding of Christian doctrine through creatively faithful engagement with Scripture in dialogue with catholic tradition(s).

Thus: We aim to publish **contributions to systematic theology** rather than merely descriptive rehearsals of biblical theology, historical retrievals of classic or contemporary theologians, or hermeneutical reflections on theological method—volumes that are plentifully and expertly published elsewhere.

We aim to promote **evangelical** contributions, neither retreating from broader dialogue into a narrow version of this identity on the one hand, nor running away from the biblical preoccupation of our heritage on the other hand.

We seek fresh understanding of Christian doctrine **through creatively faithful engagement with Scripture.** To some fellow evangelicals and interested others today, we commend the classic evangelical commitment of engaging Scripture. To other fellow evangelicals today, we commend a contemporary aim to engage Scripture with creative fidelity. The church is to be always reforming—but always reforming according to the Word of God.

We seek **fresh understanding of Christian doctrine.** We do not promote a singular method; we welcome proposals appealing to biblical theology, the history of interpretation, theological interpretation of Scripture, or still other approaches. We welcome projects that engage in detailed exegesis as well as those that appropriate broader biblical themes and patterns. Ultimately, we hope to promote relating Scripture to doctrinal understanding in material, not just formal, ways.

We promote scriptural engagement **in dialogue with catholic tradition(s).** A periodic evangelical weakness is relative disinterest in the church's shared creedal heritage, in churches' particular confessions, and more generally in the history of dogmatic reflection. Beyond existing efforts to enhance understanding of themes and corpora in biblical theology, then, we hope to foster engagement with Scripture that bears upon and learns from loci, themes, or crucial questions in classic dogmatics and contemporary systematic theology.

Finding the Textbook You Need

The IVP Academic Textbook Selector
is an online tool for instantly finding the IVP books
suitable for over 250 courses across 24 disciplines.

www.ivpress.com/academic/